Transport and Communications Innovation in Europe

The **European Science Foundation** is an association of its 54 member research councils, academies and institutions devoted to basic scientific research in 20 countries. The ESF brings European scientists together to work on topics of common concern, to co-ordinate the use of expensive facilities, and to discover and define new endeavours that will benefit from a co-operative approach.

The scientific work sponsored by ESF includes basic research in the natural sciences, the medical and biosciences, the humanities and the social sciences.

The ESF links scholarship and research supported by its members and adds value by co-operation across national frontiers. Through its function as a co-ordinator, and also by holding workshops and conferences and by enabling researchers to visit and study in laboratories throughout Europe, the ESF works for the advancement of European science.

This volume arises from the work of the ESF Network for European Communications and Transport Activities Research (NECTAR).

Further information on ESF activities can be obtained from:

European Science Foundation
1 quai Lezay-Marnésia
67080 Strasbourg Cedex
France

Tel. 88 76 71 00
Fax 88 37 05 32

TRANSPORT AND COMMUNICATIONS INNOVATION IN EUROPE

Edited by
G. Giannopoulos and
A. Gillespie

Belhaven Press
London and New York

Co-published in the Americas with Halsted Press, an imprint of John Wiley & Sons, Inc., New York

Belhaven Press
(a division of Pinter Publishers Ltd)
25 Floral Street, Covent Garden, London, WC2E 9DS, United Kingdom

First published in Great Britain in 1993

Co-published in the Americas by Halsted Press, an imprint of
John Wiley & Sons, Inc., 605 Third Avenue, New York, NY 10158–0012

British Library Cataloguing in Publication Data

A CIP catalogue record for this book is available from the British Library
ISBN 1 85293 269 4

Library of Congress Cataloging-in-Publication Data

Transport and communications innovation in Europe / edited by G. Giannopoulos
  and A. Gillespie.
    p.   cm.
    Includes bibliographical references and index.
    ISBN 0–470–22001–5
    1. Transportation – Europe – Technological innovations.
    2. Telecommunication – Europe – Technological innovations.
    I. Giannopoulos, G.A., 1946– .   II. Gillespie, A.E.
    HE242.T69   1993
    388′.094–dc20   93–10001
                                                                          CIP

ISBN 0–470–22001–5 (in the Americas only)

Typeset by Mayhew Typesetting, Rhayader, Powys
Printed and bound in Great Britain by Biddles Ltd of Guildford and King's Lynn

Contents

Part III   Some Key Issues Concerning Transport and Economic and Spatial Organisation

Part IV

List of Figures

List of Tables

List of contributors

Alan Bieber is Director of long range studies at the Institut National de Recherche sur les Transport et leur Sécurité (INRETS), in Arcueil, France. He has taught transport at the Ecole Nationale des Ponts et Chaussées for 17 years. His main fields of research are demand forecasting and economic evaluation for large transport projects, such as TGV lines.

Roberto Camagni is full Professor in Economics at the University of Padua and also teaches at the Bocconi University in Milan. He is the President of the Italian Regional Science Association and of GREMI (Group de Recherche Européen sur les Milieux innovateurs).

Roberta Capello is research fellow at Bocconi University in Milan. Her major research field is industrial and regional economics. She is currently undertaking a PhD in the Economics Department at the Free University, Amsterdam on externality effects associated with telecommunications networks.

Heikki Eskelinen is senior researcher at the Social Sciences Section of the Karelian Institute, University of Joensuu, Finland. His current interests are in comparative Nordic research on regional development within the context of international economic integration.

Joao Francisco dos Reis Simoes is a transport engineer, working at the Instituto Superior Technico in Lisbon.

Michel Frybourg is ingénieur Général des Ponts et Chaussées. Beginning his career as a highway engineer from 1968–82 he directed the Institut de Recherches des Transport. An Associate Professor at the Ecole Nationale des Ponts et Chaussées, he is also President of ENOES (Ecole Nouvelle d'Organisation Economic et Sociale).

G.A. Giannopoulos is Professor of Transportation Engineering in the Civil Engineering Department of the Faculty of Technology at the University of Thessaloniki, and is currently head of the Civil Engineering Department. He has a PhD in Transportation Engineering from the University of London. The author of five books and numerous articles, he is currently a member of the EC's DRIVE and TELEMATICS programmes Management Committees.

Andrew Gillespie is a lecturer in Geography and researcher within the Centre for Urban and Regional Development Studies at the University of Newcastle upon Tyne. He is currently Acting Director of the ESRC-funded Newcastle Programme on Information and Communications Technologies (PICT) Centre. His main research interests are in the implications of new information and communications technologies for the development of cities, regions and rural areas.

P. Papaioannou is Lecturer at the Department of Civil Engineering of the School of Technology, University of Thessaloniki. He has an MSc in Transportation from Bradford University and a PhD from the University of Thessaloniki. His current interests are in public transport and in the application of new technologies in this field.

Françoise Potier is Director of Research at the Institut National de Recherche sur les Transport e leur Sécurité (INRETS), in Arcueil, France. She is currently working on national and international travel evolution, with an emphasis on tourism and week-end travel.

Roberta Rabellotti is research fellow at Bocconi University in Milan. Her major research field is development economics. She is currently undertaking a PhD course in Development Economics at the Institute for Development Studies, University of Sussex.

Cees Ruijgrok is a researcher at the TNO Institute of Spatial Organisation in Delft. He is an expert on the development of logistics systems.

Ove Svidén spent 16 years at Saab Scania Aerospace Corporation, 5 years as a manager for Energy Forecasting with Volvo and 4 years as Systems Engineer within the EC's DRIVE programme in Brussels. He has a PhD on scenarios for long range infrastructure planning of transportation and energy systems from Linköping University.

Erik Swyngedouw is lecturer in Human Geography at Oxford University and fellow of St Peter's College, Oxford. He holds masters degrees in agricultural engineering and urban and regional planning from the University of Leuven and a PhD in Geography and Environmental Engineering from John Hopkins University.

Sten Wandel is full Professor and Head of Logistics and Transport Systems Division at Linköping University. He holds a PhD in Industrial Engineering from Stanford University. He currently participates in the OECD Scientific Expert Group on 'Advanced Logistics and Communications in Road Freight Transport Operations'.

Preface

This book has been written as part of the work of the Europe 2020 group of the Network for European Communications and Transport Activities Research (NECTAR) organised by the European Science Foundation (ESF).

NECTAR was launched in 1986 in order to improve channels of communication and the co-ordination of research efforts in the fields of transport and communication between researchers and research institutions in Europe. Its first main task was a systematic evaluation of the state of the art of current research in transport and communications in Europe through a survey involving some 500 experts in the nineteen ESF member countries. In a second phase NECTAR has focused on four core research areas: (1) Barriers to Communication; (2) Europe 2020: Long-term Scenarios of Transport and Communications in Europe; (3) Supply and Demand Behaviour in Transport and Communications; and (4) Transport and Communications Policy.

The Europe 2020 group has looked into the long-term implications of transport and communications in Europe taking into account foreseeable changes in technology, industrial structure and social attitudes. Its work has resulted in two books: *The Geography of Europe's Futures* by Ian Masser, Ove Svidén and Michael Wegener; and this book, *Transport and Communications Innovation in Europe*, edited by George Giannopoulos and Andrew Gillespie.

The editors wish to acknowledge the contribution of all the members of the Europe 2020 group, beyond the attribution of the individual chapters. In particular, we wish to acknowledge the contribution of Sten Wandel, of the University of Linköping, whose editorial help during the initial stages of the work is much appreciated.

George Giannopoulos
Andrew Gillespie
November 1992

Chapter 1

Introduction

G. Giannopoulos and A. Gillespie

Innovation, as Joseph Schumpeter established, provides the driving-force behind long waves of economic development. In this book, our aim is to provide a long-term perspective on innovation in the spheres of transport and communication. Transport and communications are, of course, essential elements of all advanced economies, and they in consequence closely reflect changes in economic and social organisation. Not only do transport and communications systems adapt in response to new demands for movement which are placed upon them by new forms of economic and social organisation, but they also, due to the transformation of spatial relationships which advances in transport and communication can bring about, make possible new forms of economic and social organisation. Transport and communications are, then, both cause and effect of economic and social change.

The premise from which we start is that the current period is undergoing particularly significant changes of a permanent and structural rather than ephemeral nature. The epochal shifts under way have been variously described, *inter alia*, as signifying a transition from an industrial to a post-industrial or information economy; from a Fordist to a post-Fordist mode of economic organisation; or from the downswing of the Fourth Kondratieff long wave to the upswing of a Fifth.

The nature of the transition, and its longer-term implications for economic, social and spatial organisation, and hence for transport and communication, is hotly contested. Some argue, for example, that spatial propinquity will once again become a dominant element of economic organisation, with the re-establishment of sectorally specialised regional economies within a global trading system. Others argue that the trend towards functionally specialised regions, reflective of a marked spatial division of labour, will lead towards increasingly globalised systems of production.

While the nature of the transition is a matter of debate, certain aspects of it seem, nevertheless, to be widely accepted; it is generally agreed, for example, that differentiated and more volatile consumer tastes have brought about a need for companies to be more flexible and responsive to their customers, while quality expectations across a range of criteria, from design to order to delivery times, have been substantially upgraded.

From the perspective of transport and communications, these shifts have profound implications.

Transport systems now have to cope with demands for more frequent movements, usually in smaller shipment sizes, over greater geographical distances, with shorter lead times, and in which a very high premium is placed upon quality of service and reliability. In order to meet the considerable upgrading which such demands represent, transport systems are undergoing a burst of innovation. This is taking a number of forms, including technological innovation, new infrastructures, organisational innovation, and commercial innovation in the wake of deregulation:

- Rapid technological innovation is taking place, particularly in the application of information technologies to the transport sector. In this process, the application of computer systems over geographically dispersed locations is resulting in telecommunications becoming increasingly integrated into transport operation. As Frybourg puts in in Chapter 2, 'the electronic transaction will increasingly trigger the transport process which in turn will be computer-controlled'.
- New infrastructures are being developed in order to take full advantage of technological possibilities. The European high-speed rail network is the prime example of a 'systemic innovation', requiring new infrastructure as well as new vehicles. In the telecommunications field, integrated services digital networks (ISDN) and their broadband upgrades provide important examples of service innovation based on new infrastructures.
- Forms of organisational and institutional innovation are taking place, which in many respects are more significant than technological innovation itself. The development of advanced logistics organisations, to take one example, is an innovation which is creating 'value-added transport services' for users, transforming the flow of goods along the logistics chain, and restructuring the transport service supply side due to the level of planning and investment needed to operate efficiently. Another example is provided by the 'hub and spoke' organisation of air travel, which creates 'virtual networks' connecting places with each other without direct interconnection.
- Commercial innovation through the creation of transport markets is increasingly taking place in the wake of the deregulation of transport and communication services. The need to establish flexible and more responsive transport services in a period of upheaval in demand requirements has necessitated the relaxation of regulatory constraints and mandatory price structures — as Frybourg argues below (Chapter 2), 'what is needed is not only the relevant information but the power to act on behaviour which only pricing can effectively achieve.'

Examining these forms of innovation within the transport and communications sectors, within an explicitly European context, constitutes one of the two main aims of the book. The second aim is concerned with exploring the complex nature of the interrelationships between transport and communication innovation on the one hand and economic, social and spatial transformations on the other. In Part I of the book, these two aims are articulated and conceptualised in Chapters 2 and 3 by Frybourg and by Capello and Gillespie respectively.

Frybourg is concerned to demonstrate the increasing importance of what he terms 'non-material investment' for the process of innovation within the transport sector, to which the application of computerised systems in particular is transforming both the operation of transport systems and the type of transport services which can be offered. Capello and Gillespie, in contrast, attempt to understand the implications of contemporary changes in economic and spatial organisation for transport and communications, particularly in the sense of the nature of the new demands being placed upon existing infrastructures. These two perspectives, the first which starts with the nature of innovation in transport and communications and the second which focuses rather on the broader socio-spatial context within which innovation is occurring, are then followed through in the contributions of Parts II and III respectively.

The approach to understanding transport and communication innovation which the book embodies is distinctive in a number of respects. First and foremost, the contributions attempt to view innovation from a social science perspective rather than from the engineering perspective which is more usual in the transport and technology fields. An important implication of this choice is that technology is seen not as impacting upon society so much as being impacted upon by society. Innovation in transport and communication systems is not then regarded as stemming primarily from the internal logic of technological advance but rather from the pressures imposed by new forms of economic development, new ways of life and new forms of territorial organisation.

A second distinctive aspect of the book lies in its attempt to explore the spatial dimensions associated with innovation in transport and communications. The links between existing spatial structure and organisation and patterns of movement and travel are of course well established; a number of the contributions to this book attempt, through the use of scenarios for example, to explore the ways in which transport and communication innovation will influence future economic and social organisation over space, and/or the impact of changing economic and social organisation on future patterns of transport and communication.

A further distinctive feature of the book is its concern with the policy issues and implications associated with transport and communications innovation. Reflecting the holistic rather than the partial approach to innovation which the book attempts to embody, the policy issues encompassed include not only those concerned with technological innovation but also with infrastructure provision more generally, with the regulation of transport and communications, with land use and regional planning, and with environmental policies. Further, a number of the contributions are concerned with examining or indeed challenging the distributional and equity implications of contemporary forms of innovation in transport and communication.

Each of the chapters addresses policy issues, and the concluding chapter attempts to synthesise these policy deliberations, focusing primarily on the European Community scale of decision-making. Europe provides a particularly interesting environment for examining innovation in transport and communications, given the significance being attached to trans-European networks in helping to bring about the integration of previously separate national economies and urban systems.

Part I: The Framework of Change

Chapter 2

The 'imaginary' in the world of transport: from mechanics to virtual networks

Michel Frybourg

A note on methodology

It is frequently asserted that the world is becoming more complex, and it is a relatively easy matter to pinpoint the different stages in this process. Each sector is evolving along similar paths, though the pace of change may differ. This evolutionary process is apparent in both the sciences and the world of business; one activity stimulates another and breakthroughs occur in those sectors which, by the nature of things, are ripe for change. It is hence only natural to draw some analogies when looking at the future of the transport sector, though we must be careful to avoid some unfounded generalisations.

The theory of numbers

Underpinning every science is the concept of numbers, first familiar as integers and later subject to three stages of complexification: first, the rational numbers (a/b) and then the irrationals (whose square is a whole number). These two groups form a set of real numbers which today is an essential tool for scientific work. But in this set the equation $X^2 = -1$ has no solution, and over the centuries it came to be realised that giving a solution to this equation would be extremely useful in mathematical calculations and would make for progress in algebra. Hence the imaginary numbers based on $i = \sqrt{-1}$ were irrational. The set of all the numbers so obtained (real and imaginary) is known as the set of complex numbers and constitutes the third stage of the process.

Let us go back into history where we will see that this development was slow, hesitant and indeed polemical. The Greeks, with Pythagoras, Aristodus and Euclid, were interested in irrational numbers, whose origins go back to at least the fifth century BC, but it was not until 1572 AD that Bombelli showed that real numbers could be designated by expressions that were in appearance 'imaginary'. Leibniz (1646–1716) saw imaginary numbers as 'an elegant and marvellous challenge to human intelligence, an unnatural birth in the world of thought, almost an amphibian existing between the world of being and non-being'. Only in the nineteenth century, with Gauss and Cauchy, were these new numbers accorded full status. The process had taken twenty-five centuries.

From the world of numbers to the economic world

Developments in economics have followed a similar path, but with a considerable time lag. The domain of the 'rational' is the production of goods and services, the 'irrational' corresponds to marketing, while the 'imaginary' corresponds to non-material investment. Our task is to demonstrate that these analogies are not arbitrary.

To assimilate the market to an 'irrational' activity is to recognise its non-Cartesian character and to realise that the supposed rigour of price calculation is not without its 'mythical' character. The determination of a 'fair price' was long associated with the regulation of profit margins, a supposedly rational approach and yet one that is totally at odds with a commercial strategy whose catchwords are flexibility and immediate adjustment to change. A Cartesian approach assumes stable data and time to analyse them, and results in an administered economy, whereas commercial activity is by essence spontaneous and demands almost instantaneous reactions that are incompatible with any 'a priori' rationality. A 'fair price' is what a good trader can expect to get!

A strictly rational approach, following Descartes, can only work if the person who uses it has all the time in the world. It supposes that objects do not change or disappear in the process of complexification, and that one can check afterwards that nothing has been forgotten. Commerce, however, requires something quite different: managing a process that is both fugitive and subjective. It is not a branch of logic — the art of proving — but one of rhetoric — the art of persuading. It calls for vigilance and readiness to dialogue so that opportunities can be seized when they arise. Cost formation for an economist becomes, for a Cartesian, the equivalent of squaring the circle, a task as dizzy-making as counting the numbers of Pi around the rotunda of the Palais de la Découverte in Paris.

But it is not enough to assimilate irrationality to commerce; we must now understand the non-material investment that so discomforts the traditional economist, who is more at home with the real numbers resulting from commercial transactions. The heterogeneous, bric-à-brac quality of these imaginary investments is not incidental. This activity has been termed a 'surrealist ragbag' into which everything is stuffed — marketing, training, software, R&D, advertising and business investment abroad.

How can we quantify the invisible and codify the imaginary? How can we give full status to the 'non-material' networks that will back up the infrastructural networks on the ground? The Gausses and Cauchys of

today have an enormous task ahead of them in conceptualising what a
new Leibniz will once again call 'an elegant and marvellous challenge to
human intelligence, an unnatural birth in the world of thought, almost
an amphibian existing between the world of being and non-being'. What
is becoming clear is that the non-material is gaining ground in all sectors
of activity. 'Imaginary solutions' are being found to real problems which
cannot be dealt with through the rationality of tangible links or the
relative 'irrationality' of immediate transactions.

Avoiding false hierarchies

It would be wrong to see the 'rational' as in a sense primitive, the 'irrational' as sophisticated and the 'imaginary' as intelligent, and this is for
three reasons. The first mistake would be to forget that each level exists
only by virtue of the reality of the previous level: there is no irrational
number without a rational number, no imaginary number without a real
number. In the same way, there is no market without the production of
goods and services and no 'non-material' investment without material
investment. The second would be to believe that progress has left the
realm of the known and traditional for that of the 'non-traditional';
while the third and most frequent error would be to place intelligence
only in the world of the 'imaginary'. Such pedantic expressions as the
'intelligent car' or 'intelligent traffic light' should not blind us to the
genius of Edouard Delamare-Debouteville who dreamt up the first motor
car in 1884.

This third error is easily explainable by the fact that people equate
engineering with the 'rational', commerce with the 'irrational;' (in that
it escapes the determinism of a priori 'Cartesian' planning — crises
become apparent only after the event), and data processing with
intelligence, as it requires no material support and permits of generalisations that a purely geometrical approach would not allow (such as
finding two points of intersection between a straight line and a
parabola). We can go along with this approach, but it needs to be
complemented by cross-fertilisation between all the phases. Though these
occurred in chronological order, this does not imply a rigid hierarchy or
that the earlier phases are in any sense more 'solid' than the latter.

Proof of this is seen in the conclusions of two members of the French
Academy of Sciences, Robert Dautray and Paul Germain, in their report
on engineering for the President of the Republic. There can be no new
technology without progress on the engineering front. The Challenger
disaster was the result of a failure of the joint sealants; the chlorine leak
in Super-Phoenix was also due to mechanical failure; and the relative
decline in the French manufacturing industry may be ascribed to a
weakness in a key area of engineering: robotic machine tools involving
both engineering and electronics. Anyone who sees driving a heavy

vehicle as a low-skill activity is in for, at best, a rude awakening, since the 'man–vehicle' unit is at the heart of one of the main safety problems facing modern society. Intelligence is everywhere — in the rational, the irrational and the imaginary.

Transport involves more than transport and civil engineering

Transport is a service activity calling for major investment by industry in both mechanical and civil engineering. As a service industry it has acquired only limited autonomy and this only quite recently. Firms and individuals have long transported goods for themselves in some measure and merchants were heavily involved in maritime transport well before the era of international shipping. Only the big merchants were able to shoulder the risks associated with maritime trading. A merchant sent out three ships in quest of spices. If none returned he had lost; one back and he broke even; two back and he had done well; and with three back he was a wealthy man.

When professional carriers appeared on the scene, they were often regulated in some way. Transport is often dependent on infrastructures, implying land requirements and hence the possibility of expropriation, which is granted to private enterprises only under concessional arrangements with the duties and obligation stipulated therein. This state of affairs rapidly results in a monopoly situation with, according to the market, price controls or subsidies and generally both.

Commercial autonomy in the transport sector is a very recent development brought about by deregulation, and freedom to set tariffs is still far from total especially in the area of public transport. Some consider that transport, in that its technological demands are low, is culturally too underdeveloped to become an independent activity, and is only just permeable to rational numbers, i.e. addition, and for the most sophisticated, the 'rule of three'.[1] Others think transport is too important an activity to be left to carriers. For them, transport is part of the communications industry which is controlled at the highest level.

Whatever the true situation, the result has been that, for a long time, innovation in this sector has tended to occur only in upstream activities, i.e. in rolling stock and vehicles, and civil engineering, rather than in management and organisation. This is largely because operators have been limited in their freedom of action. Hence, progress in the transport sector tends to be seen essentially in technological terms, rather than in terms of commercial and organisational innovation where the potential for development is in fact considerable. Transport is only now starting to open up to irrational numbers and wake up to the power of imagination.

The key discoveries in the history of transport have been the invention of the steam-engine which sparked off the development of railways and steamships, the internal combustion engine which made automobile and air travel possible, and the electric motor which allowed the development of city metro systems. These developments were, of course, accompanied by progress in material science and in mechanics which provided better performance and made it possible to build the necessary infrastructures at a reasonable cost.

During this time discussion focused on railway administration, the co-ordination of transportation, quotas, compulsory tariffs for road transport, etc. For their part, the airlines were barely consulted about the major aeronautical programmes — their early fleets were made up of converted bombers. The role of the transport operators was to manage their operational maintenance staff and, exceptionally, to manage the infrastructure. But they were not free to decide on investment (physical or financial quotas), wages and tariffs.

Commercial innovation

It is often claimed that 1978 marked the start of a trend towards greater liberalisation in the transport sector with the adoption of the Airline Deregulation Act under the Carter Administration. There is some truth to this, but one should not forget such precursors as the decline of natural monopolies, developments in the public services, the role of transport auxiliaries, the development of transport on its own account, rental and charter services, as well as the example set by sea transport. As early as 1965, Simon Nora noted that the prime task of public enterprises is to supply their market at the least cost to themselves and the community.

Changes in the concept of public service have come about not only through the demise of dominant technologies and the wider possibilities offered to users, but also as a consequence of abuses of corporatism which expanded at the expense of continuity of service to the consumer and cost effectiveness (especially in regard to economies of scale) to the taxpayer. These considerations explain the general public's attachment to 'its own' post office and railways. With the re-emergence of competition, the government saw itself obliged to encourage more commercial dynamism in the transport industry to the benefit of users who now became its customers. This dynamism implied much greater autonomy of management. With the greater commercial freedom they now enjoyed, transport enterprises could shift from a supposedly 'rational' administrative system to a more 'irrational' system characteristic of the competitive world of commerce. Transport was now open to commercial innovation.

A box is a simple idea, but a profitable one

The concept of containers, familiar throughout the world today, goes back to Malcolm Maclean. From 1934 to 1955, Maclean ran a haulage firm and then set up a company which was to become the world's No. 1 container operator for three decades: Sea-Land, two words which sum up what multi-modal transport is all about. Maclean's idea was to transport goods rapidly and cheaply over long distances by avoiding the many different regulations of the United States governing the size and weight of road vehicles. The present standards, which are indispensable to the growth of containerisation, have been set up by the International Standards Organisation (ISO).

It is worth mentioning some of the main stages in the history of containerisation. The first container-carrier, Gateway City, dates back to the late 1950s: a few hundred Twenty-Foot Equivalents (TFE). Since that time there have been some three generations of container-carriers and capacities have risen from several hundred to 2,500/3,000 TFEs, culminating in the twelve giant container-carriers belonging to US Line (another Maclean company) with capacities of 4,300 TFEs. Admittedly, US Lines went bankrupt and the ISO was partially destabilised by the Super High Cube, but the momentum continues unabated. Mr Chang, the rather shadowy shipping magnate who started business in May 1968 with a second-hand cargo, set up the Evergreen Company which now provides a round-the-world service using twenty-two third-generation ships calling at nineteen ports in both directions.

This example of a radical innovation that owes nothing to technological progress in vehicle manufacture is not unique. It is worth noting too that the idea of containers, a simple but extremely profitable idea, has in the space of twenty years completely revolutionised shipping lines and port facilities as well as jobs in dockhandling and transit. It has also radically changed the system of customs tariffs, the traditional *ad valorem* duties largely giving way to FAK (freight all kind) duties. Such developments remind us that transport is a service activity in which progress is measured in terms of improvements in levels of service; technology is only one factor among many others.

The return of competition

The Carter Administration's decision to deregulate the transport sector owes nothing to the current vogue for free-market economics; at most it may be seen as pointing the way ahead. The decision was based essentially on the need to find new sources of productivity. At the time it was thought that the productivity gains accruing from technological progress in aircraft design would soon lose momentum and would at best simply offset what were expected to be ever-rising fuel costs.

The hope was that gains could be expected more from savings in operational costs as a result of increased competition (better management, more efficient use of fleets, networks and capacities, as well as of tariffs, wage cuts, etc). Transport can be viewed as a system and innovation can come from any of the components of the system and/or from closer integration of its elements. The system comprises infrastructure, vehicles and operating techniques.

Containerisation is an example of an operating technique. Competition is an excellent alkaloid, a stimulant in small doses, and in high doses, a poison, as Auguste Detoeuf has so ably put it. To stimulate transport, all one needs to do is to free it from administrative rationality (quotas and compulsory tariffs) and industrial rationality (progress in materials and equipment), so allowing it to be permeated, first by the 'real' (systems innovation) and then by the 'imaginary' (organisational innovation).

Systems innovation

Rolling stock and track

The TGV (*train de grande vitesse* — high-speed train) and the VAL (automated light vehicle) fall within the realm of the 'real', but, contrary to what is often said, they go beyond the mere application of technological progress in engineering and are more in the nature of a systems innovation. The TGV was developed to meet the challenge of non-traditional suspension systems (air cushion and magnetic) which were deemed too bold and costly because they were not compatible with existing infrastructures. The TGV's main innovative feature was the possibility of using a new line with 'motorway characteristics' in order to attain higher operational speeds that were previously limited by the curvature of existing tracks. This radius of curvature was determined by the need for rail tracks to be sited so as to avoid excessive gradients. The innovation here is a systems one in as much as a TGV on an ordinary line is no faster than the conventional *train corail*.[2] The operating speed does not depend only on the critical speed of the bogie but also on the curvature of the track. It was discovered, or rather rediscovered, that engineering technology could only be fully exploited through a complete overhaul of the whole system, including trains, infrastructure and operating techniques.

The VAL was a response to the authorities' desire to endow the smaller major cities (with populations of under one million) with a transport system having the qualities of service of traditional metros at comparable cost. This meant that the lower capacity of the system (smaller trains or vehicles and less traffic) needed to be offset by greater manpower productivity. The only way to achieve this was to use auto-matic driving systems that did not require each unit to be manned. The VAL does, however, require a major initial investment (of the same magnitude as a metro) and one that is much higher than for a tram system which does not use grade-separation. As the recent debate in Strasbourg showed, competition between the two is quite fierce: lower initial investment for trams versus low operating cost and greater flex-ibility for the VAL. A comparison between the two must take into account the whole system (segregated or protected corridor) and not just the rolling stock.

Fare structure and operating technique

The integration of the various components of a system is not just the result of technical decisions on, say, a new line with different characteristics or an automatised driving system. It may arise as the result of commercial decisions. A case in point is the *Carte Orange* used in Paris, a monthly card valid for all forms of transport, or tickets allowing passengers to make connecting journeys. The introduction of the *Carte Orange* radically changed the way Parisians used their transport system, including surface transport. Its cost is warranted for essential commuter journeys and any other trips are in a sense free. It becomes a second car and people no longer hesitate to take a bus for a short trip or to change lines. The Paris network (metro and surface lines) has become a fully integrated system. This is even more true for the suburban system (RATP plus SNCF suburban trains).

A commercial policy consists above all of adjustability to the diver-sities of supply and demand. A bus on a scheduled service travels in both directions and may not always be available at rush hours. Passengers travel for different reasons (business or pleasure) and under various constraints, especially in terms of time. The maximum tariff acceptable to a user is very variable, according to his or her reasons for travel, or the type of goods to be transported. Commercial innovation consists of finding the optimum combination of tariffs.

Fare bands for train travel according to time of day and year constitute another system designed to 'confine' business and pleasure travel within certain periods. The idea is to canalise business and tourist traffic into relatively 'watertight' compartments so that business travellers, in exchange for the higher fares they pay, can expect guaranteed seats, convenient time schedules and frequent services, while other users can enjoy cheaper travel within the limits of available seating or be assigned special time slots.

Deregulation has paved the way for a range of activities that have yet to find their point of equilibrium. The market for the sale by travel agents of 'straight' airline tickets, i.e. with no other service, is still relatively undefined. Alongside this official market is the practice of discounting tickets of certain airlines by the 'bucket shops' under conditions of somewhat dubious legality. These practices reflect the 'irrational' aspect of an industry which is seizing opportunities as they arise and is introducing flexibility into a system where a priori rules would put a brake on the market. But a market is not a natural system; it is a sophisticated product which can only function with a number of quite complex rules. It needed to invent imaginary numbers, i.e. computerised systems and virtual networks based on terminals (hubs) and their interconnections (spokes).

Computerised systems

Computer-reservation systems (CRS)

Effective intercity transport operations require an efficient seat reservation system. Manually operated systems had become totally impracticable by the 1960s, due not only to the increased traffic, but also to the move towards deregulation (greater amounts of data to be handled by an ever-increasing number of operators and routes). The increasing number of connecting journeys made possible by the 'hub' system could only be dealt with efficiently by multi-airline reservation systems. **Computer reservation systems** (CRS) introduced in the 1980s have had a major impact on the three areas of business, technology and finance.

First, business. The possessor of a CRS enjoys a close relationship with the travel agencies, has a more effective marketing system and, above all, retains control over all the marketing information. The advantage of CRS is hence to provide real-time computerised access to the market. With CRS not only can general information available to all be displayed but also airlines' own products, special rates, extra services. The sale of airlines' own connecting services can be 'pushed' at the expense of others.

The owner of a CRS retains the passenger file and hence is free to compile a customer list which can be subsequently used for promotional purposes. The system also covers such ancillary services as hotel reservation, car hire, package tours and even non-tourist activities such as banking, travel loans, ticket sales by mail, insurance, currency exchange, theatre bookings, etc.

Now, the technological implications. Given the pace of technological change, the growth in services offered and the sheer volume of data to be handled, the designers of these systems must constantly strive to offer their customers even more sophisticated services. The costs involved in such developments are enormous.

The third factor, financial, following directly from the first two, is an extremely important one. Booking systems have become distribution systems, a sales tool which boosts company sales and increases turnover.

Moreover, the need to be linked into a system is essential. It is indeed a question of business survival as these systems provide travel agencies with a global package comprising all the tools (invoicing/accounting/customer follow-up, etc.) required for decision-making. In the coming world of ever-expanding data exchange using new communication systems and remote sales, the electronic transaction will increasingly trigger the transport process which in turn will be computer-controlled.

Understanding the process requires an analysis of the competitive economy and of the comparative advantages offered by **electronic data interchange** (EDI) for commercial transactions. Computerised reservation systems are only one example of the benefits it can bring, which include the exchange of commercial documents such as orders and invoices without use of paper.

Electronic data interchange (EDI)

The competitive economy has given strategic importance to the logistics and computer technology of communications (as distinct from the use of computers within companies), so that companies which fail to take this aspect into account in their boardroom deliberations will be seriously disadvantaged. Expressions such as 'just-in-time' or references to the five Olympic zeros — no stock, no time lag, no fault, no breakdown, no paper — point to a new form of logistics based on tighter flow management and rooted in the desire to enhance productivity and meet the challenges of the competitive economy. Another set of five zeros uses three acronyms of US origin: JIT (**just-in-time**) for the first two, TQC (**total quality control**) for the next two, and EDI (**electronic data interchange**) for the fifth.

The mid-1970s (which marked the end of thirty years of post-war economic expansion) was a transitional period during which a supply-dominated economy, a sellers' market where it was sufficient to produce in order to sell, gave way to a buyers' market where the ideal was to produce only that which was already sold. Production capacity had moved into surplus and firms could develop only through efficient marketing. Marketing techniques resulted in segmentation of the market, product diversification, smaller stocks and faster turnover. In many industries it became increasingly difficult to acquire a competitive advantage or to differentiate one's product. The market had reached maturity, and prices, production techniques and the functional characteristics of the products were, to all intents and purposes, the same. There was little customer loyalty or brand identity. In this situation service became the deciding factor.

In every industry where the customer must have flexible and rapid access to the supplier, telecommunications provide a means of redefining the service. Two tactics have been employed: (1) providing the customer with a terminal linking him directly with the various company departments and its internal networks; (2) tailoring the system to customer needs through the provision of additional facilities or a more convenient service ('tracking' procedures for goods monitoring). The aim is to reduce the spatial and temporal barriers impeding access to the firm and to use the terminal to create a new relationship with it. The transaction costs may be transferred to customers by asking them to enter and validate their transaction. This direct contrast also allows for the provision of extra services and information. For example, when a client at the Hotel Scandinavia pays his bill, he can also receive his boarding pass for Scandinavian Airlines (who own the hotel) and check in his luggage. Similarly, supermarkets have transformed their cash registers into computerised bank tills with, in addition, supply control capability. These examples show the EDI can help break down inter-industry barriers.

The major companies have realised that once they have set up a network, the extra cost for new services may be quite low. If a company installs an EDI network before its competitor, it enjoys the advantage of being first on the scene since the customer is unwilling to have more than one terminal and this dictates his choice of supplier. The owner of a point-of-customer contact, such as a reservations terminal in the case of an airline, or more generally a workstation for transactions, provides a facility for non-traditional services and a means of enhancing customer loyalty.

The existence of a workstation and hence the availability of information in numerical (i.e. computer-processable) form can be a valuable aid to decision-making. The ground is being laid for the systems of tomorrow, whatever their appellation (expert systems, decision-making tools). In a service company, whether a carrier or a forwarding agent, the key collaborator in a competitive market is the person effecting the transaction. His effectiveness can be considerably enhanced if he has access to the relevant 'real-time' information enabling him to do business for his company in optimum conditions.

Significant changes have occurred in international trade in recent years. To a certain extent, these changes have been supported, and perhaps stimulated, by changes in information systems and telecommunications. In the 1990s, many observers expect to see more significant changes. These are exemplified by what is happening in Europe. The Single European Market will bring about significant changes in trade within Europe and between Europe and its trading partners, especially Japan, the Dynamic Asian Economies and North America. At the same time, the deregulation of telecommunications in Europe, and related deregulation and privatisation activities in other countries are creating the potential for major changes in all aspects of the offering of telecommunications and related information systems services, such as value-added networks. Further significant progress is being made in the development of data transmission standards for electronic data interchange (EDI), especially among manufacturers and their suppliers, distributors and customers.

It appears likely that in this context there will be significant changes in patterns of trade, in the economic competition between cities, regions and countries, and in the firm and industry structure in general and especially in manufacturing and distribution, integrated logistics and transportation, and in finance.

Virtual or informal networks

While it is relatively easy, technically if not legally, to 'dematerialise' commercial documents and to transform, say, the verbal agreement of a horse-dealer into keying in the appropriate validation on computer, it is a much more risky business to break loose from the constraints of infrastructures that have physically marked our cities and countryside for upwards of a century. The star-structure of the Paris metro is both the cause and the effect of the centralisation of Paris and ensures that the city will continue to develop on similar lines. The small gauge of the Paris metro has protected it from the ambitions of the large railway companies by giving an urban vocation to an investment which, in its early stages, was not intended for commuter travel. Perhaps transport can hope to find two intersections — an origin and a destination — between a straight line (representing potential demand) and a parabola (representing the available infrastructure). In brief, is it possible to renew this 'unnatural birth in the realm of thought' of imaginary numbers and create 'this amphibian existing between being and non-being'? To answer this question we must study the interconnection between hubs and spokes and the informal networks of associated firms.

Interconnection

The decision to link up the RER (express metro) of the RATP (the Parisian Metro Company) and the suburban services of the SNCF (French railways) was taken in 1971 following a mission to Japan. Many engineers were lukewarm about the project and the experience in London had been disappointing. The aim was to examine railway regulation on the hypothesis of joint use by convoys having different modes of operation: single route for the metro and different destinations according to convoy for the SNCF. It is now clear that the decision to link up was prompted by the technological feasibility of so doing through progress in electronics. Now that trains could come into the heart of the capital, the physical barriers — the consequence of two distinct gauges — and the psychological barriers — a disregard for Parisians' travel needs — had been removed. It became possible to exploit the star network for cross-city suburb-to-suburb trips and was a major step forward towards the creation of a virtual network.

The TGV interconnections consist in physically linking axes that are being built (Sud-Est and Atlantique), approved (Nord-Transmanche) or projected (Est). The interconnection is a structural modification. It involves direct links and hence is a fundamentally new departure from the traditional spoke pattern with Paris at its hub. In 1970 the combination of radiotelephony and computer science led the transport authorities to speak of interconnection in the electronics field, as well as of integration with the RNIS (service-integrated numerical network). In the RATP there has been internal integration with the *Carte Orange* (bus and metro) and external interconnection with the SNCF. Inter-firm communication using EDI systems is another form of interconnection.

The decision to interlink the TGV lines was a key element in the decisions taken on 9 October 1987. The new connecting line that will skirt the East of Paris will link up the already existing TGV Sud-Est, the TGV Atlantique, and the TGV-Est which is under study. It will serve the Paris Airport of Roissy and will hence allow new multi-modal transport combinations. The new network will provide links between the different regions and with the rest of Europe. The Île-de-France interconnection should be completed at the same time as the TGV Nord and the Channel Tunnel.

In the area of road traffic, new information systems are helping drivers to choose between different routes, especially in urban areas and during peak holiday periods. Radio guidance has existed for many years but with limited effectiveness. The 'green routes', varying traffic signal systems and the *bison futé* system of alternative itineraries have extended its possibilities. A new generation of guidance systems is being studied in two Europe-wide research programmes, PROMETHEUS and DRIVE. Experimental guidance systems are also under study in Berlin (ALI-SCOUT) and London (AUTOGUIDE). New systems using in-car computer technology hold out new possibilities for a more efficient use of the infrastructure as well as a more flexible use of the existing networks, i.e. supplementing the real network by an appropriate virtual network, in a word another form of interconnection.

Hubs and spokes

This United States idea is a consequence of airline deregulation and denotes a series of privately-owned terminal hubs which have had a far-reaching effect on factors of production. Each company has 'its own' terminal constituting a natural monopoly and providing economies of scale through an interconnecting system that reduces the number of direct flights.

The hub system is not new and is natural in an activity which demands high-capacity aircraft, full loads and high frequencies to provide a good level of service, i.e. a reasonable quality of service at a reasonable price. Bulking is a necessity for freight services and the concentration of freight has been a fact of life for ports for many years now, success breeding success. The same phenomenon is apparent on the railways where the grouping of individual wagons in the marshalling yards is more efficient when the traffic is high. What is new with these terminals is their networking structure and computerised management which have made them so much more efficient. What we are witnessing is not so much a qualitative change but a change in their very nature.

While the frequency of the delivery of supplies to a factory is determined by full vehicle loads, 'just-in-time' production requires smaller but more frequent deliveries. In order to maintain costs at an acceptable level, the 'real numbers' solution would consist of making two half-load deliveries. This is a bad compromise. The 'complex numbers' solution would consist of organising a delivery schedule with a fully loaded vehicle and delivery to four factories from a single terminal. To do this on a large scale, recourse is needed to 'imaginary numbers', i.e. computer science. An example is the SNCF's ETNA which combines an 'ordinary' system (the train leaves when it is full) with an 'accelerated' system (the train leaves on time) to give an optimised real-time system. The runaway success of the express freight delivery service is one outcome.

The productivist logic of real numbers allowed quality of service to suffer at the expense of economy of means, but despite this, the familiar parcel post service and the SERNAM[3] rail freight service remained a permanent headache since they were always in the red. In countries loyal to a public service tradition, these activities were phased down in an orderly manner: some savings, not too much loss of quality and a gradual lightening of the traffic load; it could always be hoped that more could be achieved at a later stage.

In the United States the market collapsed and the situation was ripe for a total overhaul that consisted in tackling the problem the other way round. Quality of service was guaranteed and it was hoped that success would ensue. The stress was on the ends rather than the means and the rationale for complete loads was supplanted by that of the computerised terminal. The risks were enormous but the success was staggering.

What accounts for such success? On the demand side, there is the sheer size of the markets, with constantly changing products, such as fashion goods and beauty products. For these industries, the plane is the only means of transport used in the United States. Quality of service too is exemplified in the speed of electronics maintenance and repair services and diversification policy. On the supply side, the possibility of calling on the most sophisticated information technologies has played a crucial role.

The success of enterprises such as the Memphis giant, Federal Express, and UPS has led to profound changes with regard to market segmentation, the organisation of intermodal transport, the hub-and-spoke structure of transport schemes, the standardisation of packaging, mechanised handling and the pricing structure. Their achievements stand as a model for 'non-material' enterprises.

Non-material enterprises

This expression does not denote a one-man outfit with a telephone, but an enterprise which invests in know-how and software, both 'non-material' investments. The first such firms to make their appearance in the transport sector in the 1970s were involved in distribution. These companies work for major suppliers like Unilever and distribute goods to the points of sale, replenish supplies on request and look after every aspect of the operation from invoicing to collection of payment. They have no trucks of their own but lease them and generally do not even own their warehouses which they rent. Their investment is entirely intangible. Network integration means that they have to subcontract some activities to others. This type of skill, which may be qualified more in terms of expertise than mere specialisation, combines communication and management techniques.

This approach, eschewing the ownership of real estate or rolling stock, has caught on. Today there are taxi firms that no longer have a fleet of vehicles and drivers, but instead sell to independent operators the right of access to a central switchboard. The Non-Vessel Operating Common Carriers (NVOCC) in the United States are maritime shipping companies with no ships. They orchestrate the movements of containers and enable shipping companies to fill their giant container-vessels. Regular shipping lines in Europe, faced with the difficulty of operating ships under their national flags, are increasingly divesting themselves of their ships to concentrate on freight handling and on-board loading, which are far more profitable activities. Tour operators are selling both flights and tourist accommodation. The recent mergers in France, which have had varying measures of success, were designed to gear up to meet the challenge of the US, British and German giants.

This situation is characteristic of a buyers' market where the customer calls the tune. It arises when there is a surplus transport capacity which puts carriers at risk. Changes in the economic climate can, however, reverse the situation, causing the supply to diminish and prices to rise. It must always be borne in mind that the non-material cannot exist without the material: there are no imaginary numbers without real numbers. However, the immense scale of some non-material investment such as that ploughed into computerised reservation systems has created an irreversible situation, with the costs of entry such that there is no alternative to joining the system and paying the price. The success of

SABRE and APOLLO with the European airlines provides ample evidence.

Conclusion

Transport, which started out in the realm of engineering, has today become such a complex set of organisations that the systems involved must call on all the resources of computer science. Information technology has become as essential to its development as industrial technologies. This should not be taken to imply that progress is not being made on the engineering side. That would be a sad thing indeed for a science of movement! The engineer's dream has always been to eliminate friction between moving parts, the myth of the magic carpet. With magnetic suspension and linear drive, he is not far from realising his ambition. Experiments under way in Emslend are conclusive. What is now needed is to achieve the right economic conditions for these new techniques to become competitive.

But whatever the progress of the transport equipment industry, such equipment must be integrated into the technical system of the transport mode concerned and its market. The technical system assumes that vehicles, infrastructure and operating techniques will evolve in harmony, as was the case for the TGV. There can be no radically new trains without new infrastructure. To sell cars that can travel at twice the maximum authorised speed for operation on infrastructures whose geometric characteristics are patently insufficient and which carry heavy and mixed traffic is nonsensical from the point of view of road safety. The technical system is a reality that must be lived with in the transport industry.

The existence of a transport market in the true sense of the term is all the more essential given the diversity of demand of travellers, depending on income, trip purpose, and physical and geographical conditions, and of goods, depending on their nature, destination, batch size and frequency of delivery; only a genuine market combining a diversity of products and tariffs can meet this multiplicity of needs. It is clear that this sector, which has been overadministered, needed to be given greater freedom, and that true cost efficiency, which is incompatible with mandatory price structures, had to be restored. It is not enough to provide users with information as in motorway information. What is needed is not only the relevant information but the power to act on behaviour which only pricing can effectively achieve.

These major technical and commercial systems will call for all the resources of science and organisational and information technologies. Complexity requires to be managed and this will require the creativity of the communications industry which is investing primarily, if not solely, in the non-material, and which has the ability to transmit the right messages to manufacturing industry on the basis of an almost instantaneous knowledge of demand. These integrated service enterprises, which are set to be the prime users of the future service-integrated numerical networks of the telecommunications industry and the value-added networks, will be able to integrate the whole process from production to distribution and thereby fulfil a logistic role which is none other than the provision of value-added transport. Transport has moved from the integer — the wheel — to the complex number — computerised systems, via the irrational number — the commercial transaction. It has hence become permeable to innovations of all kinds that Jules Vernes could scarcely have conceived of, fascinated as he was by the science of movement.

Notes

1. Rule one applies to determine the fourth element of a proportion, when the other three are known.
2. The attractive 'coral-coloured' trains, which replaced the traditional green wagons in the 1970s.
3. A subsidiary of the SNCF, responsible for parcel service delivery by rail.

Chapter 3

Transport, communications and spatial organisation: future trends and conceptual frameworks

R. Capello and A. Gillespie

Transport, communications and spatial organisation: an historical perspective

Introduction

Few changes are having a greater impact on the ability of firms and countries to compete in global markets than the recent and ongoing revolution in telecommunications and transport. The new capabilities of information processing and transmission, as well as the enhanced mobility of people and the movement of freight, are profoundly altering features upon which the competitiveness of firms and the comparative advantages of regions depend.

The key forces generating a new industrial and spatial structuring are embodied in the radical technological changes currently under way in the telecommunications and transport industries. Communications and transport networks can be regarded as the 'carriers', in both literal and symbolic senses, of new systems of industrial and spatial organisation.

The idea of communications and transport as the carriers of new industrial and spatial forms is of course not new. Many commentators have drawn attention to the historical association between advances in transport and/or communications technologies and changes in the nature of society, changes in the way the economy is organised, and changes in spatial structure and organisation.

In one sense, the very existence of the city can be understood as the spatial response to the severe limitations upon the movement of people, goods and information which prevailed before and during the early stages of the industrial era. As Schaeffer and Sclar (1975, p. 8) put it, 'to avoid transportation, mankind invented the city'.

Adopting a historical perspective (Table 3.1), it is clear that technological advances in transport and communication have been instrumental in the establishment of a series of major economic, social and geographical developments (we purposely do not use the term 'caused';

Table 3.1 Association between major transport and communication developments and spatial form of production, 1850–1950

	*1850	1900	1920	1930	1950
Movement of Information	Telegraph	Local Telephone			International Telephone Networks
Movement of Freight	Long/Medium-Distance Railway		Van		Lorry Aeroplane
Movement of People	Long/Medium-Distance Railway	Suburban Railways Urban Electric Trams		Motor Bus	Car Aeroplane
Spatial Forms of Production	Urban Production Agglomeration	Expanded Metropolitan Areas Production Agglomeration		Suburbanisation of Production Multi-Locational Enterprises	
			Development of International Business Organisation		

Note: * Dates present the time by which inventions were sufficiently diffused to permit social and economic innovation to take place.

the complex question of the nature and direction of causality in the relationship between technology and society we will return to later).

The period of industrial urbanisation (1850–1920)

The explosive growth, in the second half of the nineteenth century, of industrialisation and its spatial expression, the industrial city, is impossible to have envisaged occurring without significant developments in the ability to transport both people and goods and to communicate information. Key innovations in the realm of transport and communication which made industrial urbanisation possible include the emergence of national railway networks, facilitating the movement between cities of both people and industrial goods; and national telegraph networks, enabling movement on the railway networks to be co-ordinated and controlled, and other information, for example on price movements, to be transmitted and exchanged between cities.

The large and spatially extensive metropolitan complexes which have become established by the early years of the present century were in turn dependent upon key developments in the short-distance movement of people, notably the suburban railway and the electric tram, and in the emergence of local telephone networks.

The period of Fordism (1920–80)

By the middle of this century, the widespread diffusion of further significant innovations in the realm of transport and communication were both making possible and reflecting a complex set of economic, social and geographical changes which we will refer to as 'Fordism'.

At the level of the metropolitan area, the most obvious change in spatial organisation in the period of Fordism was that of the suburbanisation of the population (Walker, 1981), a development intimately associated with the widespread diffusion of car ownership and usage. Urban fields, or 'daily urban systems', had by now spread well beyond the physical confines of the urban area to encompass and incorporate previously rural territories and communities.

Still at the urban regional level, the previous constraints upon the movement of goods, which had kept productive activities close to the centrally located rail termini, had been successively removed by the diffusion of the short-distance goods van, and subsequently by the advent of long-distance goods transport by lorry (Moses and Williamson, 1967).

These sequential changes permitted, in the era which we are characterising as Fordism, a considerable expansion and extension of the locations in which production activities could be viably situated. In conjunction with other characteristics of land and labour markets, including the suburbanisation of population outlined above, these improvements in the transport of goods facilitated the suburbanisation of manufacturing, and in due course the so-called 'urban–rural shift' of certain types of manufacturing activity.

Above the level of the individual urban region, transport and communication improvements were again instrumental in making possible the systems of long-distance national, and increasingly international, integration and co-ordination upon which Fordism depended. The growth of the Fordist multi-locational enterprise, with its complex functional spatial division of activities, required an interlocking set of mechanisms for the efficient movement of goods, people (in the form of managers, sales and marketing staff, etc.) and information. Containerisation, high-speed rail travel, intra- and inter-metropolitan motorway networks, national and international air travel and national and international telephone and telex networks can be regarded as the essential underpinnings of the Fordist system of industrial and spatial organisation.

A 'post-Fordist' transport and communications?

What of the current period of transformation, from Fordism to some yet to be defined 'post-Fordism'? What will be the spatial form of post-Fordism, and how will transport and communications limit, modify, facilitate or encourage its development?

This chapter is concerned primarily with the adjustments and developments taking place in communications and transport in association with the emergence of what we contend is a new paradigm of industrial and geographical organisation. The outlines of this new paradigm are discernible in contemporary developments, but its eventual, fully articulated form is not yet clear. Indeed, there is considerable debate about precisely which features of the contemporary transformation will emerge as the defining characteristics of the new paradigm, and which, on the contrary, will come to be seen only as temporary features of the transition from one paradigm to another.

Further, the current period of transition provides not one but a number of competing paradigms, with the future outcome not yet certain or determined. Each of these competing paradigms has different implications for transport and communications. Exploring these different future scenarios, as a basis for understanding what the long-term requirements for transport and communications in Europe will be, forms the subject of this chapter.

Our approach to analysing current transformations and
future possibilities

The significance of contemporary developments in transport, communications and spatial organisation, coupled with the lack of certainty about their interrelated outcomes, is reflected in a growing literature (see, for example, Soekkha et al., 1990; Nijkamp et al., 1990; Brunn and Leinbach, 1991; Brotchie et al., 1991; Hepworth and Ducatel, 1991). In contributing to this debate, our approach contains a number of points of departure from conventional approaches:

1. First of all, this study is based on a **simultaneous analysis of both transport and communications**. The analysis of technological innovation which we develop proceeds on the basis of a strong interrelationship existing between transport and telecommunications technologies, an interrelationship witnessed for example by a host of information technology (IT) applications to the transport sector. This relationship goes well beyond simple technological linkages and manifests itself in the joint capacities these technologies have to impact on the spatial structure of the economy. Just-in-time organisational forms of production, for example, require both advanced telecommunications infrastructures as well as a modern, efficient and reliable transport system. The lack of one of the two infrastructural systems would inevitably lead to inefficiency and to difficulties in sustaining this spatial-organisational form of production.

2. Secondly, the analysis is based on a constant awareness that **although technological changes in telecommunications and transport are the catalyst for spatial dynamics, they are only necessary but not sufficient conditions for these dynamics**. There are two reasons for this assumption:

    •   technological changes are developed and generated on the basis of economic, industrial and institutional forces governing their development trajectories. By this we mean, for example, the institutional changes governing the telecommunications sector, which acts in effect as a 'gatekeeper' for the development of new information technologies. At the same time, the way in which industrial firms in the telecommunications sector react to the threat of possible competition, by developing co-operation agreements with other firms, for example, necessarily has an impact on the development trajectories of these technologies;

    •   Even with a rapid development and diffusion of these new technologies, changes in spatial structure and organisation only take place if they are accompanied by modifications in locational preferences at the level of the firm. This is also true at an industrial level, where locational patterns reflect the industrial and economic equilibria arising from interlinked locational preferences.

3. Another distinct feature of the present study is that **despite most frequent analyses trying to capture a direct link between technological changes and spatial patterns, this study stresses the interrelationship between technological changes, new organisational forms of production and spatial trajectories**. The organisational variable is regarded as a fundamental and crucial 'bridge' to capture the linkages between technological changes and spatial dynamics. The relationships between these variables are neither linear nor uni-directional, being best regarded as a circular set of interconnections, making the definition of the original causes of changes not easy to define (see the next section on interrelationships and causality). To present the argument in a linear narrative way, the circle must be 'broken into' at some point. Although we have chosen here to break into the circle at the point of technological change, reflecting the context within which we are writing, we contend that other starting-points would be equally valid, and indeed may be more useful in understanding the nature of contemporary transformations.

4. The present study **adopts a two-level approach, a micro and a macro level, for studying changes in organisational and spatial structures**. The micro level refers to the firm, i.e. to changes in the intra- and inter-corporate organisational structure and in the spatial organisation of production. These changes could manifest themselves through a new division of labour and of functions and through a new spatial division of labour. The macro level is related to the industrial system as a whole and underlines changes in universal industrial behavioural rules, in regulatory regimes and in the spatial structure around which industrial systems are organised.

5. A final characteristic of the analysis is that **no single, unique trajectory of change in the industrial and spatial structures can be identified for the future**. The development trajectories for these industrial and spatial structures are obviously related to the development of transport and telecommunications technologies, but these in turn depend on the development trajectories of some other crucial elements, including technological innovation, the diffusion and application of technologies throughout the industrial system, and the institutional framework within which diffusion takes place — concerning, for example, the structure of markets and how they are regulated, standards issues, etc.

    These elements can follow a number of different development paths, each of them leading to a different pattern of usage of transport and telecommunication technologies and consequently to the constitution of different industrial and spatial structure scenarios. For these reasons, in this chapter we refer to differing possible scenarios in the development of the industrial and spatial structure and we consider which of them is most likely to take place, given some key considerations. Before considering these scenarios, however, the next section explores in rather more detail the complex nature of causality in the relationships between transport and communications and spatial organisation.

Understanding interrelationships and the circular nature of causality

As established in the previous section, our concern in this chapter is with the nature of the interrelationships between transport and communications on the one hand, and organisational and spatial structures on the other, during a period of major structural change, which is affecting all of these elements, and the relationships between them, simultaneously. With so many simultaneous changes taking place, understanding the direction(s) of causality is by no means straightforward. In this section, we begin to 'unpack' the complex interrelationships at work, and in so doing attempt to establish the framework which we will use in the following section for presenting a range of future transport and communication scenarios.

Technology and the relationship between transport and communication

One of the driving-forces affecting both transport and communications is of course technological innovation. Although there are some important developments taking place in the technologies of transport, such as high-speed trains and 'clean engine' systems, most recent innovation in the transport field is best regarded as examples of what Freeman et al. (1982) describe as 'incremental' forms of innovation. More radical innovation in the field of transport and communications is associated, firstly, with the application of informatics and telematics to the transport sector, for example in road informatics systems and in goods transport logistical systems; and secondly, with the digitalisation of telecommunications networks, which has made possible computer-mediated communications and broadband communications. (These innovations are examined in Part II of the book.)

In an important sense then, information technologies and the associated 'informatics revolution' lie at the heart of the innovation process in both transport and communications. A form of 'technological convergence' is thus affecting the relationships between the two, opening up new complimentarities and potential synergies, most evident in the way telematics networks are becoming integral to an increasing array of transport operations. At the same time, however, technological advances in the telecommunications field are providing new opportunities for substituting electronic communications for physical transport. The nature

Table 3.2 Major areas of innovation in transport and communication

Mode/Movement of	(Physical) Transport	(Electronic) communications
Information	express courier services	— high-speed fax — electronic mail — computer networks (e.g. for CAD) — videotex/teletext

People	— high-speed train
	— road informatics
	— information and booking
	  systems
		— workstations with
		  slow-scan video images
		— video-conferencing

Goods	— logistical systems	— EDI
		— facsimile transmission of
		  printed material (e.g.
		  newspapers)
		— computer networks for
		  just-in-time delivery

of these potential complimentarities and substitutions is suggested in Table 3.2, which provides some examples of changes associated with technological change in transport and communications as they affect the movement of information, people and goods.

For the **movement of information**, innovation is concentrated primarily in electronic communication rather than in physical transport. Although express courier services, supported by sophisticated logistical systems, have proved an important innovation in the movement of information, substituting for slower and less reliable mail services, it is in digital telecommunications that the most significant developments are occurring. Building upon the rapid growth of (analogue) facsimile transfer, digital networks such as ISDN offer the prospect not only of high-speed fax but of public electronic mail services and an increasing range of applications for moving specialist information in digital form, such as computer-aided designs.

For the **movement of people**, significant innovations are occurring in both transport and electronic communication. The physical movement of people is being assisted by innovations as diverse as high-speed rail, road informatics, and on-line information and booking systems. The electronic movement of people, or rather their video images, seems to be suddenly 'coming of age', not in the long-heralded video-phone but rather in the rapid growth of corporate video-conferencing, made possible by a combination of more affordable broadband satellite networks and data compression techniques which are allowing moving images to be transmitted over 'medium-band' terrestrial networks. A number of European

PTTs, for example, are experimenting with slow-scan video images transmitted over '2 B + D' 64kb/s ISDN networks.

For the **movement of goods**, significant innovations are again found in both physical and electronic forms of movement. As Chapters 5 and 12 below demonstrate, advanced logistical systems are revolutionising the transport sector, while the growth of **electronic data interchange** (EDI) applications are making an important contribution from the telecommunications side. Additionally, mention should be made of the electronic movement of certain types of 'goods', notably printed material such as newspapers or insurance policies, which can be transmitted as facsimile images or digital records and printed simultaneously at remote locations.

Technological innovation is, then, affecting not only the development of transport and communications but also the interrelationship between them. New complimentarities, as well as some new substitution possibilities, are being created by innovations in the physical movement of information, people and goods over transport networks, and their electronic communication over telecommunications networks.

The implications of innovation in transport and communications for organisational and spatial structure

From the point of view of our objectives in this chapter, the significance of the types of technological innovation considered above lies in the way they interact with, or modify, or limit, the behaviour of organisations and, in the longer term, the spatial organisation of the economic system. The complex nature of the interrelationships between these various elements, particularly as concerns causality, can best be illustrated by means of examples. Below, three such examples are used to demonstrate the relationships between changes in transport/communications, organisational behaviour and spatial structure. Each has a different causal 'starting-point', for there is no single direction of causality, the different elements being bound together in a web of two-way interactions.

EXAMPLE 1: TECHNOLOGICAL INNOVATION
The first example starts with a technological innovation, EDI, which is, simultaneously, both a transport/communication innovation, affecting the flow of information associated with the movement of goods, and an organisational innovation, affecting the relationship between customer and supplier. EDI can have significant implications for the behaviour of the firm and for organisational structure more generally; it can contribute to improving the internal efficiency of the firm, through automating existing labour-intensive procedures; it can improve the competitive position of adopters, by speeding up their response to customer orders; and, in the longer term, through reducing transaction

costs, it can even shift the boundary of the firm by affecting the 'make-or-buy' decision (Williamson, 1975).

EDI can also be expected to have implications for the spatial organisation of production systems: by reducing one element of transaction costs, and by improving the overall efficiency of the transactional system, EDI is likely to contribute to the spatial extension of production linkages, and hence to the viability of global production systems. Further, as EDI becomes more widely adopted and centrally embedded into the organisation of production, the ability of locations to support sophisticated electronic communications for EDI will become a prerequisite for inward investment. In the longer term, therefore, it can be suggested the EDI will affect, at a variety of scales from the urban–rural to the international, the relative locational attractions of different places for productive investments.

Finally, the 'wheel comes full circle' (appropriately enough, given the nature of the example), with these EDI-led organisational and spatial adaptations imposing new requirements upon the transport system, for example to support larger volumes of long-distance freight movement.

EXAMPLE 2: ORGANISATIONAL CHANGE

Our second example, based on an actual firm (documented in more detail in Capello and Williams, 1992), breaks into the transport/communication/organisational behaviour/spatial organisation web of interrelationships at a different point; it starts not with a technological innovation but with a perceived need for organisational change. The firm in question, which produces agricultural fertilisers and pesticides, recognised that its marketing effort was inconsistent and fragmented. The existing marketing effort was dispersed around its many production sites, and the firm decided to centralise the marketing function into three sites.

The reorganisation of the marketing function within the firm thus had an explicit spatial dimension, and at once imposed new requirements upon the firm's communications infrastructure. A new computer communication network was implemented, linking the head office with the three new regional sales and marketing offices. At the same time the pattern of business travel within the firm changed substantially, both between the head office and the three marketing centres and between the sales offices and the firm's customers.

EXAMPLE 3: SPATIAL RESTRUCTURING

The final example, like the second an actual firm (documented in more detail in Goddard, 1990), starts from the need to reorganise the spatial structure of the firm, this time in response to a geographical shift in the firm's markets. The firm, based in the north of England and making timber doors and window frames, saw its existing northern market contract substantially with the demise of council-house building in the 1980s. Southern markets were growing vigorously with the boom in 'do-it-yourself', but serving these markets necessitated meeting much shorter order-to-delivery cycles than the firm was capable of with its existing production organisation.

The geography of the firm's production organisation was completely restructured, without having to close existing sites or open new ones, and a computer network implemented in order to support a very different set of interlinkages between the firm's production sites and with its final markets. As a result of this reorganisation, patterns of movement of both intermediate and final products have changed completely, and the volumes of movement substantially increased. The higher transport costs have, however, been more than compensated for by production economies of scale and by the firm's improved responsiveness to customer orders which the computer network has made possible, resulting in increased market share and improved competitiveness.

Breaking into the circle: choices and implications

As these examples demonstrate, there is no single direction of causality in the complex interactions between transport, communications, organisational behaviour and spatial structure. The circle by which they are interconnected can be broken into anywhere, in the sense of a change in any one element of the system then affecting each of the other elements. The 'starting-point' adopted in any examination of these inter-relationships is nevertheless significant, indicating a choice, a concep-tualisation of the main dynamics of the system of interconnections under investigation.

A familiar, indeed conventional, approach to understanding the types of interrelationships with which we are concerned would be to focus on the 'impacts' of new technology; starting therefore with the major changes taking place in the technologies of transport and communica-tions, and following through their impacts upon organisational behaviour and spatial organisation, an approach adopted for example in the EDI case outlined above.

In the remainder of this chapter, however, we choose a different starting-point, reflecting the conceptualisation with which we started of transport and communications as 'carriers' of particular paradigms of industrial and spatial organisation. Our contention is that Europe is moving towards a new paradigm of industrial and spatial organisation, one which is different in certain key respects from the model of growth which has been hegemonic in Europe since the 1950s, and which we labelled in the introduction as 'Fordism'. Just as transport and communications developed along certain paths during the Fordist era, helping indeed that paradigm to be realised, to be viable, so a new paradigm of economic organisation, a successor to Fordism as it were, will make new demands upon the transport and communications system.

It follows that if we wish to try and understand what transport and communications will be like beyond the immediate and relatively predictable future, say in Europe 2020, then it will be necessary to attempt to first understand what type of industrial and spatial organisation will be prevailing at that time. If we are right in our contention that the present period of restructuring is indicative of a new paradigm of economic organisation, then a reading of what it is that is new about that paradigm (and indeed what it is that is not), at least as it is likely to affect the demand for transport and communications, will be an essential starting-point.

This is not of course to deny the strong element of circular causality that we have discussed above, for future developments in transport and communications will no doubt facilitate forms of industrial and spatial organisation which are not currently viable. Our belief, however, is that starting with the changes now occurring in such organisation, and tracing through their implications for transport and communications, will prove to be a better choice in predictive terms than starting with a new technology-led prediction of transport and communications in the year 2020, and then trying to read off the 'impacts' they are likely to have on economic and spatial organisation.

We are surely all too familiar with the inadequacies of futurological predictions based on the supposed power of new technologies to 'transform' society and its spatial organisation. The strong element of wishful thinking behind such predictions often seems to be motivated by a sense of frustration with the complexities and perceived inadequacies of society as it is presently constituted. Rather than grappling with these complexities in the real world, how much easier it is to envisage a new society, constituted around the liberating potential of new technology. The field of transport and communications research is not unfamiliar with this type of discourse, which can be regarded as harmless or dangerous depending on your point of view; either way, it is not science, or social science, and should be left to the realm of science fiction.

Our own conceptual preference is then to start not with the impact of changes in transport and communications on economic and spatial organisation, but rather with the less superficially exciting, albeit more challenging, task of considering the implications of changes in economic and spatial organisation for transport and communications.

Transport and communications and the spatial structure of Fordism

The concept of 'Fordism' is a broad and far-reaching attempt to capture the essential characteristics of what the French Regulation School define as a distinctive 'model of development' under capitalism. According to Leborgne and Lipietz (1988), a model of development involves a conjunction of three sets of relationships; firstly, a 'technological paradigm', a set of general principles which govern the evolution of the organisation of labour; secondly, a 'regime of accumulation', the macro-economic principle describing the long-term compatibility between levels of production and of consumption; and, thirdly, a 'mode of regulation', the forms of individual and collective adjustment which enable the regime of accumulation to be sustained.

Fordism is one such conjunction, which Matthews (1991, p. 125) suggests 'is now seen as the dominant political-economic framework of the twentieth century'. This framework or growth model became established in the United States in the inter-war period and diffused to Europe in the period of post-war reconstruction, producing 'a twenty-five year golden age' of capitalism (Lipietz, 1986), but which has since the 1970s sustained a number of interrelated set-backs which have undermined its continued viability.

The dominant 'technological paradigm' under Fordism can be summarised as one of mass production and Taylorist work organisation, the 'regime of accumulation' that of a mass consumption counterpart to mass production, and the 'mode of regulation' as the combination of collective wage bargaining, the hegemony of large corporations, Keynesian demand management and the welfare state (Leborgne and Lipietz, 1988; Boyer, 1988). Our concern below is only with the first of these three interlocking elements, that which deals with the organisation of the Fordist system of production. We begin by outlining the main features of this system, paying particular attention to its spatial organisation, before considering Fordism's transport and communications requirements (see Table 3.3 for a summary).

Fordist industrial and spatial organisation

The basic rationale behind mass production was the reduction of cost by standardising the production of parts, and the use of repetitive methods to substitute for skilled labour. Piore and Sabel (1984) characterise the rise of the mass production system as a first 'industrial divide', differentiating it from craft and batch production methods. Although these previously established forms of industrialisation continued to coexist with Fordist mass production, the enormous productivity improvements which the latter made possible rapidly came to dominate in those sectors, such as cars and consumer durables, for which mass markets could be developed. As articulated by Scott (1988):

These sectors, in their classical form, are distinguished by a search for massive internal economies of scale based on assembly line methods, technical divisions of labour and standardisation of outputs. The Fordist elements of the system comprise, in their essentials, the deskilling of labour by means of the fragmentation of work tasks while integrating the human operator into the whole machinery of production in such a manner as to reduce to the minimum discretionary control over motions and rhythms of work. (p. 173)

Table 3.3 Fordist spatial organisation and transport and communication requirements

Industrial Organisation	Spatial Organisation	Transport and Communication Patterns	Infrastructure Requirements
Micro Level			
— functional specialisation	— spatial division of labour within multi-locational enterprises	— long-distance intermediate product movement to assembly sites	— reliable long-distance goods transport — standard quantities, predictable in advance
— economies of scale	— corporate control hierarchy related to urban hierarchy	— long-distance final product movement to markets	— reliable air communication, and rail travel in a national context, to maintain corporate span of control
— vertical integration	— metropolitan labour markets	— long-distance movement of people to maintain corporate span of control	— reliable national and international telephone and telex systems
— 'hard' automation	— regional functional specialisation (division of labour)	— vertical information flows, intra-corporate information exchange predominates	— availability of private circuits for internal voice and data communication
— hierarchical control	— nationally and internationally extended production systems	— commuting to large urban and suburban production sites	— urban and suburban mass transit for labour force
— mass production	— linkages maintained over long distances — no spatial clustering		— goods transport and information networks are predominantly national and international in scope, permitting the connection of cores with peripheries
Macro Level			— little need for local communications networks
— vertically integrated systems			
— large-firm dominated			
— 'lowest cost' supply linkages (dual sourcing)			
— mass consumption of standardised goods			

The technical embodiment of Fordist production principles, the semi-automatic assembly line (Aglietta, 1982), can be seen as a device not only for increasing output but, as importantly, for gaining control over the pace and organisation of production, combining the technical requirements of a shift from batch to flow production with a new drive for management control (Matthews, 1991).

This form of 'hard automation' proved very successful in achieving high rates of productivity growth for standardised, mass-produced goods. An appropriate vehicular analogy for Fordist production organisation at this micro level would be the steamroller: a large, rather cumbersome, but crushingly efficient piece of machinery designed for and dedicated to a particular task, and extremely difficult to deflect once it is in motion. These same characteristics, however, proved rather less effective when the erosion of mass markets and the need for constant product innovation required not a steamroller but an adaptable all-terrain vehicle!

At the level of the industrial system as a whole, Fordism was characterised by large, vertically integrated firms. Partly this stemmed from the internal economies of scale in production associated with its technological basis, but of considerable importance too was the need to co-ordinate and reintegrate the considerable technical division of labour which Fordism engendered. Quite simply, this co-ordination and re-integration task was more effectively handled, and with lower transaction costs, by the corporate hierarchy than by the external market.

The spatial form of the Fordist system of production organisation was of course integral to that system, for, as Walker (1988, p. 385) argues, 'it is impossible to separate the organisational from the geographical', as 'capitalist organisation is constituted in and through spatial relations'. At the broad regional scale, Allan Scott (1988) has described the spatial form of Fordism at the peak of its development as:

associated with a series of great industrial regions in North America and western Europe, as represented by the Manufacturing Belt of the United States and the zone of industrial development in Europe stretching from the Midlands of England through northern France, Belgium and Holland to the Ruhr of West Germany, with many additional outlying districts at various locations. These locations were the locational foci of propulsive industrial sectors driving forward, through intricate input–output connections, dense systems of upstream producers. (p. 173)

The geography of Fordism was associated in particular with major metropolitan regions, for it was the large city that provided the agglomerations of labour required for mass production. However, although this spatial form characterised what we might describe as 'early' Fordism, its spatial expression evolved and changed over time. Schoenberger (1988, p. 255) suggests that this evolutionary tendency involved a shift from 'initial massive industrial agglomerations in the core to decentralisation and increasing dispersal of production towards the periphery'.

This shift reflects an internal dynamic within Fordist production which, more so than any previous form of industrialisation, came to use space and spatial differentiation as active elements of accumulation (Harvey, 1987). The Taylorist principles of work organisation embodied in the Fordist mass production system involved a constant search for ways of improving profitability through the division of labour. The 'technical disintegration' of the production process into separate shops within a plant and then into an inter-plant division of labour was so sharp that it could be increasingly realised as a 'territorial disintegration' (Leborgne and Lipietz, 1988), in which different plants could be optimally located according to the type of labour they needed.

The spatial form of the industrial system thus underwent significant changes with the evolution of Fordism. The earlier form of geographical specialisation based on sectors became a functional specialisation associated with the increasing refinement of the division of labour within the firm, with certain regions coming to specialise as centres of corporate control, others as concentrations of research and development, others as semi- or unskilled production 'branch plants' (Hymer, 1972; Lipietz, 1975; Massey, 1984). The 'spatial division of labour' within 'late' Fordism soon became international as well as interregional, as the progressive deskilling of elements within the production process enabled the large, vertically integrated Fordist corporation to take advantage of even cheaper unskilled labour in the Third World periphery (Frobel et al., 1980; Lipietz, 1986).

Fordism's transport and communications requirements

The increasingly complex spatial organisation of production which evolved under Fordism imposed very considerable requirements upon the transport and communications system (Table 3.3). Indeed, it is clear that the pattern of production characterised above as 'late Fordism', with its high degree of territorial disaggregation and dispersed production, would not have been viable without significant innovation in both transport and telecommunications. As noted by Frobel et al. (1980, p. 36) in their analysis of the new international division of labour, this form of industrial development is predicated upon 'a technology which renders industrial location and the management of production itself largely independent of geographical distance'.

How, and to what extent, were these requirements met? In the transport field, significant improvements have taken place since the 1960s which have benefited exactly the type of long-distance, regular, standardised commodity flow demanded by the (late) Fordist production system (Pedesen, 1985). Containerisation and the long-distance motorway networks which have so facilitated freight movement by truck, can be regarded then as the necessary transport concomitants of Fordist production organisation. As van Hoogstraten and Janssen (1985) have argued in the case of The Netherlands:

it is more than contingent that the generalisation of the network of motorways, spread from the western part of the Netherlands over the rest, has run concurrently with the decentralisation of production.

In addition to the routinised long-distance movement of intermediate and final production, Fordism also required that reliable systems of voice communication be in place to permit the long-distance control and co-ordination of spatially dispersed production. Beyond voice telephony, the advent of computer networking in the 1970s clearly further facilitated the process of decentralisation. Thus according to Perrons (1981, p. 251), 'neo-Fordist labour processes, based on electronic information systems with automatic feedback mechanisms . . . meant that locations in peripheral areas were technically feasible'.

The vertically integrated nature of Fordist production organisation places considerable emphasis on intra-corporate flows of information. One of the main requirements of Fordism in terms of communications infrastructure is, in consequence, the provision of point-to-point voice and computer networks by means of leased circuits. The evidence concerning the geography of computer networking in the UK shows that such networks are indeed used almost exclusively for intra-organisational communication (Daniels, 1987), and suggests further that the use of dedicated private circuits is high in those regions most clearly associated with the type of decentralised branch plant production associated with the late Fordist spatial division of labour (Diamond and Spence, 1989).

The Fordist system of production organisation thus placed very considerable demands on transport and communication infrastructures and networks. Leaving aside the (rather sterile and probably unresolvable) question of whether the requirements of Fordism stimulated the necessary innovation and infrastructure investment, or whether this innovation and investment 'led' the development of new forms of production organisation which evolved in order to exploit the new opportunities, it can be concluded that Fordism is clearly associated with major improvements in long-distance transport and communication.

Without such improvements, it is evident that the model of decentralised production organisation that we have characterised above as late Fordism would not have been viable, for this model demanded both the efficient long-distance movement of intermediate goods as well as final production, and the space-transcending control and co-ordination of complex multi-locational enterprises.

The crisis of Fordist production organisation

There is by now a substantial body of literature on the reasons why the Fordist system of mass production ran, in the 1970s and 1980s, into increasing problems. Some see the breakup of mass markets due to changing consumer taste as the key; others the undermining of Fordism's production heartlands by the rise of low-wage industrialisation in the Third World; others again the technical rigidities of Fordist production organisation itself.

The idea of Fordism reaching limits determined by its own internal logic is associated in particular with the French Regulation School, following and building upon the work of Aglietta (1982). He concentrated on the limits of Taylorist task fragmentation, and on the technical limitations of the assembly line in a period of unstable market conditions. Roobeek (1987) sees Fordism as coming up against a series of problems of control, problems which include not only the control over the labour process within the factory but also control over the complex spatial divisions of labour which Fordist production organisation had engendered.

Although improvements in transport and communications had been instrumental in the emergence and evolution of Fordist production organisation, there were clearly limits to the Fordist system's ability to transcend space and to overcome distance. As with so many of the other characteristics of Fordism, these limits became critical when more volatile and segmented market conditions necessitated much greater flexibility and responsiveness. Responses to the crisis of Fordism would thus need to address, *inter alia*, the limitations imposed by spatial organisation and by transport and communication systems. It is to these responses, to the possible successors to Fordism, that we now turn.

Transport and communications and the possible successors to Fordism

A reinvigorated 'neo-Fordism'?

One significant possibility which needs evaluating is that developments in transport and communications networks and systems can help to resolve the crisis of Fordist production organisation. Following Piore and Sabel (1984), Rubery et al. (1987) argue that competitive success now depends not on achieving economies of scale in established mass markets, but rather on securing new markets, developing new competitive strategies for meeting changing demand requirements, and increasing the responsiveness of the organisation to market changes. One of the present authors has suggested elsewhere (Gillespie and Williams, 1990; Gillespie, 1991) that developments in telematics offer important possibilities of achieving a more 'flexible Fordism'.

The scope for establishing a reinvigorated form of neo-Fordism has been considered by a number of writers (see, for example, Leborgne and Lipietz, 1988; Mathews, 1991). However, even if some of the control and co-ordination problems of Fordism can be overcome by means of innovation in transport and communications systems, there remain questions over the long-term viability of Fordist principles of production organisation. As Mathews (1991, pp. 131–2) contends:

Fordism, with its Taylorist fragmentation of jobs, deskilling and divorce of conception from execution, is becoming less and less relevant. It was 'productive' and 'efficient' only under the very special conditions prevailing within mass production.

In the new reality of segmented, rapidly changing markets, in which a considerable competitive premium is placed upon product innovation and upon responsiveness to market shifts, the hierarchical fragmentation of the Fordist system of production organisation is simply no longer optimal. This of course is not to deny that 'Fordist' enterprises can adapt to the changing circumstances, and re-establish the basis for profitable production, as many clearly have been able to do. We would argue, however, that in so doing they have shed many of the key defining characteristics of Fordism. In the remainder of this chapter, we turn our attention to two different interpretations of a post-Fordist industrial future, and to the transport and communication implications of these competing scenarios.

The 'flexible specialisation' scenario

INDUSTRIAL AND SPATIAL ORGANISATION

The 'flexible specialisation' model of industrial organisation was formulated by Piore and Sabel (1984), drawing upon an interpretation of developments in the so-called third Italy. Conceptually, this model rests on the assumption that the economic weaknesses of Fordism need to be overcome, and a new industrial and spatial structure of the economy established, possessing a number of different, indeed oppositional, characteristics to that of Fordism. Thus if Fordism was primarily concerned with mass production, mass consumption and the exploitation of economies of scale, the flexible specialisation scenario rests on the idea of product customisation, volatility of markets and demand, and the exploitation of economies of scope (Table 3.4).

Because of its oppositional view to Fordism, the school of thought is heralding, indeed often celebrating, a 'post-Fordist' future, one which marks a radical change and a break with the previous model of industrial development. It is at once evident that the 'second industrial divide' predicted by Piore and Sabel conceptually implies the development of a

Table 3.4 Flexible specialisation scenario

Industrial Organisation	Spatial Organisation	Transport and Communication Patterns	Infrastructure Requirements	Policy Options and Priorities
Micro Level — small batch production — economies of scope — customisation — functional integration — decentralised decision-making systems — soft automation	— complementary regional and urban systems — specialised labour markets — spatial clustering	— long-distance final product movement to markets — short-distance intermediate product movements — frequent short-distance movement of people — long-distance people movement (sales and marketing) — high requirements for intra- and inter-firm exchanges of information — horizontal inter- and intra-firm information flows	— flexible final product transportation system — short-distance frequent intermediate product transportation system — fast long-distance final product transportation systems — efficient local telephone and fax networks — local computer networks	— development of regional transport system — development of digitalised networks at local level (bottom-up approach) — tension between frequent freight movements and capacity of roads (improvements of roads)
Macro Level — vertically disintegrated systems — firms networks — segmentation of markets — co-operative inter-firm linkages (single sourcing)				

new industrial order, in which the industrial and spatial forces of equilibrium are related to quite different economic and industrial features and to new corporate strategies. Moreover, associated with the flexible specialisation scenario is the potential for the different development pattern of transport and communications systems, because of the different transactional and relational economic structures they will be required to support.

The generation of this scenario will thus have profound implications for both the micro and the macro level. At the micro level, the emergence of the 'flexible specialisation' system rests on the assumption that mass production will be replaced by an industrial organisational model concerned rather with small batch production, regarded as a more suitable model of production organisation for dealing with dynamic markets, displaying both high levels of vulnerability and volatility of demand.

A consequent outcome of batch production is the exploitation of economies of scope rather than the traditional economies of scale (directly concerned with mass production and consumption). Economies of scope are those economies of joint production resulting from the use of a single set of facilities to produce, or process, more than one product, under dynamic market conditions (Chandler, 1986; Teece, 1980; Jelinek and Goldhar, 1983).

Moreover, the flexible specialisation scenario will generate a radical shift of demand away from mass consumption products in favour of differentiated, personalised outputs. Demand for a variety of products will increasingly replace demand for cheap and standardised products, and this will create more scope for the development of small, specialised firms. Demand needs will then increasingly generate a process of customisation of products, thus rejecting the idea of mass production and favouring a more differentiated production model.

In this scenario, the functional specialisation of Fordism will be replaced with functional integration, conceptually overcoming once again the limits of the present structure. It has in fact long been recognised by organisation scholars that the profound functional specialisation of the large enterprise, designed to achieve economies of scale and higher professional know-how, presents the risk of internal segmentation and bureaucratisation, and in particular a loss in terms of the efficient exploitation of information arising from everyday operations in each department (Camagni, 1988). A functional integration model can, it is argued, overcome this inefficient and rigid structure, a structure which is completely inadequate in periods of high market volatility. Cross-functional work can generate useful synergies between functions, especially in terms of innovation.

The model of the large hierarchical firm, designed to be the most efficient industrial model of production, will increasingly give way to more decentralised organisational forms, in which the transfer of intermediate responsibility to lower levels in the organisation takes place, assisted by the capabilities of the new technologies. By facilitating on-line remote communication and decision support, these technologies can help to decentralise decision-making processes to peripheral areas and to lower organisational levels.

All of these changes in intra-firm organisation are supported and fostered by developments in so-called soft automation, by which is meant automation technologies consisting of a high percentage of software components and with a high reprogrammability capacity. The exploitation of economies of scope can be achieved only through the use of reprogrammable technologies, able to produce a variety of products with the same capital resource.

Major changes will also affect the industrial system as a whole, and once again the new rules governing the industrial and spatial structure of the economy will have characteristics that are opposed in many ways to those that prevailed under Fordism.

The model of the large, vertically integrated firm, with its strongly centralised decision-making power, will be replaced with vertically disintegrated systems based on a series of specialised medium-sized and small firms. Under the scenario we can thus envisage a radical segmentation of markets, reconstituted into 'firm networks': a group of small and medium-sized firms, legally independent from one another, but very much vertically integrated within a particular production process through co-operative inter-firm linkages. Moreover, these inter-firm linkages are likely to be based on single sourcing relationships (Antonelli, 1988).

On the basis of the characteristics of this industrial system it is relatively easy to configure its future spatial structure. The high degree of specialisation of interlinked firms will lead towards the development of complementary regional and urban systems, specialising in different final products and based on local specialised labour market needs.

A spatial clustering will be the expected consequence, characterised by frequent linkages taking place over short distances; the development of specialised local areas, or 'industrial districts', such as Prato and Silicon Valley, in which the industrial system is governed by a high level of product specialisation, can be regarded as contemporary exemplars of the flexible specialisation scenario (Becattini, 1988; Scott, 1988; Camagni and Capello, 1990).

TRANSPORT AND COMMUNICATIONS PATTERNS AND INFRASTRUCTURE
REQUIREMENTS: POLICY OPTIONS AND PRIORITIES

The picture of the industrial and spatial system drawn above is the basis for the configuration of possible transport and communications development patterns, their future infrastructure requirements and appropriate policy options to support this scenario (summarised in Table 3.4).

The high specialisation level achieved by firms and production areas will generate long-distance final product movement to markets, because of the highly spatially segmented market division. For intermediate goods, conversely, the spatial clustering phenomenon and the development of local industrial districts will result in short-distance intermediate product movements (cf. Pedersen, 1985).

Another consequence of the spatial clustering and of the development of local districts is the frequent, short-distance movement of people involved in meetings; frequent face-to-face contact can be regarded as essential for generating and maintaining the co-operative and trust-based relationship upon which the flexible specialisation model of production organisation rests. For sales and marketing activities, conversely, long-distance travel is to be expected, necessary because of local (urban and regional) product specialisation and of the high degree of market segmentation.

Vertically disintegrated systems require a well-developed information axis, around which both inter- and intra-corporate information flows will be transmitted. These information flows, both intra- and inter-corporate, will be used primarily to transport horizontal information, i.e. information among functions at the same level in the hierarchical structure, or, in the case of inter-corporate information flows, among firms at the same level in the production chain. This type of highly specialised and disintegrated production system requires a strong mechanism to ensure synergies, both between functions and firms, resting on a well-developed information system.

These patterns of transport and communication — of goods, people and information — require a future implementation of transport and communications systems able to cope with and support the new industrial and spatial structures. Unpredictable, fluctuating quantities of goods movement, for example, require a highly flexible transport system, able to cope with frequent movements of small quantities, rather than with the predictable, less frequent, larger volumes of transported goods that characterised Fordism.

The highly disintegrated local districts' model will thus increase both short-distance, frequent, intermediate-product movements as well as long-distance, frequent, final-product movements, and will necessitate reliable, frequent, regional interconnected passenger transport networks, efficient local telephone and fax networks and local computer networks.

Considerable effort is already being made in Europe to upgrade and improve long-distance transport and telecommunication networks. Consequent to the above discussion, however, a further important policy priority in the future development of transport and communications infrastructures would be to focus on the upgrading of local and regional transport and communications systems; the development of regional and metropolitan light railway networks, for example, or local digital telematics networks.

The SPRINT project, developed in the Prato area (a local district in Italy), provides an interesting example of the latter. The attempt has been to create a local digitalised computer network, interconnecting all economic agents of the area and providing them with a local inter-company networked information axis (De Braband and Manacorda, 1985; Mazzonis, 1985; Rullani and Zanfei, 1988; Zanfei, 1986). The failure of the SPRINT project can be explained, first, by its premature appearance in an area without a developed telematics culture, and second, by the threat it posed to the established power relationships embodied in the existing transactional structure (Capello and Williams, 1992). However, in the 'flexible specialisation' scenario of the future such obstacles are likely to be overcome, both by a diffused telematics culture and by profound changes in the division of labour, in which more symmetrical and synergetic horizontal linkages will become established.

The development of this scenario will inevitably heighten the tension between the frequent freight movements required and the capacity of the road network to absorb such movements. Consequently, policy priorities should also be given to projects designed to improve roads at regional and national levels.

The 'network firm' or 'global-local' scenario

INDUSTRIAL AND SPATIAL ORGANISATION

Some doubts must remain over the prospects for both the 'neo-Fordism' and the 'flexible specialisation' scenarios. While the first rests on the assumption that the 'crisis of Fordism' can be internally resolved and overcome, and a new or at least modified regime built upon the old industrial and spatial organisation, paradoxically the flexible specialisation scenario is based on the over-idealistic view that a completely different industrial and spatial structure can be developed with completely opposite features to those of Fordism (see Amin and Robins, 1990 for a critique of the empirical and theoretical validity of the flexible specialisation scenario). Whereas the neo-Fordism view thus maintains that little of importance has changed, the flexible specialisation view maintains that little of importance remains. Our own view lies some-where between these oppositional extremes. On the basis of empirical evidence supporting it, a third and more likely scenario can be envisaged, which we term the 'network firm' or 'global–local' scenario, built on the assumption that the inadequacies of Fordist mass production are over-come, but with less radically oppositional outcomes than those predicted (advocated?) by the flexible specialisation school.

This intermediate position is likely to appear at both micro and macro levels (Table 3.5). At the micro level, instead of envisaging the exploita-tion of either economies of scope or of scale, a new equilibrium between the two will be more likely. In fact, the development of economies of scope stem from the exploitation of reprogrammable production

Table 3.5 Network firm or global–local scenario

Industrial Organisation	Spatial Organisation	Transport and Communication Patterns	Infrastructure Requirements	Policy Options and Priorities
Micro Level — new equilibrium between economies of scope and scale — quasi-vertical integration — systems automation — functional integration	— new management of territory (same geography of the economic space of the firm with different functional location) — new logistical platforms — tendency for clustering around innovative firms	— long-distance movement of both intermediate and final products — much long-distance movement of people between firms and within the firm (among different functions) — high requirement for intra- and inter-firm horizontal and vertical information flows	— development of air freight and other long-distance goods movements coupled with short-distance frequent delivery road-based local systems — high-speed trains — airports — long-distance computer networks — modern personal communication services (video-conferencing, electronic mail)	— integrated transport and communication networks — development of international computer networks, EDI, ISDN — avoiding missing networks — spatial planning (creation of urban distribution platforms)
Macro Level — network firms — asymmetrical but stable linkage arrangements between producers and suppliers				

technologies, which require very substantial capital investment, thus necessarily requiring large-scale production to be economically viable, i.e. the exploitation of economies of scale. Thus, instead of completely replacing economies of scale, economies of scope will rather complement and coexist, exploited not only in the 'information handling activities sphere' (Jonscher, 1983), but also in the area of production activities (Capello and Williams, 1990).

Moreover, empirical evidence suggests that the development of new industrial systems strengthens a 'quasi-vertical integration' as the most efficient organisational form of production. There are various intermediate forms of 'quasi-organisation' that are assuming an ever more important role as an alternative to full vertically integrated or vertically disintegrated production systems. In the terminology of Williamson (1975), these intermediate forms of organisation will arise between the two opposite alternatives of 'make or buy', and can be described as the 'make-together' alternative (Camagni and Rabellotti, 1988; see also Chapter 11).

The 'make-together' type of organisational form rests on the need to create synergies and complementarities through partnerships, due in part to the increased complexity and specialisation of products and markets. The traditional models of the large, vertically integrated company on the one hand, and of the small, autonomous, single-phase firm on the other, will be replaced with a new type of large 'network firm', with strongly centralised strategic functions and extending in several directions, and with a new type of small enterprise, integrated into a multi-company local network. Across the network, a system of constantly evolving power relationships govern both the dynamics of innovation and the appropriability of returns to the partners involved.

The 'network firm' will be attracted towards diversified mass production, which is the result of the contemporary exploitation of economies of both scope and scale, and by 'systems automation', i.e. not isolated 'islands of automation', but rather integrated automation systems, through local area networks (LANs) or wide area networks (WANs). Moreover, the integration process will take place between currently stand-alone procedures, with the positive consequence of an automation of inter-sphere and inter-function procedures. At the level of bureaucratic procedures, then, functional integration is likely to occur. The 'network firm' will inevitably centralise control at the level of strategic functions, but with the implementation of modern technologies, control over bureaucratic and routinised functions will be decentralised.

The industrial system coming out of this scenario is a reinforcement and generalisation of the concept of the 'network firm', consisting of large firms, leading in their respective market specialisation, competing with a host of smaller firms. At the level of suppliers, the existence of a 'network firm' will generate asymmetrical but stable linkage arrangements, the asymmetry depending necessarily on the unequal division of power among competing firms.

With respect to spatial organisation, the outcome which can be envisaged from this scenario is far less dramatic and severe in its changes than the one suggested above by the 'flexible specialisation' scenario. Despite the widespread assumption that the intrinsic capacities of new transport and communications technologies will reshape the geography of firms, it can be argued that the spatial extent of firms will remain, or at least could remain, largely the same.

This assertion is backed by empirical evidence, which suggests that a very different spatial organisation can be achieved without the relocation of activities (Goddard, 1990). On the contrary, what will change is the way in which firms exploit their economic space, putting in place a new management of territory within the existing locational parameters of the firm (Williams and Taylor, 1991). In particular, following efficiency and effectiveness aims, firms will try to rationalise their fixed locational assets by physically integrating previously disjointed functions, thereby achieving better economic performance.

Another way of using and exploiting territory more effectively is through the development of new logistical systems, which may well lead to adjustments in the geography of corporate space. The development of central locations for stored goods helps in rationalising materials purchases and intermediate-goods movements, the efficiency of which derives from highly computerised storage systems (Ruijgrok, 1990).

TRANSPORT AND COMMUNICATIONS AND INFRASTRUCTURE
REQUIREMENTS: POLICY OPTIONS AND PRIORITIES

A different development pattern emerges from this third configuration of a possible industrial and spatial system (see Table 3.5). This scenario requires long-distance movement of both intermediate and final products, accompanied by an increase in short-distance final-product movement, co-ordinated through new logistical systems. The consequence is a more intense movement of both intermediate and final products from production sites to storage centres and from them to the final market. Globalisation of markets strengthens this phenomenon, augmenting the spatial distribution of products and thus their physical movements.

A rather strong pressure for long-distance business travel derives from this scenario, necessitating high volumes of movement between firms and (spatially diffused) customers, and between functions of multi-site firms (each of which is expected to be located in one place, avoiding duplication and thus inefficiency). The 'network firm' scenario additionally implies a high volume of business travel associated with co-operative agreements, which may well be international in scope, complemented by well-developed and advanced satellite-based video-conferencing systems.

Moreover, the 'make-together' form of organisation implies a high volume of information transmitted between firms in the form of horizontal inter-corporate information flows. At the same time, high volumes of vertical inter-corporate information flows characterise this scenario, corresponding to the information requirements for asymmetrical but stable linkages with suppliers. Intensive intra-corporate information flows will also be necessary in order to develop the types of 'new management of territory' outlined above, involving the relocation of part-functions in one place, thus rationalising decision-making processes. It is clear that with such a relocation of activities in space, firms will need a constant flow of information, both horizontally (to develop decision-making processes) and vertically (because of the decentralised control system).

From the above discussion, a simple consideration comes immediately to mind concerning the infrastructure requirements associated with this scenario. In an industrial and spatial system based on intense long-distance movement of people, goods and information, a wide range of transport and communications systems infrastructures will be necessary, including air freight systems, short-distance frequent-delivery road-based local systems, high-speed trains, air passenger travel, long-distance computer networks, and advanced personal communication services (i.e. video-conferencing, electronic mail).

Some clear policy priorities emerge from this scenario and from these infrastructure requirements. All policies enhancing long-distance transport and communications infrastructures are in this respect useful and efficient policies. The development of international computer networks with **electronic data interchange** (EDI) applications will be required to deal with the mass of information associated with the new logistical platforms, as will the implementation of ISDN (the **integrated services digital network**). With respect to this scenario, then, a top–down policy approach to the development of advanced networks, rather than the bottom–up local network approach embodied in the previous scenario, is much more effective and efficient, dealing with the implementation of international 'information highways' rather than local telematics networks and applications.

This scenario has then clear implications for the development of transport and communications infrastructures. Not only is this new industrial and spatial scenario built on the assumption that long-distance, reliable transport and communications networks are implemented, but it rests on the idea that these networks have to be 'integrated networks', both geographically and technologically speaking. The integration of these networks permits the development of the industrial and spatial system outlined above, for a 'quasi-vertically integrated' form of organisation requires both an advanced communications infrastructure and a highly reliable complementary transport system.

The integration has to take place at both a geographical and technological level. At a spatial level, we are referring primarily to international networks, designed for long-distance transport and communications. Networks which are confined to national territories, whether for the movement of information or people, will be of limited use in sustaining the types of industrial organisation predicted under the network firm or global–local scenario. Technological integration is clearly vital for the development of international interconnected networks. Standards problems have to be overcome, both in the telecommunications and transport arenas, in order for genuinely borderless infrastructures to be developed.

With respect to this issue, a group of international experts have developed a project on 'Missing Networks in Europe' for the Round Table of Industrialists, primarily concerned with identifying the discontinuities which exist in international networks in both transport and communications sectors. The result has pointed out that both telecommunications and transport networks could perform much better if missing networks were addressed at five different levels (Nijkamp et al., 1990):

- hardware   (physical infrastructure)
- software   (logistics and information)
- orgware   (institutional and organisational setting)
- finware   (financial and funding arrangements)
- ecoware   (environmental and safety effects)

The interest in incorporating 'missing networks' becomes more crucial once a spatial and industrial system is envisaged in which economic transactions are developed primarily at an international scale and where synergies among firms take place globally.

Conclusions and policy recommendations

Of the three scenarios presented above, the most likely appears to be what we have described as the 'network firm' or 'global–local' scenario. There are few grounds for expecting that the Fordist model could be reinvigorated, even if some of its limits and weaknesses could be overcome. Once the nature of markets and the regulatory system has shifted, as it has clearly done with Fordism, there are few reasons to suggest that the old system with its attendant model of production could return. However, the 'rejection' of the Fordist model for the future does not need to lead to accepting the directly opposing model envisaged in the 'flexible specialisation' scenario. This scenario is idealistic but unrealistic, with little empirical evidence to suggest that we are moving towards this kind of regulatory system. On the contrary, the empirical evidence suggests rather a third kind of scenario, an intermediate model of production between the assumed rigidity of Fordism and the anticipated flexibility of 'post-Fordism'.

Some clear policy recommendations for the transport and communications infrastructure can be drawn, on the assumption that the 'network firm' scenario is the one most likely to be represented in 'Europe 2020'.

Long-distance movements of people, freight and information seem likely to increase in importance as national territorial systems dissolve, and in consequence the emphasis in infrastructure provision needs to shift towards advanced international transport and communications networks. Physical discontinuities in both transport and communication networks have to be avoided, if the new industrial and spatial system in Europe is to be effectively supported.

The transport and communications infrastructure requirements of this scenario go well beyond the geographical and technological integration of networks. The 'network firm' scenario rests on the assumption that a complete integration between transport *and* communications networks will be developed. The increasing importance of standardisation and harmonisation refers not only to the two sectors separately, but also to their combination. The strength of infrastructural development in this scenario is related to the implementation of technological and geographical integration of elements in *both* the transportation and communications systems.

Spatial planning of transport infrastructure needs therefore to be developed in conjunction with the territorial planning of communications infrastructure. An efficient and reliable logistical system requires a contemporary existence of both advanced telecommunications systems and transportation networks. Integrated logistical systems require information systems and communication facilities that lead to improved control possibilities and to more efficient deliveries of stored goods in time and space (Ruijgrok, 1990).

A final consideration concerns the need for integrated transport and communications systems to be developed in conjunction with broader spatial (urban and regional) planning. Only in this way will transport and communications networks be developed on the basis of the real needs and necessities of the newly emerging industrial and spatial system. This assumption refers to the idea that transport and communications technologies in themselves are not sufficient forces for generating indigenous local economic development. On the contrary, they have to be thought of as strategic instruments to be exploited with reference to broader spatial economic planning. In this way, supply-driven transport and communications projects with little or no connection to real demand requirements and needs can be avoided, and the future development of these leading technological infrastructures can be conceived rather in terms of their contribution to the creation of an integrated economic system for 'Europe 2020'.

References

Aglietta, M. (1982) *Régulation et crises du capitalisme: l'experience des Etats Unis*. Second edition, Calmann-Levy, Paris.

Amin, A. and Robins, K. (1990) 'The re-emergence of regional economies? The mythical geography of flexible accumulation', *Society and Space, Environment and Planning D*, 8(1), pp. 7–34.

Antonelli, C. (ed.) (1988) *New Information Technology and Industrial Change: The Italian Case*. Kluwer Publishing, Kingston-upon-Thames, Surrey.

Aydalot, P. and Keeble, D. (eds) (1988) *High Technology Industry and Innovative Environments: The European Experience*. Routledge, London.

Becattini, G. (ed.) (1988) *Mercato e Forze Locali: Il Distretto Industriale*. Il Mulino, Bologna.

Boyer, R. (1988) 'Technical change and the theory of "regulation"', in Dosi, G., Freeman, C., Nelson, R., Silverberg, G. and Soete, L. (eds) *Technical Change and Economic Theory*. Frances Pinter, London.

Brotchie, J., Batty, M., Hall, P. and Newton, P. (eds) (1991) *Cities of the 21st Century*. Halstead Press, Longman, Cheshire.

Brunn, S.D. and Leinbach, T.R. (eds) (1991) *Collapsing Space and Time: Geographic Aspects of Communication and Information*. HarperCollins Academic, London.

Burns, T.J. and Stalker, G.M. (1979) *Direzione Aziendale ed Innovazione*. Franco Angeli, Milan.

Camagni, R. (1988) 'Functional integration and locational shifts in new technology industry', in Aydalot, P. and Keeble, D. (eds) (1988), op. cit.

Camagni, R. and Capello, R. (1990) 'Towards a definition of the manoeuvring space of local development initiatives: Italian success stories of local development — theoretical conditions and practical experiences', in Stohr, W. (ed.) (1990) *Global Challenge and Local Response*. Mansell, London.

Camagni, R. and Capello, R. (1991) 'Nuove tecnologie di comunicazione e cambiamenti nella localizzazione delle attività industriali', in Lombardo, S. (ed.), *Nuove Tecnologie dell'Informazione e Sistemi Urbani*, forthcoming.

Camagni, R. and Rabellotti, R. (1991) 'L'innovazione macro-organizzative nel settore tessile-abbigliamento', *Sviluppo e Organizzazione*, 108, pp. 2–8.

Capello, R. and Williams, H. (1990) 'Nuove strategie d'impresa, nuovi sistemi spaziali e nuove tecnologie dell'informazione come strumenti di riduzione della incertezzo', *Economia e Politica Industriale*, 67, pp. 43–70.

Capello, R. and Williams, H. (1992) 'Computer network trajectories and organisational dynamics: a cross-national review', in Antonelli, C. (ed.) (1992) *The Economics of Information Networks*. Elsevier, London.

Chandler, A. (1986) 'Scale and scope: the dynamics of industrial enterprise' (mimeo).

Daniels, W.W. (1987) *Workplace Industrial Relations and Technical Change*. Frances Pinter, London.

De Braband, F. and Manacorda, P. (1985) 'Scenario telematico e territorio: lettura di un'esperienza in Corso'. Research Report, October.

Diamond, D. and Spence, N. (1988) 'Infrastructure and Industrial Costs in British Industry'. Report for the Department of Trade and Industry, HMSO, London.

Freeman, C., Clark, J. and Soete, L. (1982) *Unemployment and Technical Innovation: A Study of Long Waves in Economic Development*. Frances Pinter, London.

Frobel, F., Heinrichs, J. and Kreye, O. (1980) *The New International Division of Labour*. Cambridge University Press, Cambridge.

Giaoutzi, M. and Nijkamp, P. (eds) (1988) *Informatics and Regional Development*. Avebury, Aldershot.

Gillespie, A.E. (1991) 'Advanced communications networks, territorial integration ant local development', in Camagni, R. (ed.) *Innovation Networks: Spatial Perspectives*, Belhaven Press, London, pp. 214–29.

Gillespie, A.E. and Williams, H.P. (1990) 'Telematics and the reorganisation of corporate space', in Soekkha, H.M., Bovy, P.H.L., Drewe, P. and Jansen, G.R.M. (eds) *Telematics — Transportation and Spatial Development*. VSP, Utrecht, pp. 257–74.

Goddard, J.B. (1990) 'The geography of the information economy'. PICT Policy Research Paper, No. 11, Programme on Information and Communications Technologies, ESRC, London.

Harvey, D. (1987) 'Flexible accumulation through urbanisation: reflections on post-modernism in the American city', *Antipode*, 19.

Hepworth, M. and Ducatel, K. (1991) *Transport in the Information Society*, Belhaven Press, London.

van Hoogstraten, P. and Janssen, B. (1985) 'New forms of industrialisation and material infrastructure in the Netherlands' (mimeo).

Hymer, S. (1972) 'The multinational corporation and the law of uneven development', in Bhagwati, J. (ed.) *Economics and World Order*. Free Press, New York, pp. 113–40.

Jelinek; M. and Goldhar, J. (1983) 'The interface between strategy and manufacturing technology', *Columbia Journal of World Business*, Spring, pp. 26–36.

Leborgne, D. and Lipietz, A. (1988) 'New technologies, new modes of regulation: some spatial implications', *Society and Space: Environment and Planning D*, 6, pp. 263–80.

Lipietz, A. (1975) 'Structuration de l'espace, problème foncier et aménagement du territoire', *Environment and Planning A*, pp. 415–25; English translation in Carney, J., Hudson, R., Lewis, J. (eds), 1980, *Regions in Crisis*. Croom Helm, Beckenham, Kent, pp. 60–75.

Lipietz, A. (1986) 'New tendencies in the international division of labour: regimes of accumulation and modes of regulation', in Scott, A.J. and Storper, M. (eds) *Production, Work, Territory: The Geographical Anatomy of Industrial Capitalism*. Allen & Unwin, Boston.

Massey, D. (1984) *Spatial Divisions of Labour*. Macmillan, London.

Mathews, J. (1991) 'Mass production, the Fordist system and its crisis', in Mackay, H., Young, M. and Beynon, J. (eds) *Understanding Technology in Education*. Falmer Press, London.

Mazzonis, D. (1985) 'A project for innovation in Prato', Paper presented at the Workshop of San Miniato, 28–30 November.

Moses, L. and Williamson, H.F. (1967) 'The location of economic activity in cities', *American Economic Review*, 57, pp. 211–22.

Moulaert, F. and Swyngedouw, E. (1989) 'A regulation approach to the geography of the flexible production system', *Society and Space: Environment and Planning D*, 7, 327–45.

Nijkamp, P., Maggi, R. and Masser, I. (1990) 'Missing networks in Europe'. Report presented at the Round Table of Industrialists, November.

Nijkamp, P., Reichman, S. and Wegener, M. (eds) (1990) *Euromobile: Transport, Communications and Mobility in Europe*. Avebury, Aldershot.

Nijkamp, P. and Salomon, I. (1989) 'Future spatial impacts of telecommunications', *Transportation Planning and Technology*, vol. 13, pp. 275–87.

Pedersen, P.O. (1985) 'Communication and spatial interaction in an era of advanced technology — with special emphasis on the goods transport'. Paper presented at the ESF Workshop on Transport Planning in an Era of Change, Zandvoort, April.

Perrons, D. (1981) 'The role of Ireland in the new international division of labour: a proposed framework for regional analysis', *Regional Studies*, 15(2), pp. 81–100.

Piore, M. and Sabel, C.F. (1984) *The Second Industrial Divide: Possibilities for Prosperity*. Basic Books, New York.

Rubery, J., Tarling, R. and Wilkinson, F. (1987) 'Flexibility, marketing and the organisation of production', *Labour and Society*, 12, 1, pp. 131–51.
Ruijgrok, C. (1988) 'Recent developments in logistics, information technologies and spatial systems', in Giaoutzi, M. and Nijkamp, P. (1988), op. cit.
Ruijgrok, C. (1990) 'Telematics in the goods logistics process', in Soekkha, H. (ed.) (1990) *Telematics — Transportation and Spatial Development*. VSP, Utrecht.
Roobeek, A.J. (1987) 'The crisis in Fordism and the rise of a new technical paradigm', *Futures*, 19(2), pp. 217–31.
Rullani, E. and Zanfei, A. (1988) 'Networks between manufacturing and demand: cases from textile and clothing industries', in Antonelli, C. (ed.) (1988) *New Information Technology and Industrial Change: The Italian Case.* Kluwer Publishing, Kingston-upon-Thames, Surrey.
Schaeffer, K.H. and Sclar, E. (1975) *Access for All: Transportation and Urban Growth*. Pelican, Harmondsworth, Middlesex.
Schoenberger, E. (1988) 'From Fordism to flexible accumulation: technology, competitive strategies, and international location', *Society and Space: Environment and Planning D*, 6, pp. 245–62.
Scott, A.J. (1988) 'Flexible production systems and regional development: the rise of new industrial spaces in North America and Western Europe', *International Journal of Urban and Regional Research*, 12(2), pp. 171–85.
Soekkha, H.M., Bovy, P.H.L., Drewe, P. and Jansen, G.R.M. (1990) *Telematics — Transportation and Spatial Development*. VSP, Utrecht.
Teece, D. (1980) 'Economies of scope and scope of the enterprise', *Journal of Economic Behaviour and Organisation*, 1, pp. 223–47.
Walker, R.A. (1981) 'A theory of suburbanisation', in Dear, M. and Scott, A. (eds) *Urbanisation and Planning in Capitalist Society*. New York.
Walker, R.A. (1988) 'The geographical organisation of production systems', *Society and Space: Environment and Planning D*, 7, pp. 377–408.
Williams, H.P. and Taylor, J. (1991) 'ICTs and the management of territory', in Brotchie, J., Batty, M., Hall, P. and Newton, P. (eds) *Cities of the 21st Century*. Halstead Press, Longman, Cheshire.
Williamson, O. (1975) *Markets and Hierarchies: Analysis and Antitrust Implications*. Free Press, New York.
Zanfei, A. (1986) 'I vincoli alla diffusione delle tecnologie dell'informazione in alcune esperienze di applicazione della telematica', *Economia e Politica Industriale*, no. 50, pp. 253–89.

Part II: Technological Innovation in Transport and Communications

Chapter 4

Transportation technology trends in Europe

M. Frybourg

Introduction

We are in the midst of significant technological change which is having a major impact on industrial structures, providing new opportunities for economic growth, and reordering the competitive standing of developing countries. At the level of the firm, technology is a tool to achieve and sustain the competitive advantage, but radical innovation is system-oriented and involves infrastructure. The paramount role of information technology has to be emphasised as an efficient tool to meet socio-economic needs. One has to highlight the potential risks and rewards of pioneering any change as a first mover, but to be a good follower also requires investment in technological know-how.

A research policy is not the result of an inventory of technological opportunities. Such an inventory is a way to hide what is important or pertinent behind the unlimited potentialities of the future. What one has to look for are the bottlenecks or alternatives, so that one can identify why what is theoretically possible is not operational now, and which alternatives are to be explored before taking up positions on a development programme. The bottlenecks are, of course, the costs, but they also include the externalities, the lack of standardisation and the incompatibilities or system incoherencies. For example non-conventional suspension systems are incompatible with existing rail infrastructure, and as a consequence, it is not possible to use existing facilities to access urban areas. Destinations outside the new track can only be reached through connections.

Two key letters will determine the evolution of the transport system: H&S, with four distinct meanings: **high-speed trains, high service** frequencies, **hub-and spoke** system and **highway safety** improvement. As regards the first, not long ago, the railway faced an uncertain future against the onslaught of airline and private car competition, but the amazing success of the TGV on the Paris–Lyon line has dispelled this fear. The same holds true for the second H&S and for the fears expressed some years ago concerning the attitude of the public towards fully automatic systems. Numerous urban transport systems with entirely automatic operation have been put into service over the last fifteen years and are working in a satisfactory way with considerable advantages in quality of service, including high frequencies. High frequencies and economy of scale are compatible only with hub terminals calling on the most sophisticated information technologies. This is true as well for freight terminals and passenger terminals in all modes of transportation. Information technologies are becoming increasingly essential for the development of transportation and must contribute to the improvement of highway safety.

In the following we examine the transportation technology trends that are apparent in Europe, in the four basic domains (H&S's) mentioned above.

High-speed trains

The French example

In the early 1970s it was acknowledged that certain motorway design principles could be adapted to railways. Instead of providing a spread service as it is the case for conventional road and railway networks, the fast motorway and fast railway routes were concentrated in main corridors serving hub cities. In the 1970s the French railways were faced with saturation of the network backbone, that is the line between Paris and Lyon. The situation was such as to call for the trebling or quadrupling of the existing track length. The associated investment was so high that the creation of a new high-speed railway seemed to be justified while the existing lines could be preserved for freight traffic, local and night passenger traffic. For the type of fast passenger train under consideration the speed is not limited by the longitudinal profile but rather by the horizontal alignments. So the new high-speed railway was built with steep grades, making it possible to adopt a highway-type profile and reduce construction costs.

The recognised success of the South-East TGV was the basis for the construction of more high-speed infrastructures. The area served by the TGVs progressively grew and extends now to the Côte d'Azur, Switzerland and the French wintersport resorts of the Alps. The traffic rapidly increased: the one hundred millionth passenger was recorded in mid-1991. The economic return established which exceeded 15 per cent made it possible to repay the loans contracted by the SNCF to finance the project in less than 10 years. The South-East TGV had hardly begun operating (1982) when the President of the Republic requested the SNCF to begin the studies of the Atlantic TGV to serve the western part of France.

The feasibility study proved favourable and the implementation of the project was decided in 1984. The infrastructural works are now completed and the Brittany service has been effective since 24 September 1989. Service to the South-West will follow this year. After further studies, in October 1987 the French government decided to continue equipping the networks with high-speed lines. Subsequently, further to the decision to construct the Channel Tunnel and to increased contacts with The Netherlands, Belgium and Germany, construction of the North TGV was decided (Paris–Lille–Calais). This will constitute the French part of the common PBKALF project to connect Paris, Brussels, Cologne, Amsterdam, Frankfurt, and London.

Finally, interconnection of the South-East, Atlantic and North TGV radial lines was decided. This section will allow a breaking away from the conventional star structure of the French railway network. It will thus be possible to create TGV connections which will not necessarily stop at Paris but rather at its periphery. At the same time, synergy with the airlines will be favoured by the direct connection with two large airports: Paris Charles de Gaulle and Lyon Satolas. All these sections will be operational around 1994.

The options that contributed to the TGV success are the following: compatibility with the existing network, specialisation of the new lines in high-speed passenger traffic, service at high speed and frequency. Terminal routes can be served on conventional infrastructures and the characteristics of the new line to be built are optimised, taking into account solely the requirements of passenger traffic. After the 380 km/h reached by TGV in 1988, the pilot German ICE exceeded 400 km/h in 1988 and the Atlantic TGV reached a maximum speed of over 500 km/h in 1990. This is why the French government issued in 1990 a master plan of the high-speed railway systems in order to schedule the future development of the network. This plan is a component of the European high-speed railway network adopted by the EC.

The European network of high-speed trains

In terms of economy, safety and environmental protection, high-speed trains are a welcome alternative to the increasing congestion in air and road travel. Aware of the challenge, the Community of European Railways — the railway companies of the twelve EC members plus Austria and Switzerland — presented, in January 1989, a project for a European high-speed network. This network will be built in several stages, gradually incorporating new links. The year 1995 will see the completion of European projects currently under way, with a total of 12,300 km of new or upgraded railway lines. These include the Channel Tunnel, the implementation of standard track gauges on the France–Barcelona–Madrid–Lisbon corridor, the international project linking London–Paris–Brussels–Amsterdam–Frankfurt across sections of 300 km/h, in an area where 10 per cent of the population of the European

Community is concentrated. The latter project has seen the implementation of the first European industrial joint venture on the development of a common train set.

Wheel-on-rail versus magnetic levitation

The Atlantic TGV constitutes the second generation of high-speed trains of which number 325 of a series production version beat the world record for rail speed on 18 May 1990, reaching 515.3 km/h. By comparison with the South-East TGV, these trains feature a wide range of innovations in the motor, braking and current collection systems which allow higher revenue speeds. The French railways have chosen self-commuted synchronous a.c. drivers, a revolutionary step forward in the design of electric locomotives developed by Alsthom. The last French record with the South-East TGV was reached in 1986, at 356.3 km/h. This record was beaten by the German ICE in May 1988, at 406.9 km/h. Two years later, the increase is over 100 km/h. The magnetic levitation system 'Transrapid' attained 412 km/h in January 1988, with Transrapid 06, and achieved 435 km/h in December 1989 with Transrapid 07. Thus, as far as speed is concerned, wheel-on rail and magnetic levitation systems are on an equal footing.

German and Japanese engineers demonstrated that it was technically possible to construct systems running at a high speed, guided and driven by magnetic fields. The engineer's dream has always been to eliminate friction between moving parts, the magic carpet myth. With magnetic suspension and linear drive, engineers are not far from realising their ambition.

However, in a market economy, technological performance alone is not sufficient. The huge investment in the magnetic system over the past fifteen years has yet to be tested as to its results in terms of improved reliability, competivity or safety of the system as well as in estimating real costs. In contrast, after the two thousand million passengers of the Shinkansen, and the one thousand million passengers that have already travelled by TGV, the above elements have proved as well that commercial speeds of 350 km/h and over can now be envisaged in the wheel-on rail technique (1,000 km in 3 hours). At such speed levels, the air resistance is the main factor and the power required to ensure forward motion is the same for the two systems, provided the transmission outputs are identical. It is clear that prospects are still good for wheel-on rail systems, particularly if we consider the possibility of running on a conventional line. Compatibility was a strategic option adopted by France in the 1970s, a difficult option whose success has well surpassed initial expectations.

High service frequencies

The need for public transport to assure the efficient functioning of
metropolitan areas in industrialised and developing societies is almost
universally accepted. Even the most diehard North American suburbanite
will concede that the public transportation service is an essential function
to be provided by 'somebody', . . . for the 'other guy' (so that he can
keep driving his automobile more freely). New fixed guideway transit
systems, or significant extensions of existing systems, have been
constructed since 1960 in the US, Canada, Europe, Japan and developing
countries: twenty-three in North America, including Vancouver, opened
to traffic in 1987 and virtually in all major cities in Europe.

These are structural differences between the competing modes that
form part of the diversity in supply in urban public transport. Unbridled
competition would lead to the elimination of socially very desirable
modes, or at least to market shares that would be socially suboptimal.
The modes must therefore be seen as complementary. In some circumstances, this complementarity will be best achieved by the clear distinction of functions, for example buses as feeder services and rail for
line-haul (sometimes called 'integration'), but in other circumstances
competition or dual working will be justified.

If we define 'new systems' as fixed guideway systems using significant
departures from conventional transit, then the systems to consider are
either **automated guideway transit** (AGT) or **Maglev** or **linear inductor
motor** or both. There are only three examples of AGT deployment in
North American cities among the twenty-three cities quoted above,
namely Detroit, Vancouver and Miami; and in Europe, the French VAL
has been in operation in Lille since 1982 and later in Toulouse and
Rennes.

Numerous transport systems with entirely automatic operation have
been in service for the last fifteen years and are working in a satisfactory
way. These systems were initially constructed for the transport services
of specific areas: airport, exhibition parks, campuses, shopping-centres.
However, at the beginning of the 1980s they made a noticeable entrance
into urban public transport with the entering into service of the VAL
system and the Japanese systems in Kobe and Osaka — although, in this
latter system, the function of 'accompanying agent' has not yet been
suppressed. With the opening in 1986 of the systems in Vancouver,
Miami, and the numerous systems under study or construction such as
the 1A-line in Lille, the D-line in Lyon, the VALs in Toulouse, Rennes
and Jacksonville, the Detroit subway, the 'TAU' in Liège, etc., we can
assert that entirely automatic devices have become everyday equipment
and now represent a variant to be seriously considered in any new urban
transport line project. The reasons for this are as follows:

- On the one hand, this driving mode presents considerable advantages, as much in the field of quality of service as in the field of easy operation of a transport system: high service frequencies:
- On the other hand, the fears expressed some years ago concerning the attitude of the public towards fully automatic systems and the safety problems that these systems could raise have been dissipated:
- Finally, the price to be paid for these advantages is considered to be acceptable by operators.

We can develop this last point by attempting to draw up a financial balance sheet of fully automatic underground railway lines. The best approach consists in proceeding to a comparison on the same line, examining the differences of costs to which two different modes of transportation can lead.

We will choose as a reference an underground railway line comparable to line 1 of the Lille metro, well known as VAL, whose main characteristics are summarised below:

length:	13km
number of stations:	18
number of trains:	36
minimum interval:	approximately 1 minute

Let us take as underlying assumption for this comparison that neither demand nor transport supply changes, that is to say that train frequencies, the duration of service periods — in the case about 20 hours — and the number of veh-km offered are the same in both cases. The demonstration would be too long to develop but the conclusion is clear: the balance sheet of a fully automatic underground railway system is positive with the option 'without platform doors', but naturally closer to the equilibrium if we choose the option 'with platform doors'. VAL is a design with platform doors but ideas are in evolution and several automatic underground railways in co-operation or in construction, for instance those in Vancouver, Miami, Detroit and Lyon, are designed without platform doors.

High service frequencies can be offered at reasonable cost only with automatic systems in the future because the balance sheet will be more positive for three main reasons:

1. the increase in manpower cost;
2. the progress of micro-electronics and the generalisation of microprocessor controls accompanied by the development of tools as aids to maintenance which could contribute to reducing cost; and
3. the appearance of system series such as line VAL to reduce the item 'studies, tests and qualification'.

The main objective of automating a public transport system is to maintain a high quality of service, chiefly frequencies, even outside peak period, thus making mass transit more attractive throughout the day and hopefully influencing modal split, and to provide extra services in the case of special events without incurring increased personal costs.

Hub-and-spoke system and relevant information technology applications

The general outlook

The **hub-and-spoke** system using single-modal and intermodal transfers is a constant phenomenon among all modes in all areas. The H&S system emanates from attempts to serve widespread geographical areas with smaller vehicles while servicing major flows with larger vehicles through consolidation and deconsolidation of traffic at hubs. It is the only way to create an economy of scale within the framework of organisational concepts in production and logistics. The H&S system is the only answer to the trend of a dramatic decrease in the shipment sizes and a consequent increase of the number of shipments to be transported induced by flexible production practice and just-in-time delivery.

In the US each air transport company has its own terminal constituting a natural monopoly and providing economies of scale through an interconnecting system that reduces the number of direct flights. This produces a concentration of traffic around the main hubs. Between 1977 and 1984 the number of take-offs handled by the hubs in France rose by 45 per cent, while overall they increased by only 8 per cent. This has led to a shift away from the notion of private air terminals to one of quasi-private airports, but the resulting congestion has given rise to government concern.

The computer revolution will probably turn out to be equally, if not more important, to the hub-and-spoke system as the container revolution. The transport sector is a phenomenal consumer of information and paper, chiefly international transport including custom, insurance and a chain of operators from the shipper to the buyer through inland transport, harbour or airport, and maritime or air transport. This is even greater when consolidation–deconsolidation are needed in a hub-and-spoke system.

If we look to production/distribution systems we observe the appearance of two new concepts:

1. JIT or JIT/TQC **(just-in-time/total quality control)** and
2. EDI **(electronic data interchange)** whose impact on the transport sector will be of paramount importance. For industry and physical distribution, information technology is a major component of their competitive strategy.

The explanation can be found in the growing influence of inventories control in manufacturing activity which needs differentiation in order to increase market share. Managers have to follow this technology change on an ongoing basis. In a situation of over-capacity, a competitive firm needs a plus through low cost and better quality, or rather a quick answer to market impulses which means a downstream command from the market to production without delay through a hub-and-spoke sourcing and distribution system. Looking particularly at transportation changes, three applications will be presented: **computer reservation system, express delivery** and **global logistic system**, which are all activities directly related to the hub-and-spoke system and **information technology** (IT).

Computer reservation systems

An efficient seat reservation system is essential to any intercity transport operator. With the growth in traffic, manually operated systems had become totally impracticable by the 1960s. The move towards deregulation further complicated the problem by increasing the volume of data to be handled (several thousand requests every hour) and by widening the choice of operators and routes. There was hence a need for multi-airline reservation systems in order to deal with the increasing number of connecting journeys made possible by the 'hub' system. The 1980s saw the introduction of **computer reservation systems** (CRS) which have had a major impact. The possessor of a CRS enjoys a close relationship with the travel agencies, has a more effective marketing system and can cover ancillary services such as hotel reservation.

The costs involved in such developments are enormous. American Airlines (SABRE) and United Airlines (APOLLO) each spent some $500 million over a period of more than ten years in developing their systems. AMADEUS, the system adopted by Air France, Lufthansa, Iberia and SAS, launched in 1987 and based on Texas Air's SYSTEM ONE, will become operational this year, with the capacity to handle 1,750 computers, the most powerful in the range.

Booking systems have become distribution systems (**global distribution systems** — GDS) and, at the same time, an essential company sales tool designed to boost company sales and turnover. Furthermore, in view of the enormous investment required, the services offered by reservations systems, previously free, are now chargeable and the charges are added to agencies' terminal leasing costs. The need to be linked into a system is universally recognised; it is a question of business survival, even if the service has to be paid for ($2 per transaction in the US). These systems also provide travel agencies with a complete back-office package (invoicing, decision-making tools, general and analytical accounting, customer follow-up, etc.). In the world to come, with over-expanding data exchange using new communication systems and remote sales, the electronic transaction will increasingly trigger the transport process which in the turn will be computer-controlled. This is as true for freight as for passenger transport.

Express delivery

Traditionally, the frequency of the delivery of supplies to a factory is determined by full vehicle loads. But just-in-time production requires smaller but more frequent deliveries (**less than truck loads** — LTL). If transport costs are to be maintained at an acceptable level, the solution would consist of organising a delivery schedule with fully loaded vehicles delivering to several consignees. In the United States, Federal Express and UPS have taken over from the postal system and the rail freight system to become veritable empires expanding at a rate of 35 per cent a year. What accounts for Federal Express's success is the quality of service required by the market and the possibility of calling on the most sophisticated information technologies. The Memphis hub is a model of its kind. Filling planes with small parcels and even letters is no mean feat.

The Memphis Federal Express giant is as much a plane operator as a computer system managing 15,000 trucks, several hundred planes and thousands of employees. It keeps its customers informed of the whereabouts of their parcel through its journey. This enterprise has changed market segmentation, the organisation of intermodal transport, the hub-and-spoke structure of transport schemes, the standardisation of packaging, mechanised handling and the pricing structure. As such it is a model for 'non-material' enterprises, but which is the answer for Europe?

Global logistic system (GLS)

The use in a competitive market economy of third-party logistics services will increase in a deregulated market because manufacturers and traders will seek to replace in-house operations. In-house logistics are often used simply because of excessive control on price and capacity in the for-hire transport sector. In addition, tight regulation stifles innovation and may have prevented or discouraged the development of innovative and large-scale services that manufacturers and traders demand from a modern third-party logistics service provides. A switch to third-party logistics services may enable a manufacturer or retailer to concentrate on their core business. But this will only work satisfactorily if the information systems of the carrier are integrated with those of the shipper. If this is achieved then high-quality service can be provided and at the same time the shippers' managers are freed for priority activities. Again, the critical support role of **information technology** in these developments comes through strongly.

The financial implications of operating a completely 'closed loop' system (where all resources such as trucks, planes, terminals and drivers are employed by the carrier, a solution adopted by 'integrators' like Federal Express) are such that some carriers will seek the benefits of scale and control without the financial commitment. They will do this through information technology. For example, carriers may wish to control their transport networks but not necessarily to own or employ all the network resources. So the prospective carriers will concentrate on aspects where they can add value such as inventory management and time-definite delivery, while leaving, say, the long-distance trucking to owner-operators. These carriers will develop logistics and transport control through information systems rather than control by ownership and 'doing'.

Major carriers can be divided into airlines or maritime liner shipping companies, integrated parcel carriers (express operators), freight forwarders and distribution companies (offering haulage and storage). A number of major European freight companies are exploring the use of information technology as a strategic weapon to promote the idea of single operator control. By integrating all the stages of the processing for a shipment on a Europe-wide basis and linking major shippers into their information systems, the carrier can develop a strategy based on 'one-stop shopping' for its customers. Nevertheless, the development of tracking and tracing systems using EDI technology and bar-codes for packages is most advanced in the parcels and express freight sector.

How do the present large carriers achieve this new global status? Only strategic alliance is possible in Europe because of the national status of these companies. Multi-modal transport is an area where there is significant scope to develop competitive advantage based on reduced costs and better resource utilisation. This type of road–rail transport using swap bodies and semi-trailers can combine the different efficiencies of road and rail, but problems relating to information flow have so far hampered developments in Europe. Development of airline passenger information systems provides powerful insights into the likely directions for cargo information systems needed by the global major carriers of the 1990s. The development and use of CRSs has given a number of airlines dramatic competitive advantages, such as higher profitability through better yield management; strategic alliance through better yield management; strategic alliance through code-sharing; better information than their rivals and increased market share through priority screen position.

Current developments within air freight suggest that airlines hope many of the advantages of CRSs and IT in the passenger field can be transferred to the cargo side. There is little doubt that there is a considerable amount of catching up to do as far as computerised systems for cargo are concerned, but only if they are able to segment the freight market as successfully as they have the passenger services. Unfortunately, far too little is yet known about the buying behaviour or organisation in the freight market and work on segmenting the freight market remains in its infancy. The trip-chain is, also, more complex than for passengers and the carrier is expected to be responsible for end-to-end movement. Information systems are nevertheless recognised as the competitive forces reshaping industrial landscapes, even in the freight transport sector. That is the main reason for the GLS project initiated by Air France, Lufthansa, Cathay Pacific and Japan Airlines. This project began in spring 1990 and it is premature to speak of its success, but we can assume that its ambition is far-reaching.

Highway safety improvement

The European research programmes PROMETHEUS and DRIVE have set ambitious goals for the development of electronic aids for road traffic, which are generally based on communication links between road and vehicles or between vehicles. In the past few years there has been much talk about the vehicle being made intelligent by different electronic systems or driving aids. We are told that road safety will be greatly improved but is it really true? Between the vehicle and the road, the driver is an actor whose behaviour and reactions should not be forgotten. If some aids offer him more safety, will he not drive faster, more dangerously? The a priori study of the electronic vehicle on safety ought to answer these questions, which go far beyond technical aspects. Researchers need to take into account behaviour science, ergonomic considerations and cost-benefit analysis supported by accident data and evaluation of the potential impact of the different electronic aids which are envisaged on the most frequent categories of accidents.

We will limit our consideration here to a more technical approach, consisting of an evaluation of the feasibility of the various equipments, particularly of the transmission links which are required for the realisation of the 'aids' under consideration. Medium to long-range links like **radio data system** (RDS) or **cellular mobile radio-telephone** are already in operation, so it might be of interest here to address only the aids based on short-range (<500m) links with the following supports: microwaves, infra-red and radiating cables. These aids are classified into three categories, corresponding to an increased complexity of the required links: road → vehicle, one way; road ↔ vehicle two-ways; and vehicle-to-vehicle one or two ways.

The safety functions may be classified into two categories according to the safety level which they require: level 1 — the function influences the traffic safety, but does not totally replace the driver who retains the possibility of assessing the situation, such as traffic lights or assistance to column driving; and level 2 — the functions in this class totally replace the driver's view and any failure may lead to severe accidents, such as anti-collision at intersections or overtaking and passing aids. The safety requirements for level 2 do not seem compatible with the conditions of production, operation and maintenance of private cars.

Road-based traffic information and road guidance, parking management and automatic tolling are considered to be technically feasible but raise some difficulties concerning frequency allocations. Functions with low feasibility characteristics and low perspectives of development are anti-collision at intersections, passing and overtaking aids and automatic driving. Naturally the analysis of a purely technical nature does not preclude other investigations based on ergonomic or economic considerations.

Conclusions

Transport, which started out in the realm of engineering, has today led to such a complex set of organisations that the systems involved must call on all the resources of computer science. Information technology has become as essential to their development as industrial technologies. When the price/quality ratio is changed by technological innovation, the influence of technology on transport begins. High-speed trains give access to the quality of domestic flight for lower-income earners. Less costly than the planes and of higher capacity, this technology offers potential support to Europe. During the last thirty years, we have observed an overall improvement in urban public transport, the renewal of historical centres and the right to transport for low mobility people. The high service frequencies of the new generation of automatic metros provide a valuable contribution to the quality of urban life.

The **hub-and-spoke** system, supported by **information technology**, is the best compromise between productivity and quality of service. **Just-in-time** delivery and intermodal terminals are the prerequisite to the continental Single Market. Economy of scale is not possible without new management techniques, rapid, dynamic decision and market reaction. **Highway safety** improvement is a necessity but the contribution of technology is not at a high level, one of the reasons being the poor potentialities of communication links between road and vehicles. Engineers need to improve technology but technological innovation is a long-term procedure and profits are at the end of the route only if good strategies are adopted, market-oriented and with the right balance between technology and management. Transport has moved from the wheel to computerised systems. It has therefore become permeable to innovation of all kinds. Starting from the modern application of the dream of the flying carpet, i.e. air cushion or magnetic levitation, innovation has extended to the creation of integrated logistics, optimising the whole process, from production through to distribution (just in time concept).

Chapter 5

Information technology innovation in road freight transport

G. Giannopoulos

Introduction

Put in a nutshell, the aim of modern information and telecommunications technology applications to freight transport[1] is to have a timely information lead, ahead of the physical transport operation, thus enabling an optimal resource scheduling of all participants of the transportation chain.

There are three general levels of **road freight operation** (RFO) which can be distinguished. **Level 1** consists of the freight management and 'logistics' functions that have to do with the planning of the transport operation in the long term; the processing of the orders; the processing of the paperwork that accompanies each transport; cost control; keeping of statistical data; the monitoring of the cargo; and general finance and administration. **Level 2** is concerned with the monitoring of the fleet of vehicles which includes functions such as route planning and vehicle scheduling; vehicle dispatching; and vehicle (or more generally mobile unit) fleet monitoring and control. Finally, **level 3** contains the functions that deal with the vehicles themselves and the goods carried. It includes route guidance; trip planning; vehicle and cargo technical monitoring and control; consignment identification; and maintenance scheduling.

Information and telecommunications technology (IT) applications have been and are being studied for all these functions and levels so as to provide for increased efficiency and safety of operation. These applications include appropriate hardware and software as well as the necessary organisational structures (orgware) that will make these applications most efficient at both the company level, and at national or international level.

During the last few years a major research effort is under way in Europe, directed to improving the performance of road (and other modes of) transport by using the capabilities of modern information and telecommunications technology. The effort is to create what is usually referred to as the **integrated road transport environment** (IRTE), i.e. the development and operation of an 'intelligent' road infrastructure and vehicle which will enable a smoother, safer and more efficient traffic flow and transportation process in general. To create this IRTE, research and development is now being funded at an ever-increasing rate. Similar efforts are under way in USA and Japan.

This chapter is based on the author's involvement, as technical director, in two major collaborative European Research projects in this field, both of the EC's DRIVE programme. The first was a two and a half years' research effort (1989–91) called EUROFRET, which dealt with the formulation of appropriate strategies at European level for the introduction of information technology innovation in **road freight transport** (EUROFRET, 1991). The second is a three-year research project (1992–4) called METAFORA, that deals with specific demonstrations concerning **mobile data communications** and EDI applications in **road freight** (METAFORA, 1992).

Current use of IT in European freight transport

In a survey among 215 European **road transport** operators, forwarders and shippers of goods carried out under the DRIVE I programme (projects EUROFRET and FLEET), the current picture of usage of IT innovation in **road freight transport** in Europe emerges as follows.

For the **freight management and logistics** functions, and more specifically for communication with other operators, forwarders, customers (shippers of the goods), or control points and customs, most companies use fax, telex or public telephone. Efforts to install **electronic data interchange** (EDI) systems to connect customs offices to the various companies are in their early stages and are going through an experimental phase of implementation. For example, in The Netherlands five out of the ten operators asked are planning to connect to SAGITTA, the Dutch customs information system (at present for imports only), but there are still problems with its implementation. Similarly the Swedish Customs Offices plan to introduce an EDI system, called **toll data system** (TDS), but it will not be operating at 100 per cent before 1993.

Generally speaking, the larger forwarder companies and those who do international haulage are currently planning to connect to EDI-based customs systems. The smaller companies have, for the time being, no plans in that direction.

For **information and document exchange** between shippers, consignees and operators, the usual way is phones, letters, telex, telefax, and lately EDI are used. EDI as a common form of data transfer (including documents) is only used within the offices of the same companies (or their affiliates) and is far from widespread among different operators, especially the small to medium-sized ones. Thus the companies that have staged usage of EDI are invariably parts of larger concerns with a well-developed and extended information system. These companies are trying to talk more and more of their customers into connecting up to their systems. They are also planning to further develop and standardise these systems. Big shippers already have a terminal of their own in their office. Sometimes also big shippers try to talk 'their' operators into the system that they are using. Smaller shippers do not seem to have plans to use such systems in the immediate future.

For **cargo tracing** almost all companies today have their drivers phone the offices at regular intervals. Generally speaking, little has been done on 'cargo tracing and tracking', although this seems to be considered a priority area (EUROFRET project, Deliverable report no. 3). A lot more rapid progress is expected within the next three or four years (1992–5). The **international distribution system** (IDS), which was established by a co-operative of twelve medium-sized operators in The Netherlands and their partners in other countries, is a bit more advanced for cargo tracking than the current practice of having the driver phoning his base each day.

For **fleet management**, and more specifically for vehicle routeing and scheduling, only some medium to large operators use computer programs. Most medium to small-size companies in the survey were unfamiliar with the existing software packages, or they thought that good planning packages don't exist. To implement changes in their vehicle's routeing and scheduling, the companies use written orders, face-to-face communications, public or mobile telephones. Mobile phones (applicable for national haulage only) are used in Sweden more than in any other country in Europe and to a lesser extent in the UK, the Federal Republic of Germany and other central European countries. In the peripheral countries (Greece, Spain, Portugal, Ireland) mobile phones are practically non-existent.

Plans to implement **vehicle location systems** based on satellites are now well on the way in the European market mainly from American companies in partnership with European ones (e.g. Geostar, LMSS of Rockwell, ETAK, INMARSAT, EUTELTRACKS). These systems now have a two to three years' lead in the market over the land-based systems, namely the GSM which has been selected as the European standard for mobile telephony.

With respect to **vehicle management and control**, the tachograph, which is obligatory all over the EC and many other European countries, is the main means of vehicle and driver control today. Additionally many operators order their drivers to fill in trip reports, giving details of any malfunctions or incidents during the trip. For the great majority of operators, however, vehicle operation and control is taken care of manually, i.e. during regular maintenance.

Efforts to improve on the tachograph are already under way. 'Black Box' monitoring systems are now appearing in the market. The main reason for buying these systems is that processing the trip reports and tachograph data is very labour-intensive, and with the new systems, savings can be realised.

As regards **route guidance**, in almost all companies surveyed, drivers are free to choose their own routes (within certain limits) on the basis of their experience. Therefore 'route guidance' systems do not appear to be high in the list of priorities of the European operators. Such systems may well be more important for the private cars but not very much so for the experienced 'truckers' except perhaps in large cities.

Finally for **finance and administration**, the majority of medium to large-size operators and forwarders in the central and northern European countries now use established computerised systems. Activities like 'freight documentation', 'order processing and invoicing' and 'costing calculation', are all automated. Most companies started computer automation in these classic fields, one at a time. This often results in many isolated software packages. Most of the large and medium-size operators would like to integrate their internal system(s) and connect them with an EDI system with the most important of their customers. Also many of the forwarders interviewed mentioned their intention to abolish the discount system that is widespread today. Instead they want an individual pricing system for their large customers. Some of the large forwarders already have such a system. These are all EDI applications.

For the lesser developed countries on the periphery, the applications mentioned above are not so widespread, although increasing use is made of isolated computer packages for specific tasks. In these countries, operators or forwarders who are affiliated with larger international transport or forwarding companies have already taken actions to link up to the EDI network systems of their parent companies.

By way of conclusion about current practices, it can be said that companies responding that they had no use planned for a particular information technology application are of two kinds: those which have no requirement, and those which are yet to be convinced of the benefits of such technology in the application.

Companies are often unconvinced of the potential contribution of information technology when the system is 'decision-making' in character (Cooper, 1989). For example, routeing and scheduling systems employ algorithms which are used to design, say, daily workloads for vehicles. Thus the task of the load planner is absorbed by the computer in the anticipation of arriving at more efficient working patterns for vehicles. However, many freight companies are concerned that mistakes will be made as a result of relying entirely on a computer-based delivery plan. As J. Cooper puts it, transport folklore abounds with accounts of how the computer was 'wrong' in some way, perhaps by routeing a vehicle across the mouth of an estuary, where no road existed. Although no modern computer-based system for vehicle routeing and scheduling would allow this to happen, the legacy of past inadequacies in systems persists. Another example is depot location and vehicle routeing and scheduling, with most of the companies asked using neither.

When the system performs a task of 'data transmission' (e.g. sales order processing, dispatched goods invoicing, etc.), it is more likely to have ready acceptance by the users. They seem to accept and value the benefits from such systems more.

The reservations of companies to the merits and benefits of information technology are many, but perhaps the most important aspect is one of responsibility. If a mistake is made in, say, the delivery schedule and a customer complains, then is it sufficient to blame the computer?

As a general rule, it is the larger-size companies which are more willing to invest in new informatics and telematics applications. Research by the Transport Studies Group at the Polytechnic of Central London (Cooper, 1989) has shown that a fleet of ten vehicles appears to represent a threshold for telematics applications. Below about ten vehicles, the operator requirement for telematics will be restricted to general management applications such as accounting. For larger fleets the applications will be more specifically related to freight transport and its associated activities.

Preferences and ranking of IT applications among European freight transport 'actors'

Of the many applications that modern information technology has on road freight transport operation, Table 5.1 shows those which can be distinguished as discrete and independent systems for which existing technology, or research and development now going on, can make a commercial application in the near or medium-term future a real possibility. In the same table, the preference expressed by European road freight shippers, agents and operators (in short called the freight transport 'actors') is shown in terms of their perceived benefits likely to be derived from each application. A first ranking, according to this survey, of the major IT applications, is given in Table 5.2.

As it might have been expected, preferences differ according to the type of company examined (e.g. forwarder, operator, etc.). A similar analysis, but based on company size (in terms of the number of vehicle units they own or use), showed similar results to the ones shown in Table 5.1.

The overall trends and preferences that can be established from the above results are summarised in the following list of the four 'most preferred' new IT applications for each major 'management level' in road freight transport among European firms:

Freight management and logistics

1. EDI networks (standardised, European-wide) for order processing, paperless invoicing, order capture, cost calculations, communication with authorities, communication with forwarders and shippers, etc.

2. On-line tracking of shipments.
3. Order capture, finding return loads.
4. Paperless invoicing and automatic notification of shipment arrival times.

Table 5.1   Typology of IT application and preference (expected benefits) among European forwarders or carriers

Type of application	Forwarders	Carriers
A. Freight management and data processing		
EDI between: forwarder/carrier	2.83 (0.577)	2.36 (1.120)
EDI between: shipper/forwarder	2.54 (0.035)	1.80 (1.390)
On-line tracking of shipments	2.87 (2.470)	2.17 (1.150)
EDI between: shipper/carrier	2.83 (2.886)	2.22 (1.190)
Order capture, finding of return loads, freight exchange	2.50 (0.660)	2.09 (1.044)
Automatic invoicing, cost calculations, cost follow-ups	2.50 (1.126)	2.10 (1.330)
'Paperless' invoicing payments	2.15 (1.280)	2.00 (1.270)
Automatic notification of shipments arrival time/delays	1.64 (1.390)	1.45 (2.420)
Automatic cargo status updates	1.57 (1.340)	1.56 (1.360)
B. Fleet management		
Automatic fleet monitoring	2.19 (1.046)	2.09 (1.150)
On-line route planning and scheduling updates for new orders	2.00 (1.358)	2.17 (1.290)
Route planning based on actual road network data (time and distance)	1.40 (1.120)	1.45 (1.220)
Trip route directions for drivers (road selection + destination findings)	1.30 (1.250)	1.00 (1.270)
Route guidance and on-line tracking of (controlled) transports (i.e. dangerous, value cargo, etc.)	1.25 (1.420)	0.89 (1.280)
C. Vehicle/driver management		
Automatic vehicle-positioning system	2.07 (1.270)	1.95 (1.320)
Automatic vehicle navigation route guidance	1.65 (1.540)	1.86 (1.520)
Electronic shipment identification at loading and unloading	2.00 (1.130)	2.00 (2.490)
Automatic debiting at toll roads etc.	1.90 (1.300)	1.85 (1.300)
On-board telefax for document exchange	1.60 (1.400)	1.20 (1.400)
Automatic driver monitoring	1.58 (1.310)	1.10 (0.930)
Automatic monitoring of vehicle performance and technical functions	1.25 (1.350)	1.33 (1.270)
Transport statistics production by on-board computer-tachograph	1.50 (1.120)	1.45 (1.260)
Automatic scheduling of vehicle maintenance	1.16 (1.460)	1.45 (1.370)
Digital communication with customs at borders	1.60 (1.490)	1.50 (1.500)

Table 5.1 contd.

Type of application	Forwarders	Carriers
Digital communication with ports/intermodal terminals	1.46 (1.460)	1.56 (1.460)
Digital communication with the sender/receiver of goods	1.34 (1.430)	1.55 (1.350)
D. RTI expectations (to be installed by authorities)		
Digital communication between vehicle and authorities	2.75 (0.460)	2.70 (0.800)
Road service information on facilities along roads, road conditions, local weather, etc.	2.60 (0.670)	2.56 (0.700)
Interactive route guidance for navigation and traffic flow improvement	2.60 (0.500)	2.47 (0.640)
User cost and automatic debiting at toll roads etc.	2.40 (1.070)	2.67 (0.620)
Autonomous vehicle navigation	2.28 (1.110)	1.75 (1.500)
Environmental control of road (control of weights, dangerous goods)	2.10 (1.280)	2.21 (1.120)

Notes: The first number is the average of markings 0–3 (0 = no benefit, 3 = large benefit expected) given by the interviewees. The number in parenthesis is the standard deviation of the answers.

Table 5.2 IT technologies and preference shown among European road transport firms

A/A	Name of IT technology	Preference*
1.	Compatible, standardised European EDI systems	25%
2.	Pan-European mobile data telecommunication (MDC)	20%
3.	Interactive route guidance systems (especially for urban areas)	10%
4.	Fax systems on-board the vehicle (Mobifax)	9%
5.	Automatic vehicle location systems	8%
6.	Digital communication between vehicle and customs at borders	8%
7.	Radio service information on facilities along roads, road conditions, local weather, traffic congestion and accidents (RDS)	6%
8.	Automatic control devices on the road (weight in motion, & dangerous goods monitoring)	6%
9.	Automatic user cost charging (road fees) and automatic debiting at toll roads	4%
10.	In-vehicle, monitoring (statistics, etc.) systems	4%

* Preference expressed in terms of percentage of answers among the 215 companies asked, in the EUROFRET survey.

Fleet management

1. Automatic fleet monitoring.
2. 'On-line' route planning (diversions for new orders).
3. Route planning (routeing and scheduling) based on actual road and weather data.
4. Route planning for dangerous goods and special cargoes.

Vehicle/driver management

1. Mobile data communications (on-board computer or telefax for document and message exchange).
2. Automatic vehicle positioning systems.
3. Automatic vehicle navigation and route guidance.
4. Electronic shipment identification.

Many of the IT applications mentioned above are already in use in Europe. Applications such as order processing, dispatching of goods, invoicing, stock control, etc. (i.e. systems belonging largely to what we called earlier 'freight management') are beginning to be widely known and already a replacement market exists as new, more sophisticated systems become available. However, it is fair to say that these applications are mainly restricted to the larger-sized companies.

Therefore, and bearing in mind the remarks in a previous paragraph about the threshold size of companies for IT acceptance, what is under question is the potential for wider application to medium-sized or smaller companies. Also the potential of application of other IT-based methods and systems not yet in the market.

Information technologies of immediate application to road freight transport: issues and prospects for development

A. EDI for freight management and related activities

EDI systems in road freight transport are generally foreseen to enable computer-to-computer communication between

- shipper (consignor) and forwarder;
- forwarder and carrier;
- shipper and carrier;
- carrier and carrier (case of intermodal transport);
- forwarder and authorities (e.g. customs, borders, etc.);
- carrier and authorities.

The most likely application of such technology include

- order processing;
- paperless invoicing payments;
- stock control;
- cost data and other information transmission;
- access to relevant data banks (communication with authorities, etc.);
- order capture (finding return loads) or the so-called freight exchanges.

CURRENT STATUS

An EDI system has both physical and logical parts. The physical parts are the data transmission channels, the switching systems, and the computers at terminals or modes in the network. The logical parts are the software, the standards and the protocols for interconnecting and using the physical part. In order to adapt a computer to telematics applications, it has to be physically adapted to treat the transmission facilities as devices for input and output, and the software must be prepared to permit interaction with the network. Therefore a crucial part for the wider adoption and use of EDI is standardisation and normalisation of EDI networks.

A most notable example of current European efforts to establish reliable EDI networks is the TRADACOMS and TRADANET system in the UK (Fenton, 1984 and 1985). The UK Articled Numbers Association (ANA), whose aim is to improve trading efficiency, is responsible for standardising trading communication in the UK. In 1982 they published two manuals under the general heading of 'Trading Data Communications' (TRADACOMS). The EDI manual sets out a standard structure and sequence for data in the most common trading documents: orders, delivery notes, invoices and remittance advice along with formats for product, price and customer master files.

Most of the current TRADACOMS users, of which there are now several hundreds in the UK, currently communicate via magnetic tape using TRADACOMS standards. Software packages for formating data to and from TRADACOMS standards are now readily available.

An inevitable off-shoot of TRADACOMS was the development of TRADANET. It was recognised early on, during the development of TRADACOMS, that telecommunications provided the most suitable medium for electronic communication, being both readily available and virtually instantaneous.

TRADANET was therefore designed as a low cost off-line, highly secure value-added network which performed protocol conversion via a computer bureau. The service provides a store and call-forward facility allowing users control over the timing of data dispatch and receipt. Each company has access, either by dial-up or leased line, to its own electronic mailbox. Messages, in TRADACOMS standards, are sent in bulk to the nearest service node; messages are sorted and forwarded to the intended trading partner's electronic mailbox. Listings allow companies to see which messages have been received and withdrawn for processing. The processing cycle from start to finish takes approximately 2 hours.

STANDARDS AND PROTOCOLS

Most of the current work is focused on formulating a European standard. The European Standards Organisations CEN/CENELEC are working in this field with two committees, while a new COST research effort (COST 720) aims at testing in practice the proposed architectures and standards. The general architecture of an EDI European standard will follow the **open systems interconnection** (OSI) reference model that has been developed by the International Standards Organisation (ISO) for all computer-to-computer communications.

However, the contents of the information to be transferred have also to be specified and somehow standardised. The recent merger of the European and US standards into United Nations rules for Electronic Data Interchange for Administration, Commerce and Transport (UN/EDIFACT) will be an important basis for the development of a standard for goods transport. It contains a set of syntax rules, trade data elements directory (UNTDED), code guidelines for message design, data segments and, when the work is ready, also standard messages. The continuation of this standardisation is of the outmost importance for a fast introduction of transport-related EDI applications.

The European Community has adopted EDIFACT as the basis for its research and design projects in this field (e.g. CADDIA and the Customs project CD). Most of the other projects in Europe dealing with EDI are also EDIFACT-based, ODETTE and COST 306 for example. EDIFACT does not require any special network standard. Magnetic tapes and diskettes are currently the most common data carriers. For EDI, X25 seems to be the most frequently used but X400 may soon develop into a more popular carrier.

EXPECTED BENEFITS AND MARKET PENETRATION OF EDI IN ROAD FREIGHT

The market penetration of EDI will of course be related to the real or perceived benefits to be derived from its application. Computer-to-computer communications are more accurate and remove the need to key data from documents. Much of the time and money spent on resolving queries resulting from inaccuracies can be saved by improving communications efficiency. Reconciliation of invoices and credit notes with delivery confirmation and/or order placement can, using for example TRADACOMS, become truly automatic. Using standard product and/or location codes in electronic communication means that essential data such as company name, address, product, quantity and value can immediately be recognised by the computer with no need for human intervention.

So by some researchers EDI is expected to reduce document handling costs by approximately 20 per cent (Wandel, 1989). Research in the US (Boodman and Norris, 1981) indicates that the potential for **uniform communications standards** (UCS), (i.e. standardised message functions) in EDI could give direct savings of $67 million per annum in the food industry alone. In addition, further indirect savings could yield a further $256 million per annum in the same industry.

If the expected benefits are substantial, it is no wonder that the expected market penetration of EDI is also substantial. In a Delphi study among company experts in Europe it was found that 45–80 per cent of all shipments are expected to have the main document on EDI by the year 2000 in Western Europe. However, it must be stressed that a key factor to EDI's penetration rate is and will always be **confidentiality**. Once this has been secured and perceived as such by the users the penetration rates should be expected to increase sharply.

Individual companies report of course much faster penetration. For example, the car manufacturer Volvo planned to have 80 per cent of the main 600 suppliers confirming shipments made via EDI before the end of 1989 and to have the goods marked with bar-coded flags, all using ODETTE standards. The largest Swedish transport operator, Bilspedition, planned to have 500 of the largest domestic customers, covering 75 per cent of the shipments, linked via the EDIFACT standard by the end of 1991. In both examples, the respective customers are offered the installation of PCs, with all the necessary software and also some additional programs, bringing extra benefits to them.

Many computer manufacturers and third-party **value-added networks** have developed their own standards and protocols in order to keep their customers (e.g. IBM's SNA is not ISO compatible). The privately owned public networks are not interested in connecting with their competitors; they believe that the largest will survive in the end. Therefore, it can be expected that there will be a large 'shake-out' and only a few European-covering EDI networks will survive.

CURRENT BARRIERS TO EDI

The following barriers to EDI in Europe can be mentioned at present (Wandel, 1989):

- Large initial investment is needed in hard, soft and orgware and training to tie to internal systems that were not designed for external communication. This might be too high a cost for small companies that only join when forced to do so.
- There is still an uncertainty about what standard to use.
- There is an inertia in the organisation due to a shortage of skilled people and appropriate corporate culture. This is particularly true for the peripheral European countries where EDI is far less developed.

- At the beginning all wait for the others before using a new system. However, there are lower costs and higher benefits when there are many users of the network.
- The internal logistic systems of the companies must change to take full advantage of the faster and better information.
- The administrative savings are about the same for all, but benefits differ depending on sector and markets.
- Difficulties exist in quantifying costs and benefits in order to justify EDI, especially to medium or small companies.

B. On-line tracking of shipments and shipment identification

CURRENT STATUS

The ability to track a shipment all the way to its final destination is a very attractive application of information technology to users at both ends of the transportation chain. It entails the ability to receive automatically messages from the shipments on to appropriate roadside units which will then transmit this information to control centres. The most promising technologies for identifying shipments are **bar-codes** and **electronic tags**.

Bar-code reading with laser scanners or cameras for remote reading is a simple method, fast, cheap and relatively reliable. Several standards exist, but generally there is no problem since the same equipment can print and read most of them. A rapid universal adoption within the next three to five years can be expected of this technology in goods transport for identifying shipments, transport equipment and paper documents. Already it is applied in the case of containers. A new Japanese code using a square divided into four equal fields, representing sixteen bits, is claimed to offer higher accuracy than linear or circular bar codes. The major disadvantage of bar-codes is problems with dirt and other obstacles when reading.

Electronic tags can also be 'read' remotely. Many can store relatively large amounts of data (e.g. the Philips Premid stores 124K). Different techniques are used to transfer the information between the tag and the reader: induction, radio, microwaves, infra-red, or magnetic resonance. The relatively high price of about ($8 per tag in 1990) makes them only applicable in situations where they can be reused, e.g. for vehicle or load unit identification. The current largest application is in materials handling, e.g. a tag in the chassis directs the assembly of BMW cars (Wandel, 1989).

STANDARDS AND PROTOCOLS

All these automatic reading technologies require unique and standardised codes for shipment number, product, address, etc. The best-known standard in this respect is the European Article Numbers for consumer products. There is also a need to standardise addresses. All shippers and transport operators should have registers of their customers, containing addresses, customer number, telephones, etc. Already in Sweden, a national data bank for **goods address numbers** (GAN) has been established.

In the same way vehicles should be coded in a standardised form. This procedure is already under way for containers and other load modules when they are used in open exchange systems, e.g. container pools.

EXPECTED MARKET PENETRATION

LaLonde (1986) reported in his survey on the expected use of bar-coding in 'forward-thinking logistically-oriented companies'. He suggested that by the year 2000, 62 per cent of the inbound and 85 per cent of the outbound shipments in the US will be bar-coded. Europe will probably opt for electronic tags so the usage of bar-codes for remote shipment identification may be lower than in the US.

Already electronic tags are being used for container identification. Wandel (1989) reports the results of a Delphi study that showed 50–80 per cent of all shipments are expected to have computer-readable addresses by the year 2000 in the US and Western Europe.

As prices are falling rapidly, e.g. magnetic resonance tags might soon be as inexpensive as bar-codes, this also indicates a potential rapid market penetration.

C. Automatic fleet monitoring and vehicle positioning

CURRENT STATUS

There is already an established market for fleet management systems in Europe. Computer-based programs which allow the user to perform tasks such as routeing and scheduling but also to keep track of maintenance intervals, utilisation levels, tax renewal dates, etc. are quite well known and used by the larger operators. There is also a variety of systems for communication between dispatchers and vehicles (ranging from CB radio at the local level, through existing PMR and cellular systems, to satellite communications). In the future, these functions may be supplemented with **automatic fleet monitoring**.

Fleet monitoring allows dispatchers to track the position, status and route taken by the vehicle under their control at any moment in time. **Satellite-based systems** for vehicle positioning and fleet monitoring, although already in use in the US and partly in Europe, are making a head start in Europe, but when the new mobile telephony system GSM (**Groupe Spéciale Mobile**) which has been chosen as the universal standard for Europe comes to some meaningful geographic coverage, it is expected to take over, so to speak, and become the more widespread technology for fleet monitoring.

STANDARDS AND PROTOCOLS

The GSM network is a digital cellular mobile voice and data telecommunications system that will eventually provide pan-European coverage for its users. The **fleet monitoring** function currently under study uses the GSM **short message service** and the GSM system's own databases to track the position of a vehicle. The presence of a vehicle in a cell gives an approximate position, and the short message service is used to call up the vehicle's own navigation system (based on a **compact disc** digital map), which provides a more precise position. If a high degree of accuracy is not needed the system could be modular, with a CD map available as an optional extra.

The operator of a fleet of vehicles requires a computer and software to access the GSM network via a gateway provided by a service provider. The service provider's primary role is that of marketing the service and creating a user base. It is expected that separate businesses will undertake this role as the GSM network operators will at least in the early years of the system be primarily concerned with setting up the network. The service provider concentrates the traffic from a group of operators (perhaps in a single town) over a leased line, packet-switched or similar telecommunications network (possibly privately managed such as the existing EDI/EPOS networks), and provides a gateway to the GSM signalling system that allows the use of fairly simple software by fleet operators and protects GSM network security.

The same system could be used for data or voice communications between the fleet operator and the mobile.

EXPECTED BENEFITS AND MARKET PENETRATION

In a study performed by Analysys Ltd for the EC's DRIVE programme (Analysys, 1989) the potential benefits of this system were assessed on plausible scenarios and assumptions. The following results were obtained.

1. **Unit cost of in-vehicle equipment** for fleet monitoring. The system was estimated to be available (in 1992 prices) at a cost to the user for the in-vehicle equipment of approximately ECU 3,400–3,600 (1 ECU approx. equals $1.3). Over the next six to seven years the cost is expected to fall in real terms by about half. The fall is a result of the expected economies of scale, increasing competition on supply, improvements on production processes and is in line with the fundamental price trends expected for the overall GSM system since fleet monitoring will only be a proportion of the total market of the GSM mobile units. The total market value of the in-vehicle equipment (for trucks only) is estimated to increase between 1992 and 1996 at an average compound rate of over 70 per cent, peaking at ECU 450 million p.a. in 1997, and falling thereof by around one-third until the year 2005 when the market grows again as replacements need to be bought. The annual demand for in-vehicle

units will be around 225,000, with a value of ECU 35–40 million per annum (from 1996 onwards). This will be large enough to sustain a small number of manufacturers.

2. **Average annual operating cost per fleet (for France, Germany and BeNeLux).** The annual cost of running the fleet monitoring system for the above countries is given by the running costs of the equipment, such as the dispatchers' labour, maintenance and so forth, but excluding depreciation. As can be expected, the larger the fleet, the more affordable the fleet monitoring function would be in relative terms. From 1995 onwards an annual cost of ECU 2,800 per fleet per year is estimated, giving a total market of ECU 200 million for Europe.

3. **Fleet monitoring market.** The potential revenue for GSM operators from fleet monitoring, even assuming a modest penetration rate of 8 per cent of freight vehicles, is very significant, growing to 40 per cent of the current total value of the cellular market across the EC by the year 2000. One EC statistic suggests that there will be approximately a total of 12 million GSM subscribers by the year 2000; of these the freight vehicles are estimated to be approximately 1 million. Hence, the fleet monitoring service might account for 8 per cent of the total number of GSM subscribers. It must be noted that the current penetration for cellular phones in the UK is 22 per cent in commercial vehicles (see MIL Research, *Comms Monthly*, March 1989). The same survey found that vehicle location and navigation systems 'would be the next most popular advances'.

4. **Opportunities for local fleet monitoring systems.** Around 80 per cent of users will only travel within a relatively small area. This means that a large part of the potential GSM fleet monitoring user base is open to competition from local systems using different technical approaches which do not rely on the wider coverage of cellular systems.

As it was said before, the effect of satellite competition for those wishing to use fleet monitoring over a wider area may be significant, as these systems are likely to have a three-year lead over GSM, but in the long run economies of scale are likely to work in favour of the GSM system.

D. Vehicle route planning (routeing and Scheduling)

CURRENT STATUS

The primary objective of route (or round) planning is to design a set of routes and schedules for the vehicle fleet, which provides the customer service at an acceptable cost. The systematic construction of efficient vehicle round plans provides an important tool for the control of cost in the short term, for adapting the fleet mix in the medium term, and even for depot location in the long term.

Currently, market considerations dictate the minimum level of customer service for the physical distribution of products to the market. Constraints on attainable performance are supplied by the legal, financial and historical framework in which the system has to operate. In principle the allocation of resources, to sustain a desired level of service, is a well-structured problem amenable to model building, assuming that operational constraints are fully identified and understood.

Transport managers often express dissatisfaction with present route planning methods. These methods are often crude and have remained virtually unaltered since inception. 'Pigeon hole systems', typically based on regional routes using some geographical determinant, e.g. post-codes, are still common. Round planning often consists of manipulating consignment notes (customer orders) between pigeon holes until a 'satisfactory' utilisation of vehicle capacity is achieved.

Computerised route planning (CRP) is now used in most countries of Europe, mainly by companies operating a multi-depot network with fleet sizes in excess of fifty vehicles. Furthermore, companies may use CRP for strategic and tactical distribution issues. The best-known computer packages in use today in Europe are the 'Dayload and Transit', HSDIST, HOVER, RARAGON, ROUTEMASTER, PATHFINDER.

POTENTIAL CRP BENEFITS AND MARKET PENETRATION

Cooper (1989) reporting on a PCL study estimated a 10 per cent saving in total (multi-drop) vehicle operating costs from daily CRP as realistically attainable. Given this level of saving daily, CRP is likely to benefit operators with fleets in excess of ten vehicles (per depot). Furthermore it offers greater control over transport operations, can improve service levels, reduce the fleet size and the use of hired vehicles and enhance the ability to ask 'what if' questions.

However, many improvements are still necessary. The successful implementation of daily CRP relies on timely and accurate input data. This level of detail of information has dissuaded many companies from introducing CRP until such systems as order processing, credit checking, stock control, order picking, etc. are themselves accurate and timely and most likely computerised. The failure of early daily CRP systems was due as much to the shortcomings in support (data) systems as to weaknesses of early CRP objectives and packages.

Within the EC, in the ESPRIT research programme, an ambitious four-year research project called PONTIFEX is currently looking into the whole problem of **routeing and scheduling** from a new perspective. The aim is to create an artificial intelligence-based package that will incorporate appropriate knowledge-based 'Shell', CRP algorithms and rules of selection, thus enabling the optimum utilisation of 'tools' for each particular application (PONTIFEX, 1989). The package is intended to be very user-friendly so that it can be used by the non-specialists, and versatile enough to be used for more than one mode of transport.

The market for computerised route-planning packages has been estimated by the author to be about 70–80,000 medium and large-sized transport companies in the twelve EC member countries and an equally large number of private 'producer' companies that operate their own fleets (TRADEMCO/TRUTh, 1992).

E. Autonomous navigation and interactive route guidance (IRG)

CURRENT STATUS

Route guidance is a concept which provides a driver with knowledge of the best route to follow through a road network. The final goals are that of relieving the driver from a somewhat difficult task, and of reducing congestion. To perform these tasks, data have to be collected, in real time, on the traffic situation, then elaborated and the final information retransmitted, in suitable form, to individual vehicles.

Two notable experiments are currently under way in Europe. These are the large-scale field trials of the TRANSLISB in Berlin and AUTOGUIDE in London (both known as the ALI-SCOUT type of systems). The TRANSLISB system in Berlin is based on the LISB infrastructure that was developed in this city (infra-red beacons at traffic lights) and consists of the following main building-blocks: localisation of vehicle, vehicle–roadside communication; route optimisation; and (later) network flow optimisation.

Relative to this field, two research projects in the DRIVE I programme, should also be mentioned:

● Project V1011 where the integration of ALI-SCOUT-type **route guidance** with **traffic control** schemes were studied; and
● Project V1007 (SOCRATES) where the extension of autonomous navigation systems with the help of GSM-derived, two-way, local communication was studied.

At the present time the European demonstration projects are devised to show how the systems will be used for guidance through the urban network, to check the user acceptance and to measure benefits.

THE NEED FOR STANDARDS AND PROTOCOLS

Again, European standards on infrastructure and applications for route guidance systems have to be defined. To illustrate the multitude of problems and tasks in this field we consider the following.

Communication from vehicle to roadside and vice versa, which is essential for dynamic route guidance, could normally be made via infra-red (ALI-SCOUT) or microwave; high throughput may be necessary (500 kbode is envisaged for the 'next generation' ALI-SCOUT). A draft Anglo-German standard has recently been proposed for infra-red transmission. Data passing to the vehicle include all pointwise information on traffic needed for the route choice (in a general case) or, as in ALI-SCOUT, the optimal route. From the vehicle, data originate on traffic flows (journey times on single links, congestion indicators, etc.).

Privacy and security aspects have to be considered in this data exchange. In planned final systems, no information suitable for on-line identification of the vehicle, or of the trip, will be transmitted.

Route optimisation could be done on board as well as in guidance centres. To cope with congestion and with time-dependent situations, both must be based on real traffic data, suitable predictions, and be dynamic. In ALI-SCOUT, provision is made for recomputing optimal routes at short time intervals. The choice of 'central' route optimisation, in principle, allows for similar inclusion of 'community' (rather than 'user') optimisation criteria.

Future developments must take into account the need for integration of **interactive route guidance** with other measures within the **traffic information** class, mainly with the RDS/TMC-based systems.

BENEFITS AND PROSPECTS FOR MARKET PENETRATION

Applications of **interactive route guidance** systems (IRG) in the field of freight transport are foreseen mainly for urban areas and rather for multi-distribution jobs. No road freight operator seems at present interested in IRG systems for intercity transport as routes seem to be well-known and understood.

On the other hand, localisation needs to be performed with high accuracy, if the route suggestions in a dense urban network are to be useful. This may call for still some research and development work to be done, but as the multiple use intelligent road infrastructure in Europe becomes a reality it will be possible to be made more and more accurately and cheaply. Then a well-defined market for such services that consists mainly of urban delivery and distribution companies as well as operators of fleets of vehicles such as taxis or ambulances will emerge and profit from the technology now in the stage of field trials.

Conclusions

There is an active field of research and practical applications for information technology and telecommunications in the field of freight transport in Europe. Indeed it seems that it is this particular field of transport that is the first to benefit from such technology. On the other hand both the IT industry and the European administrations (led by the EC) are now setting out the policies and standards for the particular applications.

Of the specific applications discussed for freight transport the most preferred today by European operators and forwarders seem to be the following:

- one or two standardised and uniform European-wide EDI networks for communication between the various 'actors' of the trade;
- on-line tracking of shipments;
- automatic fleet (and driver) monitoring;
- automatic vehicle-positioning systems.

There seem to exist today a key division in telematics which influences the acceptance of systems by companies. When the system performs a task of 'data transmission' (e.g. sales order processing, dispatched goods invoicing, etc.), it is likely to have ready acceptance. By contrast, the 'decision-making' systems, such as those for depot location, vehicle routeing and scheduling, or for strategic planning, are regarded more circumspectly by companies. The reservations of companies are many, but an important aspect is one of 'responsibility' and mistrust.

As a general rule, it is the larger-sized companies that are more willing to invest in new information technology and telematics applications. A fleet of ten vehicles would appear to represent a threshold for the acceptance of such applications. Below about 10 vehicles, the operator requirement for telematics will be restricted to general management applications such as accounting. For larger fleets the applications will be more specifically related to freight transport and its associated activities.

Regarding the main IT applications in the various freight operations, the following points were made earlier on and are considered important to be mentioned again here:

1. For EDI communications the European Community has adopted EDIFACT as the base for its projects. Work now goes on at an increased rate for standardised and uniform message types as well as transmission networks. Magnetic tapes and diskettes are currently the most common data carriers. For EDI, X25 and X400 seem to be the most frequently used.

2. For on-line tracking of shipments all automatic reading technologies require unique and standardised codes for shipment number, produce, address, etc. The best-known standard in this respect is the European article numbers (EAN) for consumer products. There is also a need to standardise addresses. All shippers and transport operators should have registers of their customer, containing addresses, customer number, telephone numbers, etc. The national data bank for **goods address numbers** (GAN) already established in Sweden is a good example of how things may develop elsewhere. In the same way vehicles should be coded in a standardised form. This procedure is already under way for containers and other load

modules when they are used in open exchange systems, e.g. container pools.

3. For **automatic fleet monitoring** and **vehicle positioning** the GSM network of radio transmission or satellite communication may be used. Already satellite technology is commercially available through mainly American companies. It seems to have a three to five year lead over GSM but in the long run economies of scale are likely to work in favour of the GSM system.

4. For **vehicle route planning (routeing and scheduling) computerised round planning** (CRP) is used in most countries of Europe, mainly by companies operating a multi-depot network with fleet sizes in excess of fifty vehicles or so. Furthermore companies may use CRP for strategic and tactical distribution issues. However, many improvements are still necessary. The successful implementation of daily CRP relies on timely and accurate input data. This level of detail of information has dissuaded many companies from introducing CRP until such systems as order processing, credit checking, stock control, order picking, etc. are themselves accurate and timely and most likely computerised.

5. Finally for autonomous navigation and route guidance, applications of **interactive route guidance** systems (IRG) in the field of freight transport are foreseen mainly for urban areas and rather for multi-distribution jobs. The main European effort in this field which is now at the stage of field trials is the TRANSLISB system in Berlin and the AUTOGUIDE in London.

It appears that we are on the verge of wider market acceptance of many interesting new applications of information technology. Freight transport is probably the first field of transport to benefit from them and make them commercially viable for a wider application.

Note

1. The innovation from information technology (IT) is one field of technical innovation from which freight transport operation benefits. A more global reference to the various other fields of technological innovation in the field of transport is provided in this book by M. Frybourg's Chapter 4 on Transportation Technology Trends in Europe.

References

Analysys (1989) 'Fleet monitoring: SECFO scenario', Working paper for the EC's DRIVE programme, Systems Engineering and Concensus Formation Office (SECFO), June.

Boodman, D.W. and Norris, R.C. (1981) 'Progress in distribution: computer to computer ordering', *Handling and Shipping Management*, September.

Cooper, J. (1989) 'Telematics in goods transport: United Kingdom', ECMT, 78th Round Table, Paris.

EUROFRET (1991) 'A European system for international road freight transport operations'. DRIVE I project no. V-1027, January 1989 – May 1991, Final Report 1991 (available from prime contractor or author).

Fenton, N. (1984) 'TRADANET success: trial enters new phase and promises benefits to suppliers and everyone else', *ANAN News*, vol. 12(4), November.

Fenton, N. (1985) *Articled Numbering and Data Communication, Managing PDM to Gain Competitive Advantages*. Conference 1985, Inst. of Physical Distribution Management, London.

Giannopoulos, G.A. (1989a) 'In-vehicle informatics applications in road freight transport'. Paper presented at the ESPRIT Workshop on *Mobile Working*, 3rd ESPRIT Conference, Brussels, 29 November.

Giannopoulos, G.A. (1989b) 'The influence of telecommunications on transport operations', *Transport Reviews*, vol. 9(1), January–March.

METAFORA (1992) 'A major European testing of actual freight operations on a road axis'. DRIVE II project no. V-2048, January 1992 – October 1994.

PONTIFEX (1989) 'Planning of non-specific transportation by an intelligent fleet expert'. ESPRIT programme, Milestone one, Deliverable September 1989 (Nixdorf-Italy, prime contractor.)

Wandel, S. (1989) 'Telematics in goods transport: Sweden', ECMT 78th Round Table, Paris.

TRADEMCO/TRUTh (1992) 'Dianomes', A computer-based package for routeing and scheduling of a fleet of road freight vehicles, a research and development programme assigned to the above companies by the Mediterranean Integrated Programme for Greece.

Annex: list of abbreviations

AGS	automated guideway systems
AHC	automatic highway chauffeuring
ANA	Articled Numbers Association
ATRP	automatic tolls and road pricing
AVI	automatic vehicle identification
AVL	automatic vehicle location
AVN	automatic vehicle navigation
CA	collision avoidance
UCS	uniform communications standard
CD	compact disk
CRG	co-operative route guidance
CRP	computerised round planning
CW	collision warning
DG	Directorate-General
DRIVE	dedicated road infrastructure for vehicle safety in Europe
ECMT	European Conference of Ministers of Transport
ECU	European Currency Unit
EDI	electronic data interchange
EC	European Community
GAN	goods address number
GPS	global positioning system
GSM	Groupe Spéciale Mobile (mobile cellular telephony and data transmission system)
IDS	international distribution system

IRG	interactive route guidance
IRTE	integrated road transport environment
ISO	International Standards Organisation
IT	information technology
MSI	motorist service information
MSS	mobile satellite systems
OSI	open systems interconnection
PC	personnal computer
PCL	Polytechnic of Central London
R&D	research and development
R&S	routeing and scheduling
RDSS	radio determination satellite systems
RTI	road transport informatics
SDK	speed and distance keeping
SECFO	Systems Engineering and Concensus Formation Office (DRIVE)
TDS	toll data system
TRADACOMS	trading data communications
TRADANET	trading data network
TMC	traffic management and control
TRUTh	Transport Research Unit, University of Thessaloniki
UCS	uniform communications standard
UNTDED	United Nations Trade Data Elements Directory

Chapter 6

Technological innovation in private road passenger transport

G. Giannopoulos

Introduction

Private road transport for passengers is undergoing a profound technological transformation that started in the 1980s and is now at the peak of its evolution. By the turn of the century the technology for both automobile construction and traffic management and control will have produced a radically different environment for road transport. This 'environment', which is usually referred to as the **integrated road transport environment** (IRTE), comprises elements that can be classified in the following five broad categories:

1. the automobile's own technological development;
2. travel demand management;
3. travel and traffic information;
4. integrated urban and inter-urban traffic management;
5. driver assistance and co-operative driving.

The key factor for the development of the new systems is computer and telecommunication technology (**telematics**). However, considerable changes are also expected due to some recent breakthroughs in energy generation technology and the mechanical systems of the vehicles.

The objectives of this transformation effort are threefold. On the one hand there is the need for increased safety for the whole operation. On the other, efficiency must be preserved and improved, and finally all this with the maximum comfort, privacy, etc. and the minimum adverse environmental and socio-economic effects.

The scale of the current problem and of the benefits to be realised is immense. Transport plays a significant role in stimulating Europe's economy and quality of life. Europeans spend more than ECU 500 billion (approximately 620 billion US dollars) on road transport products and services every year. More than 10 per cent of the average family budget is devoted to transport. Car ownership has been increasing steadily by 4 per cent a year and there are already now some 120 million cars in Europe. International traffic increases by 5 per cent a year, whilst on main motorways freight traffic has increased by more than 10 per cent in 1990 alone. However, investment in new infrastructures has suffered a reduction of about 50 per cent between 1975 and 1986: from 1.1–1.2 per cent of the GNP to 0.6–0.7 per cent. In addition, in the countries of the European Commission alone an average of 55,000 people have been killed, 1,700,000 injured and 150,000 permanently handicapped by road accidents each year during the 1980s. Apart from the human suffering involved, the financial cost of this has been estimated to be at least ECU 50 billion per year (EEC, 1990). So there is certainly a lot of scope and incentives to change the current situation and technological innovation is the moving-force behind this change.

The purpose of this chapter is first, to give a concise overview of current progress and status in the application of technological innovation to all five of the elements of IRTE mentioned earlier, and secondly, to discuss the policy issues and implications of this new emerging situation.

Technological development of the automobile

The past decade and current trends

During the last decade several technical problems related to the automobile have been solved and new technological fields have been developed to solve these problems. Together with the introduction of chemistry-based technology, such as catalysts for exhausts, great advances have also been made in engine combustion and the electronic and mechatronic systems for controlling combustion. As a result, automobiles exhibit high reliability with superior performance and low fuel consumption. The increased demand for the technology providing this high performance has in turn stimulated the development of new technologies in the chassis and drive-related systems, such as electronically controlled suspension, four-wheel steering, constant four-wheel drive and anti-locking brakes. Optimum control systems using electronic technology have also been adopted for these components, besides the technology providing high engine performance. Furthermore, the industry has begun to accelerate the introduction of communications techniques, the development of new materials and the utilisation of computer-controlled mechanisms.

Technological developments have been advanced further to improve safety and to reduce exhaust pollution and fuel consumption. New safety technology has been introduced to improve the basic functions of automobiles and to increase their operational safety. To control these new systems and others, new technology has begun to contribute to the improvement of automobile performance. It includes the multiple use of electronic technology and the manufacture of some parts using new materials, such as ceramics, fibre-reinforced plastics (FRP), and fibre-reinforced metal (FRM).

Also, safety devices such as air bags, comfort equipment such as air conditioners, and information systems such as automobile telephones and navigational systems have begun to become popular, and equipping automobiles with intelligent systems has also been promoted to enrich automobile life.

The trends in automobile technology as seen for the next decade up to the year 2000 and beyond can be described as follows.

VEHICLE CONTROL AND SYSTEMS

With the advances in microelectronic technology, the application of electronic control systems is expected to gradually be expanded to engines, driving-systems, and chassis. Future electronic technology will aim at securing both sophisticated auxiliary driving functions and high safety by providing overall control. The increase in the number of elderly and women drivers accelerates the need for greater safety, including controls for easier driving and automatic transmissions. This technology will develop further to create automatic driving-systems linked with communications technology.

Promising new technologies for vehicle control are fuzzy control, **very large-scale integration** (VLSI), and photoelectric **integrated circuits** (IC); also, the intelligent sensor, which detects external environments such as the condition of various vehicle components and road surfaces, and the mental and physical condition of drivers.

The results of such technological development are expected to enable automobiles to operate at high speed and thus notably improve transportation efficiency and convenience.

COMMUNICATIONS TECHNOLOGY

To develop automobiles into an overall transportation system, it is essential to secure communications with the infrastructure.

Automobile communications technology originated with the driver navigation system and will be developed into a guidance system providing support for elderly people and further into information techniques for automatic driving.

Intermobile-station communications will also be developed and enable automobiles to have systematic contact with other high-speed transportation modes (see later sections). Also, mass-storage technology, such as high-density digital optical recording, and technology that maximises the use of wide informational communications systems, such as communications satellites, will be implemented.

NEW MATERIALS

New automobile materials that have drawn attention are **fibre-reinforced plastics** (FRP) and **fibre-reinforced metal** (FRM). These are produced by compounding resin and fibre with ceramics. FRP and FRM have already been used for automobile components and will be used more widely in the near future. The use of ceramics is important because this material has properties that cannot be provided by organic and metallic materials. Ceramics have so far been used primarily for sensors as functional materials, but they will also be applied to ceramic gas turbines and ceramic engines to greatly improve engine efficiency.

Following the implementation of new materials, the technology for the recycling or disposing of them without pollution will also need to be developed.

The prospects for the twenty-first century

As we move into the twenty-first century the current technological advances will further magnify into new systems and techniques and also towards greater integration of the automobile into its urban and inter-urban environment and greater social acceptability of its use. This is the major difference over current trends. The following areas are characteristic of the prospects for the twenty-first century.

USE OF NEXT-GENERATION COMPUTERS FOR CAR DESIGN
The technology to create fifth-generation and neural computers is being developed progressively. They will have a great influence on automobile development systems and production technologies.

Even in the current automotive development process, supercomputers are used to analyse structure and aerodynamic performance. Also, **computer-aided design** (CAD) and **manufacturing** (CAM) are also used. To meet the more detailed needs of users, integrated computer technology will be introduced.

The introduction of next-generation computer technology will not only stimulate an increased development of production technology, but will also widen the control functions of automobiles and accelerate the creation of very human-like automobiles that will have functions such as pattern recognition and judgement.

USE OF BIOTECHNOLOGY METHODS AND TECHNIQUES
The effects and future prospects of biotechnology have been clarified in the medical, chemical and agricultural fields, but its influence on automobile technology has not yet become clear.

However, it is universally recognised that there are technological factors with the potential to influence future automobile development, which are available in the organs of living creatures and which are used to detect obstacles and to reduce movement resistance of travel, such as in bats, dolphins and birds. Therefore, it is very likely that innovations in automotive technology for sensors and actuators will occur as biotechnology progresses.

MORE ENVIRONMENT-FRIENDLY VEHICLES

The number of people sensitive to environmental issues increases as society becomes more affluent. The technology for reducing exhaust pollution, which was developed in the 1970s, has definitely contributed to alleviating the problems. However, new technology to reduce exhaust pollution will continue to be developed, and this has strong potential.

The automobile industry must continue to improve the technology for reducing pollution, such as that caused by NO_{-x}, and it will continue to contribute to the maintenance of social environments in co-operation with related industries, such as the petroleum industry.

To maintain the global environment, technological development must also be accelerated in the automotive industry to contribute to the solution of problems, such as the emission of fluorocarbons and the 'greenhouse' effect.

NEW ENERGY SOURCES

The quantitative expansion of mobility in the motorised society of the twenty-first century coupled with the depletion of the current sources of fossil fuels, and also because of increased environmental concerns, will increase the search for new energy sources.

As such, the performance of batteries and motors for electric automobiles will be improved along with the operating distance per charge. They will become more popular as community cars within cities. Also, automobiles using a wide range of new energy sources will increase, such as methanol cars, gas-turbine cars using fine-ceramic materials, and hybrid cars that can use different energy sources. They will be used for physical distribution, such as in mass-transportation systems.

The technological progress in fuel cells, solar batteries and superconductivity will stimulate research in their application to automobiles and to a practical implementation of cars that will operate on new energy sources.

AUTOMOBILES DESIGNED FOR THE 'INDIVIDUAL' AND NOT THE 'MANY'

Great importance is expected to be attached to individuality, and automobiles will become increasingly custom-made for a particular set of users. Besides the creation of a reasonable transportation system, there will be an increased awareness of the social implications of the use of automobiles in providing private and comfortable rides incorporating functions such as communication by voice or data with the office, on-line information on travel and leisure opportunities, etc.

Automobile functions will become even more sophisticated and diversified. A wide variety of cars will appear as custom-made automobiles for different uses, such as leisure vehicles, commuter cars, and cars with low prices and low fuel consumption. Many types of highly individual automobiles will travel around the cities and suburbs.

Travel demand management

Scope and rationale of demand management

The management of travel demand includes a number of functions and measures that are needed to preserve capacity and operation of the road network from unlimited and uncontrolled increases in traffic. With correct action at this level, two main objectives can be achieved:

1. Move the travel demand to more suitable modes; and
2. obtain a better distribution of traffic both in time (modifying departure times) and in space (influencing route choice).

It must be emphasised that **demand management** measures must be planned *in parallel* with all the other applications of new technologies within the **integrated road transport environment** (IRTE) implementation. This is because by the application of RTI measures, the road traffic efficiency will be increased. At the same time, the attractiveness and accessibility of the road network will be increased, and at least two effects will take place:

1. More people will travel; and
2. people will be diverted from other modes to road traffic or vice versa.

The overall objective is to achieve another 'equilibrium' as shown in Figure 6.1.

Whereas normal traffic management allows more traffic (demand) to be satisfied at the same level of journey times (point A2), demand management reduces both the demand and the travel times to a new equilibrium (point A1).

'Technologies' to be used

Demand management actions are of different natures and levels. They involve the planning level as well as the operational one, from the traffic restriction in town centres to the application of time and route-dependent road-pricing schemes. Because the main goal is the better use of alternative transport facilities, the public (or collective) transport infrastructure must be improved, enlarged and made more efficient. Investment in this line will have to be planned as an essential part of the management of demand.

Also all the demand management actions have to be integrated with the other technological innovations at all levels. For example, data

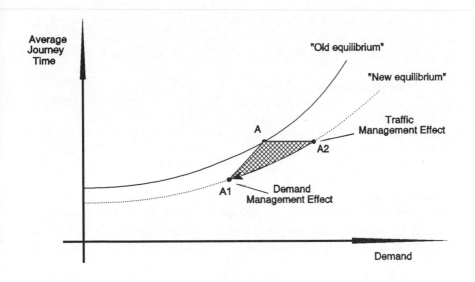

Figure 6.1 Diagrammatic representation of the effect of Demand Management

collected from the traffic control system has to be used for establishing demand restrictions. Moreover, the actions taken have to be made known to various levels of 'information' and 'control' subsystems.

Our impression is that demand management actions are probably due in the near future, and they need an early agreement at European level, not only on the applied principles, but also in standard technologies for communications. Also the operation will need correct integration with the other innovation systems.

Travel and traffic information

General

In this area many technological breakthroughs have been established, some of which are now at the point of general application in Europe. Somewhat more detail is therefore justified in their presentation.

'Travel' information can be regarded as the generic term for a number of possibilities to provide the traveller with news relevant to the current situation and with useful suggestions for a good travel choice. The information must be available to the traveller at home, at the workplace and in public areas. Information provided must be sufficient for the traveller to plan his journey to the required destination and should include traffic, tourism, time, distance, cost and regulatory data.

In order to assist in the realisation of the **travel information** function, a series of databases will need to be constructed and placed on-line for interrogation by the traveller. It is likely that a network would be required, capable of granting the co-ordinated access to a number of special databases.

The main problem areas for travel information are therefore those of 'data collection', 'forecasting models', and 'co-ordinated database network'. The latter is considered to be the most important. The communications network, together with the equipment needed for user interaction, will develop in the near future in an independent path, derived from existing technology such as Minitel, Teletext, ISDN and similar.

By contrast **'traffic' information** is a term used mainly from information given to the drivers and/or passengers *during* their trips in order to help them make on-the-spot decisions or warn them of relevant events etc. There are three basic levels of **traffic information**:

1. information describing actual abnormal traffic conditions and short-term forecasts (traffic jams, accidents, roadworks). This information will have to be interpreted and correctly used by the driver; it could be broadcast by radio channels or displayed via **variable message signs**;
2. information of traffic events, as before, but such to be used by on-board equipment for dynamic navigation;
3. specific and individual information provided to the driver, via suitable channels and on-board equipment, containing direct suggestions on suitable (or best) routes to the destination.

In IRTE, the goal of traffic information is twofold, i.e:

1. to provide the user with help in finding the route; and
2. to maintain the road traffic flow in stable 'equilibrium' by avoiding local congestion and shortening individual journeys. In the latter sense, 'traffic information' is a powerful tool for 'controlling' traffic. As such, it concentrates on all the related problems (such as 'what' information has to be given 'where' and 'when', what will be the influence on traffic as well as the acceptance by individuals etc.).

Systems and technologies used

The presentation in the following uses the classification established earlier by project COST 30 and the OECD (see COST, 1985; OECD, 1987; OECD, 1988).

Class 0 **Autonomous navigation aids.** These are wholly self-contained in-vehicle systems that help the driver to locate his position on the road network and to navigate to this destination. They do not need a communication link but could be enhanced by the use of one or more of those described below.

Class 1 **Area broadcasting systems.** These are usually radio broadcasting systems, and are used to communicate traffic information to drivers over a wide area.

Class 2 **Local roadside transmitter systems.** These also broadcast traffic information, but usually only within the area immediately surrounding a road junction, or similar 'points'.

Class 3 **Mobile radio systems.** These provide two-way radio communication over a wide area between drivers in their vehicles and a control centre.

Class 4 **Local roadside transceiver systems.** These also provide two-way communication between drivers in their vehicles and a control centre, but usually only on the approaches to a road junction.

The interrelation of the five classes of systems and their place in the driver or traveller information system is shown in Figure 6.2.

It is worthwhile to present briefly the technologies and systems developed to date in the above classes.

CLASS 0: AUTONOMOUS NAVIGATION AIDS

Most autonomous navigation aids rely on a dead-reckoning method to deduce location. This usually involves fitting the vehicle with both distance and heading sensors in order that the vehicle's progress from a known start position can be continuously monitored and updated. A few systems, however, deduce location using a trilateration technique such as provided by the radio location systems, DECCA Navigator and Loran-C, or the satellite navigation systems, DAVSTAR GPS; while some, particularly in the case of public transport or fleet vehicle systems, use roadside position beacons.

There are basically three types of self-contained systems: **simple directional aids; map displays;** and **route guidance aids.** In addition to a location subsystem, all require a keyboard — into which the driver enters codes for his start position and his required destination; a microcomputer — for 'reading' the imputs from the location subsystem and keyboard, and for computing the position and guidance data; and a display unit — for displaying, or in some cases announcing, the resulting guidance advice to the driver.

Simple directional aids show the driver the heading and remaining crow flight (i.e. straight line) distance to his destination. The heading information is usually displayed as an arrow which physically identifies for the driver the direction he must take at the next junction. These

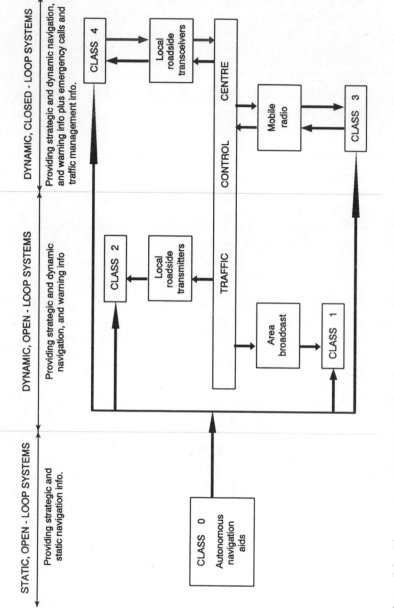

Figure 6.2 Placement and relationship between classes of driver information systems

systems tell the driver something about where he is in relation to where he wants to go, but cannot tell him what routes are available, or guide him over the 'best route'. Examples include: DRIVEGUIDE, NAVICOM, CITYPILOT and ALI-SCOUT — though in the last example only when the vehicle unit is operating in an autonomous mode.

Map display systems show the driver both his present position and his required destination on a continuously updated map display. The data needed to describe the street network for a large town may occupy several Mbytes. Map display systems therefore require an additional and high-capacity memory unit, such as a **compact disk read only memory**, to hold the 'electronic map', the vehicle and the destination, which are usually displayed together on a TV-type display built into the vehicle's dashboard. The location information given by the map display system is therefore presented to the driver in a more usable form — he can see where he is in relation to where he wants to go, and what routes are available to him; but by themselves, these systems are unable to advise him which route is 'best'. Examples include ETAK and CLASS.

Route guidance aids provide the added step of identifying and guiding the driver over the best route. They require additional data which describe not only the locations of junctions and the course of the roads which make up the network, but also the impedances they offer to traffic. A suitable algorithm is then made to operate on these data to deduce the minimum impedance (i.e. 'best') route. Distance is often used as a measure of impedance since it is the easiest to establish. However, drivers would generally prefer minimum time, or cost (i.e. a trade-off between time and distance), and sometimes 'most scenic'.

The CARIN system combines the **route guidance aid** approach with a **map display** system. Drivers using CARIN can see their position in the network and receive advice as they approach each junction on their journey to guide them over the 'best' route. Most route guidance aids, however, like a more recent CARIN version, attempt to alleviate the obvious safety hazards incurred by drivers trying to read maps while they are driving, and at the same time save on costs and data storage requirements by relying on simpler displays which give turn instructions at each major intersection as the journey progresses. Examples include EVA and the TRRL NAVIGATOR, which provide spoken and visual displays to advise the driver the turn direction he should take, and the signposted name or road number which he should follow, at the next junction.

CLASS 1: AREA BROADCASTING SYSTEMS

The preferred technique for Europe at the present is to use facilities of the **radio data** system (RDS) defined by the European Broadcasting Union (EBU, 1984). This system, which has now been adopted by several major broadcasting companies, enables digital messages to be superimposed on normal VHF radio programme broadcasts. The next generation of car radios will be equipped to decode the messages. The channel capacity is around 1200 bits per second, and some 25 per cent of this could be available for traffic messages. The system is seen to have considerable potential and the European Broadcasting Union is co-operating with the European Conference of Ministers of Transport to define a standard.

Two types of messages will be transmitted for the area served by a transmitter:

1. **Network data**. These describe permanent changes to the road network caused, for example, by new road-building. It is anticipated that drivers would renew their 'electronic maps' annually so that these messages need only describe changes which had occurred during the current year. Network data messages would be broadcast once or twice a day.
2. **Hazard warnings**. These describe major traffic incidents such as accidents, roadworks, bad weather conditions, etc. These data can be integrated into the electronic maps carried in a Class 0 device, or displayed directly on a cheaper hazard-warning-only receive unit. Hazard warning messages would be in real time.

Examples of Class 0 systems which are being developed to incorporate data messages transmitted over the **radio data system** are CARIN, EVA and the TRRL NAVIGATOR. The Eureka project CARMINAT, which will integrate the CARIN and ATLAS system, also proposes to use RDS.

CLASS 2: LOCAL ROADSIDE TRANSMITTER SYSTEMS

These systems represent a logical extension of the previous Class 1 **area broadcasting systems** to provide a higher density of transmitters, ultimately perhaps to equipping individual junctions. In this configuration they are more versatile and may be used in one of three ways:

1. as hazard-warning-only transmitters to broadcast information about an incident in the immediate vicinity. HAR (Highway Advisory Radio) is an example. In the United States, two frequencies, 530 KHz and 1610 KHz, are allocated for use by HAR. They respectively fall just below and just above the standard AM broadcast band and can therefore be received on most car radios.
2. **Local roadside transmitters** can be used as simple location beacons as used in public transport vehicle location systems. A wide range of techniques have been tried or proposed, including a coded pattern of buried magnets; short-range radio broadcasts; buried loops; leaky co-axial cable; microwave and infra-red transmitters. Current Japanese work uses radio transmitters to broadcast position codes which can be detected and used for location fixing, and automatic reinitialisation, by a range of **autonomous navigation aids** (Shibata, 1986; Giannopoulos, 1989).

3. **Local roadside transmitters** can be used as complex **beacons** (or, more correctly, as **electronic signposts**) to download hazard warnings, network updates, and route guidance advice for use in a Class 0 **map display** or **route guidance aid** unit. AUTO-SCOUT (an early version of ALI-SCOUT) is an example of such a system. In this, an infra-red communication link is used to transmit network and guidance data into a special vehicle unit which is a hybrid of the **route guidance** and **simple directional aids**. When the driver sets off on his journey his vehicle unit acts in autonomous mode, i.e. as a **simple directional aid**. When he encounters a 'beacon', he receives data which can be interpreted by his vehicle unit to guide him over the 'best' route to his destination, i.e. his vehicle unit acts as a **route guidance aid**. He then follows the advice until either he encounters another beacon and receives more advice; or he leaves the guidance network.

CLASS 3: MOBILE RADIO SYSTEMS

Cellular radio systems exist, or are proposed, in several countries. They involve dividing up the coverage area (i.e. a country or region) into abutting 'cells' whose radii vary from about 16 km in rural areas, down to about 2 km in busy urban areas. Each cell is then served by a fixed **transceiver** unit which has available several duplex (i.e. two-way) radio channels over which communication with mobile units can be set up. The cells are generally grouped in clusters of seven, which between them share the several hundred channels allocated to the system by the Post and Telecommunications Agency. The clusters are then repeated through the coverage area. Channels are therefore reused, but not by immediately neighbouring cells. Interference effects are thus minimised, while the use of the available channels is maximised.

The transceivers for each cell are interlinked and computer-controlled so that a vehicle crosses the boundary from those available to the transceiver serving the next cell without any apparent break in communication. Moreover, the system interconnects with the Public Switched Telephone Network. Cellular systems therefore effectively extend the public telephone network into vehicles, and anything which can be achieved on the public network can, in principle, be achieved on the cellular system.

One cellular system that appears to gain pan-European acceptance now is the GSM (Groupe Spéciale Mobile) based on work of the SOCRATES project of the EC's DRIVE programme.

Vehicle and area selectivity are inherent in the system because communication is set up between a transceiver which serves a known area and with individual vehicles. Data gathering and message updates would be handled in a similar way as described for the Class 1 and 2 systems above.

No international standard exists for cellular radio systems. But the

European Conference of Post and Telecommunications (CEPT) are currently working to define a standard for a digital pan-European system working in the 950 MHz region for the mid-1990s.

CLASS 4: LOCAL ROADSIDE TRANSCEIVER SYSTEMS

Early examples of these systems include ERGS and ALI. They use a two-way communication link between roadside units placed on the approaches to major intersections, and special in-vehicle units. The roadside units are controlled from a central computer and respond with a guidance instruction on receipt of a destination code transmitted from a passing vehicle. The guidance instruction is then displayed for the driver, usually on a visual display which mimics the layout of the junction ahead.

All of these early systems used inductive loop technology to provide the communication at a precise location along the road. Later developments, such as the initial proposals for AUTOGUIDE in the United Kingdom, have also favoured buried loops: mainly because the technology is well proven, and because the loops themselves can act as vehicle detectors.

However, the ALI-SCOUT system from Siemens Germany has favoured infra-red, while similar work in Japan favours a radio or microwave communication link.

The ALI-SCOUT system was designed to be evolutionary in three phases. The first phase uses a Class 0 **simple directional aid** to provide autonomous navigation. The second phase involves the addition of Class 2 **complex beacons**. The third phase involves the addition of an infra-red link for communication from the vehicle back to the roadside beacons so that participating vehicles can communicate their trip times to the infrastructure. These data can then be taken into account by a control centre in order to update the guidance advice given by the roadside units in real time.

Japanese work has favoured Class 0 **map display** devices as the basis for vehicle units, with location updating provided by Class 2 **simple (radio) beacons**. Present developments are looking at microwave as an alternative to radio beacons, and an enhancement to provide two-way communication between the roadside and vehicle units. This two-way microwave link would be used in a similar way to the two-way infra-red link employed in ALI-SCOUT.

Integrated urban and inter-urban traffic management

General functions

Technological innovation in this area has to do with data collection and analysis as well as with the actual traffic management and control techniques that are used.

The key word here is 'integration', meaning multiple use of facilities for data collection and a global integrated architecture of control and surveillance systems for all types of traffic including freight and public transport. For example, the same data required for traffic control can be used for a traffic information system with **variable message signs** (VMS), **radio data** transmission to drivers (RDS/TMC), and so on. In fact there are no clear separations between **traffic information** and **traffic control** since providing the drivers with information is a way of influencing the traffic.

Within the area of **traffic management control** the following functions are of particular importance:

- **Flow control** which includes all control measures that can be taken in order to improve the flow within specific links of a network. They are mainly used when links are of particular relevance for traffic (in terms of road infrastructure and/or traffic flow). A typical example is represented by links in a motorway network.
- **Intersection control** which provides the control of intersections, both in an urban and an inter-urban context. It contains the possibility of co-ordination with adjacent intersections (e.g. **green waves**) and also with the overall network control (e.g. **area traffic control**).
- **Network control** which can be composed of the following elements: Environmental monitoring network surveillance; origin/destination computations; traffic prediction; route optimisation.

Technologies and concepts of an integrated urban traffic management system

The **urban traffic management** context is the one in which probably the largest number of systems has been developed and put into practice in the past. These systems include many types of UTC (**urban traffic control**), AVM (**automatic vehicle monitoring**), **parking management** and (**variable message signs**). All systems have a significant role in controlling and managing traffic in towns. However, in the various European towns, systems and infrastructures are based on different methodological and technological solutions. This section is not therefore intended to give an outline of all urban traffic management systems and their subsystems

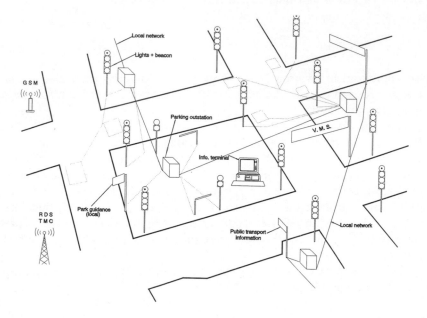

Figure 6.3   Diagrammatic representation of an integrated urban traffic
management system

with their improvements. It is only intended to show how the elements
of a truly integrated urban traffic management system can work
together, within a feasible architecture, in an integrated environment: the
urban IRTE. Most of the information in the following comes from the
work of SECFO within the DRIVE programme (see SECFO, 1990).

Figure 6.3 shows in a diagrammatic form the various elements of an
integrated urban road traffic environment as it should be reasonably
expected to be developed by the turn of the century in most major European cities. The **elements** of this environment are the following.

RDS/TMS STATION(S)
These stations will be used to broadcast traffic information to vehicles
equipped with RDS/TMC receivers. Some points need specific mention
here:

- Due to the amount of information which could be transmitted
  concerning the urban and suburban network, there is a definite need
  for selective and efficient time and space specific methods for presentation to the driver.
- Parking (static and dynamic information) as well as public transport-
  related information should also be included.

● Possible use of the same information by other subsystems (e.g. 'local networks') has to be considered.

GSM NETWORK

The GSM-based idea relies on the existence of a **cellular mobile telephone** communication system with the unit being carried within the vehicle. Conceptually, the driver can obtain direct communication with a remote centre (or other holder of the same or compatible equipment, as well as telephone subscribers) and can be contacted when required. The idea has been used for a number of years now and has been proved to be success-ful, if costly. However, with technological changes from analogue to digital methods, as demand increases sales, and with more market competition, the combined effect is to bring the prices tumbling down. The digital method will allow for efficient data transmission. Thus with the technology in place and the price becoming competitive, it is worth considering the definition and implementation of a set of transport and traffic applications.

Thus in spring 1987, a decision that transmission techniques should be used all over Europe was taken, and up to February 1988 by a subgroup of CEPT named GSM (Groupe Spéciale Mobile) the technical functions of the cellular radio communication system were specified.

In order to ensure a co-ordinated system implementation all over Europe a Memorandum of Understanding has been signed by fifteen Western European countries committing themselves (beside other issues) to

● introduce the pan-European mobile telephone system as from 1991; and
● develop common technical standards.

The countries will allocate the same frequencies for operating the new services so that motorists will be able to travel from one country to another and still use their phones. At present four difficult — and incompatible — versions of cellular telecommunication are in use in Europe and GSM is expected to change all that.

LOCAL NETWORK

There is a need for communications channels which allow the various 'control and information centres' operating at the urban level to exchange information with their respective 'local controllers'. The common solution to this need is normally the establishment of separate networks, including specific centres with their 'local controllers' or 'terminals'. As the integra-tion between different subsystems increases, there will probably be also an integration at the network level forming the so-called local networks. The way in which specific subsystems will be joined together, as well as the particular solution for the communication network(s) will always depend on the particular town, the previous development and the existing infrastructure.

In a theoretical model, all possible solutions are included on the assumption that a 'local network' will connect all the 'centres' to all the 'outstations' (see Figure 6.3). This should also include the capability of connecting the 'outstations' to each other, as required by some UTC applications.

LOCAL CONTROLLERS FOR SPECIFIC TASKS

In Figure 6.3, a number of 'outstations' are shown. They represent general, multi-purpose local controllers, capable of all the action needed at the local level for a small area of the town. This way of partitioning the tasks to be solved by space consideration is definitely not the only way nor is it necessarily the best. Until now specialised controllers, devoted to specific tasks, have been in use. If some integration at that level is needed (with special regard to UTC and IRG), such in-depth redesign will not be achieved. Moreover, many different technological solutions can be accepted at that level. Only the interfaces with the driver need to be part of the standard approach.

UNIFIED SHORT-RANGE COMMUNICATION LINK

In Figure 6.3 a number of 'beacons' integrated within the traffic signal infrastructure are shown. They represent the roadside realisations of the **unified short-range communication** (USC) link described in later sections. Again, neither the physical representation as beacons nor the integration with traffic signals are critical to the system architecture. They are only part of a possible realisation. What is relevant to be noted here is that, in the town, a large set of two-way channels (vehicle–roadside) need to be established, if **interactive route guidance** (IRG) and **user financial infrastructure** (UFFI) are to be realised.

Once this USC network is working, it will be used for providing many functions such as:

- IRG including 'congestion avoidance' and similar high-level measures;
- **electronic road pricing**, as part of UFFI;
- a set of individual functions related to parking management (parking guidance and reservations, debiting, etc.);
- a set of functions intended to improve the UTC schemes. These will extend from data collection tasks to actions directed to the vehicles, such as 'on-line speed recommendation', 'green waves', 'intersection departure advice', etc.
- facilities for public and private management.

GENERAL INFORMATION DISPLAY

In Figure 6.3 some **variable message signs** (VMS) are included, as well

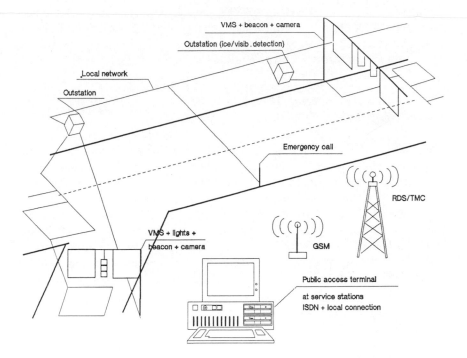

Figure 6.4 Diagrammatic representation of an integrated inter-urban traffic management system

as two kinds of specific displays (one related to public transport located at the bus stop, and the other devoted to the local guidance to a parking space in a specific parking garage). Other types of information could also be provided.

TRAVELLER INFORMATION SYSTEMS
Options considered in the previous section on traveller information must be shown in the urban context. Information must be accessible from public facilities, as well as from home, workplace and, perhaps, vehicles. This information must allow for a multi-modal use of the transport system. This is stressed in Figure 6.3 by putting 'public access terminal' within the parking area. Many other candidates can be envisaged, such as railway stations, motorway exits, service stations, etc.

CONTROL, MANAGEMENT AND INFORMATION CENTRES
Finally, an upper level of the urban IRTE system, now shown in Figure 6.3, is composed of a number of centres, both public and private, dealing with different pieces of the same task, namely, urban traffic management. A wider view of traffic management/control could include (in

addition to the usual UTC and AVM, or the new IRG and TMC) fleet management, pollution monitoring, town police centres, etc. Furthermore, since the town is part of a region, the regional centres as well as the motorway network control could also be integrated.

Technologies and concepts of an integrated inter-urban traffic management system

For motorways and other high-level inter-urban roads a similar integrated environment to the one described for the urban scene can be envisaged. Most technologies to be used are the same as the ones described for the urban context and are not described again here.

The overall picture of a feasible integrated inter-urban management system is shown in Figure 6.4. Its basic elements are again RDS/TMC stations, the GSM network (or a satellite-based communication systems which for inter-urban travel can also be used without problems and is indeed being used), the 'local network' communication systems with its outstations, a USC (unified short-range communication) link, variable message signs, emergency call stations, and some overall control and management centres.

Driver assistance and co-operative driving

The main technologies included in the area of driver assistance and co-operative driving are those linked with **intelligent cruise control** (ICC), **interactive route guidance** (IRG), **co-operative detection and ranging** (CODAR) and the already mentioned **unified short-range communication link** (USC). They all aim at providing the driver with the necessary information for safe and more efficient driving in all environments.

Intelligent cruise control (ICC)

Early forms of cruise control have been available since the late 1960s. They operated on the engine in order to maintain a pre-set speed in order to relieve the driver of speed-keeping and thus provide for more relaxing driving.

Modern ICC is intended, as a development of this original concept, to increase safety and efficiency. For this purpose vehicles will be equipped to 'sense' other elements of traffic within their proximity zones and the cruise control will provide *speed and distance keeping*.

To reach this goal two main problems are to be solved: the first is the detection and range-finding of the front vehicle; and the second the actual friction measurement (e.g. rain, ice). Both are still far from being solved in an economic and universally acceptable way.

A qualitatively new approach has been taken within PROMETHEUS by the introduction of the 'co-operative' concept. The basic assumption is that the process of detection and range-finding will be supported by the vehicles to be detected, which will have on board simple equipment (transporters or reflectors).

This line of research is considered by many as being the most promising in reaching ICC. Different steps can be envisaged in the path to a full ICC implementation. In early versions, ICC is purely an advisory system. Acoustics signals provide suggestions on correct distance and the driver is alerted when driving too close. When distance is not critical, speed is maintained.

In further versions, speed can be automatically controlled in all normal situations, by suitable application of acceleration and smooth deceleration, so as to keep a safe distance.

In the full future version, emergency braking and gear control will be added. It must be noted that the ICC described so far, in all versions, does not relieve the driver from observing the traffic and the road in front of him all the time. He must also steer the vehicle, keeping it in the right place on the road. When ICC detects that operating conditions are not met, perhaps because of dangerous surface conditions, the driver will be alerted in time and will be able to take action without risk.

Intelligent cruise control can be developed far beyond the safe distance and varying friction and speed concept as described above.

Once the co-operative option is taken, and a low-cost transponder is standardised, it will be possible to equip all the road-users, including motor bikes, cyclists and pedestrians, thus increasing the general safety level.

A further development will be to make ICC part of an advanced **collison avoidance** system. This will require a careful integration of on-board equipment with roadside facilities in addition to more advanced sensors. Moreover, it will also require a thorough examination of the legal aspects through Europe.

Finally, ICC could evolve to full application of the co-operative driving concept, i.e. speed, distance and lane-keeping and manoeuvre decisions in normal traffic or 'convoy driving', i.e. automatic control of close convoys, in reserved lanes.

All of these developments are definitely not within the time range of the next ten to twenty years.

Thus the main point for an early implementation of the ICC is the choice of the method and technology for detection and range finding. The 'co-operative' nature of today's feasible solutions leads to the conclusion that an early agreement, on a European scale, between all the interested actors is preliminary to all development.

Interactive route guidance (IRG)

Interactive route guidance is a concept which provides a driver with knowledge of the best route to follow through a dense road network. The final goals are that of relieving the driver from a somewhat difficult task, and that of reducing congestion. To perform this task, data have to be collected, in real time, on the traffic situation, then elaborated and the final information retransmitted in suitable form to individual vehicles. Again, European standards on infrastructure and applications have to be defined.

Route guidance systems have received a lot of attention in present years due to the high potential for traffic enhancement and for user as well as market acceptance. If we restrict ourselves to the analysis of systems allowing for two-way exchange of information, on a quasi-continuous and local basis, some current experiences are worthy of mention:

● the large-scale field trials derived from the infra-red-based ALI-SCOUT system, i.e. the LISB in Berlin and AUTOGUIDE in London. A draft Anglo-German standard is being proposed for infra-red transmission;
● the early CACS system and the ongoing developments of RACS in Japan.

In the DRIVE programme, two research contracts dealt primarily with problems related to this field:

● V1011 where the integration of ALI-SCOUT-type **route guidance** with **traffic control** schemes are studied;
● V1007 (SOCRATES) where the extension of autonomous navigation systems with the help of GSM-derived, two-way local communication is under research.

At the present time the demonstration projects are devised to show how the system will be used for guidance through the urban network, to check the user acceptance and to measure benefits. They are based on *ad hoc* made subsystems; integration within an IRTE will come later. Some feasible extensions are already planned, e.g. the TRANSLISB in Berlin started in early 1990 to show the use of the system for **freight transport**.

Until now, IRG has been tested and demonstrated almost as a stand-alone system. Due to its high potential, the following points will be major items of consideration in the coming years:

1.   IRG, as defined above, could be the most powerful 'traffic data collection' subsystem. These data should be provided to the other members of the traffic management loops. A strong interaction may

be devised with the traffic control class, with which also the control policies have to be integrated.
2. IRG will make use of powerful, bidirectional, vehicle-to-roadside links. Since other subsystems will need similar capabilities, effort should be put into the early definition of an integrated use of unique facilities.
3. The on-board equipment needed (other than for the communication) include dead-reckoning sensors, processors, display, and speech synthesiser, plus in some cases a road map. The same elements are needed for RDS/TMC-based information systems. There is a definite need for integration.
4. Basic data on the road maps should, of course, be the same as for other subsystems (independently from the map being used on-board or at a central site).

Co-operative detection and ranging (CODAR)

As becomes evident from the previous descriptions, a major feature of all co-operative driving systems is the problem of range finding and detection. To solve this problem current technologies focus on systems that rely on the feature that the object to be detected reveals itself upon request.

Such affordable detection and range-finding systems could be based on radar. The object to be localised should reflect the signal to the transmitter in a characteristic and well-defined way. As a characteristic reflection, one can consider simply a much stronger reflection than occurring from other objects hit by the same signal. A shift in frequency or even some kind of modulation could offer more features.

For achieving a significantly strong signal reflection, a surface of specific material is sufficient. Shifting frequency or modulating the incoming signal requires inexpensive electronic elements, called **transponders**. Thus, reflectors or transponders attached at the rear of a vehicle (e.g. integrated into the licence plate) would be sufficient.

After this is achieved, further applications can be studied. There is no technical reason for example why such elements should not be carried by other road-users or be used to mark the border of the road or dangerous elements.

Objects within the safety area could be reliably detected and the distance determined. Depending on the sophistication of the transponder used, it would be possible to discriminate between vehicle, road marks, etc.

Using transponders capable of making the reflected signal with a small amount of information, the interrogating vehicle system could receive additional data from the vehicle in front, for example speed and position. This would open up the possibility of more advanced driving control concepts to come in the more distant future.

Although available technology should be sufficient for realising the CODAR concept, further research is needed to define an optimal system concept in terms of costs and benefits and with regard to its gradual implementation.

Unified short-range communication link (USC)

Vehicle-to-road communication systems tailored to special traffic applications are at present already in operation. Microwave communication is the basis for various **automated identification systems**. Infra-red transmission is used for exchanging traffic information between vehicles and roadside beacons. The implementation of the IRG concept as described previously depends for example substantially on a short-range communication link between vehicles and roadside systems.

The features of the communication process required for these applications are in many respects different from that of CODAR or vehicle-to-vehicle communication. However, the communication requirements for automated identification, automated debiting or the exchange of traffic information with roadside beacons are rather similar. Therefore it is very useful to aim at the definition of one unified short-range communication link for this class of applications.

Some simple analysis within the DRIVE programme (SECFO, 1990) leads to the result that an attractive degree of modularity for the IRTE could be achieved if a unique multi-function device (referred to as '**USC car-interface**') in the vehicle is used to communicate with the different application systems outside and inside the vehicle. Figure 6.5 gives an example.

Policy implications and implementation issues

'Technological innovation' has been seen through this chapter as a term encompassing a wide range of products and applications not only for the mechanical parts of the vehicles but for the whole 'environment' in which they operate. The formulation of this so-called **integrated road transport environment** (IRTE) is based on advanced telematics applications, most of which have been outlined in the previous section. It also requires a whole new organisational framework and governmental commitment so that the systems to be implemented are truly international and universally applicable.

We are already faced with a situation where European, US and Japanese governmental organisations and industrial actors are competing with one another to be the first to supply the newest technological innovations in the market-place.

For Europe a number of policy and implementation actions are

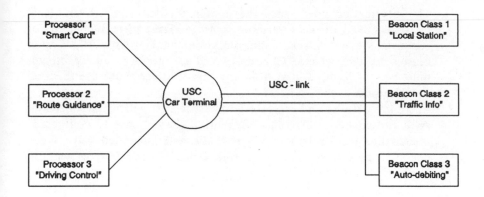

Figure 6.5 Structure of a unified communication system
Source: SECFO, 1990.

necessary in parallel with the ongoing research to solve technological problems. The most important of these actions by area of technological innovation are discussed in the following. These are the result of ongoing research and discussions principally at the EEC (EEC, 1990; SECFO, 1990) but also at other forums, notably the ECMT, OECD, etc.

On the **demand management** issue actions are probably due in the near future, not only on the applied principles but also on standard technologies for communications. There has to be early agreement on this if some concerted action is to take place. For example, the technologies for road pricing, and the principle of it, have been discussed for several years now but agreement on a common attitude is far from being reached. Another point to be made here is that the operation of any demand management action will have to be integrated with the other subsystems of the IRTE.

Concerning the **travel and traffic information** technologies, the most important issue is that of 'data collection', 'forecasting models', and 'co-ordinated database network'. The latter is considered to be the most important. The communications network, together with the equipment needed for user interaction, will develop in the near future along an independent path, derived from existing technology such as Minitel, Teletext, ISDN and similar. Apart from the quoted areas, where joint research and development effort is needed, there is no evident need for high-priority work in regulations and standardisation. End-user facilities for trip planning can be provided without difficulty by a series of different service providers.

For traffic or driver (which is more enlarged) information applications, the problems of data collection etc. mentioned before are the same, but here we have two additional differences:

1. The information must reach the user in the car. Apart from visual messages given through **variable message signs**, there is a need for common, well-established communication channels from information centres to the vehicle. Channels, media, interfaces and protocols must be standardised in such a way that a driver could use them all over Europe.
2. There are definite and relevant costs associated with data collection. As a consequence, different information centres have to collect and interchange traffic data in a systematic and integrated way. When possible, data have to be retrieved from existing sources without newly built infrastructure.

What is needed is, first, a preliminary indication of a possible choice of communication media and standards, and secondly, a reliable and well-established network of databases. On the other hand, it is to be noted that intense research and development is needed for a number of models, methods and systems.

In the field of integrated urban and inter-urban traffic management there is a definite need for work to be carried out on standards now, before any implementation takes place. The following points are most important:

●   Agreement on standards for the USC (unified short-range link). This is, perhaps, the most difficult task. On the other hand, the possibility of using the same channel for IRG, UFFI, as well as for other services and traffic management will open the door to a series of major improvements.
●   Early commencement on an 'intelligent marketing' action, directed at local authorities. This action should concentrate on the possibilities offered by the urban IRTE, together with the need for a series of integrated local prerequisites. This will, in turn, allow the creation of the European database network. Large towns and large-scale demonstrations should be included first in this action.

Similarly for the inter-urban traffic management the idea of USC (unified short-range link), IRG and automatic debiting have, until now, developed separately. If unification is possible, it should be considered now. Since some form of road pricing (toll) will probably be universally in operation in Europe, integrated electronic toll payment should be considered first.

There is also a need here for action directed towards motorway management in order to obtain provision for traffic data collection and exchange. This is, of course, a prerequisite for the creation of a European network of traffic databases or, at least, of regional networks.

Relative to the same broad area of integrated traffic management and concerning the specific technologies mentioned earlier, the following issues can be raised.

The success of the RDS/TMC will depend on the quality of the broadcasting features as well as on the accuracy, completeness and timeliness of the information broadcast.

The collection of actual, up-to-date traffic data is of great importance. The introduction of the RDS/TMC infrastructure should be accompanied by the enhancement of existing (or installation of new) systems for monitoring traffic behaviour and detecting abnormal conditions. Due to the interregional nature of RDS/TMC, a strategy for co-ordination of different information centres is needed.

Furthermore, the common standards for traffic message coding and for the transmission/reception protocol need to be finalised, a common position of the member states on the procedures for acquisition and distribution of traffic and road information needs to be defined and traffic data bases to be agreed upon.

In the field of GSM various RTI applications on the basis of the GSM **cellular radio network** will most probably emerge on their own. Market forces are already strong enough to generate RTI products with attractive cost–benefit ratios. However, additional effort is needed to make the best use of open options in the GSM specification for road traffic applications. Therefore, based on the results of the investigations on dedicated GSM systems, harmonised requirements of particular GSM functions must be defined.

Here it must be stressed that a Europe-wide application of GSM will require substantial investment and commitment by all EC members and other European countries. For example base stations for each cell, with cell radius in towns 3–4 km, will require about 5,000 stations in total all over Europe. A full area coverage of more than 95 per cent will only be achieved for instance in Germany after 1995. Other countries are expected to complete their share after the year 2000.

For **driver assistance and co-operative driving** systems and their major functions of **intelligent cruise control** (ICC), **co-operative detection and ranging** (CODAR) and **interactive route guidance** (IRG), the following can be observed.

The early implementation of the ICC requires the choice of the method and technology for detection and range finding. The 'co-operative' nature of today's feasible solutions leads to the conclusion that an early agreement, on a European scale, between all the interested actors is necessary. Also possible commonalities in on-board equipment (if any) with the other elements of the IRTE, together with the integration of roadside-based functions have to be carefully analysed.

Intelligent cruise control offers such great improvements in safety, efficiency, environment and comfort in driving that already many of the automobile companies or their suppliers are engaged in developing it for commercial use.

Interactive route guidance, on the other hand, can be envisaged in the near future only for dense and congested road networks as found in medium to large-size European towns. This is due to the nature of the system itself, as well as to the time required by the local authorities to decide and to the effort and time needed for starting the system operation. On the other hand, IRG is a 'local' measure, in the sense that its effectiveness in a town will not depend on conditions 'outside' the town itself. Thus a European agreement on the general acceptance of the system is not necessary, although some action could profitably be directed at local authorities to show them the benefits and features of the system.

However, the conditions for integration with the other systems should also apply for IRG within the DRIVE programme. These conditions were stated as follows:

- A standard for vehicle-to-roadside, short-range, two-directional communication has to be agreed upon. The agreement should touch both the physical link and the protocol. The standard should take into account other possible applications of the same channel (automatic debiting, toll collection, etc.).
- Compatible standards for all the route guidance methods have to be decided in order that the same in-vehicle equipment could operate well in different areas. Common digital road maps are included, as well as agreement on integrated functioning of IRG and RDS/TMC-based systems.
- An 'open' architecture has to be considered for 'in-car' systems, jointly from car manufacturers and electronics suppliers, to relieve the installation problems and, where possible, to allow for multi-function use of part of the equipment.

Finally, as regards CODAR, a basic European approach to a suitable implementation path is still to be found. The elements of this approach are to be found in both PROMETHEUS and DRIVE projects and common efforts must be made to ensure that feasible options in this field are picked up and realised. Soon, efforts have to be made to get an official (CEPT) statement on a frequency band, for the possible implementation of CODAR systems (80 GHz are currently under discussion). This will concentrate R&D and provide a reliable basis for the technological investment required. The same is true for the development of a unified short-range communication system. As there are already systems available, a unification will only be possible for the next generation of systems.

All these above points indicate the need for decisions and concerted action that have to be taken now in order to ensure the compatible and integrated application of the technological innovations that have been described in the previous sections.

The stage has been set and rigorous action is already under way both in EC and other governmental and intergovernmental European bodies.

European car manufacturers have also taken up the challenge and their interest in common action is manifested by their readiness to contribute by launching the Eureka programme PROMETHEUS.

It is hoped that through proper co-ordination and the market competition forces already at work, we will soon see in Europe a radically different road passenger transport scene.

References

COST project 30bis (1985) 'Electronic traffic aids on major road — Final Report', EUR 9835, Commission of the European Community, Luxembourg.

EBU (1984) 'Specification of the radio data system RDS for VHF/FM sound broadcasting'. Doc. Tech. 3244, European Broadcasting Union, Brussels.

EEC (1990) 'Operation 1992: integrated road safety information and navigation system (IRIS): rationale for action'. DGXIII/F, p. 3.

Giannopoulos, G.A. (1989) 'The influence of telecommunications on transport operations', *Transport Reviews*, vol. 9, no. 1, pp. 19–44.

JMIF (Japan Motor Industrial Federation) (1989) 'Future of the Japanese automotive industry: a report of the Consulative Committee on the Automobile Industry', published by Kenishiro Ohishi, Japan Trade and Industry Publicity IUC, pp. 35–40.

OECD (1987) 'Dynamic traffic management in urban and suburban road systems', Paris, 1987.

OECD (1988) 'Route guidance and in-car communication systems', Paris, 1987, pp. 30–58.

SECFO (1990) 'Early IRTE scenario'. Deliverable WP2/2 of DRIVE project V1057, System Engineering and Consensus Formation Office—SECFO, pp. 41–50.

Shibata, M. (1986) 'Development of in-car information systems. Annual report of roads', Japan Road Association, Tokyo.

Chapter 7

Clean fuel and engine systems for twenty-first-century road vehicles

Ove Svidén

Introduction

This chapter discusses the needs for new clean engine/fuel concepts that can meet the emission requirements and fuel supply limitations for another century or so. Why do we need a new system? What are the problems? What options do we have? What technical principles can we use? How can a new system be engineered and introduced? When can we expect to see the positive effects of it on traffic?

The aim of this chapter is to describe a system approach towards a sustainable and clean road transport for the twenty-first century. The scope is limited to fuels and energy conversion systems for road vehicles such as cars, trucks and buses. The method is best described in the book *The Systems Approach* (Churchman, 1968). The overall objective for a sustainable mobility is analysed in terms of requirements of fuels and engine systems.

The overall conclusion is that interesting new systems options can emerge if the fuel supply system is related to the energy conversion method applied. If a very clean fuel like hydrogen is selected, a number of new direct conversions to electricity emerge. Furthermore, if petroleum fuel resources beyond the year 2020 are not sufficient to supply the world demand for mobility, a new primary energy source has to be exploited in order to develop and distribute the clean new fuel required. By natural and historical analogy, these changes in primary energy substitutions take many decades to develop.

The chapter is divided into five parts. First comes a problem discussion with roots in automobile history and energy forecasting. Then comes a system analysis of the technical requirements of a clean energy conversion system in dynamic traffic use, followed by a section on a systems approach to an ecologically efficient solution.

Why a new engine/fuel system? The problems

An historical background

Why and how was a new engine/fuel system introduced one hundred years ago? The steam-engine of that time for ships and rail transport were too heavy and not efficient enough for use in light vehicles. An efficiency of about 3 per cent and a long delay between starting the coal fire and getting some steam out of the boiler made these engines less appropriate for vehicle use. A wave of inventive actions took place in the latter part of the nineteenth century to find a new solution. All efforts were geared to the problem of making a quantum jump in efficiency. (It was also to be a trimmed motor cycle engine that was able to lift man in a sustained powered flight for the first time in 1903.)

How was this quantum jump in efficiency achieved? The solution was to move the combustion into the cylinder. The ideas for the combustion engine can be traced back to the mid-nineteenth century inventions and patents. Solutions combining cannon barrels, pistons rods with cogs acting on a cogwheel on the axis on a horseless vehicle could be patented at that time. In the 1870s, Nicolaus Otto found that a mixture of flammable gas and air could be spark-ignited within the cylinder of a piston machine. After testing two, four and six-stroke cycles, he found the four-stroke cycle most efficient. A flammable gas could be obtained from gasification of a waste product called petrol that come out of the petroleum refinery process aimed at producing paraffin for lamps.

With a large dose of oversimplification one can say that the fuel for automobiles was chosen for its technical merits by the inventor, without much regard to its future supply problem. The ideas of explosive internal combustion, IC for short, kicked automobiles into motion and pushed the expansion of automobility. And it must be remembered that the fuel and engine principles were conceived without regard to the environment. These new concerns for the engine design came a century later.

At the end of the last century, Rudolph Diesel was obsessed by the idea of making a combustion engine even more efficient than Otto's. Diesel looked into high compression engines with spontaneous ignition. This could be achieved with coal powder or liquid fuel injected into the four-stroke engine. The high compression needed improved precision between piston and cylinders. The efficiency of a Diesel engine could be made higher than the Otto engine, at the price of more precision technology in the engine and the fuel injection system.

The automobile industry has stayed with the above two engine/fuel principles for about a century now. The conversion efficiency has been gradually improved. Large investments in automated production of the engines have made the price of this 'component' small in relation to the total price of the vehicle. For the car market, with its high sensitivity to first price, the petrol engine has been the rational choice at low energy prices. For commercial vehicles the economy of low price fuel and good lifetime economy has spoken in favour of the diesel engine. The refinery industry has made long-term investments in crackers (forty years' lifetime) to be able to give a higher yield of petrol to supply the growing car population. It must also be noted that not even a decade of the so-called energy crisis with doubled fuel prices could change the fuel and engine principles selected a century ago.

The present problems

In 1962 Rachel Carsons's book *Silent Spring* acted as an alarm bell for the environment issue. Since the end of 1960 the environmental issue has started to be taken seriously. The smog problems in California and Tokyo could then be related to the automobile emissions. A set of new requirements appeared. Nitrogen oxides (NOx), sulphur oxides (SOx), carbon monoxides (CO), unburnt hydrocarbons (HC), other volatile organic compounds (VOC), soot particles and noise from automobile engines had to be limited. A scheme of gradually more stringent require-ments were adopted. And the automobile engineers found solutions. Lean-burn engines, electronic injection, computer-controlled spark igni-tions, exhaust recirculation systems, etc. were developed. A three-way catalytic converter appeared to clean some 80 per cent of the remaining CO, NOx, and HC in the exhausts. The Otto and Diesel principles survived. And after a hundred years of improvements these principle solutions still have a potential for development. And still some of these achievements are not asked for in Europe!

The air quality in California has improved significantly during the last two decades after legislation about the use of catalysts and other measures to clean the road vehicle emissions. For example, exhaust pipe emissions of light-duty vehicles during certification have decreased by approximately 90 per cent from 1970 until the present, but actual in-use data show less emission reduction. The growth of population and traffic now needs further action. An advanced Air Quality Management Plan was approved by the Board of California South Coast Air Quality Management District in March 1989. This AQMP calls for another 80 per cent reduction in emissions of nitrogen oxides and volatile organic compounds within a time span of twenty years (Lloyd et al., 1989) This legislation will require the development of new cleaner fuels for road vehicles in California, but will not necessarily ban the use of the IC engine principle.

The governments in the state of California and Japan must be given a large credit in their bold decisions to raise the environmental requirements for automobile usage. This has spurred R&D in the auto-mobile industry. The congestion problem in Japan has led them to take some further steps, costly but environmentally efficient. Taxis are obliged to use liquid petroleum gas, LPG, as a fuel that is much cleaner than petrol. Electricity generation and heating in the Tokyo area has shifted over to natural gas, carried over the oceans from the Middle East and Indonesia in frozen form, LNG. Ninety per cent of daily commuting to the Tokyo central business district is done using electrically driven above-ground and underground trains. Tokyo transport and traffic are now a good example of what can be done with a systems approach, using available technology and demand management to curb the environmental problems. These costly systems solutions can in my mind only be explained by the fact that cleanliness is a higher virtue in Japan than elsewhere. They are also realists. They clearly state that they do not yet have an ultimate solution to the emission problems. Car population is growing and traffic volumes are increasing. Japan does again come closer to the smog margins.

In parallel to the above, a set of alternative engine systems for road vehicles have been studied during recent decades. A wave of new technical inventions have appeared. The search for a new automobile engine has become and R&D issue. Three solutions with continuous rather than intermittent IC combustion seem promising: the gas turbine, Stirling and modern steam-engines. Aerospace systems technology and materials have been used to make these systems competitive with the 'title defenders', the Ottos and Diesels. A systematic electrical battery research was started in the 1970s. Electrically powered vehicles are a solution to ecological requirements. But energy to weight ratios for batteries is still more than a hundred times lower than for petroleum fuels in a tank. Research institutions inside and outside the automobile industry have engaged in different solution principles, but not one of these electrical systems or alternative combustion engine systems has yet reached the market. A main contributing factor for this was the decade of the so-called oil crisis, when the efficiency problem again came to dominate over the emission problems for a decade. The economy was not suitable for bold long-range investments.

The energy supply problem was brought to the industrial societies as a political shock in 1973 by a short cartel action to limit supply gradually and thus get a higher price for oil. (This initial OPEC action was in itself a counteraction to the oil companies' decision some years earlier to cut national revenues to host countries.) The cartel action from OPEC acted as an alarm bell. The industrial world overreacted to the OPEC signals, and required quick reductions in the use of oil and also costly improvements in automobile engine efficiencies. This did not solve the long-range supply problem, however, and only delayed the point in time when oil had to be substituted for other primary energy forms. The rational argument from OPEC on limiting supply was that there were not sufficiently large reserves of crude oil to motivate the investments called for. During the 1960s the growth in oil consumption was no less than 7 per cent per annum. OPEC took on the unpopular role of telling the world to stop expanding the use of oil. And they have asked in vain for an agreement with consuming countries for the long-term planning of the rational pricing and use of the diminishing oil resources.

A large amount of research, development and systems engineering has been done by the automobile industry in recent decades. Ford spent fifteen years in developing a gas turbine alternative to diesel engines for heavy trucks. It was developed into a marketable product with about the same efficiency as the diesel. It was introduced in the early 1970s. But Ford had to withdraw it, partly from the lack of a nation-wide service network for it. Volkswagen have done research on piston engines combined with an external compositor for a cleaner continuous combustion. Saab-Scania supported for some years a development of a radically new and clean steam system, with a design tailored to the automobile usage requirements. Fiat has studied several hybrid systems. In a dual mode trolley-bus Fiat uses a nickel–cadmium battery for regenerative braking and acceleration via an electrical motor working together with a diesel engine for autonomous driving. Volvo has developed a Cumolo bus, using a hydrostatic motor/generator and pressure accumulator to store energy from braking to the following acceleration. This makes it possible for the diesel engine to work on a steady low emission level without a puff of smoke and noise when accelerating at stations or street corners. Twenty-five of these buses are now in pilot service in different Swedish communities.

Some important long-ranging work with a different system approach to cleaner vehicles has been performed over recent decades by Daimler-Benz. Hydrogen has been identified as the cleanest fuel we know. It can be catalytically burnt in a fuel cell to produce stable levels of electricity at high efficiencies. A hybrid storage system for hydrogen has been developed and proved to be industrially feasible. Eventually these R&D efforts for electricity generation from hydrogen proved that a higher overall efficiency could be obtained if the hydrogen was used directly in an Otto engine, than being converted into electricity (Buchner, 1978)!

A set of storage and handling techniques have been developed for a gradual introduction. As a first step, air-conditioning systems can be designed using exhaust heat and shifts between high and low temperature hybrid storages. Hydrogen can be used as a clean fuel for idling power levels. Together with petrol for power, the combined combustion will be radically more complete and clean if performed in this hydrogen/air mixture. Then the last step is to have hydrogen as the only fuel. Fleets of vehicles have tested these hydrogen concepts for many years in field trials in Berlin (TüV Rheinland, 1984).

But so far the concerned automobile industries have not introduced it on the market. The obvious reason is of course that a hydrogen vehicle is dependent upon an ample supply of hydrogen and service stations for it. However, a new company has been formed including the convinced specialists in the hydrogen supply and automobile industries. This entrepreneurial spirit is a good indicator for the future.

Why has not more happened yet, especially in Europe? The value of a clean environment is not yet sufficiently appreciated! The above paragraphs indicate the problems and also that there exist solutions that have not been exploited yet. We can expect a future wave of innovations, i.e. an engagement by entrepreneurs in industry carrying a selection of the inventions further into products and market introduction. According to Marchetti (1980) we live in a learning society with waves of innovations following some years after the invention waves. A peaking innovation wave is expected in the 1990s.

Future problems

The petroleum supply problem is still valid. World-proved reserves to production ratio is forty-one years according to recent statistics (BP, 1989). Ultimately recoverable reserves can be two to three times larger. But transport fuel demand world-wide is growing by some 3 per cent per annum. Even if we start to prioritise the use of oil for transports, we shall have to abandon petrol and diesel distillates derived from petroleum as a prime energy supply in some thirty to forty years time. What will be the next dominant primary energy resource? Natural gas? Synthetic fuels created from gas and coal with nuclear power as primary energy? Or do we have to abandon hydrocarbon fuels altogether due to the carbon dioxide (CO_2) problem?

Should we jump directly to the use of synthetically produced hydrogen as the cleanest fuel we know? When must we abandon combustion altogether due to limited oxygen resources in the atmosphere? Do we even have to abandon the heat engines due to their thermal pollution of the environment? Do we need a fuel/engine system in vehicles if we can solve the motorway transport problem with magnetic levitation and propulsion?

The above-mentioned petroleum supply problem will force the world to a new fuel solution within thirty to forty years. Can we wait so long for a clean fuel solution for transport? Does the global ecology require a clean solution earlier? What are the requirements for a new fuel engine concept to make it a feasible principle solution that can be developed to meet the most stringent requirements expected during the coming century? And who are the actors that can make it happen?

By the turn of the century, most probably, we must have a scientific base for a crucial system decision on which fuel/engine system to chose. By 2010 we must have validated data from field tests and pilot projects on emissions and fuel supply, efficiencies and cost. On these types of results the long-term investments decisions for fuel supply and engine mass production can be made. By 2020 then the new fuel/engine system may start to make an impact. By then we ought to know if we chose the right systems approach some twenty years earlier. If confirmed, the new fuel supply/energy conversion system for road transport may be the year 2030 be mature enough to fulfil its role as a viable ecological long-term alternative to the Otto and Diesel engines.

Who are 'we' to decide about these things? As individuals, most readers of this chapter will be retired from professional life before this transformation process is over. As individual consumers we might hesitate to make an ecologically sound investment in the engine in our own vehicle, so that the drivers and passengers in the vehicle behind in the congestion get cleaner air to breathe. The value of the environment and a secure long-term energy supply is still rated too low. But things are happening fast now also in Europe.

The environmental problems are now judged to become the biggest issue for the European Community in a few years' time. Then this transportation fuel supply/energy conversion system problem might get its ECU millions in seed money, required for the research of a best systems solution. And as it is a wide-ranging systems solution we are looking for, the search must include the automobile industry, the energy and power industries as well.

For the problems discussed here most individuals and organisations feel too small to handle them. Automobile industries with their ten to twenty years' projects have to yield to the oil industries with their forty to fifty years' investments. A national government has difficulty in imposing requirements on the local automobile industry if some 80 per cent of its products are sold for use in other countries. And the automobile industry acts on wide markets and does not have any well-organised and competent customer to supply the industry with relevant and standardised requirements. The industry has to raise the risk capital itself that is needed to develop solutions to the new requirements. And the fuel supply industry has no competent counterpart for its extremely long-term investments.

The transnational automobile and energy industries need a utility as a counterpart for the rational long-range planning to solve the problems discussed above! The lack of this transnational utility organisation will make national or industrial efforts in this domain remain as 'interesting inventions'. But to make the secure energy supply/ecological conversion system into a fruitful innovation that reaches the market and solves our ecological problems, this new pan-European utility organisation will be essential.

Telecommunication services are traditionally sold as services from a utility. This can also become the best way to sell the **road transport informatics** services in the near future. In a similar fashion, clean road transport can be regarded as a service to the users and the neighbours of the roads. Thus the early organisation of an RTI utility can be the natural starting-point for an organisation that later is in a position to sell clean road transport as a service. This can mean that the future clean fuel engine system of the automobile is included as a sealed power-pack. And its environmental performance is guaranteed by the organisation that charges for its use. The cost of clean vehicle power then is separated from the ownership of the vehicle.

System analysis and technical requirements

The world total primary energy supply

Historically the primary energy supply has shifted from wood to coal to oil in a regular pattern. Fuel wood was the dominant primary energy for the world by the year 1800, when coal started to become an efficient substitute. In the beginning of the twentieth century coal became the dominant primary energy form in the world economy. By then the oil industry had started to grow faster than the coal industry. Now for the last two decades crude oil has been the dominant resource in the world primary energy mix.

The slow but determined substitution process for different primary energy forms during the last few centuries can be seen from Figure 7.1.

The idea that primary energies compete for the energy market like the varieties of a species for the resource of a niche, give a conceptual framework and a mathematics to deal with the evolution of the energy markets. The excellent fitting of the equations (smooth lines) with the statistical data for more than one hundred years give much weight to their use for forecasting. The fast rise of nuclear by respect to a business as usual market penetration equation is probably due to the fact that nuclear sells wholesale and has not the necessity of laying its own distribution grid. (Marchetti, 1988)

By the year 1988 the **world total primary energy** (TPE) consumption in tonnes oil equivalents, TOE, percentage share of total, and growth trend 1987–8, was as presented in Table 7.1.

As can be seen from Table 7.1, crude oil is the dominant primary energy resource in the world energy mix for 1987. Some 50 per cent of the crude oil is feedstock for transport fuels such as petrol, jet kerosene, diesel fuels and heavy bunker oils for marine use. And it is assumed that oil will maintain its dominance for another twenty to thirty years and that an increasingly large part of it will be reserved for the transport sector in the coming decades. So, when we talk of primary energy reserves for transportation in the next two to three decades, we will have to look to the crude oil supply for an answer.

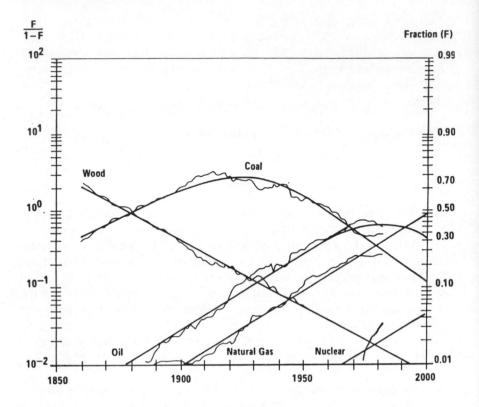

Figure 7.1   World primary energy substitution (GWy/y)

Source: Nakicenovic, 1985

Note: The world total primary energy substitution. The diagram shows how the *relative share* of different primary energy forms have developed historically. The fraction (F) of an energy form is presented against the others and thus the sum of all fractions add up to one. If presenting the ratio $F/(1-F)$ in a logarithmic scale, as above the S-formed penetration curves are represented as straight sloping lines. On top of this change in the mix of primary energy forms, a world total primary energy (TPE) growth of 2.3 per cent average per annum has been observed for the last 150 years.

Table 7.1   World total primary energy consumption

	TOE	Share	Growth
Crude oil	3,039	38%	3.1%
Coal	2,428	30%	3.7%
Natural gas	1,631	20%	3.9%
Hydroelectric	537	7%	0.5%
Nuclear	439	5%	8.0%
World TPE	8,074	100%	3.7%

Source: BP.

Fuels for road transport

By clean fuel we mean a chemical substance that is clean in its large-scale production from a primary energy, clean and safe in storage, easy to handle and clean in its combustion when used in engines. From crude oil and the petroleum refinery processes can be achieved a range of hydrocarbon fuels with different combustion characteristics and cleanliness. Let us look further into this range of possibilities in our search for a clean synthetic fuel.

Hydrogen itself is a highly reactive matter with a high energy-to-weight ratio. Carbon is a matter which can take many stable forms as well as it has a respectable energy-to-weight content. Between pure hydrogen and pure carbon exist a range of stable hydrocarbon molecules and fuel products as shown in Table 7.2.

Table 7.2 Hydrocarbon fuels

H_2	Hydrogen gas, the cleanest fuel we know
CH_4	Methane, dominant component of natural gas
C_2H_6	Ethane, gas component from biomaterial decay
C_3H_8	Propane, the light gas component of liquid petroleum gas
C_4H_{10}	Butane, the heavy gas component in LPG
C_5H_{12}	Pentane, the lightest fluid component in petrol
C_8H_{18}	Octane, the heaviest component in petrol
C_nH_{2n+2}	Jet kerosene
.	Diesel fuels
.	Light fuel oils
.	Heavy fuel oils
.	Bunker oils
.	Asphalt
.	Coke
C	Carbon, the prime component of coal

The heavier commercially available hydrocarbon fuels at the lower end of the list in Table 7.2 are not single molecule fuels. They are blends of hydrocarbons including a multitude of other molecules like alcohol, additives, trace elements and environmentally unwanted components like sulphur, vanadium and sand. The heavier the fuel, the more unwanted components it can contain. In the petroleum refinery process the unwanted components can be 'filtered' away by gasification and condensation of crude oils at different temperatures. E.g. sulphur and nitrogen components can be contained in fuel oils and diesel fuels but not in petrol. And petrol can act as a solvent and thus contain components that cannot be part of LPG or methane fuels.

From the hydrocarbon fuels mentioned above a range of derivatives like aromatic hydrocarbons like benzene and naphthalene can be achieved. By chemical engineering hydrocarbons can be transformed to

Engine Power Output

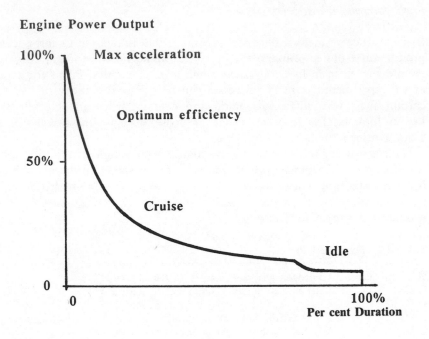

Figure 7.2 Principal diagram for a vehicle engine's power and duration

alcohols and vice versa. Methanol, CH_3OH, and ethanol, C_2H_5OH, are the alcohols related to the methane and ethane hydrocarbons. These alcohols can be used as fuels in themselves or blended with petrol, giving the blend a higher octane number.

When any hydrocarbon blend is ignited a large number of chemical transformations start to happen within microseconds. This chemical 'firework' is only partially understood (Gardiner, 1982). When the combustion is done intermittently as in IC engines, even more questions arise. But some principles remain. The simpler and lighter the fuel, the fewer the emission problems. The more continuous the combustion, the better we can control its side-effects. The lower the flame temperature of the combustion, the smaller the amounts of NOX that will be formed (at the price of lower efficiency if a heat engine is used). The lighter the hydrocarbon fuel, the less carbon dioxide is released into the atmosphere. But at the same time we have to remember that the lighter the fuels are, the more gaseous and bulky they are to store and handle.

The dynamics of energy conversion

The requirements of an automobile engine are unique and extreme (see Figure 7.2) Full power is used for a fraction of the time when the engine is used. The design point (about 70 per cent of peak power), where the engine has its best performance, is not much used in traffic. Cruise power below 20 per cent of maximum is used for most of the time in traffic. Of the total energy spent in an automobile engine 90–95 per cent is used for power levels below 20 per cent of maximum. Some 10–15 per cent of the running time the engine is idle, only supplying the auxiliary equipment with power. Less than 10 per cent of the energy content in the fuel has been spent in the useful movement of the vehicle through the city's stop-and-go traffic. In an annual perspective the car and the engine are used only some 5 per cent of the lifetime of the automobile. In between operations the car is parked with zero energy conversion.

One of the major problems with the energy use in road vehicles in traffic is the quick and large changes in power. The load change from idle to maximum acceleration to cruise and back to idle has to be managed within a fraction of a second to cope with the power needs in city traffic. And as can be seen from Figure 7.2 it is not the efficiency of the engine itself that has to be improved. The systems problem is to use a power conversion principle that is well adapted to the traffic rhythm!

It is a remarkable technical achievement to produce these bursts of power between cruise and idling from within one single heat engine. The Otto and Diesel engines do it by organising a number of explosions in a row and letting the expanding gases push the pistons. The power is then conditioned by the use of flywheel, clutch, gear shifts and transmission to give an acceptable smooth torque at the wheels. And it has been an industrial achievement to develop this complex energy conversion and power-conditioning machinery into a relatively cheap mass produced component for vehicles.

Alternative engine systems

The IC engine ideas were conceived a century before the environmental issue. Now we have approached a limit beyond which we cannot accept a further growth in intermittent combustion due to its noise and air pollution. If we accept chemical fuels as the most efficient energy storage, then the combustion of it must at least be continuous, or even better, catalytic. A number of alternative engine systems have been studied in this century, without reaching the market yet. However, each of them offers some new possibilities that can be useful for a future engine systems synthesis.

An engine concept developed during the twentieth century is the **gas turbine**. It has abandoned the IC principle for a continuous combustion in a combustion chamber under pressure with warm walls designed around a stable flame and flow. Gas turbines have in principle much lower emissions than IC engines due to this. However the striving for high conversion efficiencies leads to the use of high flame temperatures and thus to NOX generation. Otherwise the continuous combustion can give a very smooth torque output from the turbine. The expanding gases are directly transformed into a rotary motion and can act as an aerodynamic torque converter. The gas turbine principle has its efficiency merits for large units above 200 kW. Smaller gas turbines do have proportionally large losses due to air friction in small ducts. And the turbine speeds go up due to small dimensions. The torque characteristics and the high RPM require an expensive gearbox for the conditioning of the output to traffic conditions. An alternative to this is to use the KTT principle (Kronogård), using a multi-axis gas turbine, and use the 'aerodynamic' torque converter, in a similar fashion as the 'hydrodynamic' torque converter acts together with an automatic gear box.

The **Wankel** engine, or rotary engine as it was called, can be seen as a hybrid between a two-stroke IC and the gas turbine. By a ingenious triangular piston/valve mechanism the internal explosions are transformed directly into a rotary movement. A balanced run and a smooth torque is achieved. The 'humming' sound and the low vibrations of a Wankel were the proof to customers. But the price for it was high: low efficiency and high emissions. The two-stroke principle and the wedge-formed combustion chamber with difficult tightening problems, between the triangular piston and the curved walls, never allowed a full and clean combustion. When it was launched as an automobile engine alternative in the 1960s, it was in a decade of growth in economy and comfort. The Wankel engine was mortally hit both by the environmental and energy-saving issues a decade later. However, if used as rotor machine for compressing air and acting as a turbine for the exhaust gases from a external combustion chamber, the Wankel principle may still be interesting.

The **Stirling** engine was conceived in the beginning of the last century. A renewed interest in the principle came with the search for a silent and clean alternative to the diesel in the last couple of decades. The Stirling engine can be identical to a diesel machine from the pistons downwards. But the combustion has been moved out of the cylinder to a separate combustion chamber. Via a heat exchanger an enclosed gas is heated before it enters into the cylinder under high pressure, expands and thus converts its energy into mechanical torque. The Stirling principle allows for a clean continuous combustion, gives less vibrations than an IC engine, but has a torque characteristic that needs further conditioning in a gearbox.

In the search for an alternative engine for transport, the steam-engine or Rankine principle has been taken up again by a number of industries and entrepreneurs. With the use of modern materials and heat transfer principles from the aerospace field, it has been shown that the steam-engine is a feasible alternative to the above-mentioned engines. The combustion is external, continuous and can be performed in ambient pressures. The steam process gives the engine a torque characteristic that fits the characteristics of today's traffic. Without a gear shift a smooth quick acceleration can be achieved from zero to maximum speed. Another feature is that the steam process needs a lower top temperature than any of the processes described above. Thus the combustion of a fuel can be done with a minimum of NOX formation.

Beside mechanical torque to the wheels a modern road vehicle uses considerable and growing amounts of other energy forms for its auxiliary equipment. Electricity is needed for the starting-motor, headlights, light signals, cooling fans, ignition, instrumentation, windscreen wipers and washing, for heating, radio/stereo entertainment, etc. Electricity is a growing consumer of energy within vehicles. And hydraulic power for servo brakes and servo steering is entering into cars. Trucks have additional hydraulic servos, motors and jacks for cranes, winches and dumpers. Buses use pneumatic power to operate their doors. The driver and passengers require comfortable heating or air-conditioning, depending on ambient temperatures.

All the above extra applications need their specific energy form at specific times in the driving cycle. In principle the conversion generators and pumps all have been 'hung' after the primary IC engine, first as options, then as special and now mostly as standard equipment to the engine complex. Electrical systems in road vehicles are designed around a generator, rectifier, a battery and cables for the distribution of electrical power to different systems. The starter engine is the largest consumer of electrical power, say in the order of 1kW momentarily for a 100 kW engine. The electrical starter system rides passively when the IC engine is operating.

When we speak of electrical vehicles we usually mean electrical energy stored in batteries and used by electrical motors in the vehicles. The batteries are charged at night using electricity from a coal-fuelled or nuclear power plant. This represents a movement of the emission problem from many small conversions to centralised power management, and is not necessarily an elimination of the environmental problem. In an automobile-size electrical vehicle, the motor and batteries are of the 20–50 kW size. The weight and price of batteries limits the usefulness of this for road vehicles in general. But it is an established solution for special vehicles like fork-lift trucks that have to operate in workshops, food storages and the like, where emission requirements are strict. There have been large R&D efforts to design a high-capacity battery for vehicle use, but the results have so far not met the requirement for an all-purpose replacement of fuel-generated power in vehicles.

Some very significant progress, however, has been reported from the development of fuel cells (Kordesch and Oliveira, 1988). During the last decade some new low price catalysts have been developed using carbon electrodes rather than porous nickel or silver ones. With a price tag for the catalysts that has been lowered by a factor of 100 during the last ten years, the fuel cell becomes interesting indeed for vehicle use. Its principle of catalytic combustion of hydrogen at room temperatures can remove most emission problems from vehicles. Some fuel cells can even accept fuels such as natural gas and methanol, but then of course with the accompanying carbon-related emissions.

The fuel cell generates electricity from the fuel by a cold catalytic process at the electrodes. The process gives its highest performance at low temperatures (and the process is not a carnot process, whose efficiency depends upon the difference in temperature between a hot combustion and a cooling medium). A fuel cell can achieve a 60 per cent efficiency at constant loads. The efficiency is reduced if the load is varied. Thus the fuel cell can best be used in automobiles if combined with another system for peak loads.

A hydrostatic system consists of pump, pressure accumulator, distribution hoses, servo motors, hydraulic valves and control units. By using high pressures, the hydraulic units can be small and powerful. The hydraulic accumulator is a heavy alternative for storing long-range energy, but it can both be charged and give back its stored energy with high efficiency. The hydrostatic system thus can be best used to convert different mechanical energies into each other. The Cumolo bus system has proved that some 60 per cent of the kinetic energy from a moving vehicle can be stored and withdrawn for a following acceleration. In normal road vehicles this energy is lost completely. The hydraulic motor/generator in the system is quite compact as the pressures used can be some twenty times higher than in the IC engine. The hydraulic tanks and the compressed nitrogen in the accumulator take up more space.

In Nordic countries an extra parking heater, with pumps, fans and a combustion chamber is often used in order to get the car warm before starting its IC engine. In arctic temperatures an IC engine does not even start without preheating. In all climates the IC engine does not work well before reaching operational temperatures. The combustion is incomplete when the cylinder walls are cold. The emissions are much greater because of this and also the fact that a catalytic converter does not catalyse before it is warm. TRRL tests have proved that the energy consumption per km can be two to four times higher at the start than with a warm engine. For short urban trips a cold engine never reaches its equilibrium operating temperature. In the UK with its moderate climate, it has been estimated that some 30 per cent(!) of the country's petrol could be saved if IC engines were properly preheated before starting (Armstrong, 1983; Pierce and Waters, 1980).

Taking the perspective of heating- the vehicle and preheating the engine, the above-mentioned engine alternatives all have their particular problems and possibilities. The gas turbine needs no preheating, and when idle it can operate as a vehicle heater. The Stirling engine needs no preheating. It is in principle a refrigeration process working backwards, and as all heat machines has a greater efficiency in cold weather when the difference is greater between cold and hot extremes. The steam process may need some seconds of preheating to get started, and half a minute before being able to work at full power (i.e. similar to most IC engines today). A lead battery needs preheating in cold climates. And an electrical vehicle might need an extra heater(!) to keep it warm, as the high efficiency conversion in the electrical motor does not give sufficient waste heat. The fuel cell operates best at low temperatures and with stable loads. Fuel residues from the process may be used for heating in an afterburner. Hydraulic accumulators lose some of their pressure and hydraulic motors work a bit slower for the first minute in low temperatures.

A systems approach towards a twenty-first-century system

By a concept systems approach is meant a feedback process of systems analysis and engineering synthesis. It is a holistic approach to problem-solving, for issues of a long-range character and with a global impact. A solution to an ecological problem cannot be found in a single sub-system or in a specialised scientific discipline. It has to be analysed in the widest possible systems context and with many methods. A systems approach towards a clean fuel/engine system solution then means that we have to relate it to the quick tempo of the combustion, the traffic process, the long-range energy supply and the shifts of values in society. It means that we have to design the system to meet not only today's requirements from traffic and the environment, but a whole century ahead of new requirements! Presently we can only have a philosophical idea about the direction and strength of the value changes leading up to these new requirements.

A cybernetic systems approach to planning means that the long-term criteria set the direction for the components with the shorter-time dynamics in the subsystems. Each system level is stabilised by its feed-back loops and a long-term input signal from the outer loops. In a stable systems hierarchy the inner loops have a higher tempo than the next outside loop and so on. And the long-term requirements from the outer loops are filtered in steps through each systems level in the hierarchy down to the very fast dynamics of the innermost loops. And the charac-teristics of these in turn constitute the achievement of the systems hierarchy.

In the preceding chapters of this paper, the difference in tempo between the technical, traffic, industrial and political systems levels have been described. Now for the purposes of our systems approach we organise these temporal phenomena into a stable systems hierarchy,

Table 7.3   Time characteristics for different systems

1. Value systems (100–1,000 year cycles)
2. Political doctrines (liberalism, socialism, environmentalism?)
3. Primary energy supply systems (wood, coal, oil, gas, nuclear)
4. Energy industry (40-year investment cycles)
5. Fuel production and distribution
6. Automobile industry (10-year product cycles)
7. IT industry (annual product cycles)
8. Road traffic (annual, weekly, daily cycles)
9. Urban traffic (stop-and-go cycles)
10. Engine power (shifts in levels within a second)
11. Combustion chemistry (milliseconds)
12. Electronic combustion control (microseconds)

starting with the longest-term systems at the top of the list and ending it with the technical inner loops (Table 7.3).

In order to take a systems approach towards a clean fuel/engine system for twenty-first-century transport, we have to go through almost the entire list above and look for options at the different systems levels and relate them both to meaningful outer loop criteria and to the impacts on the inner loops and end results. The following sections seek to structure this complex systems problem.

The twenty-first-century primary energy supply

The **total primary energy** (TPE) demand and supply must be treated on a global scale. Historically world TPE has grown by an average of 2.3 per cent per annum during the last 150 years (see Figure 7.3). During the last fifteen 'crisis years' TPE growth was only 2.1 per cent p.a.. Assuming this 'limited' TPE growth for another 110 years, the world TPE demand will be ten times larger by the end of the next century than it is today. By then the global population is forecast to have reached 10–12 billion (UN). But even if the population has stabilised at that level in the year 2100, the growth in standard of living and mobility is expected to continue. Thus the energy consumption and the share of energy for transportation may still be growing at the end of the next century.

The world demand for transport fuels represents today some 20 per cent of TPE. This proportion could double to 40 per cent by the end of the next century. This means that by the year 2100, some four times more energy than that is now used totally by the world society could be used in vehicle, ship, train and jet engines. The energy conversion in those engines then has to be twenty times cleaner than today, if accepting today's burden on the environment as a limit!

If assuming ultimately economically recoverable crude oil resources to be three times larger than today's known reserves, we must abandon oil

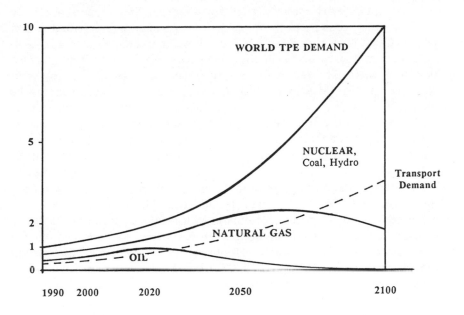

Figure 7.3 World total primary energy demand and supply, relative to 1990

as the primary energy for transport about the year 2020. If assuming ultimately recoverable natural gas resources to be ten times larger than oil and some fifteen times larger than today's known reserves of natural gas, we shall also have to abandon natural gas as the primary energy for transport before the end of the same century. These date years are indicated in Figure 7.3 where the supply and demand curves cross each other.

Regarding natural gas, a European perspective is also needed. The confirmed reserves of natural gas available for Europe from within the continent and from sources in western Siberia, the Middle East and North Africa are some eighty times larger than the present annual consumption. These are the reserves of gas found as the result of oil exploration. The reserves yet to be found when systematically searching for natural gas can be much larger. The ultimate resources of natural gas for Europe are probably at least one magnitude larger than today's confirmed reserves. Also worth mentioning are the thick seams of coal found in the North Sea when drilling for oil. These coal resources are potential reserves for the production of substitute natural gas SNG, using *in situ* mining methods.

But according to Figure 7.3 the petroleum supply of oil and gas will not be sufficient to meet demand for the latter part of the twenty-first century. The primary energy needed for the expanding wedge is as we see it today some second and third generations of nuclear power and fusion power. Using nuclear fuel recycling and breeder techniques, there is sufficient nuclear fuel available in the world to meet demand. It is assumed that both electricity and hydrogen fuels can be produced at low unit costs. It can also be assumed that the complete nuclear processes can be managed in a clean and safe way. The non-combustion principle of fission and fusion offers the possibility of leaving the atmosphere out of the process. In the long term this environmental merit of nuclear energy, i.e. both fission and fusion, may prove to be the most important asset.

Natural gas and water can solidify naturally as methane hydrates at certain temperatures and pressures. Extensive hydrate deposits have been discovered beneath the Siberian permafrost. There is also geological evidence for vast resources of methane hydrates in the oceans outside the continental shelves. These untapped resources may be large enough for centuries of world gas supply (Hodgson, 1978). However, the carbon dioxide problem may hinder us from using it. It can be the environment rather than the supply that sets the limit.

The clean fuels for transport

If the long-term energy supply problems can be solved in the way discussed in the previous section, then a number of new fuels have to be defined, produced on a large scale and distributed on a continental scale. It is not possible to define these new fuels yet. It has to be done in close connection with the primary energy supply side and the vehicle engine research and development. But in respect to their environmental properties, the following list of basic alternatives will probably have to be considered in a systems approach:

● hydrogen
● methane
● methanol
● LPG, liquid petroleum gas
● synthetic petrol
● synthetic jet kerosene

Furthermore, there is a range of non-fuel alternatives that have to be investigated in a systems approach. If we include alternatives with electricity transmission to vehicles, we also have to look into the following possibilities:

● Electricity by trolley on motorways (Ross and Hamilton, 1980).
● Electricity by open-ended transformers in the road (Ross, 1992).

The future traffic dynamics

In the section on the dynamics of energy conversion the present city traffic dynamics problem was described. It can be assumed that in essence this will remain also for the future. However, a number of **road transport informatics** (RTI) functions are now in development within the PROMETHEUS and DRIVE programmes, which can smooth the traffic flow in the future. With co-operative driving by vehicles with intelligent cruise controls, and by interactive systems between traffic signals and vehicles, the number of stop-and-go operations can be decreased. This means that the number of peak power accelerations will be reduced and the idling time for the engine system will be shorter.

Ideally a constantly flowing traffic can be envisioned as an end result. Then the requirement for peak power is relevant only for the very start of a journey. But it is doubtful that drivers will ever accept that their automobiles have acceleration characteristics similar to a heavily loaded truck and trailer equipage. It might be more important then to equip heavy vehicles with the appropriate acceleration power, so as not to be a disturbance in the traffic flow! Today, trucks have the capability to decelerate as fast as smaller vehicles, but seldom have the acceleration power to be a 'good neighbour' in the traffic flow.

The energy conversion system

To meet the requirements from both the ecological system and the traffic process levels, a future energy conversion system must probably be designed around a set of new principles in a clever combination. Based upon the reasoning in the previous section and the above systems requirements, we will in this section give some impulses to a new class of energy conversion systems.

If the long-term objective is to design a radically much cleaner fuel/engine system, we have to make its combustion as clean as we can. A number of alternatives can be mentioned in descending order of cleanliness:

- cold fusion (not technically feasible yet);
- cold catalytic combustion (for electricity generation in fuel cells);
- continuous combustion (for thermo-ionic electricity generation);
- continuous external combustion (for Stirling or steam-engine);
- continuous internal pressurised combustion (for gas turbines and Wankel rotor machines).

The last three of the above alternatives have a continuous combustion. This opens up the possibility for a design of the engine 'around the flame' and its requirements. To 'care for the flame' can be a virtue for these new engines, meaning in essence that the flame and its dynamics can be disconnected from the traffic dynamics. If only a smooth change in the flame is allowed due to environmental reasons, then peak loads must be arranged outside the heat engine system.

Another possibility from a continuous combustion is the electricity generation 'in front' of the heat engine system. The thermo-ion principle for instance is similar to the old radio tubes. If one of the electrodes is heated and the other is cooled, the ironic atmosphere between them produces an electrical current. This is a Carnot process and the thermo-ion principle works well in the temperature range 1,500–1,200 degrees Centigrade. If a substantial amount of electricity is generated this way, if can via an electrical motor give extra torque when needed in addition to the torque from a heat engine that uses the rest of the heat from the flame after the thermo-ionic process. In this way the role for the heat engine is somewhat reduced. It can then act as a bottoming cycle.

The cleanest available technology for base load electricity generation is the fuel cell. Here the combustion is catalytic and cold. The dynamic characteristics of the fuel cell makes it serve best for base load electricity generation. The unburnt fuel residues may perhaps be used in an after-burner and a heat engine related to it. This can boost the overall energy conversion efficiency for stable loads.

To solve the traffic conditioning problem, with short bursts of peak power, the combustion process must probably be left out altogether. A new technology for effective storage of limited amounts of electricity is the 'super-capacitor'. In a hybrid system this technique might be useful for regenerative braking and fast accelerations afterwards. The high torque requirements, especially for heavy vehicles, might otherwise be solved by a compact high-pressure hydraulic motor/generator and accumulator system. This system also has the potential to accumulate energy from regenerative braking of the vehicle.

An intermediate possibility of storing energy for peak loads is the accumulation of steam for a steam-engine or boost of a IC piston engine. In comparison with the hydraulic pressure accumulation, no regenerative braking is possible with the steam principle. However, it definitely speaks for the steam heat engine use in automobiles.

If we, in a systems approach, put all the above-mentioned systems on top of each other, in a monstrous hybrid machinery, with the best possible use of their different characteristics, the accumulated result may best fit the power demand curve in the principal order presented in Figure 7.4.

The monstrous 'systems rig' in Figure 7.4 will most certainly not be realised as a practical engine solution. But it can serve us as a starting-point for systems analysis. The systems engineering question will later be to create a functioning system including as few as possible of the above components. But this cannot be done before we know more about the possibilities and limitations of the above-mentioned components. We do

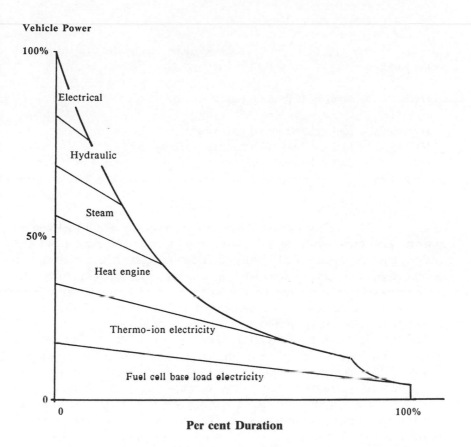

Figure 7.4 Hybrid principle, power and duration diagram

not even know if these components are the best ones or the only ones to be considered. The systems rig is created to test an idea: design electrical motors, accumulators, combustion and heat engines into an integrated and controlled system, where all components help achieve the crucial peak power, while at the same time the combustion is kept ecologically clean, smooth and silent.

In comparison with the above systems rig it is worth mentioning that the energy conversion system in present-day road vehicles includes a wide range of subsystems around the basic IC engine. A number of motors, generators, hydraulic pumps and servos ride piggy-back on the prime mover. In a hybrid systems solution these elements should be designed and controlled so as to act in synergy for the crucial peak power generation.

Five tentative clean fuel/engine systems

In this section six different hybrid systems solutions are suggested conceptually:

Hybrid 1.   Hydrogen-fuelled piston engine;
Hybrid 2.   thermo-ion electricity/motor system;
Hybrid 3.   fuel cell/steam-engine system;
Hybrid 4.   fuel cell/gas turbine/hydraulic system;
Hybrid 5.   fuel cell/hydraulic system;
Hybrid 6.   battery/supercapacitor/roadway-powered electrical vehicle

The Hybrid 1 is the obvious first solution for a clean fuel/engine system. The fuel is hydrogen and the engine is a derivative from the century-long development of Otto and Diesel engines. It is designed and optimised for the compression, ignition and fuel injection and catalyst to make the most efficient use of the hydrogen fuel characteristics. This solution also recognises the economy and vested interests in the use of already established mass production of piston engines.

The Hybrid 2 system aims at the market for 1.30 kW engines for mopeds and small vehicles with limited range. It is designed to use petrol, LPG, alcohols and/or natural gas as fuel for its therm-ion conversion of combustion heat directly into electricity. With a large battery for boost and thyristor technology for control of accelerations and limited regenerative braking, the Hybrid 2 solution can be regarded as an on-board electricity generation addition to an electrical vehicle. The fuel combustion takes place in a continuous combustion chamber at moderate temperatures. The system is designed to make the best use of the remaining petroleum reserves.

The Hybrid 3 is a more efficient and clean hybrid solution for the mass automobile market of engines in the range 30–100 kW for light vehicles. It is designed for the use of pure hydrogen fuels for its fuel cell conversion to electricity for base loads. It has a steam-engine system as 'bottoming cycle' and can accumulate steam for peak accelerations. The hydrogen is stored in hydrides and catalytically combusted in the fuel cell. Unburnt residues of hydrogen fuel are burnt in a compositor for the steam generation and for comfort heating. The steam booster gives the vehicle a unsurpassed smooth and quick acceleration when required, without gear shifts.

The Hybrid 4 system is the very efficient hybrid engine system recommended for heavy vehicles. The high-capacity fuel cell provides base power. A gas turbine system is used as bottom cycle. It also acts as a turbine booster of hydrogen and air for the pressurised fuel cell to make it work as efficiently as possible. In addition to this the accumulation of hydraulic pressure from regenerative braking can give the important boost for acceleration. The end result is that heavy vehicles using this hybrid system can now accelerate as quickly as the smaller passenger cars.

The Hybrid 5 uses a fuel cell with accumulator and a hydraulic system but no intermediate heat engine. The system has a high proportion of electricity and hydraulic system for servo power and for boost accelerations. The thyristor control of electricity to each wheel motor can give a limited power of four wheel drive, adding anti-spin and anti-skid quality to the ride. The high and low temperature hybrid storages provide air-conditioning. Comfort heating is mostly electrical, in seats, floor and doors.

The Hybrid 6 is an electrical vehicle hybrid. It uses a combination of electrical techniques at their best: the battery is used for base load during short trips. The supercapacitor is used for regenerative braking and boost for accelerations. The roadway power is included for range. Electricity is transferred by induction to vehicles when driving on special highway lanes. The on-board conditioning system distributes electricity to the permanent magnet motors in each wheel. Anti-skid and anti-spin are part of the features of this all-electric hybrid system.

How the ecologically efficient hybrid systems will be eventually designed is far too early to forecast. The above speculations and conceptual systems engineering are only intended to indicate some possibilities. It is the role of a major systems approach and R&D programme to find the appropriate hybrid fuel/engine systems for the next century.

Conclusions

It is concluded that it is not possible to solve the global emission problem with a technical fix in the vehicle engine system or an additive to the fuel. The environmental cause and effect chains go back to the long-range supply of primary energy. This relationship gives the vehicle emission issue its time dimension.

Some three to four decades ahead the world will have to abandon crude oil as a primary energy for transportation fuels. This event can be dramatic if a substitute supply is not planned well in advance. It also provides mankind with an opportunity to redesign the complete energy supply and conversion chain from mining and refining to the combustion in the vehicle engines in such a way that it can meet the global ecological criteria.

The overall conclusion is that interesting new systems options do appear if the fuel supply system is related to the energy conversion method applied. If a very clean fuel like hydrogen is selected, a number of new direct conversions to electricity emerge. Furthermore, if petroleum fuel resources beyond the year 2020 are not sufficient to supply the world demand for mobility, a new primary energy source has to be exploited in order to develop and distribute the clean new fuel required. By natural and historical analogy, these changes in primary energy substitutions take many decades to develop.

It is far too early to forecast which clean fuel will be selected and how the ecologically efficient hybrid systems will be eventually designed. In this chapter the speculations and conceptual systems engineering are only intended to raise the issues and to indicate some possibilities. It is the role of a major systems approach and R&D programme to decide upon the appropriate hybrid fuel/engine systems for a sustainable future.

Policy implications

This chapter includes a systems approach to the problem. The end result of this process should be an ecologically acceptable road transport environment.

The systems approach is based upon a philosophical assumption that the environmental issue is a 'century question' similar to what industrial growth/liberalism and equality/socialism have proved to be. By the concept systems approach is meant a feedback process of systems analysis and engineering synthesis. It is a holistic approach to problem-solving, suitable for issues with a long-range character and with a global impact. A solution to an ecological problem cannot usually be found in a single subsystem or in a specialised scientific discipline. It has to be analysed in the widest possible systems context and with many methods.

A systems approach towards a clean fuel/engine system solution then means that we have to relate if not only to the quick tempo of the combustion and the traffic process but also to the long-range energy supply and to the shifts in lifestyles in society. It also means that we have to design the system to meet not only today's requirements from traffic and the environment, but a whole century ahead of new requirements! It will be the emerging new ecology ethics that sets the ultimate criteria for the systems approach.

This policy summary ends with a recommendation: create a European Systems Approach Programme with the task of penetrating in depth the possibilities for a clean fuel/engine system. Invite experienced designers and systems analysts from the energy industry, power industry and the automobile industry to participate in an initial systems approach study. A following pre-competitive R&D programme should then be given such resources that it can come up with a feasible set of systems alternatives and policy options no later than the year 1999. The result must be of such a quality that from it a desirable, economic and ecologically safe path towards a sustainable future can be selected.

References

Armstrong, B.D. (1983) 'The influence of cool engines on car fuel consumption'. TRRL Supplementary Report 822.

BP (1989) *BP Statistical Review of World Energy*, July.

Buchner, H. (1978) 'The hydrogen/hydride energy concept', *International Journal of Hydrogen Energy*, vol. 3, pp. 385–406.

Churchman, C. West (1968) *The Systems Approach*. Dell Publishing, New York.

Gardiner, W.C. (1982) 'The chemistry of flames', *Scientific American*, February, vol. 246, no. 2.

Grübler, A., Nakicenovic, N. and Schäfer, A. (1992) 'A dynamics of transport and energy systems: history of development and a scenario for the future'. Paper of *Energy and Life* World Energy Council Congress, Madrid.

Harman, Willis (1988) *Global Mind Change*. Knowledge Systems Inc., Indianapolis.

Hodgson, B. 'Natural Gas: the search goes on, *National Geographic*, 154(5), pp. 632–51.

ICENES 3 (1983) *Third International Conference on Emerging Nuclear Systems*, Helsinki, June.

Kordesch, K. and Oliveira, J.C.T. (1988) 'Fuel cells: the present state of the technology and future applications, with special consideration of the alkaline hydrogen/oxygen (air) systems', *Journal of Hydrogen Energy*, vol. 13, no. 7, pp. 411–27.

Laithwaite, E.R. (1974) 'Linear propulsion by electromagnetic "river"', *International Hovering Craft, Hydrofoil and Advanced Transit Systems Conference*, 13–16 May, Brighton.

Lloyd, Alan et al. (1989) 'Air quality management in Los Angeles: perspectives on past and future emission control strategies', JAPCA, *The Journal of Air & Waste Management*, May, 39, no. 5.

Marchetti, Cesare (1980) 'Society as a learning system: discovery, invention, and innovation cycles revisited', *Technological Forecasting and Social Change*, vol. 18.

Marchetti, Cesare (1982) 'When will hydrogen come?', IIASA Working Paper WP-82-123, November.

Marchetti, Cesare (1988) 'How to solve the CO_2 problem without tears'. Plenary speech, 7th World Hydrogen Conference, *Hydrogen Today*, held in Moscow on 25–29 September, IIASA.

Marchetti, Cesare (1988) 'On society and nuclear energy: a historical analysis of the interaction between society and nuclear technology with examples taken from other innovations'. Final report for European Atomic Energy Commission, represented by the Commission of the European Communities, December.

Nakicenovic, N. (1985) 'The automotive road to technological change: diffusion of the automobile as a process of technological substitution'. IIASA WP-85-19.

Pierce, T.C. and Waters, M.H.L. (1980) 'Cold start fuel consumption of a diesel and a petrol car', TRRL Supplementary Report 636.

Ross, H.R. and Hamilton, W.R. (1980) 'Santa Barbara electric vehicle project, Phase 1 feasibility study'. Santa Barbara Metropolitan Transit District, 1980.

Ross, R. Howard (1992) 'Roadway powered electric vehicle system development in California, the urban electric vehicle'. OECD Document.

Silverleaf, A. and Svidén, O. (1991) 'Some reflections on clean fuels and engines for the 21st century road vehicles', based upon a round table discussion at the *ECOLOGY 90 Congress* in Göteborg on 28 November, INTRA, January 1991.

Svidén, Ove (1971) 'Hybriddrift for Bilar'. TP-71:16 Saab-Scania.

Svidén, Ove (1982) *The Gasistor: A Systems Approach to a Hybrid Engine System for Automobiles*. EKI Transportsystem, Linköping University.

Svidén, Ove (1983) 'Automobile usage in a future information society', *Futures*, December.

Svidén, Ove (1986) 'A 21 century world gas scenario', *Futures*, October, pp. 687–91.

Svidén, Ove (1989) *SCENARIOS, On Expert Generated Scenarios for Long Range Infrastructure Planning of Transportation and Energy Systems*. Linköping University, June.

Svidén, Ove (1991) 'Clean fuel and engine systems for the 21st century road vehicles'. Background paper for the ESF/NECTAR working group on Transport, Communication and Mobility, Scenarios for Europe 2020, November.

TüV Rheinland (1984) *Alternative Energy Sources for Road Transport METHANOL, Preconditions for Introduction of Alcohol Fuels*. Verlag TüV Rheinland.

TüV Rheinland (1989) *Alternative Energien für den Strassenverkehr, WASSERSTOFF ANTRIEB in der Erprobung*. Verlag TüV Rheinland.

Chapter 8

Technological innovation in urban public transport

P. Papaioannou and J.F. Reis Simoes

Introduction

Public transport within the European Community (EC) is today a very large and significant sector of the transport industry. The twelve EC countries have a total fleet of approximately 400,000 buses, not to mention the equivalent potential of metropolitan railways and other similar systems that operate in parallel. Of these buses, 112,000 operate in urban areas and the remainder in extra-urban areas. Table 8.1 gives a more detailed picture for each country. Similarly, Table 8.2 gives the figures on the situation expected in the near future.

From surveys carried out recently (CASSIOPE, 1990, Del. 3) covering 41 per cent of the total bus fleet in the EC, it was found that 27 per cent of the **public transport operators** operate less than 100 buses, 30 per cent of the companies have more than 300 buses, while the remainder, 43 per cent, have fleets of intermediate size. From the same survey it was also revealed that usually there is no competition in the **public transport operation** within one urban area. This is common in France, Italy, Spain, Greece, Portugal and partially in Germany. In Benelux, Denmark, Germany and the United Kingdom the situation is slightly different, since there is often competition between two or more operators in the same city or in a bigger conurbation.

Public transport functions and domains

Public transport operation is complex and it gets more complex with increasing size. Regardless of ownership patterns, city patterns and legal or other system particularities, every public transport operator performs certain functions which always have the same characteristics and attributes. These functions may look different, or may have different names, but certainly there are strong similarities underneath. Of course in many cases there are functions not found in other operators, or there is also the case where specific functions are performed in a different way. From an operational point of view, every company has its own layout

Table 8.1   Total public transport fleet of EC countries

| Country | Number of buses, coaches and trolley-buses | | | | |
	1970	1975	1980	1985	1986
Belgium	10,000	12,000	12,500	12,400	12,200
Denmark	5,000	6,000	7,000	8,000	8,000
France	41,000	52,000	65,000	71,000	72,000
Germany	47,000	60,000	70,000	69,000	70,000
Greece	10,500	13,300	16,800	18,600	18,500
Ireland	2,000	2,000	3,000	5,000	5,000
Italy	32,900	43,800	58,100	76,300	80,000(est)
Luxembourg	600	700	700	700	700
Netherlands	9,000	10,000	11,000	12,000	12,000
Portugal	5,000	6,000	8,000	10,000	11,000
Spain	31,000	39,000	43,000	42,000	42,000
UK	79,000	80,000	78,000	75,000	76,000
Total	273,000	324,000	373,100	400,000	407,400

Source: CASSIOPE Project, DRIVE programme.

and its own organisational structure. The company's size, state of owner-ship, legal and economic environment as well as other internal or exter-nal factors, are some of the elements that affect the organisation of a public transport operator, govern the hierarchy pyramid and impose restrictions on his operation. In this respect it is difficult to divide the whole operation into separate elements in the same way for all operators.

However, from a functional point of view, this is easier, due to the common characteristics underlying the most important functions of any public transport operator. Recent research indicates that there are seven main 'domains' or 'functions' in an urban bus operation. These func-tions, which exist in more or less every company dealing with transport-ing passengers, are the following:

1.   Real-time control (operations management);
2.   Scheduling;
3.   Passenger information;
4.   Fare collection;
5.   Maintenance;
6.   Strategic planning;
7.   Management information.

The above functions can be further divided into subfunctions which in practice describe the various processes that take place during the opera-tion of a Public Transport Bus Company.

A short description of the content of each function is particularly useful to better understand the functional categorisation and try to determine the state of advanced transport telematics penetration in public transport.

Table 8.2 The present and future urban public transport bus operations in the EC

Country	Urban Population Millions			Number of Metropolitan Areas and Bus Operations							
				100 to 500,000 Inhabitants		500 to 1 million Inhabitants		1 to 5 million Inhabitants		More than 5 million Inhabitants	
	1980	2000	2020	1980	2000	1980	2000	1980	2000	1980	2000
Belgium	8.8	9.0	9.2	3	2	1	2	1	1		
Denmark	4.3	4.6	4.5	3	3			1	1		
France	40.5	47.0	51.1	81	109	8	10	4	5	1	1
W. Germany	52.2	53.4	50.9	94	102	12	14	9	16	1	1
Greece	6.0	8.0	9.5	1	1	1	1	1	1		
Ireland	1.9	2.7	3.8	1	1	1			1		
Italy	38.9	45.4	48.4	68	72	10	12	8	10	1	1
Luxembourg	0.3	0.3	0.3	1	1						
The Netherlands	12.6	14.5	14.4	33	39	4	5	2	2		
Portugal	2.9	4.3	6.4	2	2	1		1	2		
Spain	27.8	36.2	42.5	66	84	7	9	3	4		1
UK	50.6	52.7	53.9	101	110	17	20	11	12	1	1
Total EC	246.7	278.2	294.8	454	526	62	73	41	55	4	5

Source: Cassiope Project, DRIVE Programme

Real-time control

Real-time control (operations management) has to do with the day-to-day operation of a public transport company. As the term indicates, the various functions have to be monitored in real time in order to be effective and useful. Managing depots, monitoring vehicles and crew as well as controlling operations are some of the subdomains of real-time control. Operations management in real time requires appropriate equipment and infrastructure which facilitate operation and allow the people responsible in this domain to perform their tasks.

Scheduling

Scheduling deals with vehicle and driver scheduling and driver rostering. The functions performed in this area are well known from a *content* point of view, but complex enough from a real-time application point of view. The problem of scheduling is always the same, i.e. to assign buses and drivers to preplanned trips, but it is applied every time in different conditions. Each network is unique, and therefore more or less different restrictions will apply. Furthermore, the scheduling tasks do not remain unchangeable, even in the same network, since many of the factors influencing the mathematical solution change in time and cause mandatory modifications.

Passenger information

Passenger information (PI) is the domain which includes all functions related to the provision of information to passengers as well as those handling the necessary data required to produce and update this information. PI refers to both real-time and off-line information, and also includes the interactive or passive, regardless of the place where this is provided. Typical examples of PI are arrival and departure times of buses, fare information, trip planning, transfer information, information about facilities for people with special needs, lost and found property, etc.

Fare collection

Fare policy, ticket issuance and distribution, ticket validation and patronage management through **fare collection** are the main functions of this domain. Nowadays fare collection can be achieved in a variety of alternative ways using sophisticated means and equipment. Automatic ticketing machines, smart cards and magnetic tickets are some typical examples. The integration of fare collection with other domains is valuable to any operator who can utilise fare collection data for the strategic planning and management tasks.

Maintenance

The domain of **maintenance** concerns such factors as repair and replacement service, breakdown diagnosis, parts inventory, staff assignment and also other functions which aim at reducing dead mileage, minimising cost and keeping high standards for vehicles. Maintenance is one of the most computerised areas and takes a large stake of every company's attention and budget.

Operators also focus — or should focus — on the following:

- the adoption of maintenance philosophy for vehicles and main parts (such as engines, gearboxes, etc.), aiming to establish a suitable balance between curative (fault repair) and preventive — systematic or condition monitoring — maintenance;
- the determining of the lifetime of vehicles and main parts;
- the design of appropriate workshops, mainly for the first levels of the maintenance activity.

Strategic planning

Strategic planning (SP) in this functional classification is the steps necessary to plan the public transport supply. Long-term commitments such as changes to route structure, location of termini, etc. are typical examples of the domains content. The term is irrelevant to the widely used term **strategic planning** which refers to the long-term planning process of a company or an organisation. In public transport SP means line network plan, rough edition of time tables and tariff plan. In this area the following functions may be also included:

- choosing the transport modes;
- establishing the medium-term plan for the renewal and increase (or decrease) of the fleet;
- improving the attractiveness of the public transport modes.

Management information

This domain has to do with the processing of all collected data required by a transport company to help company management to exercise their duties in the best possible way. To achieve this goal, it is necessary to establish a **management information system** (MIS) which is the key tool to any organisation. Data processing can take place at various levels, with a different degree of detail and with a different viewpoint. However, for management information only certain information and indices are of use. These are the ones which assist managers to make decisions and to draw up policies. Management information when combined with other data, such as external data to the company, data from the environment, etc., are the basic inputs for the medium and long-term process of a company.

Technological innovation in public transport domains

Software development

During the last decade there has been significant progress in the development of both hardware and software in the field of public transport. Many software houses took advantage of the new equipment, designed to accommodate message and data transfer, and they developed new products in order to facilitate their users. The criteria taken into account by these developers in targeting the solution offered by their products do not always follow the above-mentioned functional categorisation of public transport operation. They were governed by the specific needs of their clients, as well as by other factors. There are several general-purpose or custom-designed packages that exist and operate today. The bigger networks tend to develop their own packages either by themselves or with the contribution of software houses. On the other hand, smaller networks prefer to utilise commercial packages which can be properly modified by the customer himself. Periodic updates improve their usability and performance, in this way permitting the user to obtain the required result at a lower cost.

The main areas covered by these packages include:

- scheduling, i.e. vehicle scheduling, driver scheduling and driver rostering;
- maintenance, i.e. parts inventory, maintenance scheduling, fuel management, etc.;
- management information systems covering the following areas: operating cost, patronage information, patronage distribution in time and space, payroll, human resources, etc.

The majority of software packages deal with the first two areas which traditionally were the first priority of every operator. The reason is that better management in these two domains means direct savings from fewer buses and cheaper maintenance. It appears that the operators in certain countries are interested in certain functions, or even subfunctions. UK operators for example tend to be interested in **payroll and accounting** systems, while French operators tend to invest more in **passenger information**. Operators from almost all EC countries pay much attention to scheduling packages, though in different degrees. For Italians, legal and other labour aspects are very important. A more representative picture will be revealed in the section examining the ATT penetration into public transport.

To present in a more descriptive way the relationship between recent developments and public transport functions mentioned before, a brief reference to the existing products for each area will follow.

Main technological innovations per domain

REAL-TIME CONTROL

Real-time control equipment is most of the time devices that help the operator in delivering his scheduled timetables. Difficulties in keeping vehicles to schedule arise from the fact that public transport buses have to share the road network with other vehicles, and therefore suffer the consequences of congestion and irregular flow. When a demand-responsive system is in operation, real-time control is necessary even in cases without congestion phenomena.

Real-time control equipment is based on the ability to locate the position of each vehicle in the network. This is usually done in two different ways. i.e. by **radio telephone** and by **automatic vehicle monitoring** (AVM). The existing systems in operation can be divided into two categories: those with permanent localisation and those with localisation at certain predetermined points. Real-time control is most effective when coupled with other measures, such as traffic control, parking facilities, exclusive bus lanes, etc. A typical example is the transport system of Nice, France, where there is in operation an AVM system capable of localising buses at certain points along the existing bus lanes.

AVM systems, most of the time are combined with other operator's systems such as **passenger information systems** (PIS), **management information systems**, and **maintenance**. This is achieved through a data base which gathers data, and after processing them dispatches the outputs to the various termini, such as bus stop displays, passenger information monitors, management information systems, etc. There are many different systems operating all over Europe. Detailed information about these can be found in reports and publications. What is of interest to be mentioned here is that these systems can be classified into three types: **decentralised** systems, **centralised** and **bus-laboratory** systems. AVM systems are developed and installed by a number of European and American suppliers, who specialise in public transport hardware equipment.

SCHEDULING

This is an area which profits mainly from the development and use of software packages. **Scheduling** is one of the most important tasks in public transport. The scheduling functions are the ones no one can avoid. Vehicles and drivers have to be scheduled even in the smallest network. Thus, a considerable amount of manual work is required in order to produce daily schedules and in turn rosters. The computer technology which has made rapid strides ahead during the last fifteen years has given the chance to the schedulers to avoid this tedious work and accomplish this task by using computer algorithms and programs. Initially, a semi-automatic method was used, but gradually, fully automatic methods were developed and employed by many operators. Today, there are a number of scheduling packages which provide a wide range of capabilities and perform several different scheduling tasks. Scheduling program systems have been developed in many countries of Europe and North America. Based on the planning phase, the various products in which these programs can be classified are shown in Table 8.3. The list in this table is not complete, but it certainly contains a large part of the existing products.

Table 8.3   Classification of scheduling packages

PLANNING PHASE	PROGRAM SYSTEMS
Planning the service level	DIANA, FABIAN, INTERNEZ, NERO, MICRONETZ, RWS
Planning vehicle and staff operations	ALLIAGES, BUSMAN, CHIC, EPON, HASTUS, HOST, INTERPLAN, MICROBUS, MFS, OPTOBUS, PADD, PRO RAILNETT II, RUCUS, STANISLAS
Carrying out and controlling the plans execution	BON, INTERBUS, FOCCS, PERDIS, RBL, MOBILE, RETAX
Analysing the completion	BAS, FAST, MODS. OV, PLANFAHRT, KORN

Source: CASSIOPE Project, *State of the Art on Computer Aided Technology in Public Transport*, EC, 1989.

The most widely used systems available today (CASSIOPE, 1990 Del. 1) are probably RUCUS (USA), SAGE (CA), HASTUS (CA), BUSMAN (UK), HOT (FRG), CHIC (FR), STANISLAS (FR), MICROBUS (FRG).

PASSENGER INFORMATION

Passenger information traditionally was limited to timetables at termini and bus stops, or to fare structure information and system maps or other

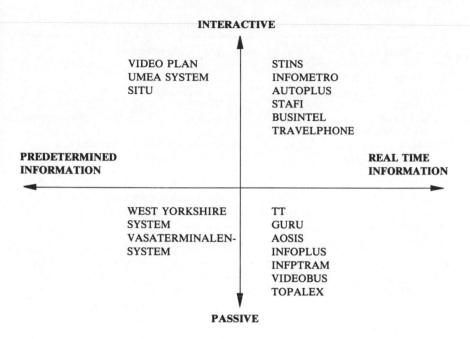

INTERACTIVE

VIDEO PLAN	STINS
UMEA SYSTEM	INFOMETRO
SITU	AUTOPLUS
	STAFI
	BUSINTEL
	TRAVELPHONE

PREDETERMINED INFORMATION — REAL TIME INFORMATION

WEST YORKSHIRE SYSTEM	TT
VASATERMINALEN- SYSTEM	GURU
	AOSIS
	INFOPLUS
	INFPTRAM
	VIDEOBUS
	TOPALEX

PASSIVE

Figure 8.1   Topology of Passenger Information Systems

printed material. In many operators, telephone information was available as well as information desks at certain central locations. Today the situation is quite different. A large number of operators in Europe operate automatic passenger information systems with various characteristics and capabilities. Often these systems are linked to AVM systems and other real-time control equipment, and provide the users with real-time information. The information supplied may be passive or interactive; also it may be real-time or not. There is a rich bibliography about **modern passenger information** systems, especially in France. A topology of existing passenger information systems classified according to the above distinctions is given in Figure 8.1.

Table 8.4 gives another picture of existing passenger information systems (Meyere, 1989) according to the location where they operate. Finally Table 8.5 contains the main features of eleven passenger information systems used in Europe (CASSIOPE, 1990, Del. 5.1).

FARE COLLECTION
Fare collection is also a domain which was greatly affected by new technology. Automatic ticket machines, banknote scanners, magnetic and smart cards, and most recently use of credit cards for multi-payment purposes are some of the most important innovations in this area. Automatic systems in fare collection are particularly useful in public

Table 8.4   Classification of existing public transport systems by location

LOCATION Name	Main Characteristic
A. HOME/WORK PLACE	
AUTOPLAS	Videotex service
STAFI	Videotex service
BUSINTEL	
Speech Datacom Services	
UMEA	Information service by telephone
TRAVELPHONE	Information service by telephone
B. STREET/PUBLIC PLACES	
AUTOPLUS	Information dispenser
STAFI	Information dispenser
STANS	
SITU	Route optimisation
C. BUS STOP/STATION	
ELSIE	
AOSIS	
VASATERMINALEN	Automatic information system
INFOMETRO	
INFOTRAM	
INFOPLUS	Waiting-time display
VIDEOPLAN	
SAI-WEST YORKSHIRE	
SAE BARCELONA	
VIDEOBUS	Waiting-time display
TOPALEX	Waiting-time display
D. ON-BOARD	
TT	Real time incidents
GURU	

Source: CASSIOPE Project, DRIVE programme, *Study of Functionalities in the Passenger Information Domain*.

transport for two main reasons: first, they result in personnel reductions, and therefore in cost reductions; and second, they are capable of gathering and processing patronage information that is needed for accomplishing tasks in other domains such as **strategic planning, real-time control** and **management information**. Magnetic or other similar cards are being used in many big cities like London, Paris, Toronto, Washington, etc.

MAINTENANCE
Automatic systems for **maintenance** are quite widespread in Europe and in other countries. The systems are more or less management systems focusing on the vehicle maintenance and technical staff management. Maintenance systems may be centralised or decentralised. In the second

case each depot has its own system and controls for all its own maintenance tasks. Sometimes a more complex situation may exist. In almost all cases a parts inventory module exists within this system to facilitate the technical management for storing and accounting purposes.

Presently there are in Europe three different lines of development in computer-aided maintenance:

- off-line repair documentation systems;
- on-line maintenance control systems;
- integrated maintenance information systems.

A significant component of almost all maintenance systems is the automatic registration and evaluation of fuel consumption for public transport buses. Such systems are used by many small, medium and large operators in Europe. Some of the well-known maintenance systems are the following:

	Country of origin
AT-ABEA	Germany
AWES	Germany
VMS (CA)	Canada
MMS (CA)	Canada
SAM (FR)	France
CGFTE (FR)	France
WIS (G)	Germany
GOS (G)	Germany

Currently there are efforts to utilise in the maintenance domain automatic systems, artificial intelligence, knowledge-based expert systems as well as computer modular and integrated systems.

STRATEGIC PLANNING

The main task within the area of **strategic planning** that has benefited from new technologies is that of network or line building.

According to an analysis which was released in 1986 by the German Ministry of Transport in Bonn, four different methods are used for line–network building as follows:

- reduction method;
- progressive method;
- 'traffic flow' method;
- 'trip sum' method;

The study compares the four methods with respect to some criteria, which include passenger and operation-related objectives, type of network, procedure of line-building and calculation of final loads on

Table 8.5 Main features of eleven user information systems

System	Country	City/Town	Facilities location and form	Peripherals	Charges	Output	Capital cost (ECUs)	Future possibilities
1. Real time interactive systems								
AUTOPLUS	France	La Rochelle	Home.W/P VIDEOTEX. Street VIDEOTEX Terminal Telephone	VIDEOTEX Terminal and Info dispenser	Tel. charge at home, free in public places	Optimus route	350,000	Connection with AVM
STAFI	FRG	Hamburg	VIDEOTEX Terminal, telephone service	VIDEOTEX Terminal and ANSI Terminal	Free	Timetable Connections Fare info	150,000	
BUSINTEL	France	Angouleme	VIDEOTEX at home or public place	VIDEOTEX Terminal, Street info. dispenser	Free in public areas. Tel. charge at home	Waiting time, Route info. Timetables general info.	150,000 (AVM not included)	Door-to-door route planning
TRAVELPHONE (Telerider)	Canada	West Midlands, UK	Bus stop telephones	Telephone	Tel. charge	Arrival time. Status info		
STINS	Sweden	Malmo Gothenburg	Terminal at stations and interchanges	Terminal printer		Alternative routes, departure/ arrival time		Automatic ticketing machine

Table 8.5 contd.

System	Country	City/Town	Facilities location and form	Peripherals	Charges	Output	Capital cost (ECUs)	Future possibilities
2. Real time passive systems								
ACSIS	Netherlands	Amsterdam	LCD at translations		Free	Platform numbers Departure time disruptions	10,500	Central control system
INFOPLUS VIDEOPLUS	France	Angouleme Angers Grenoble Reims	TV screen at bus stops and public places		Free	Info on destinations, disruptions, general info	11,700 (AVM not included)	CGA-HBS AVM system
VIDEOBUS	France	Nice	At bus stops Display of moving light along the line		Free	Waiting time		
TOPALEX	France	Caen	Visual display at bus stops		Free	Waiting time for next bus		
TT	Sweden	Stockholm	Displays at interchanges and major bus stops	Remote control terminal	Free	Next bus arrival, real time incidents, other info.	10,000 per unit 85,000 development cost	

Table 8.5 contd.

System	Country	City/Town	Facilities location and form	Peripherals	Charges	Output	Capital cost (ECUs)	Future possibilities
3. Pre-determined interactive systems								
UMEA SYSTEM	Sweden	UMEA	Info. given by any phone		Phone call charge	Next bus route no. departure time from a certain stop	11,500	Assign call numbers to each bus stop
SITU	France	Paris Caen Nantes Valenciennes	Street info. dispenser, Home equipment	Street–home terminal printer	Free	Alternative routes with additional info. frequencies, speeds, walking time	850,000 database for Paris 35,000 per unit	Micro-computer VIDEOTEX service

lines. Presently only one package offers a fully automatic design of public transport network, the one developed by Volvo Transportation Systems (VTS).

Most of the other packages use interactive approaches in the design of bus routes and transit infrastructure. The best-known are: IGTDS, Transcom, Transtep, NOPTS, VPS, ULoad, TRANSPLAN, Maditac, EMME/2 TERESE, DIANA, FABIAN; also, NERO, BRAM, FRACAS, MINUPT, MOTORS, QRS, PALETTE.

MANAGEMENT INFORMATION

In recent years **management information systems** (MIS) have been developed at a fast pace mainly due to the information technology advances. Information systems where MIS belongs usually refer to the following:

- information retrieval system (IRS)
- data base management system (DBMS)
- management information system (MIS)
- decision support system (DSS)
- question–answering system (QAS)

Each of the above-mentioned systems performs a specific role which is best utilised by the people interested in the output it produces. Most of the time the information system is a mix of two or more of these systems and it is structured in a way appropriate for the goals of its user. Today there is a wide range of software systems in operation which provide information for part or the whole of a transport operation. However, they often support other domains too. Some times an MIS need not be designed for public transport operations but only for general use. On the other hand it is most common to develop a MIS together with other automated systems specific to public transport. Some typical examples are the TRANSMIS system, developed in California, USA, which has provisions for scheduling, run-cutting, rostering, assignment, payroll, labour distribution and report generating; the system of New Jersey Transit capable of controlling facilities, scheduling, maintenance and fare collection; and the Allen County Regional Transit Authority System which provides accounting and payroll information, vehicle history, service productivity, etc.

USA and Canada are considered to be the countries with the most advanced MIS. A complete software suite developed in Canada in early 1985, the **transit information communications and control system** (TICCS) contained the following components:

ATIS	service analysis, automatic telephone information system
AVLC	automatic vehicle location and control
COBA	communications, operator and bus assignment

FIN	financial interfaces
MMS	materials management systems
MS	mini-scheduler
MST	management support tools
PCC	passenger counting collection
PID	public information display
PP	payroll/personnel
QS	quick scheduler
RC	run-cutter
ROS	rostering
SLP	slip administration
TOB	timekeeping and operator bidding
VMS	vehicle maintenance system

The GOTIME system developed by the Metro Transit of Nova Scotia Canada was another package similar to TICCS.

Current state of new technology penetration into public transport

By the term **new technology** here, we mean mainly the **advanced transport telematics** (ATT) systems mentioned in previous sections.

It is really hard to estimate the current state of ATT penetration into public transport. There are two dimensions: the quantitative and the qualitative. Public transport statistics kept by UITP (the International Union of Public Transport based in Brussels) or other organisations such as UMTA, CUTA, or other national agencies give an indication of the first dimension. However, they cannot present a comprehensive picture of the situation with respect to the level of automatisation obtained by public transport operators. The most recent and updated source of the state of new technology applications, or advanced transport telematics (ATT) as they are known, in public transport is perhaps the survey carried out by the CASSIOPE Consortium in the DRIVE programme which took place in 1989. According to the data gathered and processed from 119 European public transport companies, representing 41 per cent of the total European fleets, the degree of automatisation varies from one domain to another. Table 8.6 gives information about the use of the various innovations by public transport operators in Europe today, based on the survey mentioned.

The figures in Table 8.6 refer to the whole sample which covers the twelve EC countries. The figures differ from country to country. For example, though 28 per cent of the networks are equipped with AVM systems, 52 per cent of them are in France, 40 per cent in Italy and only 14 per cent in the UK. Similarly in passenger information equipment France comes first whilst the UK and southern European countries (Greece, Portugal and Spain) appear to be far lower. With respect to

Table 8.6 Percentage use of technological innovation by public transport operators in Europe in the corresponding areas

Equipment/function	Sample
Real Time Control	
Percentage of networks equipped with AVM	28%
Percentage of fleet equipped with AVM	65%
Counting steps	28%
Clock on board	64%
Voice communication management	74%
Assignment of vehicles	53%
Radio data transmission	33%
Vehicle monitoring	30%
Vehicle identification	30%
Incident/emergency management	36%
Lateness/earliness notification	29%
Scheduling	
Timetable planning	74%
Printing timetables	74%
Vehicle scheduling	73%
Driver scheduling	65%
Driver rostering	65%
Passenger information	
Current vehicle location	9%
Cancellation of service	13%
Route optimisation	7%
Fare information	47%
Official schedules	51%
Fare collection	
Automatic on-board ticketing	48%
Automatic fraud detection	16%
Smart cards	3%
Hands-off ticketing	2%
Origin–destination data	20%
Recorded ticket issue in bus	27%
Maintenance	
Computerised logbook	38%
Tele-diagnosis	17%
Tele-maintenance/repairs	16%
Computer-aided maintenance procedures	17%
Parts/inventory management	63%
Strategic planning	
Network adaptation	42%
Fleet optimisation	33%
Impact of route stop changes	29%
Impact of service level changes	28%
Interchange minimisation	25%

Table 8.6 contd.

Equipment/function	Sample
Management information	
Management computers	
Mainframes	44%
Mini	50%
Micros	70%
Management information systems	33%
Cost accounting database	38%
Personnel database	51%
Vehicle database	48%
Regulation/law database	14%
Road system database	15%

Source: Based on a survey of 119 public transport companies, performed in 1989 by the CASSIOPE Consortium DRIVE programme.

computer equipment, the UK and Italy come first, followed by Germany and France. Northern countries seem to have a preference for mainframes and minis, and southern countries for micros.

The CASSIOPE survey revealed that large computer systems are used for scheduling and other management tasks, such as payroll and accounting, strategic planning and maintenance.

Smaller systems on the other hand are used for management information and scheduling in small networks. Most of the time large and small computers are not linked.

Other results obtained from the survey with respect to the ATT penetration into public transport indicate that 35 per cent of the networks were equipped with the following **scheduling** packages:

STANISLAS (FR)	7 sites in France
CHIC (FR)	6 sites in France
HASTUS (CA)	5 sites in Denmark, Spain, Italy and UK
PRO (G)	5 sites in Germany
BUSMAN (UK)	4 sites in UK
HOT (G)	4 sites in Germany
MICROBUS (G)	3 sites in Luxembourg and Germany

In the domain of **Passenger Information Systems** (PIS) the situation is quite complex. Several networks operate PIS with different characteristics and attributes. Beside the systems description previously, some other systems also exist; the Canadian products SAGEPAS/INFOBUS and GOTIME provide both passenger information in real time and management information. In France 31 per cent of the operators use **telematic Information** (Minitel) which can be linked with an AVM system. Among all European countries France is the leading user of Passenger Information Systems.

Technical innovation in mechanical systems for buses

Technological advances have been significant in **mechanical systems** too. The suppliers of vehicles and other mass transit equipment, trying to gain a bigger share in the markets of Europe and North America, have come to offer a variety of extras required in current operation conditions. At the same time safety regulations are now much more stringent, resulting in better quality systems from a safety point of view. Also, the need to reduce maintenance cost and time and to automate much of the work done manually has forced manufacturers to load vehicles with a number of computerised systems which ease the everyday driver's life. As a result of all these we see today in operation modern comfortable vehicles and/or trains equipped with security and other sophisticated systems. The various areas in which improvements have been made lately include:

- safety (braking systems, seat design, vehicle interior design)
- security (alarm and other emergency systems, drivers' and vehicles' protection)
- passenger comfort (ergonomics, noise, air-conditioning, ventilation)
- vehicle aesthetics
- warning systems for the vehicle's mechanical parts
- energy efficiency
- air pollution

A short description of the most common technological advances in public transport and in particular in buses (Giannopoulos, 1989) will be given in the following.

Regeneration of braking energy

Urban buses, which operate in stop-and-go mode, brake very frequently. Fuel consumption can be reduced by partial regeneration of braking energy. There are various types of systems. For example, one well-known system uses a mechanical accumulator (flywheel) which accumulates energy during braking and gives it back to help the engine during acceleration. Another system utilises a pressurised gas accumulator.

Both systems demand a continuously variable transmission. During the braking phase, the vehicle's kinetic energy is transmitted via the continuously variable transmission from the driving wheels to the energy accumulator, raising the pressure in the hydraulic storage tank or increasing the rotation speed of the flywheel, as the case may be. During the acceleration phase the above process is reversed, thus 'giving back' the energy that otherwise would be lost during the braking phase.

The energy accumulators should be kept as small as possible in order to minimise weight and keep accumulator losses as low as possible. A two-axle bus should not need an energy accumulator capacity larger than 200–300 Wh. Energy savings of 20–30 per cent, depending on the operational mode of the vehicle, may be possible.

Alternative fuels

Alternative fuels such as methanol, LPG, LNG, etc. have already been used in urban buses with mixed results. The main advantages include:

1. Exhaust gases are free of sulphur and soot, as well as smoke, thus making these fuels environmentally more acceptable.
2. There is not such a great dependence on fossil fuels.

Disadvantages include:

1. Because of the 'closed' system (under pressure or low-temperature) the fuel system is more sophisticated and the lower calorific value of these fuels makes a fuel tank of roughly double volume necessary for a given operating range.
2. Fuel consumption in relation to calorific value is, because of the Otto combustion system, higher than that in the case of diesel combustion.

Buses using such alternative fuels are already in full operation in Vienna, Berlin, Auckland, Los Angeles and other cities.

Optimisation of the diesel engine and the transmission

Fuel consumption of urban buses is greatly influenced by the special operating mode of these vehicles, which comprises the following phases: full throttle acceleration, travel at constant road speed, braking and stop. As distances between stops diminish, overall consumption is increasingly influenced by the amount of fuel used in the acceleration phase. This fact has been taken into account in industry's efforts to optimise this drive cycle with a view to both reducing the fuel consumption and improving the efficiency of the bus engine. The following improvements have been investigated and have been gradually introduced in buses in recent years:

IMPROVEMENTS TO THE ENGINE
- improved fuel injection system (injection nozzles, injection pressure);
- matching of torque curve to the specific operating conditions.

IMPROVEMENTS TO THE AUTOMATIC TRANSMISSION
- matching of torque converter;
- lowering of 'headshift' point;
- reduction of losses at idling speed and of losses through friction;
- optimal choice of gear ratios and of number of gears.

IMPROVEMENTS TO THE VEHICLE
- optimal choice of rear-axle ratio;
- reduction in rolling resistance and drag.

The above improvements have resulted in a reduction of about 15 per cent in the fuel consumption of city buses without reducing performance.

Reduction of driver influence on the driving 'style' offers additional potential for fuel saving. 'Intelligent' control systems which can register and process fuel consumption characteristics are being investigated. Such engine-transmission management systems will enable the driver to programme his bus for optimal fuel consumption or for top performance, whichever is desired.

Electric buses

Electric drive systems have long equipment lives, require little maintenance and do not have polluting emissions. Against these advantages is the disadvantage of higher initial costs. 'Electric' buses may be of three main types.

The first type concerns the normal trolley-buses operating in many cities and taking their energy from overhead wires, a fact that creates flexibility and visual obstruction problems.

The second type is the battery electric bus taking its power from batteries. This technology is still under development. Its main problems are the weight of the batteries and the small 'autonomy' of the bus before recharging them.

The final type is the so-called dual-energy bus, operating with two completely independent drive systems, one diesel and one electric. In areas where the diesel operation is environmentally unacceptable (e.g. tunnels, CBDs etc.), the bus is switched to electric operation. In all other areas it operates as a normal diesel bus. The main advantage of such dual-mode buses is the flexibility they offer with respect to the protection of the environment, while they do not have the disadvantages of the electric mode buses, mainly the frequent recharging of their batteries, as in the case of the all-electric bus, or the overhead wires in all their network of lines as in the case of trolley-buses. A large fleet of dual-energy buses is planned for the city of Seattle in the USA, while cities around the world are considering the same option.

Automatic guidance systems for buses

Automatic guidance is an effort to make buses match the efficiency of **light rail systems** in terms of speed and capacity. They give the possibility for otherwise normal buses to become 'track guided', thus dramatically improving their line capacity characteristics like any other rail system. There are two alternative forms of bus guidance.

MECHANICAL OR TRACK GUIDANCE

Mechanical guidance systems necessitate specially equipped buses and tracks. Relevant equipment on the bus consists of a rigid feeler arm with a feeler roller bolted to the steering knuckle. The guide curbs on the road can be of metal or concrete. The curb rails and the roadway form a trough in which the bus is driven. This trough gives the bus a protected right of way. The feeler rollers are pressed against the curb rails and follow their course.

The bus following a track guidance system is steered along the course of the 'guide' curbs solely by the feeler device. A setting device on the feeler arm allows track width to be adjusted and feeler roller wear to be compensated. This track guidance system makes a marked reduction in bus lane width possible. The resulting savings in construction costs are particularly significant for such works as tunnels, bridges, etc. The best-known of such systems are developed and already in trial operation by both MAN and Mercedes in Germany.

Problems arise with mechanical guidance at junctions. Here the following possibilities exist:

1. Normal junctions without guidance system. Here the bus is driven, like any normal bus, by its driver on the driving wheel.
2. 'Active' points. These are guidance structures resembling rail crossings. They are, however, complicated and should only be used where a central control room is responsible for setting the points.
3. 'Passive' points. Here the bus driver determines the direction he wants to follow and directs the vehicle until the feeler roller touches the guide rail on the appropriate arm of the junction. A control system regulates the adhesion pressure on the guide rail. Steering right or left is done by the driver through a switch on the instrument board.

A version of the track guidance system which does away with the curb-like guidance tracks and uses only a central, very light, track in the form of a 4 cm 'crack' in the roadway, is the GLT (for **guided light transit**) system developed by GN of Belgium and soon beginning operation in Rochefort, Belgium.

The greatest advantage of the GLT system is its simple and non-obstructing guidance structure. This advantage is particularly important at junctions, which, because of the very light 'track', can be negotiated easily by all vehicles.

ELECTRONIC TRACK GUIDANCE

This is done by a pilot cable buried in the roadway, through which an alternating current flows, generating an electromagnetic field fed by an emitter at the roadside. The equipment on the bus consists of antennae, a supplementary hydraulic servo-steering system and the electronic controls. For safety reasons the entire system is usually of dual-channel (redundant) design.

The two steering channels alternate constantly. Each of these two functional groups of the active system of electronic steering unit can steer the vehicle independently.

A simulation computer and a fail-safe monitor guarantee safe and reliable operation. All conceivable errors and failures, even fracture of the pilot cable, can be so monitored and corrected as to completely eliminate danger.

The great advantage of the electronic guidance is the simple and non-obstructing solution for the guidance, which now does not require any impeding structures on the road surface. This fact greatly simplifies switches and crossings. Both 'active' and 'passive' junctions are possible in simple form, e.g. by switching the current in the control centre from one pilot cable to another or by the driver's switching to different frequencies in the pilot cable

Some concluding remarks

The advances in technology, which were briefly described above, show that the bus can be much more than just a vehicle 'swimming' along in the general traffic stream and having stops which are nothing more than just a post on the edge of the pavement. The developments already on the horizon show that it is well worth exploiting the unused reserve of the bus as a means of mass transport in urban areas. The components of the whole system, i.e. the 'vehicle', the 'roadway/bus stop' and the 'operational control', can be improved so as to form a comprehensive package from which each public transport authority can tailor a system fitting perfectly into its overall transit concept.

The bus has the great advantage over rail transport in that each individual measure or action that is planned can be immediately put to practical use, allowing a system to be built up stage by stage. In times of economic uncertainty, when difficulties are encountered in financing large-scale public investment, the appeal of public transit operations can be considerably increased for a relatively modest capital investment by upgrading the bus to a 'bus transit system'.

The above real possibilities are worth examining seriously according to the specific needs of each urban area. Needless to say, for the bulk of the normal day-to-day operations for public transport in the majority of urban areas, the internal combustion (thermal) buses, as we have known them to date, will continue to dominate the scene for many years to come.

Policy implications and issues

The existing and the expected developments in the area of public transport — and not only in this area — due to the rapid advances of the new technologies, call for appropriate national and European policies especially in the light of the forthcoming European unification. The basic elements, with respect to transport, characterising the new era already present in our lifetime are as follows:

1. Passenger needs will be increasing at a fairly high rate due to mobility and population increase. Public transport can, and has to, play an important role.
2. The competitive environment promoted by the EC will normally result in lower operating costs and increased productivity. RTI-based systems will be necessary to meet the new conditions.
3. The supplementary role of transport modes is continuously increasing. Both public and private transport, either urban or extra-urban, tend to complement each other rather than compete with each other.

Today, there seems to be a strong determination by the decision-makers and the politicians to take measures towards better living conditions, energy savings, etc. Governments (and the EC) will in principle have to intervene when:

● marked mechanisms fail to produce an overall 'desirable' system;
● they are directly involved as main 'beneficiaries' or 'intermediaries' (e.g. suppliers of frequency channels or communication lines); and
● they want to enforce, through RTI systems, other wider policies concerning the overall transportation system in the area.

In each of the three cases above, one can see a number of goals and objectives of intervention which have to be stated here because they will define (and restrain) the level of intervention and corresponding strategy. The most important of these goals are as follows:

- to restore equity in the use of public transport (with the free application of market mechanisms some groups of users may be at a disadvantage);
- to induce competition in cases where this is low. For example where there is no strong 'seller' or 'buyer' of RTI applications in the market.
- to avoid unnecessary development of incompatible systems through the introduction of appropriate technical and functional standards;
- to develop the necessary wider infrastructure that is the prerequisite for the development of successful systems;
- to provide minimum levels of service when the government itself is the provider of public transport (as in the case of many local governments);
- to induce use of the system in a way that produces wider benefits and not only more patronage for the operator. An example of such 'use' is to provide on-line data on passenger needs and preferences for the adjustment of the service very much in the way that monitoring the flow of vehicles is used as an input for adjustments to the service by the traffic control system;
- to integrate passenger information functions into larger information systems aiming at encouraging the use of the town; information about parking facilities, electronic newspapers, telereservation, etc. (with the implementation of multi servicing communication networks);
- to allow for time savings on the part of the user, by facilitating the use of a European network with the same knowledge (e.g. basic information functions).

The technical innovations of the last decade have been already partially incorporated in all domains of public transport, namely operations management, scheduling, passenger information, fare collection, maintenance, planning and management information as well as in the mechanical systems themselves. The degree of the new technology penetration varies from country to country and operator to operator, depending on a number of factors which affect and direct the decision-makers each time. The ownership status, the size, the competition, the operators' traditional attitude towards innovation and the overall and local economy are some of the most important ones. The adoption of suitable policies from central and local governments to promote and encourage the use of new technologies in the area, coupled with the appropriate financial motives should remain and/or become a high-priority aspect of all partners involved. The potential benefits from such a policy, it is believed, will be spread to the majority of people either directly or indirectly. The expected benefits among others include better and enhanced public transport passenger service, environment improvement, promotion of the public transport role, reduction in accidents and pollution, and as a result of the above, better living conditions in urban areas. Therefore, public transport with this new role can be and must be a part of the new integrated road transport environment for Europe.

References

CASSIOPE Project (1990) DRIVE Programme, Deliverable 3, *Operator Needs and Overall Requirement Report*, March.

CASSIOPE Project (1990) DRIVE Programme, Deliverable 1, *State of the Art on Computer Aided Technology in Public Transport*, March.

CASSIOPE Project (1990) DRIVE Programme, Deliverable 5.1, *Study of Functionalities in the User Information Domain*, May.

Giannopoulos, G. (1989) *Bus Planning and Operation in Urban Areas*. Avebury, UK.

MAN (1985) *Development for a Future Bus Transport System*, MAN Commercial Vehicle Division, March.

Meyere, A. (1989) *Urban Transport: Information for Passenger and New Technology*, EMCT.

Chapter 9

A scenario on the evolving possibilities for intelligent, safe and clean road transport

Ove Svidén

The objective of this scenario is to show possible paths of development. The role of the scenario is to synthesise the requirements and possibilities discussed in the previous pages into a feasible solution that in time can solve the environmental problems we have today. The scenario is meant to give the reader a hint of a feasible path of development in the future. The scenario is only meant to present a development that can happen. It is not necessarily a forecast of what will happen. The scenario is normative in its character. It shows one possible path towards a desired ecological road traffic. It is not an exploratory scenario with many alternative possibilities. The scenario is a tool to motivate the reader for the systems approach and R&D work. This is needed to provide us with such facts so that we can select the proper path towards the future.

It is assumed that it is not possible to solve the global emission problem with a technical fix in the vehicle engine system, or an additive to the fuel. The cause-and-effect chains go back to the long-range supply of primary energy. This relationship gives the vehicle emission issue its time dimension. The scenario is designed to give an impression of what we have to do during the next couple of decades, by seeing it from a century perspective. To give the scenario and the evolution it describes an easily grasped time dimension, it is formulated as stages for the years 2000, 2010, 2020, 2050 and with the year 2100 as a visionary and philosophical round-off.

The change in primary energy usage is one of the slowest moving changes we can observe in our society. New attitudes and lifestyles also change over long periods in time. The scenario is based upon a philosophical assumption that the environmental issue is a 'century question' similar to what liberalism and socialism have proved to be. Thus the environmental movement started as a protest against and critique of present society. The issue has now reached a level of concern that has made us start with the removal of some obviously harmful substances and by-products of our civilised life. It can later lead up to a global mind change (Harman, 1988), new scientific facts and engineering tools that enable us to create our support systems to be ecological by design. This can then end in a completely new ecological lifestyle, different living and working patterns and with new technological means for transport, communication and mobility.

The scenario also makes another assumption, that the **road transport informatics** (RTI) evolution, that just has started, can make only a limited improvement to the environment. However, the RTI programmes in Eureka and the EC can as a side-effect provide a number of technical/economical/organisational tools to manage also the long-range fuel/engine issue.

To grasp the future possibilities conceptually now, we have to base our reasoning on established language. To escape the limitations of this, a number of new word combinations and a few acronyms have been created. They indicate desirable synergies and possible future products. The acronyms are used to shorten the text, and are defined when first used.

The year 2000 scenario

Let us first see how far the road transport informatics (RTI) evolution has come. Assume that the dumb sun visor in cars has now been replaced with an intelligent one: a road transport informatics unit, called the RTI unit, in front and above the driver. It is small as the visor including chips for **European route guidance, parking guidance** and **automatic debiting**. It has a smart card reader for the TRAC (**transport access card**). It contains a transmitter and receiver for communication with roadside beacons. It has a matrix display at its lower end with a fresnel lens. The driver can see one row of symbols and a line of text on it as projected some 2 metres ahead of him. He can see the symbols with his peripheral vision. He can read text without major adjustments to his eye focus. He can scroll through presented information using a little joy-stick for his thumb on the steering-wheel. He can enter a command with the other key on the wheel. When at standstill, he can flip the RTI unit down to get access to a complete keyboard and display for general inputs, programming of standard destination addresses, etc.

The RTI unit can be installed in a car within an hour at a cost of ECU 200. (Many buy two units. The desktop one is used for trip planning.) The purchase and the installation can be done at any local RTI shop, franchisers to the transnational EUROADS utility organisation (European Utility for Road Operation, Administration, Development and Services). The proper use of all RTI functions can be learnt by using the desktop PC driving simulators. The local EUROADS shop can also give the help and driving instruction needed. The follow-on tutoring then is included as a function in the RTI unit. The pan-European installation of roadside beacons, traffic control centres and training of their personnel is also organised by EUROADS and performed by their regional service. Also included in this service is helping local traffic management with the trimming and updating of traffic light control systems to perform to the agreed European standard. In the EUROADS service handbook is included advice for parking and demand management as a means of curbing city congestion.

The first use of the **European route guidance** is to assist car drivers in selecting the best parking options and guide them to it in an efficient way. The parking fee is debited automatically from the smart card. Coming to a service station to 'fill her up' also includes the automatic fill-up of parking money in the smart TRAC card from cash payment or from the owner's bank account. The cash flow from these **automatic debiting** of user charges forms the capital for the escalating implementation of European **route guidance** organised by EUROADS. The use of the RTI unit for all types of personal navigation is so efficient and enjoyable that it hides the fact from most users that they have accepted a parking meter with automatic enforcement in their car! This is the first important step for creating the cash flow needed for the future road infrastructure development needed for traffic efficiency. It will also be used as a means for road users to 'pay their way' to an ecologically efficient road traffic.

The commercial vehicle fleets and public transport vehicles are scrapping some of their outmoded and redundant radio communication equipment in favour of the RTI units plus mobile telephones. They also install and use extra RTI chips and software as add-ons. Functions thus tested are **dispatch planning, vehicle location and load management.** Commercial vehicles and executive automobiles used as mobile offices are also installing the chips and co-driver servos needed for **intelligent cruise control** with speed and distance-keeping to the vehicle in front. A **lane keeping** function is also tested. But these are possible to use on motorways and in the fast lane on some main roads only. Commercial vehicles act as pioneer consumers for RTI functions. Lines of commercial vehicles in dense formations on the main roads and motorways are also more common now than ten years ago.

Drivers and automobile clubs do not like the situation where there are long slow lines of heavy vehicles to overtake. The accompanying emission and safety problems are not acceptable. Union action puts pressure to obtain a better working environment for the truckers. They do not like to be travelling efficiently behind other diesel vehicles, with an odour of high pollutant emission. Similar requirements come from bus passenger in urban areas. After the successful introduction of catalysts for cars with petrol engines, the diesel exhaust and odour problem has become more apparent. Reformed diesel and fuel mixtures of 20 per cent diesel fuel and 80 per cent methanol or natural gas are being used more frequently to reduce the problems. Trucks and buses equipped with extra pressure tanks for compressed natural gas can be seen in sensitive urban areas. This is not so much the result of good foresight or European planning but rather the afterthoughts from a number of traumatic smog catastrophes in the early 1990s.

Regarding the supply of primary energy, the changes in Europe are slow but determined. Between the years 1990 and 2000, total primary energy in Western Europe will have grown by 2.1 per cent annually compared with the average 2.4 per cent p.a. for the previous nine decades. Oil has fallen in its relative position from 45 to 40 per cent of TPE in a decade. Natural gas has increased its share from 15 to 20 per cent in the same time. Coal has remained at 20 per cent. And the share of nuclear power has grown from 11 per cent to a plateau of 13 per cent of TPE. Crude oil is still the dominant primary energy form, but natural gas is 'the rising giant' for Europe. But Western Europe is still far behind the Commonwealth of Soviet States which have increased their natural gas share from 39 to 45 per cent in the same decade.

In parallel with the above events in society, the pan-European R&D Programme for Emission Control, Transportation Fuels, Energy Conversion and Supply has been silently working for seven years. It has been a joint venture between the Commission of the European Communities and the European automobile, oil and power industries. The end result of this work is that some new clean fuels are recommended. They have to be produced and distributed on a large scale. The implementation plan suggests a gradual move towards hydrogen as the long-term solution and methanol as the most feasible intermediate fuel. For the coming decades, **liquid petroleum gas** (LPG) and **compressed natural gas** (CNG) are proposed as clean fuels derived from the petroleum refinery process of crude oil and natural gas. The second part of the proposal includes three hybrid engine systems designed to make the most efficient use of the clean fuels above.

In summary then, by the year 2000, traffic will have become a bit more efficient with electronics. The traffic environment is determined by the use of petroleum products and conventional petrol and diesel engines. The organisation EUROADS has been established with vested interests from governments and the automobile, energy and IT industries. It now has the authority to purchase the development of future ecologically efficient fuel/engine hybrid systems.

The year 2010 scenario

Standardised RTI systems are now mandatory in the European Community for all new cars produced. The RTI impacts on traffic are now becoming visible. Traffic is denser, due to growing transport demands, but the flow is smoother and more efficient. Safety levels are only slightly better than a decade ago. A small positive effect on the environment from RTI has been screened by the growth in traffic volume. The somewhat cleaner air surrounding traffic today is due to the use of clean fuels and catalyst-equipped engines. The operational driving task is regarded more and more as a boring nuisance. The joy of driving has been lifted to a tactical level, as a play with information. The road-pricing functions let the drivers experience directly the cost to society of their driving in congested traffic and within emission-sensitive areas. The tutoring function represents a new game drivers can play with themselves to improve their performance when driving.

The EUROADS utility has become a strong transnational corporation. It acts as a 'technology pull' agent and as a competent systems buyer of RTI, not only of products from the IT industry. EUROADS acts on the strength of a long-range clean fuel implementation plan and from a responsibility through its national companies for the administration of cash flow from all pan-European road usage into R&D. Based on its operative engagement and service provision, EUROADS can formulate the requirement for new RTI systems. EUROADS has the role of speci-fying functions and requirements for future European traffic. With the accumulated cash flow from the road-pricing functions they get the financial authority to specify and plan the future. By the year 2010 the goals for safety improvements will be of prime concern. Also EUROADS has financed the systematic and long-range R&D and Demonstration Programme for the new clean engine/fuel system required to meet the long-range ecological needs. In parallel with this the crucial hydrogen fuel distribution system is now being planned.

By the year 2010 the hybrid engine systems will be industry projects still at the laboratory stage, trying to prove themselves capable of a quantum jump in ecological efficiency. EUROADS is in a position to license them for use on a limited scale in real traffic. Fleet tests and pilot schemes are being arranged to prove the feasibility of the new family of hybrid solutions. But they are still the challengers. It is still the petrol engines and diesel engines that have the market. With catalysts and cleaner fuel mixes, and with many other add-on/after-thought solutions, it is still the Ottos and Diesels that give the traffic its pulse. With a 3 per cent average growth in traffic volume per year, traffic has doubled since 1987.

As road users are now paying their way, via the road-use pricing scheme, to more efficient, safe and ecological road transport system solutions, they are regularly informed about R&D progress. There is a wave of rising expectations. Now the drivers are beginning to realise the limitations in the old technology of noisy, vibrating, IC engines, manual gear shifts, manual chokes, and cold starts. At the same time automobile industries still make a good profit out of their automated engine manufacturing plants invested in some decades ago. The hybrid engine projects are carried further by a set of new company conglomerates with know-how and venture capital from the petroleum industry, power industry and those automobile industries with a engine development tradition. Most automobile manufac-turers are becoming more systems and market-oriented. They are looking forward to the time when they can buy the power pack as a component to add among others to their 'fashion products'.

There is a plan for long-term hydrogen supply, but no volume production and distribution yet. The clean hydrogen fuel can be seen as a derivative from uranium, used as the primary energy. In the first generation atomic plants of the last century, only some 1 per cent of the atomic energy content was used. A residue was left that was still 99 per cent fuel. It became obvious that the nuclear power of the twentieth century was only a very first step towards a more integrated nuclear fuel processing and power plant system. The Three Mile Island incident and the Chernobyl accident showed that there were lessons to be learned. But it also proved that nuclear safety is manageable. The safety level of nuclear power has been achieved with very few lives sacrificed compared with the development of the accepted safety level for air travel. Millions of lives, however, still have to be lived before road traffic is made safe by design.

By the year 2010 a number of second-generation nuclear power plant designs will have proved their reliability and safety. They are tailored to the nuclear fuel reprocessing cycles. These power stations are designed for a range of applications ranging from district heating, electricity generation and hydrogen generation. The nuclear fuel cycle is designed for, and will interact with, the above power plants. The fuel generation and reprocessing is designed to be a closed feedback loop. In principle, the nuclear fuel residues from the twentieth century can be recycled to 'fuel' the entire twenty-first century! At the end of the process (and of the century) an energy-consuming fusion torch is suggested to transform the squeezed-out nuclear fuel residues into stable and non-radiating matter.

Large infrastructure investments are needed for the development of the nuclear-hydrogen fuel cycles. A hydrogen pipeline distribution system is needed. EUROADS helps finance this via the operation of its road-use pricing scheme. Such a 'user cost for infrastructure' scheme is needed to generate the cash flow for the very costly investments in the clean hydrogen fuel supply and distribution along the roads of Europe. The pan-European EUROADS utility organisation is asked to take a wider responsibility for the supply of hydrogen fuels, and add the 'clean road transport' as a new service to the road users. With a vested interest in EUROADS, the automobile and energy industries can now more safely pursue their development of the new hybrid engines.

The year 2020 scenario

The **road transport informatics** evolution now has proved its merits for traffic efficiency. The equipment has proved its reliability. It can now be used to control a number of safety functions. This also means that all road vehicles by law also have to include automatic gear shifts, ABS brakes with anti-spin and anti-skid functions, and servo-controlled engine and brake functions to make their RTI safety functions work. These are expensive add-on systems to the traditional twentieth-century vehicle concept. But they are integrated in the design of the new hybrid engine systems. This gives these challengers a flying start for their market introduction. But by 2020 their market share will be still only some 10 per cent. So their impact on emission levels in the year 2020 will be hardly noticeable on a continental scale. However, as public transport has acted as prime consumers of qualified hybrid engine systems for their buses, you will be able to feel, smell and hear the improvements in city areas.

Even if all new heavy vehicles, buses and some automobiles by now are manufactured with hybrids of some sort, the traffic on the roads is still dominated by vehicles with petrol and diesel engines, even if their production has almost finished (in Europe). Some of the automated engine factories have moved to other continents, some of them are still left in Europe. The engines are then exported to the less-developed regions of the world.

The IRTE, an **integrated road transport environment** for Europe has now taken shape and traffic is now characterised by a more mature and cultivated appearance. The original goal on transport and traffic efficiency increase has been met. The optical 'noise' from signs and message boards along roads is beginning to disappear. Most signs had to be taken away as they became redundant and their inflexible information is in conflict with effective RTI-assisted driving.

Commercial traffic with heavy trucks, buses, para-transit, delivery vans and executive cars is made even more efficient by the use of **integrated transport management functions** in addition to the above. Also the possibility of **lane-keeping functions** are tested. In a few high speed lanes columns of cars can move in close formation at speeds of 100–150 km/h. The requirement is that the car-following platoon is led by a vehicle fully equipped with high grade RTI facilities. In a few slower lanes at night you can see lines of heavy vehicles with human drivers only in the first vehicle.

EUROADS concentrates on trimming the integrated road transport environment in Europe. The traffic efficiency goals have been met by means of the Road Transport Informatics. Road traffic safety has been improved, yes, but not to the level possible with the new integrated hybrid engines with their servo-control functions. EUROADS has a responsibility to secure the supply and distribution of hydrogen fuel on a pan-European scale. When this hydrogen fuel implementation programme is finished by the year 2017, the vehicle engine industry conglomerates could start marketing their 'components' to the automobile industries.

By the year 2020 hydrogen fuels, which have been used by the space industry for decades, may now start to be used also as prime fuel for airline operations. The know-how and experience from this aerospace pioneering helps EUROADS to establish a network of service stations capable of maintaining and servicing these new machines. As the hybrid engines have a reliable and MTBF (**mean time between failures**) that is two orders of magnitudes better than the Otto's and factor of 10 better than the Diesel's, the service level is expected to be very low. But service personnel have to be trained in the rapid removal and plugging-in of a new hybrid power pack in 30 minutes flat. It is part of the new EUROADS service improvement programme.

By the year 2020 natural gas will have become the dominant primary energy fuel in the world energy mix. Some of the natural gas will be transformed into hydrogen with the help of nuclear power. This is done in power plants above petroleum fields. The hot carbon dioxide obtained from the steam reforming of natural gas is then used for tertiary petroleum recovery. By reinjecting the carbon dioxide into the petroleum layers of old fields, their yield can increase at the same time as the carbon dioxide is buried. A mixture of hydrogen and natural gas is then delivered to the European conurbations for use in industry, homes and transport.

Natural gas is by now also the important feedstock to the fast growing plastics industry. Carbon fibre structures are gradually replacing the steel in automobiles. The slender elevated highways proposed for high-speed light vehicles are to be built in stiff carbon fibre sections. The building industry is starting to look at carbon fibres for housing structures in general. This use of carbon plastics materials is a way of reducing the carbon content in fuels, and thus also in the long-term of reducing the carbon dioxide in the atmosphere.

The year 2050 scenario

Pan-European road traffic is now efficient, safe and clean by design. Ecological road vehicles run smoothly on their high-capacity **trans-urbia network**. Its roads, fibre-optics, electrical power and gas energy supply link every single home with all the services of the city.

The road transport system serves the users and society well. Traffic is humane and inherently safe by design and operational control. The new ecological vehicles are silent and clean. The sealed hydrogen/hybrid power pack is by now a standardised component, mass produced and serves anonymously in all brands of road vehicles. The four 'intelligent servo wheels' of a modern car perform their steering, propulsion and retardation duty with unprecedented comfort and high safety margins.

The road transport informatics technology is now mature and thoroughly tested. Systems are 'shaken down' to their essential functions, and are now working with unprecedented reliability and high availability. The on-board RTI unit, now on one megachip, includes the functions for **integrated European route guidance, automatic debiting, speed guidance, dynamic speed keeping, lane keeping, car following** and basic **collision**

warning. The **tutoring function** can compensate for most types of driver handicap. The **road-pricing scheme** is efficiently distributing the costs to those who benefit, and raises the capital needed for further infrastructure improvements. The intelligent roads define the structure of the dispersed **trans-urbia** with its high **info-Mobility**.

Transport is effective. Mobility is high. People rely on safe and efficient road transport for their dispersed living and working patterns outside the stagnating city cores. And car driving is now more related to local airports and their service and club facilities than to city commuting. Road transport and traffic volumes, however, are decreasing, as regional and continental air transport is taking over more and more in Europe. The facilities for meetings and conferences around airports are becoming the hubs of real power and influence, rather than the old city centres.

The emission problem is in essence solved by the integrated hydrogen supply and conversion systems. The natural gas distribution grid is now gradually transporting more hydrogen than methane. When speaking of energy supply in the year 2050, it is worth noting that in the press, in daily speech and in people's minds, the word gas is used more and more as a synonym for energy since natural gas became the dominating primary energy after oil in Europe. Together, the old electricity grid and the gas grid now give a very high degree of reliability in the energy supply.

Some of the electricity and the hydrogen is produced locally from wet solar cells on the roofs of the family homes. Most of it, however, still comes from natural gas and nuclear power. Some of the natural gas is upgraded via nuclear power and steam-reforming to hydrogen energy. This removes the carbon content from the gas in the form of carbon dioxide. Part of it is reinjected in old oil fields for tertiary oil recovery. Part is used in the production of carbon fibre plastics. By the year 2050 it will be used as the dominant building material for cities, vehicles and transport infrastructure, replacing the heavy concrete and steel used in the last century. Prefabricated carbon fibre homes and office buildings are airlifted from the factory to the place of use.

For Europe, the intelligent road transport and traffic integration has had similar effects, as had the Rhine Commission and its improvements on river transports for the unification of Germany. The integrated road transport environment improvements have spread like waves over Europe and are now exported to the economically vital Middle East and Africa. EUROADS is rich, powerful and a corner-stone for the united Europe spanning the continent from the regions of Ireland to DR (Democratic Russia), and from LL (Liberated Lappland) to Israel.

The automobile industry with its ten-year product cycle had first to relate to the IT industry and its one-year tempo, then yield to the energy industry and its half-century-long development cycles. The surviving automobile industry has developed into transcontinental GISCs (**giant industrial system complexes**), thus evading some of the more shortsighted continental politics with its geographical limitations. The gas energy conversion systems, both on the supply side and the vehicle side, are produced by the energy GISCs. The creative dialogue between government and industry goes on at international airpolis, with the public ecosophic debate over TV as catalyst and democratic feedback.

The year 2100 scenario

Different forms of nuclear power give the world its primary energy. The natural gas pipeline and gas distribution network is called HYGRID now because the gas coming to consumers is clean hydrogen. All the carbon content in natural gas is now removed and used for the plastics and carbon fibre industry. All industrial and household hydrogen is catalytically combusted. The transportation sector uses hydrogen as its prime fuel. A number of Hybrid engine systems transform the hydrogen energy into desirable forms for comfort, levitation and propulsion.

The natural gas resources made it possible to finance the building of HYGRID. Now this very network is also used for the hydrogen era. Together with the electricity transmission grid and supply network, the continents now have a secure and clean energy supply. Whenever a pipeline of cable has been laid or a road, rail or vacuum tube connection has been built, the appropriate fibre-optic cables have been included. This means that the communication infrastructure by the year 2100 is following the energy and transportation networks. High-quality information can be achieved in all buildings over the entire pan-Europe. The micro-cell mobile telephone network makes most of the telecom facilities available also in vehicles.

Euromobility is high with the ecological vehicles on the intelligent roads. Vacuum trains in tunnels and on elevated tubes transfer passengers and light goods quickly between the mega-cities. Air travel with silent vortex lifts STOL aircraft between 5,000 local airports in Europe, giving good access to all regions. Heavy goods transport is provided with airships (filled with waste helium gas from the fusion reactors). The building industry is distributing all its carbon fibre houses, office and industry modules by using these airlifts.

The large-scale primary energy production for the future is now coming from fusion power — in the sun! Each new house has its wet solar cell system that absorbs the solar energy and transforms it into electricity and hydrogen. Hydrogen is used for storage, personal transport and also for the nearby industrial processes.

The crucial environmental problems are solved now. The decentralised living and working pattern is now predominant. The industry modules are commuted to the people by airlifts. The service modules provide the households with goods and fresh food. People travel on average one hour per day as was also the case a hundred years ago. But now in the year 2100, the trips are longer, less frequent and for pleasure. The commuting to work syndrome has been replaced with travel for creative development work, social contacts, education, recreation and other personal growth activities.

The lifestyles have had time to change in order to lead the way to the above-mentioned dispersed society. Now, in hindsight, it can be said that it was the change in human attitudes and values from an 'analytical science-based industrial growth' paradigm to the holistic environmentalism that started this evolution. It was the new holism, life sciences, environmentalism and systems approach that in the end provided the creative researchers of the twenty-first century with an appropriate answer to the fusion problem. And now by the end of it we see the possibility of using it in our transport vehicles for the twenty-second century. For an automobile, a fusion cell cluster, including the hydrogen fuel for its entire lifetime, can be built into a 100 litre and 100 kilogram compact power pack. This is at least what the network of fusion inventors claims. But before we take a stand on the issue, we need to perform a major pan European systems approach study on the issue.

Reference

Harman, W. (1988) *Global Mind Change*, Knowledge Systems Inc., Indianapolis.

Chapter 10

Technical changes in the telecommunications sector

R. Capello and R. Camagni

Introduction[1]

The aim of this chapter is to highlight technical change taking place in the telecommunications sector, justifying and explaining from a technical point of view the development of a new techno-economic paradigm (Freeman et al., 1982).

In fact, structural changes taking place in the economy are partly the result of a great and pervasive technological revolution, opening the way for greater exploitation of information flows and for wider access to information (see next section on the main features of the new technological paradigm).

Computer networks have been defined as the 'quintessence' of information technology (Gillespie and Williams, 1988) for their capacity to manipulate, transmit, store and process a larger amount of information. This chapter deals with technical changes under way in the three major components of computer networks — transmission, switching and terminal equipment — obtaining in this way a broad-based analysis of the changing technical process (see the third section on technical changes).

Technological changes open the way to the development of a wide variety of services and networks with different technological profiles. Possible future development trajectories are presented (see the fourth section on future developments), for both networks and services, in order to show the increasing importance and the strategic use of these services to achieve better economic performances for corporate users.

Technical changes generate positive economic effects if they are interrelated with organisational changes, creating the possibility for adopting the present economic structure for technical solutions which are different from technical innovations of the previous techno-economic paradigm. The competitiveness of firms and comparative advantages of regions increasingly depend on the use of information-intensive techniques rather than on the capital-intensive techniques which were typical of the last techno-economic paradigm. An analysis of the interrelationships between technical change and its economic effects will be presented from the basic premise that technological change is an *exogenous* factor of change, but that nevertheless the economic impact of this change is far from being evident and obvious. The simple adoption and diffusion of new technologies is in fact a necessary but not sufficient condition for achieving better economic performance (see the fifth section on the economic impact).

The strategic importance of the development of the telecommunications sector for the competitiveness of territorial and industrial systems suggests some public policy recommendations, which are presented in the sixth section.

Main features of the new technological paradigm

Many economists have emphasised the importance of the contribution of technological change to economic development. Measuring the exact relationship of economic growth to technical progress is fraught with difficulties, but, for example, Solow (1957) estimated that 80 per cent of growth in the US economy between 1909 and 1949 could be attributed to technological change. Schumpeter (1939) underlined the role of technological change in his theoretical approach to economic growth, explaining the cyclical patterns of growth and employment in terms of technical and organisational innovation.

More recently the relationship between technological change and economic development has been emphasised by Freeman et al. (1982), as well as by Perez (1983), who divided technical innovations into three classes — incremental, radical and revolutionary — and defined periods of growth as the result of a 'goal-matching' between the emerging 'techno-economic' paradigm and the socio-political and legal institutions.

At present, a new techno-economic paradigm is being established as the result of radical technological changes in the electronics sector and, in particular, in microelectronics. These radical technological changes create a new basis for economic development, abolish new rules of competition and impose different organisational structures on economic operators. The core fundamental technologies (active components, data-processing hardware, telecommunications switching-equipment and software) generate by their interaction a host of incremental innovations and from them a new wave of economic development.

The technological revolution taking place in the last two decades allowed a process of *integration* amongst different sectors. The typical example of this phenomenon is the integration between computer science and telecommunications, creating what the French termed the **telematics** sector.

At the same time, the computer has become more and more *central* to the development of communication and information structures: the integration of hardware and software systems characterises the present

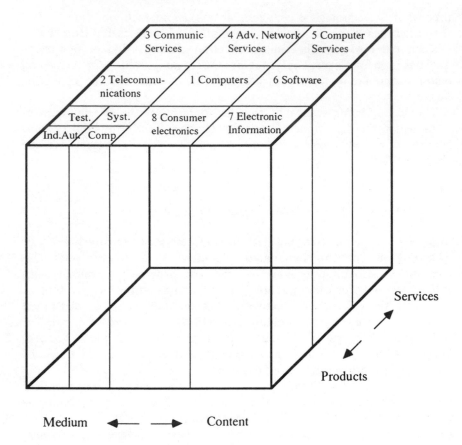

Figure 10.1   The information technologies map.

Source: Camagni, 1986.

technological development. In a technical sense, convergence involves the ability to use a single technology across areas which used to be regarded as separate: notably data processing, word processing and telecommunications. Microprocessors, for example, perform crucial roles in all three areas (Arnold and Guy, 1987).

The emerging process is described and synthesised in Figure 10.1, a revised version of the famous Harvard information map. The process under way is characterised by two integration levels:

- A first level is amongst four traditional pre-existing systems: communication services, computer services, electronic information and professional electronics. As a result of this integration process, new areas, or new 'systems', take place, and are presented in the overlapping areas of the four traditional systems in our map.
- A second level is a general integration of all areas or 'systems' with

Table 10.1 The information technology market — 1986 (millions of US dollars)

	USA	Japan	Europe 4*	Total 6 major countries	Other countries in the world	World
Computers	44,239	21,095	24,666	90,000	24,794	114,794
Software	16,298	2,570	6,768	25,636	5,291	30,927
Services	27,837	6,527	12,899	47,263	10,976	58,239
Office machines	10,624	1,180	3,904	15,708	3,511	19,219
TLC	24,080	7,920	13,006	45,006	14,104	59,110
Total limited IT	123,078	39,292	61,243	223,613	58,676	282,289
Others	97,259	47,569	43,239	188,067	56,176	244,243
Total IT	220,337	86,861	104,482	411,680	114,852	526,532

Note: * France, Italy, UK, Germany.

Source: Camagni, 1987.

the core area, that of the computer. Traditional hardware systems, such as switching and terminal equipment, are today characterised by both hardware and software components.

If the information technologies map is interpreted in that way, it becomes a useful operational instrument to evaluate the information technology market. Figure 10.2 represents the market of **information technologies** in six major countries (USA, Japan, Italy, France, Germany, UK) in 1986. The areas are proportional to the value of their markets (see Table 10.1).

The implementation of these new technologies is a very complicated process, concerning all sectors of the economy, and of society as a whole. It is also an expensive process in terms of the financial, human and capital resources involved and requires many organisational changes within the economy and society. The widespread generalisation of the new technological paradigm in the economy as a whole is dependent upon the adaptive capacity of social and political institutions to the requirements of the new economic order. Change is necessary in numerous institutions, including education and training; industrial relationships; managerial and corporate structures; management styles; capital markets and financial systems. It has been argued that 'the structural crisis of the 1980's is in this perspective a prolonged period of social adaption to this new paradigm' (Freeman, 1986). The diffusion of a new wave of innovations based on new technologies creates many changes. The aim of this chapter is simply to highlight the technological changes creating and supporting this new paradigm.

Technical changes

The last two decades have been characterised by a continuous development in information communications networks and facilities due to fundamental and pervasive technological changes. The integration of telecommunications and computer science brought about the birth of a new sector, namely the 'telematic' sector, and consequently the creation of new services and communications networks.

For an in-depth analysis of technological innovation taking place in the last two decades, a separation of the different computer network hardware components is extremely useful. A computer network system consists of three major components:

1. transmission equipment;
2. switching-equipment;
3. terminal equipment.

In each of these subsystems profound and radical changes are taking place.

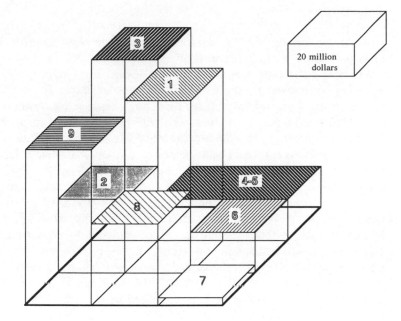

1 = Computers   2 = Telecommunications   3 = Communication services
4 = Adv. network services   5 = Computer services   6 = Software
7 = Electronic information   8 = Consumer electronics   9 = Professional electronics
9.1= Electr. components   9.2= Electr. for Ind. Automat.   9.3= Systems electronics
9.4= Electronic testing, measure and medical equipments

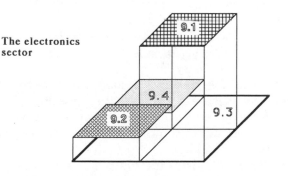

The electronics sector

Figure 10.2 The market of information technologies in six major countries*
                1986

Note: * USA, Japan, Germany, France, Italy, UK.

Source: Camagni, 1987.

Transmission equipment

Concerning the transmission equipment, both the physical infrastructures and the nature of the transmission are changing.

Physical infrastructures have usually been combinations of copper wires and microwaves, these being the ones available for transmission media. Both these infrastructures now have replaceable systems.

In 1962 the invention of the laser made possible the transportation of information through fibre-optic cables. This innovation has still been developing in recent years and generates not only a radical increase in transport capacities of the network, but also improves the signal quality, reduces noise and interference: in fact, while the traditional copper cables require the 'regeneration' of the message every 2–3 km, fibre-optic cables can transport it for 50 km without the necessity of 'improving' it. Moreover, fibre-optic cables provide wideband infrastructures, a characteristic which helps the integration between traditional communications services and 'new value-added' services (Camagni, 1986).

The development of fibre-optic is still continuing: one of the first applications of fibre-optic in Italy appeared in 1985 (e.g. the creation of a fibre-optic network within the Trade Fair in Milan) Capello, 1988 and 1989), but there are problems and realisations in long-distance networking projects because of the high financial resources required.

The other traditional transmission medium, microwave radio, can now be replaced with satellites. These were introduced commercially around the mid-1960s and opened the way to inter-continental communications. With this new means communications costs diminished by 40 per cent in comparison with the use of copper wire cables.

In addition to development in transmission media, the nature of the transmission system, consisting of one or a number of separate data-carrying circuits, is also likely to change. With the applications of microelectronics and 'integrated circuits' in telecommunications equipments, the 'digitalisation' of the transmission system can be exploited. Electric impulses are no longer waves transmitted with an analogue system, rather information is coded and transmitted following the binary system.

The earliest forms of data transmission, necessitating a digital transmission system, were achieved by the modification of standard PTT voice transmission lines. Output data signals are generated in a digital form by the computer, and are then modulated into an 'analogue' format voice line by the use of **modem** (modulator–demodulator). Initially signals of 110 digital bits per seconds were available. Gradual improvements, especially in line quality, led to 300, 600, 1,200, 2,400, 4,800 and 9,600 bps (bytes per second).

From these innovations a drastic reduction in transmission costs is expected, as well as an improvement in communications quality as far as speed and reliability are concerned.

Switching-equipment

As concerns switching-equipment, current innovation has improved electro-mechanical switching into digital electronic systems.

The most efficient and modern switching-equipment is the 'packet data' system, typical of the so-called packet switched networks.

Data are in this case carried over a computer network in 'packets', each of which holds the sender's and the recipient's addresses on the network. In this way, each 'packet' of information follows the carrying lines free at the moment of its transmission. Packets are then put together at the destination, where they arrive following different trajectories, and information is reconstructed by means of a packet assembler. The result of this form of switching is a much more rational exploitation of the network with accompanying increases in quality and speed of transported information.

The 'digitalisation' process under way in both transmission and switching systems opens the way for the exploitation of a single network to transport voice, data, texts and images. The aim of all industrialised countries in the development of telecommunications is the implementation of an **integrated service digital network** (ISDN), whose role would be the unique transmission structure. All developed countries, apart from Italy and Spain, are experimenting with the use of this new infrastructure. Meanwhile, networks have been introduced in order to offer subscribers efficient transmission lines and communication facilities, separate from the traditional telephone network, whose improvement and modernisation is a primary task for all national services providers.

The creation of modern transmission infrastructures allows the delivery of a wider range of services, namely 'value-added services'. Their feature is to be able to transmit and elaborate information at the same time. Audio and video-conferencing, videotex, teletex, EDI, electronic mail, just to quote some of them, are all the result of this technological revolution.

Terminal equipment

Finally, terminal equipment is also subject to drastic changes. The technological process occurring in this respect can be summarised in the idea that terminal equipment is transformed from simple hardware machines to complicated and sophisticated hardware and software systems. The 'intelligence' of the network was in the past strongly centralised in large mainframe machines located in computer centres. The current trend is a process of 'decentralisation' of part of the central memory capacity to network terminal equipment, allowing in this way the more efficient functioning of the network because of a more fully distributed memory capacity. The results of this process include, for example, telefax machines capable of memorising time and destination of a communication, and transmitting it at the required time, and teletex machines with internal memory being able to remember arrival times of communications and whether each communication has been collected.

Future developments

The radical technological changes taking place explain the increasing range of networks and communication facilities characterising the recent past. Generally speaking, and in view of the previous discussion, the new technologies in the field are expected to implement in the future:

- **digitalisation**, which makes it possible to process much larger amounts and new forms of data (such as moving images);
- the use of **optical fibres**, which makes it possible to transmit information at considerably higher rates and at much lower cost;
- the integration of **microelectronics** components and software;
- the development of **satellite links**.

These technological advances, which will sooner or later render current techniques obsolete, will bring about a decisive improvement in the way in which the human voice, data and images are transmitted and processed, and will make possible the much more widespread use of communication networks which fully exploit their interactive potential (OECD, 1988a and 1988b).

Networks

In addition to the traditional telephone network, a new advanced communications infrastructure with different technological profiles will be developed in order to speed up the availability of the advantages of rapid transmission rates to corporate users. Digital networks such as the **public data network** (PDN) in Great Britain, **Transpac** in France and **Itapac** in Italy, each using packet-switching networks, allow a quick and efficient communication linkage amongst business and institutional subscribers. The development of dedicated leased circuit networks (for intra-organisational or closed group uses) which provide sophisticated services, often in advance of those provided on public switched networks, has created incentives to reduce artificial barriers to the transmission of voice and data signals between networks and for a reduction in restriction on the uses which can be made of different types of facilities.

The countries of the European Community have committed themselves to the ISDN concept: a single network that will serve a wide variety of user needs by supplying a broad range of telecommunications services.

The development of this infrastructure is based on common technical standards in all EC countries, thus assuring the physical interconnection of the network across countries.

ISDN, working at speeds of 64,000 to 160,000 bits per second (bps) will transfer two to seven pages of text per second. Switching and connection time is to be no more than 2 seconds between any users' terminals, and generally much lower. ISDN will also be much more flexible than existing public switched networks, including such features as user-to-user signalling to help establish application protocols before connection, and point-to-multi-point transmissions.

Technical potentialities have already generated the possibility for a broadband telecommunications network that works in the range of 10 to 100 megabits per second. Fibre-optics happens to fit that need, and currently the telecommunications carriers are debating the possibility of skipping narrowband ISDN and moving directly to broadband ISDN via fibre-optics, at least for service to the office, if not the home (Casali, 1986; Solomon, 1987).

The technological features of ISDN will allow subscribers to communicate data, text, images and voice on the same physical infrastructure with a guaranteed interconnection amongst countries, because of common communication standards.

The introduction so far of ISDN in selected OECD countries shows different geographical penetration of this technological innovation (Zanfei, 1990).

The problem in the implementation of this network is not technological, which entirely depends on the amount of financial resources involved in the implementation of the project, which vary from country to country, but the definition of the value of this network for corporate users. In the USA ISDN has already been used to signify, rather than 'integrated services digital network', the words 'innovation subscribers don't need'. This negative attitude towards the implementation of the ISDN underlines the existing gap between the supply of technological potentialities and the real needs of users. The implementation of such technologies is related to innovation in subscribers' uses, rather than to innovation in technologies *per se*.

All developed countries are investing financial resources in the development of modern communications infrastructures. It has been recognised that these are strategic means for the economic and social development of nations. The enormous amount of financial resources involved, shown in Table 10.2 for four selected European countries, explains the strategic importance of the development of these infrastructures. More significant is the share of national GNP accounted for by investments in telecommunications, which has grown from 1981 to 1987 in Italy, Germany and Great Britain, while in France it has remained constant at high levels (Table 10.3).

More than ever, this technological development can create a gap

Table 10.2 Investments in telecommunications (billions of Italian lire)

	Italy	France	Germany	United Kingdom
1981	2,756	4,918	5,699	3,326
1982	3,669	4,992	6,633	3,496
1983	4,460	5,136	7,150	3,527
1984	4,935	5,572	8,550	4,339
1985	5,348	7,621	10,213	4,863
1986	5,535	8,526	11,035	4,721
1987	5,983	7,998	11,999	5,060
1981/87	32,686	44,763	61,279	29,332
1988	7,315	–	–	–

Source: Capello, 1991.

Table 10.3 Share of investments in telecommunications of GNP (percentage value)

	1981	1982	1983	1984	1985	1986	1987	1988
Italy	0.59	0.67	0.71	0.68	0.66	0.61	0.61	0.68
France	0.74	0.67	0.64	0.63	0.76	0.79	0.70	–
Germany	0.73	0.75	0.72	0.78	0.85	0.82	0.82	–
United Kingdom	0.57	0.54	0.51	0.58	0.56	0.57	0.58	–

Source: Capello, 1991.

amongst countries, allowing more developed nations to have a higher rate of adoption. Italian development policies, for example, are limited by the modernisation process of the traditional telephone network, absorbing at the moment a very high percentage of national resources devoted to the telecommunications sectors and thus postponing the full implementation of modern networks.

Services

The resulting convergence of telecommunications, data processing and audio-visual media will alter the nature of telecommunications and considerably widen the range of services proposed. The number of potential new services is virtually unlimited, with each differing in some degree from the others (Table 10.4). This increase in variety is essentially due to two major factors: **digitalisation**, since digital systems are by their very nature transparent to the signals they carry, unlike analogue systems; and the **effects of microelectronics** in terms of the price, reliability and size of the available hardware.

These technological innovations will initially make it possible to improve and generalise the existing services: the telephone, telex, teletex and low-speed data transmission. However, they will above all lead to the creation of new telecommunications infrastructure and the development of entirely new services, which can be divided into two groups:

- **second generation services**, which presuppose the improvement of the existing infrastructures with digital data transmission. Demand for this category of services is already making itself felt. Such demand comes from business users and concerns electronic mail, text processing (including electronic storage and retrieval), high-resolution videotex, audio-conferencing, etc. Demand for services of this type has grown considerably (Figure 10.3) and is expected to reach 10 per cent of traffic by 1993, from only 3 per cent at the beginning of the 1980s (Scarpinato, 1991).
- **third generation services** or broadband services (person-to-person communications incorporating text, voice and pictures), the introduction of which will require new telecommunications infrastructures (fibre-optics or satellites). Some of these services are being offered to business or residential users under experimental programmes designed to test their impact and feasibility. The demand for these services has to be generated and will initially stem from businesses, before gradually spreading to homes.

The adoption process of these services depends on what has been defined as the 'telecommunications learning cycle' (Bar et al., 1989). During the first stage, companies use networks to replace existing labour-intensive processes in a straightforward attempt to reduce their costs and speed up their operations. This stage has also been defined as the 'substitution' phase (Camagni and Capello, 1989), in that new services substitute for coastering facilities, improving their efficiency and quality. For example, companies use fax or electronic mail instead of the Post Office to send letters and memos, or on-line file transfers rather than shipment of magnetic tapes or discs.

During the second stage, or 'innovation' phase, companies use telecommunications to transform the way their employees interact and work, exploiting the technology's potential to articulate more efficient and effective work processes.

The first stage is easier to achieve, in that the adoption of these services does not alter in any particular way the organisational structure and the division of 'power' within a firm.

The aim of this technological innovation is a higher degree of efficiency and better service quality. In the second stage, many problems can occur in the adoption and use of these new services. Different internal organisational rules as well as a change in the approach to work are the prerequisites of such innovations but are difficult to achieve. This obligatory interrelationship between technology and organisation, in

Table 10.4 Examples of telecommunications services

Class	Communication form	Narrowband	Broadband
			Example of teleservices
Communicative services			
	Video	– Teleworking*	– Videotelephony – Videotelephone conference – Videoconference – Surveillance – Fund transfer – Two-way TV
	Voice	– Radiomobile	
Dialogue services	Data	– Data communication – Transactions – EDP* – Teleworking* – Telemetry and alarms	– High speed data communication – File transfer – Computer-aided services (CAD/CAM)
	Document	– Text communication – Facsimile	– High speed facsimile – Images/moving picture documents
Messaging services	Video		– Videomail
	Voice	– Voice mail – Secretarial assistance*	
	Document	– Electronic mail	– Text/graphics/moving picture documents

Table 10.4 contd.

Class	Communication form	Example of teleservices	
		Narrowband	Broadband
Retrieval services	Videotex	– Videotex – Secretarial assistance* – EDP*	– Broadband videotex – Teleshopping – Computer-aided education – Consumers' advisory – Film retrieval – High resolution document and image retrieval
Distributive services Distribution services with non-starting-point-oriented access	Broadcast	– Hi-fi stereo	– Video broadcasting – TV, HDTV, HQTV,** 3DTV – Pay TV, STV
Distribution services with starting-point-oriented access	Distribution upon selection Broadcast	– Hi-fi stereo on demand	– TV on demand – Teletext – Cabletext

* Classification of these services depend on considered application.
** MAC standard TV.

Source: Casali, 1986.

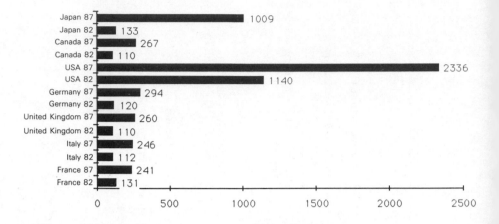

Figure 10.3   Data transmission: implementations in six major countries
Source: Italtel.

order to achieve through technological development better economic performance, slows the adoption process of these more sophisticated services. Furthermore, this process is problematic because of the underdevelopment of the high technology infrastructures which form the basis for the widespread implementation of 'second-generation' services.

The economic impact of new information technologies

Technological development is an exogenous factor to economic development. Nevertheless its economic impact is highly dependent upon different features and different capacities of the economic system to accept and exploit technological change, turning it into better economic performance.

From a user's perspective, the rapid increase in communications potential embodied in the new communications technologies opens the way to the exploitation of competitive advantages on the basis of the achievement of more information and knowledge. Competitive advantages are now based on the capacities of new technologies to transmit, process, store and elaborate a greater volume of information (Gillespie and Hepworth, 1986).

Thus, the higher technological potentialities present major opportunities for firms to achieve competitive advantages. However, despite general belief, these opportunities are not provided by the simple adoption of these technologies, but by their **innovative use**. By innovative use we refer to the application of these technologies to produce new products, new processes and new transactional structures. The development of on-line services in the banking sector, i.e. points of sales, cash dispensers, home-baking, provided by the development of inter-banking computer networks systems, are a clear example of innovative use of these infrastructures. By the same token, process innovation can be generated by the use of these new infrastructures by enabling 'islands of automation' (such as flexible manufacturing systems) to intercommunicate, either within a single site (local area networks) or among a multitude of sites (wide area networks). As a managerial innovation, computer networks operating over space through telecommunication channels have obviously greater increased the ability of multi-site organisations to control and integrate their activities over space (Antonelli, 1988; Fornengo, 1988; Rullani and Zanfei, 1988).

The impact of **information and communications technologies** (ICTs) upon business performance can be analysed in terms of increased efficiency, greater effectiveness and enhanced competitive advantage. Increased efficiency is achieved, for example, by reducing costs and maintaining existing output levels by using technology as a substitute for other inputs (i.e. clerical staff). Effectiveness is concerned with the capacity to deliver more and improved products within the existing resource base. Competitive advantage is obtained by the exploitation of ICTs to achieve more strategic information and to generate product, process and managerial innovations.

The innovative and strategic use of ICTs, generating positive effects on business performance, is strongly associated in its development with deep organisational changes. In fact, innovative use of these technologies implies the interrelationship of technology and organisation as two inseparable variables (Mansell, 1990; Zeleny, 1985).

Technologies in themselves appear as neutral devices, as a pool of opportunities available at a given cost and can be interpreted as some quasi-public goods. But what really matters, and what is not at all a public good, is the cultural and organisational capability of exploiting their potentialities through a creative blending of technological devices, organisational styles and business ideas.

This aspect becomes clearer by conceptualising the firm in terms of its transactional structure (Coase, 1937; Williamson, 1975). From this perspective, the adoption of new ICTs has to be seen within the context of an existing array of transactions, both within and between firms, which shape the nature of the organisation, particularly the division of functions and labour (Capello and Williams, 1992). In particular, these organisational changes manifest themselves in processes of functional integration, creation of new functions and changes in the relative importance of simple functions in the decision-making process, these changes being profoundly dependent on the existence of new telecommunication technologies governing transactions. At the same time, ICTs can generate requalification of staff, integration of previously differentiated jobs, changes in the relative importance of jobs, automation and routinisation of activities. Thus, the adoption and widespread use of ICTs can bring about, and may in fact be dependent upon, organisational change.

Innovative use of ICTs undoubtedly requires a high level of organisational changes, as stated above. The consequent implication is that the diffusion of new technologies among users requires deep and *ad hoc* learning processes, regarding both the technical aspects of new communications systems, and, more important, the possible interrelationship between technology and organisation.

It would be misleading to assume the existence of a direct and immediate effect of technological change on the economic performance of firms. It is a chance given to adopters to achieve a better economic performance, but the capacity to exploit these possibilities depends on individual corporate strategies and on the capacity of each firm to link the technological changes to business and organisational strategies.

Policy recommendations

The technological complexity and difficulty in the use of modern technologies suggest that the development of new communications technologies is a difficult process and its diffusion over time and space requires 'public policy' stimuli.

The relatively limited diffusion of computer networks is demonstrated by both official sources and empirical data.

In the UK, for example, OFTEL (Office of Telecommunications) publications indicate the limited use of private circuits, central to computer networks, achieving only 10 per cent of British Telecom revenue in 1988. Further, that 90 per cent of private circuits are analogue and that these circuits represent 75 per cent of private circuit revenues, 25 per cent being derived from digital circuits. Moreover, 75 per cent of all private circuits are within the same exchange area and that the City of London is the main geographic market.

The relatively limited diffusion of computer networks is also demonstrated by a recent survey of organisations.[2] Whilst 40 per cent of respondents used a computer network, and over 65 per cent of these organisations had installed their computer networks since 1985, the broad diffusion of computer networks into the functional structure of organisations has remained relatively undeveloped (Capello and Williams, 1992).

The pattern of use of these computer networks suggests that the development trajectory of new technology is still in its first stage.

Thus, inevitably, public policy support should create a pressure on those mechanisms that in diffusion processes generate accumulation rates through spin-off effects.

Public policy should thus encourage computer network development in areas with high potential demand density, i.e. central regions, where mechanisms such as network externalities could generate positive cumulative effects, and thus, where critical mass could be achieved in a shorter time.

Positive network externalities, in fact, arise because the total number of subscribers has an important effect on the user-value of each additional subscriber, and each additional connection has important effects on the user-value of the network of existing subscribers (Allen, 1989; Antonelli, 1989; Hayashi, 1992). This mechanism is more efficient when applied in central areas, where the user-value of the network of subscribers is higher.

Related to this idea is the assumption that most economically developed areas are legitimated to be 'networked' first, in order to develop a cumulative process. A top–down public policy is thus suitable, implementing 'information highways' between metropolitan areas. A bottom–up development policy, focusing on network development in local areas, risks generating a development model with few possible interlinkages among 'islands of networks' and thus presenting a high risk of failure because of its local characteristics.

For instance, Italy witnesses the inadequacy of 'bottom–up' policies in the telecommunications sector, with many local projects stimulating geographically restricted advanced telecommunications networks. The SPRINT project in Prato (Tuscany) (Zanfei, 1986), or 'Lombardia Cablata' in Lombardy, are two examples where local advanced networks were implemented and modern services offered, with the result that they were a complete failure (Camagni and Capello, 1990; Capello, 1988). Their failure was in part contingent upon the local development of these networks, which could be interpreted rather as 'white elephants' instead of efficient projects generating real interest from the demand side.

A top–down approach, i.e. an approach starting with national projects and then developing local ones, is in this respect a more appropriate public policy to generate cumulative adoption processes. Nevertheless, to be efficient, these policies have to consider the geographical asymmetry in networks, which is created by following a top–down approach, only as a timing difference in investments among regions. These asymmetries must not turn into discontinuity, reflecting different investment intentions. In this case, in fact, discontinuity would become a structural difference between central and peripheral regions, the latter being penalised by the lack of modern infrastructures, therefore losing the possibility of achieving advantages typical of central locations, i.e. agglomeration economies, and thus the possibility of overcoming the limits of a peripheral area.

By the same token, public policy should be concerned with the existence of 'missing networks' at an international level. This concern should go far beyond the simple physical infrastructure, and should take into consideration a series of concerns, as a recent study for the Round Table of Industrialists has pointed out (Maggi et al., 1991):

- hardware (physical infrastructure)
- software (logistic and informatics)
- orgware (institutional and organisational setting)
- finware (financial arrangements/funding)
- ecoware (environmental and safety effects)

In this study it was concluded that the telecommunications sector could perform much better. To improve the current situation in Europe telecommunications the following suggestions were made:

- The introduction of a base European telecom network, including standard facilities, uniform rules and tariffs, and services.
- A separation of responsibility between regulators (government, policy) and operators (implementation (orgware)) is needed.
- Avoidable barriers to entry should be minimised (orgware); the existence of monopoly should be avoided.
- Since deliverable technologies are changing too fast, a sustainable basis for regulation is missing. Improving competition should then be the keyword (orgware).
- Telecommunications prices should be cost-related (orgware).
- Use the outcome of current ENS applications (e.g. the European nervous system) in transportation, banking, environmental protection, health care, education (orgware, hardware, software, ecoware and finware) to develop Europe-wide applications.

These suggestions reflect a demand-side-oriented policy, neglecting monopoly as a useful market structure in highly technologically dynamic sectors, and interpreting competition as a key force for rapid diffusion processes in an era of a networked economy.

Conclusions

The aim of this chapter was to highlight the technological changes in the field of telecommunications within the context of the emerging 'information economy'.

The integration of two separate sectors, namely computer science and telecommunications, has opened the way to the creation of radical changes in the way information is transmitted and utilised. Thus, the competitive advantages of firms derive from the exploitation of information-intensive techniques rather than capital-intensive production (Gillespie and Hepworth, 1986; Gillespie and Williams, 1988). In fact, the capacity of processing, manipulating, storing and transmitting information is becoming strategic to the achievement of better economic performance.

At the same time, the convergence towards a more computerised communications system has provided subscribers with a wide range of 'value-added services' characterised by a higher efficiency and quality in the transmission process.

The telecommunications sector, like the transport sector, can thus be regarded as a cluster incorporating basic innovations in the neo-Schumpeterian sense (see Freeman and al., 1982); it represents a techno-economic discontinuity leading to a qualitative jump in socio-economic and technological conditions in our society, on the basis of the micro-electronics sector (including e.g. transistors, integrated circuits, microprocessors, computers, laser technology).

In this perspective, the telecommunications sector becomes strategic to the competitiveness of territorial and industrial systems: ICTs thus represent a chance given to economic systems to achieve better economic performances. Nevertheless, they also represent a new threat which territorial systems (national, regional and urban) have to face in the near future. The lack of ICTs infrastructure can represent the way territorial systems can be isolated from development processes and from integration processes, characterising modern economies: integration among European countries, between Western and Eastern European economies.

From this perspective, then, the telecommunications sector and its future development become strategic for the understanding of the future economic position of each country, and thereby of the competitiveness of national, regional and urban territorial industrial systems in the 1990s.

The telecommunications sector is not the only sector of strategic importance for economic development. The competitiveness of economic systems will also be dependent on the widespread development of technological potentialities in the transport sector, as is witnessed by other contributions in this volume. The exploitation of the technological potentialities in both sectors will ensure a strategic economic position for European countries, as these sectors are the vehicle for both European integration and intra-European competitiveness.

Notes

1. Although the chapter is the result of the common research work of the two authors, R. Capello has written most of the chapter apart from the second section which has been jointly written.
2. The project has been developed at the Centre for Urban and Regional Development Studies at the University of Newcastle upon Tyne and financed by ESRC (Economic and Social Research Council) under the PICT Programme.

References

Allen, D. (1989) 'New telecommunications services', in *Telecommunications Policy*, September, pp. 257–71.

Amin, A. and Goddard, J. (eds) (1986) *Technological Change, Industrial Restructuring and Regional Development*. Allen & Unwin, London.

Antonelli, C. (ed.) (1988) *New Information Technology and Industrial Change: The Italian Case*. Kluwer Academic Publisher Books, New York.

Antonelli, C. (1989) 'Induced adoption and externalities in the regional diffusion of information technology', in *Regional Studies*, vol. 24(1), pp. 31–40.

Antonelli, C. (ed.) (1992) *The Economics of Information Networks*, North Holland, Amsterdam.

Arnold, K. and Guy, K. (1987) 'Policy options for promoting growth through information technology'. Paper presented at the seminar on *Information Technology and Emerging Growth Areas*, Paris, 24 and 25 September.

Bar, F., Borrus, M. and Coriat, B. (1989) 'Information networks and competitive advantages: the issues for government policy and corporate strategy'. OECD–BRIE Telecommunications User Project, Paris.

Camagni, R. (1986) 'Introduzione all'onda informatica', in Freeman, C. and Soete, L. (1987) *Onda Informatica*. Edizioni del Sole 24Ore.

Camagni, R. (ed) (1987) 'Le tecnologie dell'informazione in Italia e nel mondo'. Final research report for IBM Italy, Milan, December.

Camagni, R. and Capello, R. (1989) 'Scenari di sviluppo della domanda di sistemi di telecomunicazione in Italia', in *Finanza, marketing e produzione*, no. 1, March, pp. 87–138.

Camagni, R. and Capello, R. (1990) 'Innovazione tecnologica e innovazione organizzativa: la telematica in banca', in *Quaderni di Informatica*, Bull Italia, no. 2, pp. 13–27.

Capello R. (1988) 'La domanda di reti e servizi di telecomunicazione nell'area metropolitana milanese: vincoli e strategie', in Camagni, R. and Predetti, A. (eds) (1988) *La trasformazione economica della città*. IReR-Progetto Milano, Franco Angeli, Milan.

Capello, R (1989) 'Telecommunications and the spatial organisation of production', in *Information Economy Series*, University of Newcastle, Newcastle-upon-Tyne, no. 10.

Capello, R. (1991) 'L'assetto istituzionale nel settore delle telecomunicazioni', in Camagni, R. (ed.) (1991) *Computer networks: mercati e prospettive delle tecnologie di telecomunicazione*. Etas Libri, Milan.

Capello, R. and Williams, H. (1992) 'Computer network trajectories and organisational dynamics: a cross-national review', in Antonelli, C. (ed.) (1992) op. cit.

Casali, F. (1986) 'From N-ISDN to IBCN: service, network and economic changes', in *Les services du futur*, Le bulletin de l'IDATE, actes des 8èmes journées internationales, no. 25, November.

Ciborra, C. (1989) *Le tecnologie di coordinamento*. Franco Angeli Editore.

Coase, R. (1937) 'The nature of the firm', in *Economica*, November, pp. 386–403.

Fornengo, G. (1988) 'Manufacturing networks: telematics in the automobile industry', in Antonelli (ed.) (1988) op. cit.

Freeman, C. (1986) 'The role of technical change in national economic development', in Amin, A. and Goddard, J. (eds) op. cit.

Freeman, Ch., Clark, J. and Soete, L. (1982) *Unemployment and Technical Innovations*, Frances Pinter, London.

Freeman, C. and Soete, L. (1986) *L'onda informatica*, Edizioni del Sole 24Ore.

Giaoutzi, M. and Nijkamp, P. (1988) *Informatics and Regional Development*, Gower, Aldershot.

Gillespie, A. and Hepworth, M. (1986) 'Telecommunications and regional development in the information society', in *Newcastle Studies of the Information Economy*, no. 1, October.

Gillespie, A. and Williams, H. (1988) 'Telecommunications and the reconstruction of regional comparative advantage', in *Environment and Planning A*, vol. 20, pp. 1311–21.

Hayashi, K. (1992) 'From network externalities to interconnection — the changing nature of networks and economy', in Antonelli, C. (ed.) (1992) op.cit.

Maggi, R., Masser, I. and Nijkamp, P. (1991) 'Missing networks in Europe', *Transport Reviews*, forthcoming.

Mansell, R. (1990) 'Rethinking the telecommunication infrastructure: the new "black box"', *Research Policy*, vol. 19, pp. 501–15.

OECD, (1988a) *New Telecommunications Services: Videotex Development Strategies*, Paris.

OECD, (1988b) *The Telecommunications Industry: The Challenges of Structural Change*, Paris.

Perez, C. (1983) 'Structural change and the assimilation of new technologies in the economic development', in Giaoutzi, M. and Nijkamp, P. (1988) op. cit.

Rullani, E. and Zanfei, A. (1988) 'Networks between manufacturing and demand: cases from textile and clothing industry', in Antonelli, C. (ed.) (1988) op. cit.

Scarpinato, M. (1991) 'Struttura dell'offerta e dinamica del mercato dei sistemi di telecomunicazione', in Camagni, R. (ed.) (1991) *Computer networks: mercati e prospettive delle tecnologie di comunicazione*. Etas Libri, Milan.

Schumpeter, J.A. (1939) *Business Cycles: a Theoretical, Historical and Statistical Analysis of the Capitalist Process*. McGraw Hill, New York.

Solomon, R. (1987) 'Electronic and computer-aided publishing: opportunities and constraints'. Paper presented at the seminar on *Information Technology and Emerging Growth Areas*, Paris, 24 and 25 September.

Solow, R.M. (1957) 'Technical change and the aggregate production function', in *The Review of Economics and Statistics*, no. 39, pp. 312–20.

Williamson, O. (1975) *Markets and Hierarchies: Analysis and Antitrust Implications*. The Free Press, New York.

Zanfei, A. (1986) 'I vincoli alla diffusione delle tecnologie dell'informazione in alcune esperienze di applicazione della telematica', in *Economia e Politica Industriale*, no. 50, pp. 253–89.

Zanfei, A. (1990) *Complessità e crescita esterna nell'industria delle telecomunicazioni*. Franco Angeli, Milan.

Zeleny, M. (1985) 'La gestione a tecnologia superiore e la gestione della tecnologia superiore', in Bocchi, G. and Ceruti, M. (eds), *La sfida della complessità*. Feltrinelli, Milan.

Part III: Some Key Issues Concerning Transport and Economic and Spatial Organisation

Chapter 11

New technologies and macro-organisational innovation: the cases of the banking system and the textile industry in Italy

R. Camagni, R. Capello and R. Rabellotti[1]

Introduction

Interest in the development of the new information and communications technologies stems from their transformative nature. As Hepworth defined them (1986 and 1989), they can be considered as 'spatial systems' in that they allow the transmission, storage, manipulation and exchange of both 'labour' and 'capital' resources in the form of information flows. Thus, they generate possibilities of profound product and process innovation to their adopters and the achievement of competitive advantages for firms and institutions in general, following new corporate development strategies and new innovation trajectories.

These new information technologies, associated with the ongoing technological revolution, can be exploited with the intention of:

- creating new production processes;
- increasing the efficiency of office functions (back and front-office automation);
- improving the control over production processes from the managerial point of view (automated factory);
- creating new distribution networks (telebanking, teleshopping);
- improving the quality of existing products;
- improving decision-making processes;
- creating new relationships between the firm and its external environment (new relationships with suppliers, teleworking, databases as external information sources).

Each of these renewal processes obliges firms and institutions to rebuild their organisational structures according to new principles for achieving economic advantage through new managerial and technological instruments.

The introduction of new technologies is an extremely complex process, the result of profound cultural, psychological, managerial and organisational changes. New technologies both allow and impose internal

organisational changes for their adopters; they support the spatial relocation of production, as well as obliging new functional divisions of labour
(Camagni, 1988; Capello and Williams, 1992). In other words, they have
the potential to reshape the organisational structure of the firm at a
micro-economic level, and of the economy at a macro-economic level,
building new forms of social, economic, managerial and corporate
organisation. Technological innovation must therefore be associated with
major organisational changes, and the study of the diffusion of new
technologies among companies must be associated with the study of these
organisational dynamics.

This chapter examines organisational changes, related to the introduction of new information technologies, occurring in two very different
sectors of the Italian economy: the textile industry and the banking
system. The two sectors nevertheless have some general features in
common. In particular, they are both traditional sectors which are
developing a strategy of revitalisation in order to face the challenge of
increasing competition.

The **banking system** in Italy is characterised by dynamic growth,
increasing instability of both internal and external markets, and a high
level of maturity of products. The increasing internal demand for financial services creates possibilities for higher marginal profits for banks,
thus exacerbating internal competition. This situation is accompanied by
a growing instability in European markets in view of the opening of the
Single Market, thus increasing international competition. Therefore, the
introduction of new technologies becomes an important strategic factor,
allowing the achievement of product and process innovations and thus
supporting a process of revitalisation of the sector.

The same features can be seen in the case of the **textile industry**: strong
international competition was generated in the sector by the entry of new
producers competing on the basis of prices and thus forcing Italian firms
to improve their price/quality ratio. New technologies have become in
this sector too a strategic weapon enabling improved internal efficiency
and effectiveness, and the achievement of competitive advantages from
profound product and process innovation.

The methodology adopted in the analysis is similar for the two sectors.
In both cases, the study has been carried out on the basis of primary case
studies conducted in some of the major Italian banks and textile firms.[2]
The chapter presents the results of these analyses. The second section
deals with the case of the Italian banking system, and the third section
with the Italian textile industry.

The analysis of the Italian banking system begins by underlining the
impact that new technologies have on the centralisation and decentralisation of functions between headquarters and branches. As the second
section of the study shows, a new balance in the spatial allocation of
functions is taking place, reshaping the functional relationships within
the system. The effects of the introduction of new information and

communications technologies manifest themselves also in a new internal functional division of labour, generating new functions and creating a new hierarchy among the existing functions. Organisational changes also occur in inter-bank relationships with the introduction of inter-bank computer networks, and the analysis points out the current trends in the development of these new technologies and their accompanying organisational dynamics.

In the textile industry, the third section of the analysis shows how the introduction of new information technologies has affected the classic organisational alternative between vertical integration and the market. As opposed to the traditional 'make-or-buy' alternative, the Italian forms of external growth and co-operative agreements, which we have defined as 'make-together', are much in evidence. The study shows that the current trend is towards more developed vertical integration on the level of strategic functions, while external co-operative agreements often occur in the product design phase, in devising *ad hoc* technological solutions and, obviously, in decentralising the various production phases. Finally, the fourth section provides a conclusion in which some comparisons between the results in the two industries are drawn.

Macro-organisational innovation in the banking system

The alternative between functional centralisation and decentralisation in the Italian banking system

It is widely believed that the principal effect of new information technologies, and in particular new computer networks, is the spatial decentralisation of activities. For banks traditionally operating in dispersed geographical areas, new communication technologies are interpreted as effective instruments for the decentralisation of functions to local branches. Direct contact with branches appears to relieve the head office of responsibility and decision-making through the possible immediate control of the work of all individual branches. Our analysis strongly revises this interpretation; the process of decentralisation is the result of very complex problems, certainly not solved by a simple on-line link between branches and headquarters.

The tendencies in the subdivision of functions among headquarters and peripheral branches are the following:

- The first effect of the use of networks for on-line data transmission is the **centralisation** of routine standardised functions, linked to administrative and bureaucratic operations. The existence of a single data-processing centre linked by networks to branches involves the centralisation of all administrative-accounting operations, which can be transmitted in real time with daily revision with the aid of computer networks.

- The availability of resources in branches, relieved of administrative tasks, has allowed the **decentralisation** of many operations of production and distribution of services. The 'specialisation' of the branches in the distribution of services and the management of contacts with the public, linked to a reduction in traditional counter tasks through the existence of self-service banking, contributes to an increase in the quality and efficiency of work carried out by branches. New technologies tend, moreover, to shift the burden of operations of 'input' of banking transactions from bank personnel to the business customer (interconnections of computers) and to the private customer (automatic machines and self-service transactions) in ways which reduce operating costs. Branches thus become typical 'points of sale', concentrating exclusively on contacts with the market, and become real instruments for monitoring demand.
- The headquarters concerns itself with the traditional activities of decision-making and control, over which the effect of the introduction of computers has only in part produced a decentralisation to branches.

A deeper analysis is necessary to explain these tendencies; the new subdivision of activities between headquarters and branches is presented in Table 11.1, which compares the past situation, characterised by automation processes, and the present situation, created by the introduction of networking in the chain of production.

Administrative activities, as previously mentioned, have become more centralised through on-line, real-time communications from the branches to the central host computer. Both accounting activities and bureaucratic/administrative activities are carried out centrally, through daily contacts with peripheral branches.

Operating activities, closely linked to the distribution of services, are traditionally the responsibility of branches, the geographical distribution of which allows an effective approach to serving the market. In the branches, the activities of financial advice and assistance to customers, already partly their responsibility, are further increased, together with financial decision-making in general. The new tendency which emerges in this area is towards the decentralisation of the distribution of specialised services (credit, loans, special accounts), traditionally centralised because of their high decision-making content. Control of these activities is made simpler with the aid of computer networks support; moreover, the standardisation of procedures, necessary for the automation and networking of the distribution of these services, limits the degree of freedom of branches, simplifying control. The on-line link also allows branches to carry out more operations through the transfer of information from central databases, useful for operational decision-making.

Table 11.1 Centralisation/decentralisation of different activities — comparison between past and present situation

	Past (Automation)		Present (Automation and networking)	
	Headquarters	Branches	Headquarters	Branches
Administrative activities		Book-keeping activities / Administrative and bureaucratic activities	Book-keeping activities / Administrative and bureaucratic activities	
Operating activities	Distribution of specialised services	Distribution of traditional services / Consulting activities and assistance to the client		Distribution of traditional services / Consulting activities and assistance to the client / Distribution of specialised services
Control activities	Management control of the branches / Management control of the bank		Management control of the branches / Management control of the bank	
Decision-making activities	Strategic and planning activities / Decision-making linked to operating activities		Strategic and planning activities	Decision-making linked to operating activities

For this reason branches tend to become the only points of contact with the market, and therefore assume a new strategic role in the management of the sensitive bank/customer relationship.

Activities of control of the general debit/credit state of the bank, and of the grouping of defined business objectives, remain the absolute responsibility of headquarters, given the importance of these activities for the coherent overall development of the bank. The current trend in banking as a result of networking is instead a change in the activities of control of the operation of the single branch. This no longer takes place daily through the physical movement and verification of paperwork on the assets of each branch. In the 'new' bank management an area of decision-making autonomy is left to branch managers, who have to achieve objectives determined by headquarters within the framework of the business development of the bank, with monthly margins and with subsequently greater decision-making autonomy in the management of a single branch.

With regard to **decision-making activities**, those concerned with strategic and planning activities remain strictly centralised and managed by headquarters. Networking allows, however, the decentralisation of decision-making linked to operating activities. In the more technologically innovative banks there is a tendency towards decentralisation of the whole procedure for giving credit for loans of up to average size.

The total automation of credit procedures, including the delicate decision-making process for giving credit, is managed by branches through terminals within the bank linked via the network to the database on the credit position of customers (internal management database). Using expert systems, evaluation takes place through the input of simple data on the customer and the immediate processing of indicators, whose deviation from standard values determines the decision to give credit. In this case, the decision is taken at branch level, relieving headquarters of an activity of limited strategic importance.

The diffusion of this standardised procedure is, however, limited, even in the more innovative banks interviewed. Some are not pushing networking in this direction because they do not think that the reduction of decision-making to simple standardised procedures is a sensible strategic choice. The results are interpreted as an acquisition of efficiency for the bank, to the detriment of greater internal control and of a more rational lending policy and liquidity management.

If we analyse the activities which through computerisation have undergone localisation changes, the common denominator is the transfer of information flows characterised by **data**, or by **uni-directional information**. The increased use of management and marketing databases linked to the network in order to obtain information for operations of advice and assistance, or the transfer of raw data for the central processing of administrative information, exclusively require the transmission of uni-directional information.

Greater autonomy in terms of the operation of branches occurs as a result of the possible link-up in real time between headquarters and branches; again, however, the transmission of uni-directional information is needed for distant control within a pre-established hierarchical framework (Camagni, 1987). What banks do not use their internal computer networks for is the support of strategic decision-making, requiring the transmission of bidirectional information. The managerial information system, understood as information flows to support strategic decision-making, is poorly supported by computer networks. The banks analysed showed little use of internal electronic mail, or of access to internal and external databases for information on the state of the market.

Bidirectional information tends not, then, to be transported through computer networks; exchanges of opinions, decisions and negotiations are messages effected without electronic support. There are many problems limiting the application of networks in this area:

- The use of networks to transmit this type of information requires a highly technically advanced structure to guarantee the security and secrecy of the messages transmitted; electronic systems which allow a hierarchy of access to information are necessary. Strategic information must be available only to high levels in the hierarchy, with the certainty that it can be obtained only by clearly specified people.
- The use of computer networks to transfer strategic information requires the overcoming of a managerial mentality linked to bureaucratic procedures, involving the checking, signing and manual control of every phase in the procedure.

Consequences of computer networks for functional organisation

In the last ten years banks have undergone an internal organisational change which can be described as passing from the **traditional bank** to the **industrial bank**. The phenomenon of the industrialisation of banks can be seen in two characteristic processes:

- the creation of new functional areas, such as marketing, typical of an industrial structure. More sophisticated and detailed information flows, typical of highly disaggregated marketing databases are of primary importance for the banking system operating in a dynamic, turbulent and unstable environment (Bracchi, 1985);
- the different nature and higher degree of interfunctional collaboration for certain functions, such as organisation, planning and information systems.

With respect to the first of these processes, the introduction of computers into banks has played an important role in the creation of **marketing activities**, which have developed very recently. The marketing function has always had a minor role and a limited capacity in banks, as banks traditionally operated in a monopolistic spatial regime. Today market conditions require instead a commercial aggression not unlike that of industrial firms, and strategies which allow development in a strongly competitive market. The bank now has to develop an information system specifically designed for marketing, with which to manage the large volume of necessary information, utilising databanks and market analysis.

Networking has a dual role in this process:

- On the one hand it increases the effectiveness of marketing in the important phase of advertising the introduction of new services.
- on the other it helps marketing by supporting the possibility of utilising specialised databases.

Marketing has increased the importance of the development and support of new computerised services offered to customers. According to market surveys, it focuses on potential **development areas** to determine the services to offer to customers. The development of new on-line services such as cash management or electronic bank receipt is based on marketing analysis, which locates promising market niches in terms of potential demand. Once the services are introduced, the marketing function locates, with specialised databases, customers with specific characteristics matched with the profile of the new services. Marketing activity is therefore fundamental both upstream and downstream in the process of creating new services, and becomes a key function for the strategic development of innovation in the supply of services.

Internal process innovations, or the utilisation of networks for the transmission of data, support the marketing function by making available databases useful in the selection of customer groups to which to offer new services. The utilisation of databases for this purpose is currently very limited in banks; the databases themselves are more limited in terms of the information available than are the databases for management purposes. Moreover, they are often not directly electronically linked to the marketing area at which they are aimed, and the movement of information is still based on the physical transport of printouts.

Most of the information which is embodied in marketing databases is, in practice, the by-product of data processing already done by banks in order to carry out their traditional activities. Moving beyond these fairly unsophisticated databases, towards those which are more adequate for marketing purposes, is limited by a number of factors:

- First, the cost of more sophisticated databases of this type is generally still very high.
- Second, a greater flexibility of database use is required. The automatic selection from a general database of customers with very specific characteristics is a requirement often lacking, preventing an efficient use of networking as a support for marketing activities.
- Finally, a high degree of disaggregation is required for marketing databases. With policies of cross-selling, once a customer has been identified for a service, promotional policies for that customer support the sale of other services.

The second change resulting from the process of networking which has developed widely in banks in recent years is the change in the nature of some traditional functions. In particular, the functions of **organisation, planning and control** and **information systems** have come to have a crucial role; the networking process has stimulated their enhanced status in the functional structure of banks, and has at the same time accentuated the opportunity for collaboration across these functions.

The link between these functions derives from the need to create 'made-to-measure' internal networked procedures, which match the needs and the existing structure of each individual bank. Networking of internal bank procedures is a typical process which develops with *ad hoc* computer networks selected on the basis of planning needs and existing organisational structures. The interlinking of organisational, planning and information systems allows the co-ordination of procedures of corporate development with those of information and internal organisational needs.

Quite differently from innovations in the distribution of services, in which products are standardised and are similar for all banks, process innovations develop in different contexts from one bank to another, and are shaped each time by the needs of the individual bank.

Innovations in inter-bank relationships: current trends

Technological innovations, both in processes and products, are the new strategic instruments for facing the strong competition in the sector. This forces the bank to radically transform its inter-bank relationships, pushing in two different directions at the same time, **co-operation** and **competition**. The creation of on-line inter-bank services, with the exploitation of inter-bank computer networks, requires a high degree of co-operation between banks, without which the introduction of these services would be impossible. On the other hand, these services and new information technologies themselves are becoming increasingly competitive instruments through which to supply a wider range of products, to provide a higher quality and efficiency of service, and to enable market niches which represent the specific needs of users to be conquered.

There are two types of external computer networks through which the banks are linked with the competitive environment: internal networks accessible by customers of the bank from home and inter-bank networks. The first represent linking networks, in public or private infrastructures, among banks and their customers at home, for the offer of 'made-to-measure' services. As research has shown (Capello, 1988), the development of these computer networks still poses many institutional management problems. There is the danger for public telecommunications operators that these specialised networks may be utilised by banks for communication with customers located in other towns or even other countries. In this way the banks and their customers can exploit the opportunity for communicating long distance or internationally at a local call cost.

Inter-bank networks allow communication between the terminals of banks world-wide (e.g. the SWIFT network). Co-operation between banks is necessary for the 'networking of the market', meaning the offering of networked services to clients. The development of services such as the cash dispenser, the credit card, point-of-sale terminals and cash management, which require electronic transfer of funds through inter-bank networks, is guaranteed by a high level of co-operation among national and foreign banks. Conversely, the competition is more open on the production side, in which the installation of modern internal private networks, sophisticated software and extensive databases gives to different banks different competitive advantages.

The current trend shows that between the two patterns of development of networking in banks (in production — internal networks; and in distribution — inter-bank networks) the networking of the market represents the sector of greater growth, both currently and in the immediate future.

Technological innovations designed for the market are more easily and quickly established in banks than are the networks and information structures used in production processes. The reasons for this phenomenon are various (Capello et al., 1990):

● First, as has been discussed, technological innovations with regard to the market are standard products, which do not require long and costly planning procedures, as is the case for production innovations; these are *ad hoc* products, tailored to the needs of each individual bank, and therefore more expensive in terms of human and financial resources.

● As a consequence of this, the organisational changes required by the networking process are limited to micro-organisational changes in the tasks of counter staff. In the case of computerisation of internal procedures, the organisational changes are many and complex, and influence the functions of the company, the delicate problem of decentralisation or centralisation of the powers of branches, and their control.

- Competition in the sector is such that for reasons of image banks are stimulated to invest in on-line services to offer to customers. The extent of diffusion of services such as cash dispensers and credit cards is such that the refusal to introduce such services immediately becomes a **competitive disadvantage** for the bank, with a risk of losing customers.

Up until now new technologies have pushed towards greater inter-bank co-operation, accepted and managed by banks in order to maintain an image in the market and towards customers. Technological innovation in banks seems up to now to have had as its aim the achievement of greater internal efficiency, while the two higher levels of economic advantages attainable (greater effectiveness and greater competitiveness) do not seem to be as clearly defined. From the analysis carried out, the adoption of new information technologies in the area of production seems to be motivated primarily by the objectives of reducing personnel costs, without a clear acknowledgement of the possibilities of new technologies in terms of decision-making effectiveness and competitive advantages.

Macro-organisational innovation in the textile industry

The Italian textile–clothing industry vis-à-vis *the 'make-or-buy' alternative*

According to Williamson (1967, 1975 and 1983), economic activities take place either within hierarchical organisations or in the market-place, depending on the relative proportion of organisational and transaction costs respectively. Transaction costs can vary depending on the specific item being exchanged, and on the uncertainty and frequency of the exchange. The market approach is most appropriate when certainty prevails, and when the items involved are standardised and transactions are random, whereas a hierarchical organisation approach works more effectively in situations of uncertainty, with non-standardised products and when transactions are more frequent (Silva, 1985).

Innovations in contractual techniques on the one hand, and in organisational techniques on the other, will shift the relative advantage towards either transactions in the market or in-house vertical integration (Monaco, 1987).

With regard to the textile–clothing sector, Mariotti and Cainarca (1986) hold that strong market orientation is resulting in an increasing vertical integration. In fact, a corporate policy focusing on the quality/fashion combination calls for manufacturing to adjust continuously to the changing market requirements and for an ever more stringent product quality control, in order to ensure consistent quality standards. This results in a marked increase in transaction costs, and in the uncertainty and frequency of external contacts. Moreover, there is the risk of strategic, highly 'fashion-sensitive' information being leaked.

A drive towards vertical integration, despite the resultant savings in transaction costs, may on the other hand entail some inefficiency within the company, owing to slower reaction times, higher organisation costs and co-ordination problems ('control loss'). For example, the crisis in large companies in the 1970s forced the textile–clothing industry in the opposite direction to that of vertical integration, i.e. towards various forms of **production decentralisation** or **industrial districts**. The factors instrumental in the success of more market-oriented organisational solutions are the cost differentials related to smaller company size, the flexibility of company structures, inter-company work-sharing in terms of specialisation by production phase and by product, and, finally enhanced external agglomeration economies associated with geographical concentration.

In this context, the Prato case is extremely significant: a vertical fragmentation strategy in the wool industry was adopted, quite naturally, in this area in the years following the Second World War. The vertically integrated model, which had been a traditional feature of the production pattern, was replaced with a number of small to medium-sized firms specialising in specific phases of the production cycle (Lorenzoni, 1985).

Against the vertical integration of the 1960s and the vertical disintegration of the 1970s are a number of intermediate forms that provide a continuous spectrum of alternatives from the market to the integrated company approach. The trend towards these intermediate forms results in new forms of inter-firm relationship, namely the establishment of co-operative relationships of a **'make-together'** type, as opposed to the traditional **'make-or-buy'** trade-off.

The reduction of learning times, the simultaneous introduction of the same product world-wide, the ability to continuously innovate technologies and to exploit every opportunity to apply internal know-how, are all essential for survival in global competitive markets, which result in a trend towards intermediate organisational forms of company development (Camagni and Gambarotto, 1988). A survey on the diffusion of these intermediate forms within the Italian textile–clothing industry (Mariotti and Cainarca, 1986) has confirmed an upward trend towards such organisational systems, particularly in the subsectors that are more 'fashion-sensitive'.

*Information technologies and the macro-organisational structure
of the sector*

Information technologies can affect the choice between market and integrated company approaches as a result of their impact on transaction and organisation costs. Specifically, the new technologies make the boundaries between market and enterprise less evident, stimulating a wide range of intermediate, **non-market, non-hierarchy** solutions, such as contractual relationships, joint ventures, franchising, etc.

A schematic view of the macro-organisational structure of the textile–clothing industry is illustrated in Table 11.2. Across the horizontal axis, a continuous spectrum of organisational forms is shown, ranging from full vertical integration ('make') to the market ('buy') across several intermediate forms ('make-together'); the entries on the vertical axis indicate the various functions that constitute the textile production cycle.

The **vertical integration** of all phases in the cycle, as can be found traditionally in big corporations, might be assumed to be becoming less and less popular, since it entails far more rigidity from a production standpoint. It can, however, reasonably be inferred that the introduction of information technology leads towards a greater vertical integration, in that some functions that were previously run separately will inevitably become integrated, following the implementation of new technological systems. For example, the introduction of CAD/CAM systems entails the integration of the design function with that of production. A further push towards integration stems from the adoption of management information systems that link up the manufacturing function to the control and commercial functions, whereby decision-making in the production area is becoming closely bound to strategic planning and to marketing policies.

On a production level, the decrease of subcontracting or 'putting out' systems, as found in three companies in our survey, is explained by the problems arising from checking product quality and the delivery terms of outside producers. These problems are evident particularly in smaller enterprises, since they have less control over third parties in their co-operative agreements.

It should be noted, however, that the flexibility ensured by the new process technologies, both in terms of lot size and of product characteristics, enables the integrated enterprises to partially overcome problems of rigidity that are associated with large companies.

Also, in connection with the technological solutions adopted by enterprises in the industry, 'in-house' projects are often implemented, both in terms of internal technology development and internal tailoring of standard solutions, as well as in collaboration with outside consultants. The need to develop new technological systems internally stems from difficulties in finding standard products on the market, particularly for the most specialised and least common production cycle phases. Owing to a

Table 11.2 The textile-clothing industry macro-organisational chart

Organisational Form/ Function	Make	Make-together					Buy
		Non-equity agreements			Consortia cooperative agreements	Industrial districts	Market
	Vertical integration	Equity	Technological financial participation	Control			
Trade Exhibition					interfacing specialised areas (Milan, Como)		trade fair services acquisition
Fashion	in-house designers	designers' joint ventures			image data banks (Carpi)		designer services acquisition
Telematics	in-house implementation			private networks with suppliers	consortia offering telematic services (ICE, Citer)	area networking (Prato, Como)	telematic services acquisition
Marketing	in-house marketing		franchising (Benetton)	franchising		district 'image'	external marketing
Process technologies	in-house implementation	establishing technology suppliers (GFT)			joint development of technology projects (ENEA Como)	area-based technology suppliers: integrated districts	technological services acquisition (Benetton, GFT)
Manufacturing	in-house production		supplying technologies to third party organisations	controlling subcontractors		decentralisation of the various production phases	
Training	in-house training				training managed through consortia	specialised training in industrial districts	training supplied by the market (technology suppliers)

very limited demand for some types of equipment, production costs are high, also because of the lack of any determined innovative effort on the part of technology producers.

The final reason for the push towards vertical integration is the increased availability of real-time information on the progress of the production cycle. In fact, the new information technologies ensure better control of the various phases of the cycle.

Table 11.2 also illustrates **equity agreements**, which provide for partners having split stock ownership. The joint ventures occasionally set up by garment-making companies with leading fashion designers can also be defined as equity agreements. The creativity of designers, as well as the benefits deriving from labelling products with a prominent name, are thus combined with the manufacturing and organisational capabilities and the sales network opportunities that are provided by the garment industry, thus creating new companies.

New companies are also established for the production of exportable manufacturing technologies, often targeted at newly developing countries, these technologies having drawn upon the know-how developed in finding autonomous solutions to in-house problems.

Also shown are so-called **non-equity agreements**, which do not provide for any split stock ownership of the partners involved. In the textile–clothing industry the financial participation of a dominant partner in purchasing technology, or, more generally, for providing the capital outlay required for the partner's activities is quite common. In the case of technology, this normally involves enabling third parties to introduce innovations. Another example of this type of agreement could be a franchising agreement, as adopted by Benetton, in that it provides retailers with the initial investment to establish their activity.

Within the category of 'non-equity' agreements are also those providing for some form of control by the dominant enterprise over its partners. Among the most common is subcontracting; these contracts can take various forms, for example, providing product specifications only or the models to be implemented, or even forms whereby raw materials are also supplied. In the sales area, franchising may involve some form of control in that it binds the shopowners in the retail network to contracts that impose the exclusivity of the product, set the prices and define the standard of service to customers.

Other 'non-equity agreements' are the co-operative agreements between individual firms and consortia, covering some joint efforts, such as the case of CITER in Carpi which, in addition to the databank mentioned previously, provides other information-related services. A databank service is also offered by ICE (Instituto per il Commercio Estero), a non-profit export agency that supports potential exporters.

Also common are co-operation agreements between companies and research institutes for the development of technological innovations, such as the case of ENEA's programme in the Como area (Lombardy) which, with a pre-existing association, 'Tessile di Como', interfaces with companies in the industry. An approach similar to that in Como is being developed in the Biella area (Piedmont), where the Città degli Studi, a research and technology transfer centre, has co-financed an analytical study on the wool-processing cycle with the Biella Industrialists Association, to be carried out by IT experts in order to identify areas suitable for automation.

Table 11.2 also shows **industrial districts** (Becattini, 1979; Dei Ottati, 1986), characterised by informal agreements and low transaction costs resulting from assiduous contacts, availability of information and established relationships. The 'industrial district' represent intermediate situations, between vertical integration and vertical disintegration; they may be considered as co-operative agreements on a territorial basis, characterised by high stability and easy information transfer. What most clearly differentiates an industrial district from the more generic inter-company agreement is the relevance to the former of historical, cultural and environmental factors, as opposed to the latter's straightforward functional integration; in the industrial district, relationships are developed by co-operative habit and by geographical closeness, and are mainly managed through personal contacts.

In an overall system of companies of varying size, involved in either production or services, all operating in the textile industry and with many interconnections, the communication of information plays a key role in production. The case of Prato is significant in this respect in that it allows an analysis of the initial results of a telematics project currently in operation.

The telematic project is sponsored by SPRINT (Sistema Prato Rinnovamento Tecnologico), a consortium for technological innovation composed of ENEA, the Prato Municipality, the Industrial Associations, various banks and the Florence Chamber of Commerce, and is aimed at the installation of a videotext system, supported by a modern fibre-optic network that interconnects all production system components (Reseau, 1985).

This project, however, has so far encountered a number of problems and resistance on behalf of users: some of these difficulties are determined by the impact of IT on consolidated hierarchical and power structures, others by the lack of cultural and organisational background to the participating parties, and finally by the difficulty of translating the operator's traditional language into a data-processing dictionary (Mazzonis, 1985; Zanfei, 1987). With regard to information control, modernisation of the communications system facilitates multi-user information access: the traditional intermediary (*impannatore*) role, which until now has involved exclusive control of market expertise, is thus jeopardised.

A project similar to that established in Prato is beginning in the Como area, where ENEA, in a joint venture with the local administration and with the Industry and Artisan Associations, has developed various projects designed to improve the organisation of small enterprises, to rationalise the transportation system, to enable commissioning companies to establish links with third parties and to improve access to market information (Reseau, 1986).

Technology development projects on an industrial district level are often concerned also with process innovations; in Prato the SPRINT project is aimed, in addition to the installation of a telematics network, at a cross-technology effort focusing on the automation of some processes, the adoption of new techniques and the automatic control of some operations, as well as energy-saving initiatives.

In addition to these public or semi-public concerns, industrial districts often develop technology supply. In so far as they host a customer base, a common occurrence is the creation of highly specialised technology producers, who offer strongly 'custom-oriented' products. In the Biella area there is, for example, an important concentration of textile CAD producers, mostly specialised in solutions for the wool industry. The district thus becomes an 'integrated district' featuring a main activity which in turn stimulates complementary specialised manufacturing and/or service activities.

Finally, the industrial district plays an important 'image-making' role in marketing for participating companies. Geographical concentration and easy product and quality identification are appealing to customers and represent an extremely effective sales tool (Camagni, 1991).

The current trends

An analytical study of the macro-organisational structure prevailing in the textile–clothing industry points to a current trend towards a concentration of strategic functions. If we look at the summary (Table 11.2) we can assume a leftward shift, that is, toward tighter cycle controls or even vertical integration, for the near future at least. In fact, there is strong evidence to indicate a centralisation of decision-making processes for commercial aspects, strategic planning, and product design as well as for the adoption of new technologies; this implies an upward shift of the strategic centre of the firm due to both the quantity and quality of information of all aspects of the company's economic system increasingly available to managers at the highest level.

Information is understood to be a strategic asset, and is therefore kept under close scrutiny at top management level. Of relevance in this connection are the conflicts that have arisen within the industrial districts where attempts have been made to relax information barriers and to implant into an open telematic network the complete range of contacts, information and inter-personal relationships that traditionally imply non-transparency, confidentiality and hierarchical decision-making.

Equally significant, though with the opposite bias, are the problems that Benetton encountered after installing the first centralised market information network, which was overlaid on a well-established structure of small manufacturers and retailers reluctant to supply all the information requested about their activities.

It appears, therefore, that information technologies have a stronger impact on the reduction of organisational costs, rather than transaction costs, in that initially at least they can be introduced more easily into areas characterised by a well-established, recognised and accepted power structure (Antonelli, 1988).

Furthermore, the complex problems and the high costs involved in the adoption of new technologies obstruct their introduction into small enterprises, confirming the 'conservativeness' of their spatial diffusion model. The new advanced technologies are particularly efficient if they are implemented using a systematic, integrated approach involving the production process as well as the management system and marketing policy. This integrated approach is difficult to achieve in phases, and is therefore less accessible to small enterprises.

In the case of 'industrial districts', the introduction of advanced technologies is sometimes slowed down because the single enterprise gains no advantage from the adoption of systemic innovations if other companies do not follow. The difficulties of the innovation process, and particularly the slow diffusion of systemic innovations, could therefore present a threat for the flexible specialisation model (Gros-Pietro, 1988).

Even if large firms can successfully exploit the new advanced technologies, there are various intermediate forms of 'quasi-organisation' of the industry that are assuming an ever more important role as an alternative to full vertical integration in some given phases of the production cycle.

The need for market resort and the search for synergies and complementarities through partnerships are due in part to the increased complexity and specialisation of products and markets. Firstly, technologies as previously stated are becoming increasingly complex and sophisticated and their use calls for consulting support; secondly, the search for variety and originality of models usually entails external creativity support; third, marketing also occasionally resorts to outside agreements that allow the expansion of the sales network with limited investments; finally, certain phases of the production cycle are often carried out by outside production units, for reasons of cost and flexibility.

The availability of a full-blown *filiere* extending from production to commercialisation and to 'fashion creation', providing access to specialised services, complementary production and a subcontracting network to carry out certain manufacturing phases in a close-knit co-operation, are all keys to the success of the Italian textile–clothing industry.

Future projections suggest a trend towards the vertical integration of strategic and control functions, thus towards the consolidation of large-scale enterprises, and at the same time towards more widespread intermediate forms of quasi-organisation *vis-à-vis* outside services and production facilities.

Thus, the external environment will play a major role, even though the traditional understanding of the industrial district is replaced with the expanding industrial district, in the sense of a wider geographical extension (Camagni, 1987). In conclusion, we can assume that the industry *filiere*, controlled by large enterprises but spatially extending over the regional or national territory, will represent the prevailing macro-organisational structure of the Italian textile–clothing industry. In other words, we believe that the traditional models of the large, integrated, largely self-sufficient company, and of the small, autonomous single-phase firm, will be replaced, on the one hand with a new type of large 'network company' with strongly centralised strategic functions and extending in several directions, and on the other hand with a new type of small enterprise, integrated into a multi-company local network. Across the network, a system of constantly evolving power relationships govern both the dynamics of innovation and the appropriateness of returns for all partners involved.

Conclusions

The analysis of macro-organisational changes due to technological innovation in two specific sectors of the economic system, namely the textile industry and the financial sector, has generated interesting results:

1. The new technologies have assumed a major role in the development–revitalisation strategy for the Italian textile–clothing industry and banking system. The introduction of information technologies in manufacturing, management and marketing has enabled the Italian textile industry to withstand the competition of newly emerging countries and to reach a leading position world-wide in the industry. Also in the banking system new technologies are a strategic instrument to cope with the increasing international and domestic competition, and play a fundamental role in the revitalisation process.

2. This strategy has involved significant changes. In the textile industry, the new technologies have allowed the enhancement of creative capabilities through the introduction of CAD, CAD/CAM systems and databanks. From the perspective of the industry as a whole, IT has assumed a fundamental role in managing vendor and market relations. The establishment of information networks within either large-scale vertically integrated companies or industrial districts has considerably increased the potential for co-ordinating different

production phases in the textile cycle, as well as for collecting and distributing market-oriented information. In the banking system, too, the introduction of IT has developed radical changes in the internal structure, such as the creation of the marketing function (typical of the industrial sector), and a deeper interrelationship among strategic functions. The functional integration process allows a more coherent and rational general planning strategy.

3. In the textile industry, the introduction of IT pushes towards a concentration of strategic functions, and to a vertical integration of all phases of production, for the near future at least. A similar conclusion has been reached for the banking system. In this case, the alternative choice of concentration versus decentralisation has generated a process of concentration of decision-making functions, coupled with the 'externalisation' to branches of all operational functions. The common idea that computer networks create a spatial decentralisation of power does not find any support in the results of our analysis. A transfer of intermediate responsibility at branch and plant level is taking place, thanks to a more efficient control system (on-line remote control), but this process is still far from leading institutions towards a decentralisation of strategic functions. In the textile industry, however, various intermediate forms of 'quasi-integration' of the industry are taking place, playing an ever more important role as an alternative to a full vertical integration in some given cycle phases.

4. The general conclusion drawn from this study is that in both sectors the introduction of new IT is associated with deep organisational changes, which are the main bottlenecks in the adoption process. This can be seen as a two-phase process:
   (a) a substitution phase, during which new technologies replace existing technologies to develop the same procedures;
   (b) an innovation phase, in which new technologies are used to develop new functions, and create product and process innovations. At this stage, technologies require deep and complex organisational changes and generate substantial economic advantages.

Our analysis has pointed out that both the textile industry and the banking system have exploited the first phase and are entering the second phase, although this will be a long and complex process which the two sectors have to face if they want to exploit to the full all the potentialities offered by these new technologies.

Notes

1. This chapter presents the results of two research projects directed by Roberto Camagni and conducted for Bull Italy by Roberta Capello and Roberta Rabellotti respectively for the banking sector (second section) and for the textile industry (third section). Though the paper is the result of a common research effort of the three authors, R. Capello has written the second section, R. Rabellotti the third section, while the remaining first and fourth sections have been jointly written by the three authors.
2. The major banks and textile industries involved in the analysis, to which we are indebted, are the following:
   (a) in the banking system:
      Banca popolare di Bergamo
      Banca popolare di Milano
      Banca popolare di Novara
      Banco di Roma
      Cariplo
      Credito Italiano
      Nuovo Banco Ambrosiano
   (b) in the textile industry:
      Gruppo Finanziario tessile
      Gruppo tessile Miroglio
      Loropiana
      Max Mara
      Missoni
      Nanibon
      Ratti
      Stamperia di Camerlate

References

Antonelli, C. (ed.) (1988) *New Information Technology and Industrial Change: The Italian Case*. Kluwer Academic Publisher, London.

Antonelli, C. (ed.) (1992) *The Economics of Information Networks*, North Holland, London.

Aydalot, P. and Keeble, D. (eds) (1988) *High Technology Industry and Innovative Environments: The European Experience*. Routledge, London.

Becattini, G. (1979) 'Dal settore industriale al distretto industriale. Alcune considerazioni sull'unità di indagine dell'economia industriale', *Rivista di Economia e Politica Industriale*, 1, pp. 7–21.

Bracchi, G. (1985) 'Manager bancario e nuova informatica', *L'impresa banca*, 2, June, pp. 21–7.

Camagni, R. (1987) 'The spatial implications of technological diffusion and economic restructuring in Europe with special reference to the Italian case'. Paper presented at the Meeting of Experts on *Technological Developments and Urban Change*, Paris, 29–30 June.

Camagni, R. (1988) 'Functional integration and locational shifts in the new technology industry', in Aydalot, P. and Keeble, D. (eds) (1988) *High Technology Industry and Innovative Environments: The European Experience*. Routledge, London.

Camagni, R. (1991) 'Local milieu, uncertainty and innovation networks: towards a new dynamic theory of economic space', in Camagni, R. (ed.) *Innovation Networks*. Belhaven Press, London.

Camagni, R. and Gambarotto, F. (1988) 'Gli accordi di cooperazione come nuove forme di sviluppo esterne delle imprese', *Economia e Politica Industriale*, 58, pp. 93–138.

Capello, R. (1988) 'Lo sviluppo di reti e servizi di telecommunicazione nell'area metropolitana milanese: vincoli e strategie', in Camagni, R. and Predetti, A. (eds) *La Transformazione Economia Della Città*, Milan: Franco Angeli.

Capello, R., Taylor, J. and Williams, H. (1990) 'Computer networks and competitive advantages in Building Societies', *International Journal of Information Management*, pp. 54–66.

Capello, R. and Williams, H. (1992) 'Computer network trajectories and organisational dynamics: a cross-national review', in Antonelli, C. (ed.) (1992) *The Economics of Information Networks*. North Holland, London.

Dei Ottati, G. (1986) 'Distretto industriale, problemi delle transazioni e mercato comunitario: prime considerazioni', *Economia e Politica Industriale*, 51, pp. 93–121.

Gros-Pietro, G.M. (1988) 'L'industria italiana e la frontiera technologica', in Benedetti, E. (ed.) *Mutazioni Tecnologiche e Condizionamenti Internazionali*. Franco Angeli, Milan.

Hepworth, M. (1986) 'The geography of technological change in the information economy', *Regional Studies*, 11, pp. 19–30.

Hepworth, M. (1989) *The Geography of the Information Economy*. Belhaven Press, London.

Lorenzoni, G. (1985) 'From vertical integration to vertical disintegration'. Paper presented at International Workshop on *Integration of New Technologies in Traditional Sectors*, San Miniato, 27–30 November.

Mariotti, S. and Cainarca, G.C. (1986) 'The evolution of transaction governance in the textile–clothing industry', *Journal of Economic Behaviour and Organisation*, 7, no. 4, 351–74.

Mazzonis, D. (1985) 'A project for innovation in Prato'. Paper presented at the International Workshop on *Integration of New Technologies in Traditional Sectors*, San Miniato, 27–30 November.

Monaco, T. (1987) 'Le modalita microeconomiche del controllo sulle risorse', in Camagni, R. and Predetti, A. (eds) *La Transformazione Economia della Città*, Franco Angeli, Milan.

Reseau (1985) 'Scenario telematico e territorio. Lettura di una esperienza in corso', mimeo, Milan.

Reseau (1986) 'Progetto telematica per la provincia di Como', mimeo, Milan.

Silva, F. (1985) 'Qualcosa di nuovo nella teoria dell'impresa?', *Economia e Politica Industriale*, 1.

Zanfei, A. (1987) 'Vincoli alla diffusione di tecnologie dell'informazione nell'area tessile pratese'. Paper presented at the conference on *Innovazione e tecnologie*, Prato, 30 April.

Williamson, O.E. (1967) 'Hierarchical control and optimum firm size', *The Journal of Political Economy*, 2, pp. 123–38.

Williamson, O.E. (1975) *Markets and Hierarchies: Analysis and Antitrust Implications*. The Free Press, New York.

Williamson, O.E. (1983) 'Vertical integration and related variations on a transaction–cost economics theme', in Stiglitz, J.E. and Mathewson, G.F. (eds) *New Developments in the Analysis of Market Structure*. Macmillan, London.

Chapter 12

Innovation and structural changes in logistics: a theoretical framework

S. Wandel and C. Ruijgrok

Introduction

Logistic changes do not occur evenly over time, because innovations tend to come in clusters. Examples of past revolutionary logistic changes include growth of coastal trading based on a new type of vessel; the industrial revolution that was made possible by the introduction of rail transport; and the shift to new distribution structures caused by the simultaneous introduction of automobiles for transport and telephones for order transfer.

We are now in the beginning of the next logistic revolution, which is based on the following three interrelated megatrends.

First, new information technology will penetrate all stages of the value-added chain (i.e. from the manufacturer through distribution and transport to the end user). The span of control and the synchronisation of the stages are expected to increase dramatically. With informatics, transport can be controlled and managed as an extension of the production process.

The second trend is the shift to more transport and to faster means of transport such as air, fast rail, and truck for larger freight segments due to improved performance/cost ratios. This trend is caused partly by improvements in transport equipment technology and by new information technology.

The third megatrend is the reduction in barriers between countries, peoples and companies. Examples include the European Common Market, the integration and transformation of Eastern Europe, liberalisation of trade, increased geographical coverage of standards, integration of the world finance markets, faster geographical diffusion of new technologies and increased international mobility of professionals and managers.

These trends are the main driving-forces for the introduction of advanced logistics in leading companies and regions. These developments are likely to have major effects on the way transportation of freight will take place in the near future, and therefore will also be very important for governmental bodies that are responsible for facilitating these developments, both in making available the required infrastructure, but also in helping less advanced companies to achieve a higher level of economic growth, while maintaining or protecting environmental quality.

For example, changes in demand and increased international competition, their implications for increased variability and responsiveness to customers' needs, and new production techniques and patterns significantly alter the relationships between manufacturers, suppliers, wholesalers and retailers. These changes increasingly determine the structure and location of industry and the national and international division of labour. These developments are leading to new demands on the transport sector and its logistics, i.e. transport logistics.

The transport sector already faces a capacity crisis in most countries. The increasing division of labour and its implications for production patterns and locations is resulting in a further tightening of the natural interdependence between transport, production distribution and related economic activities, often dispersed over different regions, countries and continents. This implies that bottlenecks in one part of this network — one transport mode, one region, or in communication — will affect other transport modes as well as product wholesalers and retailers, and hence employment and economic performance in general.

To meet the new challenges and at the same time overcome the capacity limits of the transport sector, a straightforward expansion of existing capacities is in many countries neither possible nor desirable for socio-economic, environmental or related reasons. However, structural reshaping of distribution and transport networks and operations have a large potential for using the limited infrastructure capacity in a much more efficient way. Advancement of logistics may even be more important than investment in road and railway infrastructure. We could summarise the tasks ahead of us by saying that we are not aiming for more, but for better.

Not only does the increased demand for transport result in greater volume, but also in qualitatively different patterns of distribution and delivery systems and hence increased costs. To cope with this new demand and the costs involved in co-ordination and integrating systems, there is a need to develop information technology-based equipment, systems and related services, i.e. advanced logistics. Therefore, advanced logistics is seen as part of the solution to the current and emerging problems of the changes in the economy, and in the transport sector in particular.

A theoretical framework

Background

Most road transport-forecasting models are based on forecasting traffic generated by the private car. Estimates of the size of the population and car ownership are the base. The theoretical framework underlying these models has been used to develop forecasts for traffic and infrastructure needs generated by the logistic activities of industry and trade. However, poor results have been achieved because the relation between industrial activities and traffic demand is very complicated and is not directly comparable with the case of passenger transport. Moreover, the relationship between production output and infrastructure needs changes over time due to shifts in organising production in time and space as well as organising transport with consolidation and intermodal transport chains. For these reasons, a more realistic conceptual framework is called for, from which more valid relations between logistics, transport operations and infrastructure provision can be identified and modelled.

Manheim (1979) has developed a conceptual framework for what he terms 'Basic prediction models', in which the two layers of transport service and transport demand are depicted (see Figure 12.1).

1. **Service models** are needed to determine, for any specified set of options, the levels of service at various flow volumes. Examples include travel times over a rail link as a function of train length, schedule, railway conditions and volume of passengers; and volume versus travel time curves as used in traffic assignment procedures.
2. **Resource models** are needed to determine the resources consumed (land, labour, capital and other direct costs; air, noise and other environmental impacts; aesthetic and social impacts) in providing a particular level of service with specified options.
3. **Demand models** are needed to determine the volume of travel demand, and its composition, at various levels of service.
4. **Equilibrium models** are needed to predict the volumes that will actually flow in a transportation system for a particular set of service and demand functions (short-term equilibrium in the travel market).
5. **Activity-shift models** are needed to predict the long-term changes in the spatial distribution and structure of the activity system as a consequence of the short-run equilibrium pattern of flows, that is, the feedback effect of transportation on land use (activity-system equilibration).

The system of prediction models is mainly developed for passenger transport but examples from the freight sectors are mentioned.

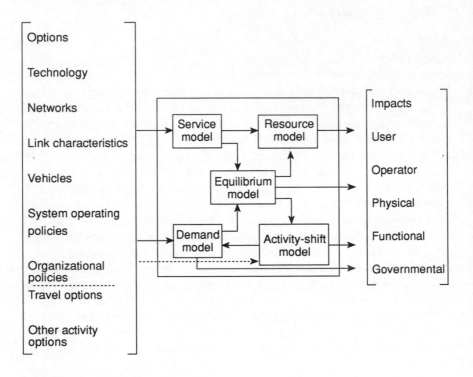

Figure 12.1   System of basic prediction models
Source: Manheim, 1979.

Extending Manheim's framework to five layers

Borg (1991) has modified Manheim's framework to better fit logistics and freight transport issues. He introduces a middle layer — transport operations — to separate the material flow from the infrastructure. Thereby, the market in the 'equilibrium model' is divided into the two markets, transport and traffic.

In order to also include informatics in the conceptual framework, we suggest a five-layered model (see Figure 12.2). The five functional layers are material flow; transport operation; informatics operation; transport infrastructure; and telecommunications infrastructure. These subsystems are then assumed to interact on four markets.

The product logistic activities of a manufacturing or trading company (i.e. logistics users) create demands for moving material and goods among nodes via links, i.e. a **material flow** system. The material flow system has nodes for production, assembly, storage and display. The demand for each link can be described in terms of ton/year, shipment size, frequency, lead time, precision and flexibility. Demand from all

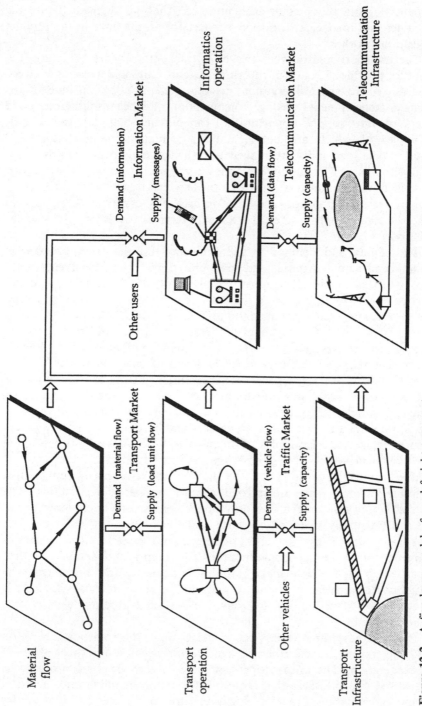

Figure 12.2 A five-layer model of road freight transport

product logistic activities at each node can then be aggregated into the total demand for freight transport services for all the links in the product logistic network.

The transport logistic activities of a transport services company (i.e. logistics providers) result in the flow of load units and vehicles between nodes, i.e. **transport operations**. In this system, nodes include modal change, transhipment, sorting, consolidation and deconsolidation. Load units provide supply opportunities for moving material and goods, examples of which are boxes, pallets, containers, swap bodies and trailers. The load units are moved by vehicles, e.g. trucks, trains, ships and aeroplanes. The supply opportunity for each transport flow can be described with parameters similar to those which described material flow. Supply from all transport activities on each link can then be aggregated into the total supply of freight transport services for all the links in the transport system.

The supply and demand is then matched on the **transport market** resulting in actual material and load unit flows. The effectiveness/efficiency of this match can be measured as load factor, unsatisfied demand, service quality level, etc. Note that there can be load unit flow and vehicle movements even without material flow on some links during certain time periods, e.g. for backhauls of empty trailers. The load units are moved by vehicles, e.g. trucks, trains, ships and aeroplanes. Vehicle movement requires traffic capacity in terms of space and time.

We define the **transport infrastructure** system as the physical infrastructure, guideways and interchanges, and the management of its usage. Examples of guideways and interchanges are roads and intersections; railways and switches; sea passages and harbours; air corridors and airports; pipelines. Examples of management of physical infrastructure are limits on vehicle loads, sizes and speeds; other traffic regulations; traffic control; allocation of the limited capacity by queuing time; priorities among road users; road charges or traffic restrictions. The infrastructure system creates supply opportunities for vehicle movements, i.e. traffic supply in terms of space and time.

Vehicle movements for both passenger and material flow generates demand for using the infrastructure. The supply and demand is then matched on the **traffic market**, resulting in actual vehicle movement. The efficiency/effectiveness of this match can be measured as vehicles per hour, hours of congestion per day, unsatisfied trip demand, trip time reliability, etc.

Each of these three layers, the material flow, the transport operation and the transport infrastructure, require information for their planning and operation. The information generated in each of these processes is translated into messages that require information handling and facilities. These information transfer facilities are provided by **informatics operators** on the **information market**. The efficiency/effectiveness of this market can be measured in a similar way as for the transport market.

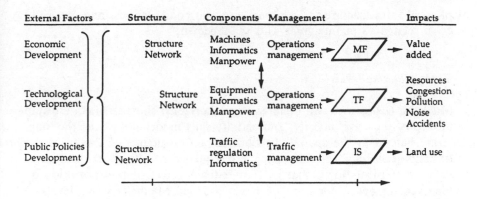

Figure 12.3 External factors, decision activities and impacts of freight transport

Furthermore this exchange generates data flows that require telecommunications infrastructure. In certain cases (e.g. EDI) this infrastructure does not exist at a sufficient level to guarantee a smooth exchange of information. Demand and supply of communication capacity is matched on a **telecommunications market**. The efficiency/effectiveness of this market is measured in a similar way as for the traffic market.

Note that the layers represent functions and not organisational bodies. Hence one organisation may cover several functional layers, e.g. some industrial companies have transport operations done on their own account and most railways still manage both the infrastructure and the transport operations. One layer may consist of several organisations, e.g. transport operations are often divided into forwarding agencies, operators and vessel owners.

Let us first focus on the three transport layers. The right-hand side of Figure 12.3 indicates the **impacts** from the activities in each layer. These impacts affect both parties inside the system under study and stakeholders outside the system via externalities, such as pollution.

Logistics create time and space utility for the products being moved, thereby enabling the logistic users to provide **value-added** to their customers. Production processes, on the other hand, create and shape utilities.

Inventories occur whenever the material flow stops or moves at less than infinite speed. **Capital** must be invested in inventory and warehouses, **end-operating costs** will be incurred for **labour**, maintenance, etc.

The transport flow also uses **resources**, such as vehicles, manpower and energy, and this creates emissions, such as **noise** and **pollutants**, and causes **accidents** and congestion. Transport flows generate costs for society as well as for the operator.

The transport infrastructure system consists of past investments in physical infrastructure in terms of **land** and constructions, and generates costs related to maintenance and management.

Three planning levels

Manheim (1979) uses two different time horizons: short-term equilibrium models of the travel market; and activity-shift models to predict the long-term changes in the spatial distribution and structure of the transport demand-generating activities as a consequence of the short-run equilibrium pattern of flows, that is, the feedback effect of transportation on land use. In our framework we have extended Manheim's two levels to the following three levels, each with its own time horizon:

- **Structure** (both physical and organisational): physical infrastructures such as new roads, rail links, new buildings at nodes; organisational structures such as business strategy; and customer and supplier networks;
- **Components**: manpower, vehicles, machines, line network, informatics, traffic regulation, signs, etc;
- **Management**: allocation of resources, traffic management, scheduling, dispatching, controlling, etc.

These internal decisions made by actors inside the system under study are influenced by environmental factors such as seen on the left side of Figure 12.3: economy, technology and public policy.

As seen above, Manheim used the two levels, activity-shift and equilibrium, only for transport demand and not for the supply side. We will use the three decision levels for all three layers. Hence the 3 x 3 matrix in Figure 12.3 is created.

The three levels of planning and decision activities of the three layers interact with each other in complicated patterns. Some decisions have consequences for decades (e.g. investment in physical infrastructure), while adaptation to new market demand and adoption of technological innovation typically have shorter cycle times. The different lengths of the cycle times create a constant state of disequilbrium in the two markets.

Many studies show that changes of logistics activities are typically demand-driven. They begin with new ways of organising the material flow inside the factory walls. When this is completed, the focus shifts to rationalising the external logistics of manufacturing and trade, resulting in a demand for new transport services. The transport operation industry responds to this shift by gradually changing its strategy, structure, organisation, components and management to meet the demand for new services. The shift in transport operation then requires new investments in, regulation of, and management philosophy for the infrastructure network.

Table 12.1 Relationship between logistics structures and transport demand

Logistic shifts	Transport demand shifts							
	Ton/ km	Geogr. cover- age	Ship- ment size	Freq- uency	Speed	Quality	Flexi- bility	Service cover- age
1. Global sourcing	+ +	+ +	+	−	+	+	−	+
2. Fewer partners			+	−		+	−	−
3. Outsourcing	+				+	+ +		+ +
4. Fewer storage points		+	− −	+	+ +	+	+	+
5. Inventory upstream		+	−	+	+	+	+	+
6. Local sourcing and production	− −	− −	−	+	−		−	−

+ + large increase, + small increase, − − large decrease, − small decrease

Advanced logistics could be adopted more quickly if new transport services and new infrastructure provision were established in anticipation of advanced logistics instead of a decade after its introduction. There-fore, it is critical to predict how a certain shift in logistics will affect the demand for transport services and how a shift in transport production will affect the infrastructure system.

Changes in product logistics

The megatrends described in the introduction are the main driving-forces for the introduction of advanced logistics and thereby for changing the demand for transportation services.

The expected relationships between shifts in product logistics on the component and management levels and on the demand for transport services in comparison with conventional logistics are analysed in OECD (1992). Here we will focus on shifts on the structural and spatial level and their relationship with transport demand (Table 12.1). Production output and the location of customers have been kept constant. Each shift is studied separately, i.e. *ceteris paribus*.

1. **Global sourcing**: Several megatrends permit geographically larger material supply and distribution chains, diminishing the need for national and local logistics. Therefore, shippers demand wider geographical coverages from their transport service companies but they expect no increase in cost, and no deterioration in quality or

speed. Hence, consolidated, multi-modal, high-quality transport increases.

2. **Fewer partners**: Companies are forming partnerships with their suppliers and sales channels, and therefore they have fewer but stronger relationships. This enables them to adapt more quickly to market changes. Higher volumes of material flow through each distribution intermediary and, hence, shipment sizes or frequency increase.

3. **Outsourcing**: Both logistic users and producers are focusing more on their core business and thus contracting out more of the production of their standard components and services. Implementation of information systems has accelerated this trend by permitting managers to control supply and distribution channels without owning the assets. Development of long-term relationships are required to achieve seamless interfaces. The number of steps, and hence the number of nodes and links, in the value-added chain increases, resulting in more handling and storage operations. JIT transport, i.e. the transport organisation that results from objectives that aim for saving from having and maintaining less inventory, is then required to counter the extra costs generated by the additional steps.

4. **Fewer storage points** and, often, only one central storage point for distribution over a whole continent, particularly for spare parts, high-value components and finished products that come in many variants. Central storage demands fast and reliable transport between the central storage place and customer. Scale and scope economies can be realised by sharing a distribution system, warehousing, an order entry system and other logistic services with other shippers in 'third party logistics systems'.

5. **Inventories pushed upstream**, in order to create more flexible types of manufacturing, require frequent shipments in small quantities to geographically dispersed consignees.

6. **Local sourcing and production** versus global sourcing depends on several factors, e.g. type of industry and stage in the product life cycle. Mature products with a high level of standardisation and intense price competition tend to be procured wherever they are cheapest in the world, while suppliers for new and customised products tend to be procured locally.

In reality several logistic shifts occur simultaneously, and the changes in transport demand from a particular company, industrial sector or geographic area is the sum of all the shifts that have taken place.

To summarise, the tonnage transported is expected to decrease due to lighter products and the average distance of transport is expected to increase due to the exploitation of scale economies in production and geographical differences in production costs. Market studies as well as actual experience also indicate shifts towards higher quality, smaller

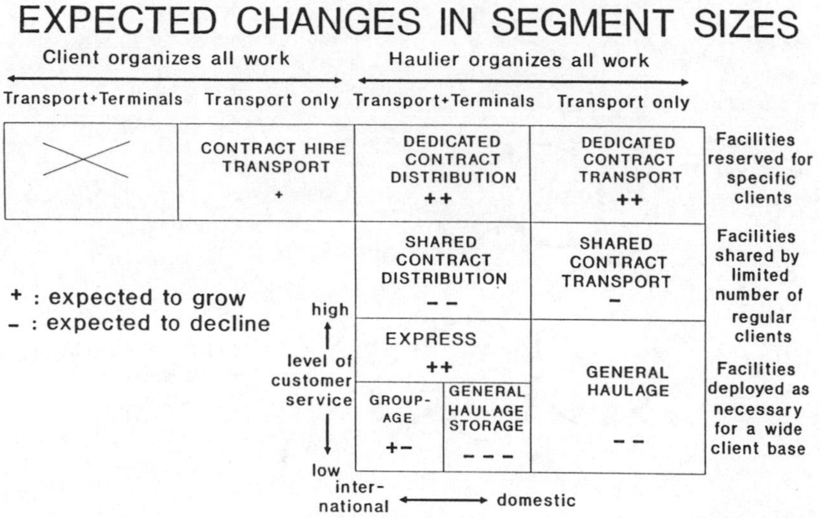

EXPECTED CHANGES IN SEGMENT SIZES

Client organizes all work   Haulier organizes all work

Transport+Terminals   Transport only   Transport+Terminals   Transport only

+ : expected to grow
− : expected to decline

Figure 12.4   Expected changes in road market segments of the European road freight market

Source: Modified from EUROFRET 1990.

Table 12.2   Estimated shares of road market segments in Europe 1990 and 2010

Market segments			
Old segments	New segments	% – share in 1990	2010
Contract hire transport	same	9.3	10.7
Dedicated contract distribution			
Dedicated contract transport	Tailormade		
Shared contract distribution	transport	8.1	25.0
Shared contract transport			
Express	same	9.8	13.8
Groupage	LTL	30.2	27.5
General haulage and storage	FTI	42.7	23.0
General haulage			

Source: Modified from EUROFRET 1990.

shipment sizes, greater frequency, larger geographic coverage, increased number of service add-ons, and, in many cases, shorter lead times and greater flexibility.

Figure 12.4 and Table 12.2 present results from a Delphi study in the DRIVE/EUROFRET project regarding expected changes in road freight transport market segments in Europe. Figure 12.4 indicates that high-

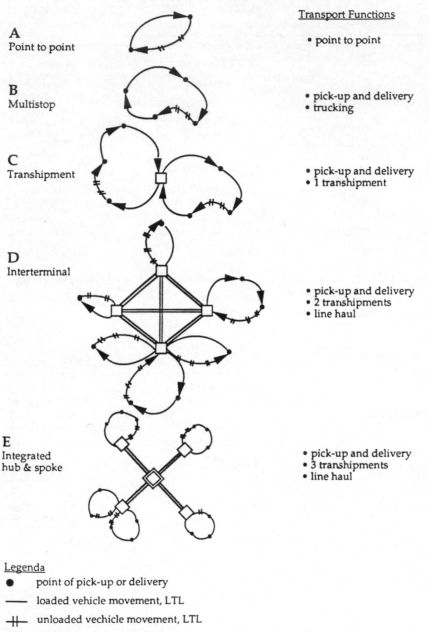

Transport Functions

A
Point to point
• point to point

B
Multistop
• pick-up and delivery
• trucking

C
Transhipment
• pick-up and delivery
• 1 transhipment

D
Interterminal
• pick-up and delivery
• 2 transhipments
• line haul

E
Integrated
hub & spoke
• pick-up and delivery
• 3 transhipments
• line haul

Legenda
●   point of pick-up or delivery
──   loaded vehicle movement, LTL
─┤├─   unloaded vechicle movement, LTL
═══   consolidated line haul, FTL
☐   transhipment or distribution terminal
▣   hub specialised on large volumes and high speed
       transhipments of packages and unit loads.

Figure 12.5   Different types of transport networks

quality road transport is expected to increase while general haulage will decrease.

Table 12.2 shows that the market share for tailored transport services is projected to triple by 2010, and express services to increase by 50 per cent. The FTL market, however, will lose half of its current market share. These changes are primarily caused by the new logistics trends.

In the next section we will analyse how the transport services industry, especially the road freight industry, is responding to these shifts in transport demand.

Implications for transport and logistics service supply

In general, five types of transport networks can be distinguished. Transport networks have evolved from simple point-to-point networks into very complicated integrated logistical networks (see Figure 12.5). What type of transport network is most appropriate is determined by the characteristics of the goods and the requirements of the customer *vis à vis* the capabilities of the transport service company.

Point-to-point type services (Type A) can be provided by normal truckers and other simple transport operators, but as more sophisticated services are required, the level of planning and the investment necessary to operate efficiently becomes intensive and more complicated. This holds true with the exception of super express services that allow point-to-point service using courier services, since they do not require investments in transhipment facilities.

A round trip multi-stop network (Type B) requires structured, efficient transport planning and routeing in order to achieve an efficient utilisation.

In addition to these requirements, a transhipment network (Type C) must have a terminal to rearrange the flows of goods to achieve optimum utilisation of load units and vehicles.

The next stage of logistical networks (Type D) uses two terminals for each LTL shipment. It often includes the interconnection between different transport modes, and therefore one must decide which transport modes should be used to route the goods. It is based on a hub-and-spoke terminal system which results in a higher frequency (i.e. more trips), greater load factors, but higher cost due to more handling per shipment.

The last stage (Type E) is the most complete network available to logistics users. If offers the greatest number of distribution services at a relatively high degree of efficiency. Distribution services offered include warehousing, administration, order processing and the control of the goods flowing via the transport network.

In Figure 12.6 we have indicated how these types of networks are positioned *vis-à-vis* logistical demands and the type of logistics organisation used. It is important to distinguish between the transportation logistics

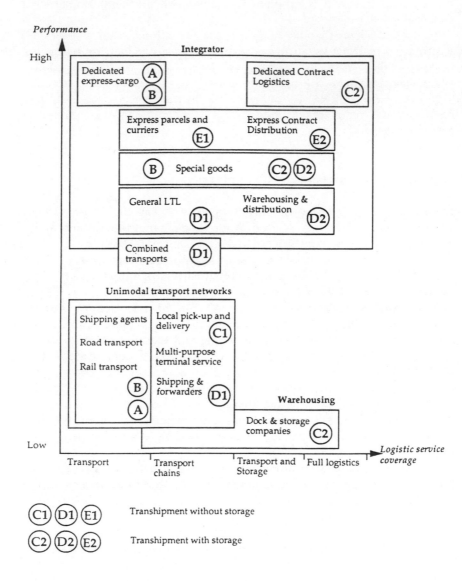

Figure 12.6   Types of logistic service providers

concept that only optimises the transportation flows on the network and the service providers that aim to optimise the whole distribution channel, e.g. making logistical decisions and warehousing goods on behalf of their customers. Only the specialised logistics providers (i.e. those offering the Type C, D and E networks) can meet the needs of logistics users who demand high performance.

The transport industry is responding to the new demand for tailored express services in several ways.

The completion of the Single European Market with the elimination of border stops makes it possible to offer overnight delivery between many places on the Continent. A hub-and-spoke system is used with air transport for the longest hauls and truck for the shorter lines, pick-ups, and deliveries. Both the Australian company TNT and the American company Federal Express offer Continental overnight services.

Fedex already has a world-wide on-line tracking system, and TNT and United Parcel Services and many others will soon introduce such systems. These companies will drive the development of mobile communication for the tracking of deliveries and pick-ups and the spread of EDI, particularly with customs agencies. The slow development in these two areas has to date prevented them from being able to offer the same service in Europe as they do in the US, although the US is five times larger than Europe.

An increasing number of transport companies are offering **third party logistics services** to shippers, where several shippers share the same distribution network and sometimes the same warehouses. The road transport informatics (RTI) must be integrated with other informatics such as inventory control, order entry and invoicing. This leads to partnerships and permits risk-sharing (Cooper and La Londe, 1990).

Preferably, the third party central warehouses should be located near the hub of a continental overnight transport system. This reduces the logistic order cycle by 50 per cent by avoiding the inbound transport leg to the hub. Fedex's Parts Bank is located near their US hub in Memphis. Spare parts for computers and human beings, e.g. hip joints, can be ordered as late as midnight and delivered with 99.5 per cent reliability by 10.30 a.m. the next day anywhere in the US.

Sometimes scheduled line-haul services are not fast enough, even if they are overnight. Hence there is a market for **super express**, where one vehicle is allocated to one shipment within one hour after the transport service is ordered. Roberts Express in the US has invested in a satellite-based positioning and communication system in order to be the market leader in this super express niche. Such systems benefit from being able to monitor continuously the position of each vehicle and to communicate with the driver. Interactive route planning in congested areas and dynamic route planning will soon be available, since the customer is willing to pay for service add-ons.

Inventories cannot be reduced to a minimum if transport service is not almost 100 per cent reliable. 80–90 per cent reliability is possible with good **quality control programs**. To achieve over 90 per cent reliability, three fundamental actions are required: each individual shipment must be **tracked** frequently; potential disturbances **detected**; and corrective action **executed**. The tracking and detection actions should be done prior to the next potential correction point. A benefit of these actions is that the performance of each link and person can be monitored, and hence, accountability is ensured.

If corrective actions are not successful using the current mode of transport, then a faster mode of transport may be needed. Therefore, contingency plans and resources have to be arranged and on-line communication established between vehicles and main offices. For example, if a swap body on a combination transport train is delayed too long, it can be taken off and moved by direct truck to the destination or, in a real crisis, by an aeroplane reserved for this purpose. Such systems are already in operation in the sea–air links from Asia to Europe, ISO containers from South America to Scandinavia, and combined JIT transport to the car industry in Detroit.

With such a 'closed loop control system' it is also possible to respond to changes in delivery time or destination, ordered by the customer after the transport has started. Hence, the lead time for changes is made shorter than transport time.

The developments in transport supply are largely dependent on developments in transport technology, information technology and the organisation of transport networks and operations (Brugge, 1991). Information technology will be dealt with separately in the next section.

1. **Transport technology** is changing in terms of load units, terminals and guideways. Load units like containers and swap bodies have become very important, and interest is now shifting to the interfaces and the points of consolidation. Terminals are increasingly using quick load systems, robotics and automatic guided vehicles (AGV) for the handling and storage of freight of different sizes, shapes and nature.

   The introduction of unit loads larger than pallets, e.g. swap bodies, containers and 2.5 m x 3.6 m mini-containers, has enabled the fast consolidation of several unit loads on one vehicle, to a train or to a ship. Such consolidation of unit loads can increase the ton per vehicle moved. If better administrative systems are also introduced, combined transport can be more economical and as reliable and fast as trucking. Breakthroughs are occurring in horizontal and automatic loading and unloading devices, the standardisation of load units and packaging techniques.

2. New **organisational techniques** in management and planning are the third element of the technological development. Technological innovation and social innovation (i.e. new types of organisations) are parallel to each other. A complex and stochastic interaction can be seen between technological and societal activities. For example, telematics helps an organisation to function properly. This applies to organisational structures within companies and more importantly to interorganisational structures like partnerships, channel management and information exchange.

New logistics patterns result in many cases in smaller shipment sizes and higher frequencies. To keep cost down and to avoid an increase in the number of trucks on the roads, shipments must be consolidated. Consolidation without losing speed and quality in delivery compared with unconsolidated dedicated distribution requires sophisticated EDI communication among all parties along the logistic chain. Typically this means on-line tracking of the parcels, not just tracking of the paper flows (e.g. freight bills), taking corrective action and preferably communicating with the driver. Furthermore, a radical advancement of hub automation, with automatic loading/unloading, sorting, storage, retrieval, picking and packing should help maintain or improve quality.

If other regions follow the US pattern, transport services will be produced in separate, reserved systems for the following parameters: shipment size, geographic coverage and speed. This means parcels and LTL are handled under different systems: area LTL, continental LTL, super express FTL and general haulage FTL.

With better consolidation technologies and corrective tracking of individual shipments, it may be economical to produce multiple services via the same system. This trend is occurring in manufacturing, as dedicated large-scale production is being replaced with flexible production, with benefits from economies of scope enabling a large set of different products to be produced.

In general it can be expected that the optimum financial equilibrium between transport, production and inventory is highly sensitive to the cost of each of these categories. The internalisation of external costs may cause environmentally friendly transport modes to be favoured and the re-evaluation of transport costs *vis-à-vis* other costs. The reverse argument is also true: if through innovation and corresponding investments in information and control systems the efficiency of transport operations increases and transport costs as a whole decrease, then an overall increase in transport services could be expected.

Changes in the supply of transport services are not decided independently. They are affected by new technologies, customer demand and external cost. In Figure 12.7 an overall picture of the interdependency between logistical change and transport supply is indicated as well as its consequences for the characteristics of transport demand.

This figure shows that many of these characteristics are influenced by a multitude of simultaneously occurring tendencies. It is interesting to see how many of these relate to the general notion of reliability. The reliability of the transport is really what many consumers require and at the same time this is the main objective for the improvement of transport services. Information technology really is a critical factor here.

In Table 12.3 a different way of summarising the main issues of this section is presented. It indicates the way in which new types of demand for logistics services create the possibility for offering new types of services.

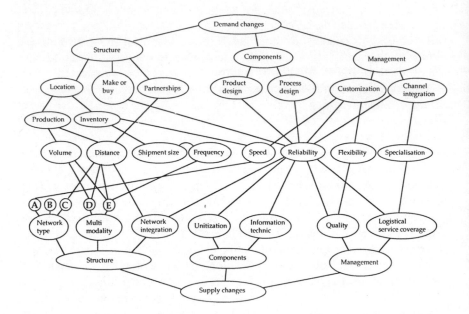

Figure 12.7   Interrelationships between changes in the demand and supply of transport services

Table 12.3   Relationship between new transport services and new logistics

New transport services	Fewer storage points	Inventories upstream order production	Contract out	World-wide sourcing	Shorter logistic cycle
Europe overnight	+ +	+ +			+ +
3rd party logistics	+ +	+	+		
Super express	+		+		+
100% reliable	+		+ +	+	
Break point				+ +	
Unit load consolidation					
City logistics	+	+			
Consignee consol					

+ Important
+ + Very important

Source: EUROFRET, 1991.

Information technologies

Information technology advancements have driven much of the world's technical innovation. The possibilities of informatics in trade and transport are practically limitless. We now face a remarkable situation: we possess most of the techniques that will be developed for the decades to come but only have a vague idea about their applications and consequences. This is especially true for logistics, e.g. the development of EDI systems (**electronic data interchange**). Bigger companies have adopted EDI and have set standards for their subsidiaries and suppliers. But in the future, smaller transport firms and governmental services (customs, traffic management, infrastructure management) will also be involved. Also the extensive programmes within the scope of DRIVE, RACE, TEDIS and EUREKA (PROMETHEUS) illustrate the high hopes attached to the evolution of transport informatics.

In the DRIVE projects EUROFRET and FLEET some thirty-eight different types of innovation in **road transport informatics** (RTI) for **road freight operations** were specified. A four-level evaluation process was used, viewing the likely importance of these developments from the perspective of the suppliers, users, society and governments (EUROFRET, 1990). The result was:

First priority
Communication with driver/vehicle
EDI with shipper
Static route planning
Interactive route guidance
EDI with port/focal points
Collision avoidance
Dynamic route planning

Second priority
Cargo/unit load tracing
Monitoring vehicle/fleet
Communication with other modes
Transport planning
Cargo/unit load tracking
EDI with customs

Definitions are as follows:

- EDI relationships existing between carrier, or integrator of transport services, and shipper/forwarder; focal and break points; and carrier and customs agencies. They cover not only freight bills but all sorts of planning and monitoring messages.
- Transport planning refers to strategic, tactical and some operative

Table 12.4 Relationship between new transport services and priority RTI functions/RTO activities

	1	2	3	4	5	6	7	8	9	10	11	12	13
Europe overnight		+	+ +					+	+		+		
3rd party logistics	+ +			+		+		+					
Super express							+ +		+		+	+	
100% reliable			+		+	+		+ +					
Break point. Unit load consolidation			+ +		+	+		+	+				
City logistics	+	+		+							+	+	
Consignee consol.													

+ Important
+ + Very important

(1) EDI between carrier and shipper
(2) EDI between nodal points
(3) EDI between carrier & customs serv.
(4) EDI between carrier and other modes
(5) Transport planning
(6) Tracing (finding)
(7) Tracking (following)
(8) Corrective actions
(9) EDI/comm. with driver
(10) Static route planning
(11) Dynamic route planning
(12) Interactive route guidance
(13) Collision avoidance

Source: EUROFRET, 1991.

- planning. It also covers tactical monitoring and corrective action of the processes involved.
- Tracing is off-line monitoring of shipment flows that is typically done by tracking the way-bill at predetermined points. The tracing information is kept in a shipment data base and used to prepare exemption reports and measure reliability levels.
- Tracking is on-line monitoring of the goods trajectory itself by manual key-punching, bar-code reading or radio frequency tags. Actual movements are compared with the plan. Deviations are reported to the shipper and consignee, and when necessary, corrective action is executed.

Table 12.4 depicts the relationship between the new transport services discussed in the fourth section and the priority RTIs.

Systems necessary to produce 100 per cent reliable transport, tracking and correction, and transport planning are the ones that require most prerequisites and information from others. Hence, to realise fully the benefits of advanced RTI functions, most systems need at least a basic level of sophistication.

With information technology, freight and vehicle flows may be monitored, and thus controlled and optimised. Key questions will be: who will have control and be responsible for correction/optimisation? And how can we protect privacy?

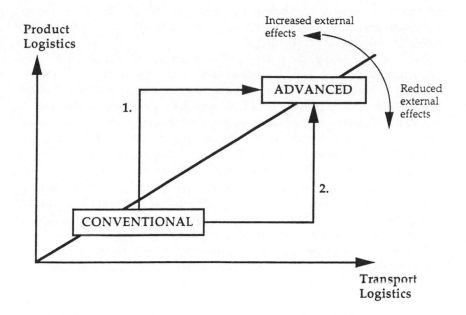

Figure 12.8 Alternative logistics development paths

Implications for informatics policies and usage

The traffic market, as compared with other markets, may be character-ised as a highly regulated market with primitive mechanisms to match supply and demand. The user is not well informed about the supply of capacity, and what he pays is rarely commensurate with his use of the infrastructure. A more direct payment for use that is differentiated in order to avoid peak hours and congested areas could be imposed (i.e. similar to that for telecommunications services).

Access regulation that is more differentiated and dynamic can contribute to improved traffic efficiency, but if the transport operators do not know the rules in advance, the reliability of their services as well as capacity utilisation will be considerably reduced. Transport operators are worried that access restrictions enforced by local authorities will make their job impossible. A scheme with dynamic and differentiated road pricing will raise certain costs, but from a logistic advancement point of view, it is preferred to access regulations.

Advanced logistic praxis always demands reliability but not necessarily speed. The transport operator has to be able to predict and keep time windows at both pick-up and delivery points. He therefore wants to avoid delays caused by traffic congestion, accidents, snow, border cross-ings or unnecessary stops at toll booths or intermodal terminals. Therefore, all such measures that can increase reliability in transit times are in high demand from logistic users. However, the infrastructure providers currently have no means of charging the user for increased reliability of the infrastructure.

The cost for using the road infrastructure could also include social costs for congestion, pollution, noise and other diseconomies. An incentive will be created for more environmentally friendly vehicles and operations. This pricing scheme could also replace strict access regulations, e.g. permitting the use of bus lanes for consolidated shipments or paying for certain priorities such as driving at higher speeds. Such advanced road pricing schemes require advanced information technology for measuring kilometres driven under various conditions, weights of vehicle, actual emission and noise production and other variables used for dynamic differentiation. This data must be collected to enable charges to be calculated and payments to be invoiced. New informatics solutions to achieve this are being tried on all continents.

Other road transport informatic innovations such as interactive route guidance, collision avoidance and, in the far future, automatic highway chauffeuring, have the potential to double the capacity of newly designed motorways and to increase the capacity of existing motorways by 50 per cent, according to some estimates in the DRIVE/PROMETHEUS programmes in Europe. Interactive road guidance permits efficient use of the whole network and avoidance of bottlenecks. Collision avoidance devices, such as intelligent cruise control, also increases capacity, albeit to a lesser degree, by allowing shorter distances and higher speeds while maintaining, or possibly increasing, safety. On-board, non-interacting road guidance using electronic maps could reduce traffic in urban areas by as much as 7 per cent.

Improvement in traffic efficiency via advanced RTI will improve efficiency in the other two layers, transport and material flow. For example, mobile communication, positioning and vehicle and load unit identification is a prerequisite for better planning and control of transport and logistic operations as previously discussed.

The mechanism described above to improve the efficiency of the traffic market is critical for short-term and intermediate-term improvements. However, the congestion and environmental problems we see today, particularly in urban areas, partly result from the inefficient use of land as related to the control of activities generating traffic demand. For example, transport-intensive activities should avoid congested areas, and land has to be reserved, perhaps subsidised, for building urban transhipment centres to allow a greater degree of consolidation in congested traffic areas.

From the above, it follows that the interest in infrastructure over the past few years has by no means risen only from the greater interest in the environment and the aim of sustainable development. Infrastructure systems are becoming more and more an issue also because of shifts in user requirements and technological innovation. In addition to improved means of transport (vehicles and vessels), upgraded regulation of traffic and transport flows, improved utilisation of network capacity and better alignment of the various transport modes and infrastructures, it is argued that the accelerated process of computerisation of our society should go together with a new way of thinking in order to find creative solutions based on fundamentally new approaches to the problems in hand. What the present situation demands from the modernisation of the physical infrastructure is not only repair, replacement and optimisation of existing systems, but technological modernisation of entire systems, including their institutional and social components.

So far, the choice has been an obvious form of modernisation of the physical infrastructure, aimed especially at combined renovation of different systems. Examples of the new way of thinking are the introduction of dynamic traffic control systems (e.g. congestion signalling, access ramp traffic control, tidal flow, rerouteing and information); various forms of logistic steering and on-line goods flow control, e.g. as expressed in the new transport concepts 'hub-and-spoke', logistic service centres, 100 per cent on time, and flexible distribution systems; and the integration of networks for picture, speech and data communication (ISDN, EDI).

The role of government in accelerating the standardisation, development and realisation of systems and infrastructures in the field of logistics is clear. For example, the construction of information networks that facilitate efficient usage of resources, and speeding up the introduction of advanced logistics in lagging industrial sectors, rural regions and in small to medium-sized companies, are urgent issues that governments must consider.

Moreover, the introduction of road–vehicle communications systems, under development in the EC's DRIVE, the USA's IVHS and Japan's AMTICS and RACS projects, will not only benefit the management and control of road freight transport but will also have a substantial effect upon road traffic itself, since pinpointed, real-time traffic information can be transmitted to vehicles, and traffic conditions can be monitored by the information received from vehicles, thus increasing the reliability, safety and efficiency of transport.

In order to obtain broader acceptance from society, further surveys and analysis of the diffusion mechanisms and impacts of advanced products as well as transport logistics are needed. This research should be aimed at clarifying the possibilities of transportation companies to reduce the necessary amount of vehicles and infrastructure through new organisation and improvements in their efficiency.

In the following, several issues to do with the role of government with regard to advanced logistics are summarised.

Many of the developments in communications and information technology and in logistics will emerge in different ways, at different times and at different speeds. It is therefore difficult and not advisable to control these developments in a top–down manner. This will cause inflexibility and inefficiency. However, the proliferation of all kinds of systems may also be unattractive, and some kind of assistance in the required standardisation, or help in achieving horizontal and vertical co-operation is valuable. This is an important task for governmental organisations.

All over the world, deregulation and privatisation of public facilities are emerging. This will create possibilities for increased efficiency through increased competition amongst companies and countries. Of course, there is a danger that monopolistic tendencies will occur, and governments should observe carefully what is happening in order to take appropriate action. This means that there is an important need to monitor the developments mentioned above. Many of the statistics that we are used to compiling are not well fitted to achieving this task. Especially in the field of communications and the organisation of logistics, some efficient form of data collection has to be developed.

It is expected that advanced information systems will expand from networks within individual companies to open networks, and that the quality of the information processed in the network will improve. It is also expected that such systems will expand from within a particular industry to large community systems and to international information systems. Many companies have already created world-wide information networks that facilitate the flow of information necessary to control the logistics. Moreover, the introduction of road–vehicle communications systems will accelerate the sophistication of road freight transport.

However, this process has only just begun. There are many obvious obstacles, such as social, technical, organisational, financial and legal barriers, to the establishment of truly integrated systems. Some of the issues and concepts which would affect the future of advanced logistics are summarised in what follows.

In order to achieve optimal usage of scarce resources, all of the costs that society has to pay in order to facilitate activities have to be taken into account, and ideally be paid by the users of these facilities. In many cases this is not easy, and at present many costs, especially those related to environmental damage, are generated but not compensated for. Of course, the internalisation of external costs — also relevant in areas other than transportation and logistics — could lead to significant changes in logistical decision-making, and therefore is of the utmost importance.

The environmental concerns are likely to emerge in the developed countries in particular. The way in which these will affect logistics operations is not very well understood yet and is an interesting area for future research. This involves the development of environmentally friendly (green) logistics, such as the recycling of waste products and the minimisation of external effects of transport operation (noise, pollution and accidents).

In urban areas, one is confronted with a lack of space and congestion.

For example, loading and unloading during normal working hours are considered to be the main cause of congestion, and the lack of parking facilities is becoming an endemic problem. Advanced logistics could be used to optimise the way in which pick-ups and deliveries in urban areas take place, among others, through the development of urban distribution centres. Also, other types of transhipment facilities that are necessary to consolidate freight flows are likely to emerge, and technological as well as organisational support is necessary to ensure the realisation of such facilities. Moreover, integrated production of a route guidance system using road–vehicle communications and the improvement of parking facilities will be alternative measures in urban policies.

In areas where the spatial conditions are such that the infrastructure cannot be improved on the ground surface, the development of underground facilities could help to overcome these problems. All of these developments will take place in various countries, and in various political and cultural climates. Such developments could be assisted by international co-ordination and co-operation, thus leading to improved economic growth and stability.

This need has been identified by some international bodies. The EC research programme DRIVE mainly focuses on informatics in the vehicle and along the road. However, some of the broader logistic issues are treated in the projects IFMS, METAFORA and COMBICOM. OECD has in its Road Transport Research Programme for these tasks set up the Scientific Expert Group TA1 on Advanced Logistics and Communications in Road Freight Transport Operations. Also within ESF/NECTAR several initiatives for further analyses of logistics issues have been taken.

Acknowledgement

The results reported in this chapter are to a large degree based on experience gained in research collaboration with colleagues in international research projects and networks as well as at our home institutes. In particular we want to thank the members of OECD Road Research Scientific Expert Group TA1, the members of EC/DRIVE project EUROFRET, and of course the members of ESF/NECTAR group Europe 2020.

At Linköping Institute of Technology, Joachim Borg's research has inspired us in developing the conceptual framework, P-O Eriksson and Karl-Erik Jonsson drew the figures, Mona Wickell helped us with typing and retyping, and Richard H. Barns corrected our English.

References

Borg, J. (1991) 'Makrologistiska studier', Department of Management and Economics, Linköping Institute of Technology, draft to forthcoming dissertation.

Borg, Joachim, Wandel, Sten and Ågren, Bertil (1992) 'On measuring macro logistics costs and performance in Sweden in relation to other nations'. The 6th World Conference on *Transport Research*, Lyon, France, 29 June–3 July.

Brugge, R. (1991) 'Logistical developments in urban distribution and their impact on energy and the environment', in Kroon, M., Smit, R. and Ham, J.v.d. *Freight Transport and the Environment*. Elsevier, Amsterdam.

Club of Rome (1991) *First Global Revolution*.

Cooper, J. (1991) 'Logistics and the environment', in Smit, H. (ed.), *European Transport Planning Colloquium*. Delft.

Cooper, M. and La Londe, B. (1990) *Third Party Logistics*. National Council of Logistics Management, Oak Brook, Ill., USA.

ECMT (1990) *Freight Transport and the Environment*. Round Table, OECD publications, Paris.

EUROFRET (1990) 'Alternative RTI strategies for RFO scenaria: scenaria for future freight operations and alternative RTI strategies', 3rd Deliverable, vol. 1, DRIVE project EUROFRET V-1027, Commission of the European Communities DG XIII, May.

EUROFRET (1991) 'The evolution of RTI in RFO: actions and impacts on the organisational structure of road freight transport', 5th Deliverable, DRIVE project EUROFRET V-1027, Commission of the European Communities DG XIII, January.

Inoue, K. (1991) 'Material for panel discussion', International Symposium on *Advanced Logistics*, Institute of Highway Economics, Yokohama, Japan, 28 May.

Manheim, M.L. (1979) *Fundamentals of Transport Systems Analysis*, Volume 1: *Basic Concepts*. The MIT Press, Massachusetts.

Nijkamp, P., Maggi, R. and Masser, I. (1990) 'Missing networks in Europe'. A study prepared for the European Round Table of Industrialists by ESF/NECTAR Network.

OECD (1992) *Advanced Logistics and Road Freight Transport*. OECD, Paris.

Round Table of European Industrialists, *Need for Renewing Transport Infrastructure in Europe*. European Round Table Secreteriat, 15 rue Guimard, 1040 Brussels.

Wandel, S. and Hellberg, R. (1987) 'Transport consequences of new logistics technologies', in *Proceedings from the Second World Congress of Production and Inventory Control*, Geneva, Switzerland, 7–9 April, World Congress, Inc. (Reprinted at International Institute for Applied Systems Analysis, RR-87-17, Laxenburg, Austria, 1987.)

Chapter 13

Rural areas in the high-mobility communications society

H. Eskelinen

Introduction

For a long time, the evolution of socio-economic and spatial structures in Western Europe has been based on the system of cities or functional urban regions. As a consequence, some countries can be considered to have become totally urbanised in the sense that they lack classical rural areas dominated by primary production and characterised by poor accessibility and depopulation. Yet some dimensions of rurality as distinctive features of spatial structures persist. For instance, the bulk of the area of each European country is used for purposes of primary production.

This chapter surveys the role of transport and communications infrastructure, as well as factors conditioning its utilisation, in the development of rural areas. A detailed investigation concerning spatial variations in the level of infrastructure networks and the services based upon them is clearly beyond reach here. The discussion considers these issues in more general terms, using the thinly populated rural areas in the Nordic countries as its main point of reference. Their experiences might have broader significance for the prospects of other rural areas in Europe, because in contrast to the rural regions in the south of Europe, those in the north have already completed the 'rural exodus' stage and they are fairly well-equipped in terms of infrastructure networks.

The second section raises some methodological and empirical problems concerning the delineation and characterisation of rural areas. Their internal differentiation and trends of development are briefly outlined. The third section focuses on infrastructure networks as a determinant of regional development within the context of rural regions. In the fourth section the potential of new transport and communications infrastructure technologies, and the constraints acting upon them, are considered. Against the background of these assessments, the fifth section analyses the prospects for the provision of services as well as for the restructuring of economic activities in rural areas. The sixth section draws a number of conclusions and considers policy implications.

Rural areas

One of the fundamental methodological problems in the analysis of rural areas concerns the role of the category 'rural' in classification and explanation. The fact that developments in rural areas are, to a major degree, conditioned by the dynamics of urbanised regions has important implications for theoretical frameworks.

As a consequence, even defining and delineating rural areas is an intricate task. Several criteria have been applied in empirical investigations, including occupational structure, historical and cultural characteristics, environmental factors, population density, accessibility and urbanisation (rural areas as non-urbanised areas). A major practical obstacle to the applicability of all these criteria concerns the availability of empirical data. In particular, most statistics are compiled in terms of administrative regions (see, for example, Moseley 1979; Phillips and Williams 1984).

Internal differentiation

The methodological starting-point for the survey is the fact that the urban–rural setting does not form a dichotomy. Nor can it be characterised as a continuum, because urban and rural features can be found in different groups and strata of people in the same community.[1] For instance, accessibility, which is obviously the first choice as the empirical delineation criterion for rural areas from the point of view of transport and communications research, is often linked more with individuals and social groups than with particular localities.

Overall, the socio-economic and spatial fabric in rural areas consists of different layers. They are restructured as a result of several processes of change which proceed in widely varying combinations in different regions and countries, and which are also influenced by natural conditions and climate.

The resulting rural areas form a complex spectrum in terms of economic base, social stratification and spatial patterns. Their internal differentiation is of such magnitude that there is questionable value in referring to the Western European rural areas in general or on average. Even population density, which is generally correlated with rurality, varies considerably in different parts of rural Europe as can be seen in Figure 13.1.

The variety of rural areas in Western Europe ranges from metropolitan fringes which are in high demand as sites of good quality housing and modern economic activities to declining peripheries suffering from depopulation and related structural problems. Some of the most remote regions have already undergone the process of marginalisation in the sense that areal economic activities have withered away; in an economy

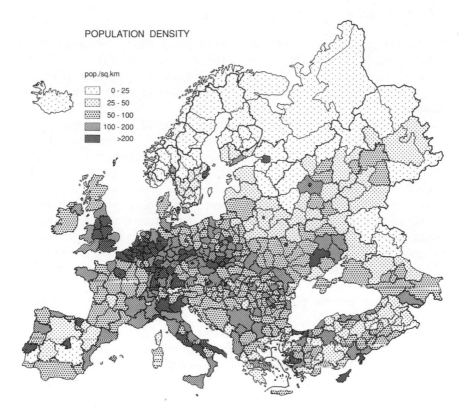

POPULATION DENSITY

pop./sq.km

0 - 25
25 - 50
50 - 100
100 - 200
>200

Figure 13.1 Population density in Europe

based on functional urban regions, these regions have been transformed into uninhabited raw material reserves or into recreation sites and symbols of environmental policies.

Typical examples of economically marginal and geographically peripheral rural regions include the bulk of Ireland and Greece, the Massif Central in France and mountainous regions in the Alps and on the Iberian peninsula. Thinly populated areas in the northern European EFTA countries belong to the same category. Yet by far the largest 'reserves' of classical rural areas in the Europe of the future are found in the former socialist countries. Their deep-seated problems are rapidly emerging as a major policy issue.

Trends of change

As far as production structure is concerned, the dominance of the primary sector has traditionally been the most distinctive feature of rural areas. In most cases, primary production refers to agriculture. However, fishing and forestry have been more important in some parts of rural Europe.

The position of the primary sector as a source of employment and income has rapidly eroded in recent decades. This structural change has derived its impetus from long-run trends in technology and demand conditions. Mechanisation has resulted in a rise in productivity, but growth in demand has lagged behind or been non-existent.

In 1960, about 27 million people were employed in the primary sector in the present EC and EFTA countries. At the end of the 1980s, the figure was about 11 million, and the share of the primary sector had declined to about 7 per cent of the economically active population.[2] Figure 13.2 illustrates country and region-specific differences, which are striking.

In the most densely populated regions of Western Europe, the share of agriculture and forestry is less than 4 per cent. In most regions of Greece, the Iberian peninsula and the former socialist countries they still employ more than one-quarter of the economically active population.

Overall, changes in the socio-economic and spatial fabric of rural areas can to a lesser degree be explained by referring to developments in primary production or activities based on it. In recent decades, the most important growth sector in rural areas have been manufacturing industries, public services and in some cases tourism and recreational activities as well.

Industrialisation — mainly in the form of the much-debated urban–rural shift — has been facilitated by regional differences in wage levels, the unionised labour force and other conditions of production. It has also been supported by various regional policy measures such as labour subsidies and soft loans. The resulting layer of economic activities, which partially consists of branch plants, has preserved or accentuated spatial differentiation in the functional division of labour. In most countries, its growth has already ceased or at least slowed down, which has contributed to a profound reorientation in the strategies for rural development. Yet there have also been examples of rural areas with growth of endogenous independent manufacturing firms, such as Småland, Sunnmøre and Western Jutland in Scandinavia, northern Portugal and central–north-western Italy.

Although the expansion of public services in rural areas has taken place in all Western European countries, it has had country-specific peculiarities as well. Particularly in northern Europe, the provision of public services to everybody irrespective of where he or she lives has had an accentuated role in the redistributive activities of the welfare state.

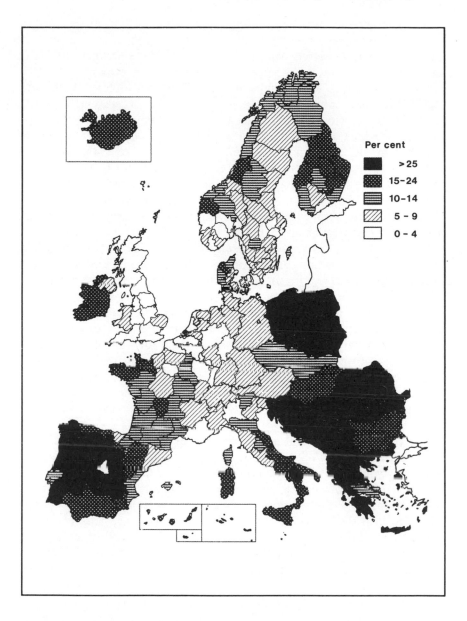

Figure 13.2 The share of the economically active population in Europe in 1985 engaged in agriculture and forestry (excl. CIS; figures on Eastern Europe concern countries as a whole).

Source: Regional utreckling i Norden.

Consequently, the rural periphery of the Nordic countries can be regarded as being in socio-economic terms to a major degree an artefact of the egalitarian welfare state (see, for example, Eskelinen 1991). In some other countries, mainly in southern Europe, the provision of public services has had a less prominent role. This has affected both their significance as a source of employment and their accessibility.

The drastic socio-economic changes in the classical rural areas have been intertwined with changes in settlement patterns and the spatial distribution of economic activities. Urbanisation and the processes induced by it (suburbanisation, counterurbanisation, reurbanisation) have proceeded in parallel with the depopulation of the most remote rural areas.[3] Yet it should be noted here that there are also in this respect clear differences between European fringes both in terms of the timing and potential repercussions of these processes. Firstly, urbanisation in its traditional form — as the 'rural exodus' — is today one of the salient structural characteristics only in some southern European countries, and even there, it is less significant than earlier. Secondly, because rural areas in the Nordic countries are much more thinly populated than in the south of Europe, even a minor outmigration from remote rural areas in these countries would lead to serious problems in the maintenance of the existing settlement structure as well as in the provision of services.

As far as prospects for the future are concerned, the main point worth emphasising is that the incorporation of rural areas into the economy at large is undergoing profound changes. The overall repercussions of this transition are far from clear, although some of the main factors are relatively obvious.

In agriculture, structural and price policies employed have resulted in massive over-production. A major policy reorientation is needed and it is bound to have considerable repercussions in rural areas. They depend on the strategies of adjustment employed by family farms. According to observations on various European countries, the options available can be classified into the following three main groups (Persson and Westholm, 1990). Some farms strive to become specialised commercial enterprises, establishing their own product development and marketing activities. The second group consists of those farms which continue their earlier production, but gradually more on a part-time basis or as a hobby. These pluriactive rural households combine agriculture with various other sources of income, such as rural tourism. Thirdly, many farming households leave agriculture altogether. The relative importance of these different modes of adjustment — and consequently, their impact on the rural socio-economic fabric — is generally conditioned by the planned international decisions in agricultural and environmental policies (see Strijker and de Veer, 1988).

Future developments in non-areal economic activities, which have rapidly grown in importance in rural regions, are influenced by the ongoing restructuring of the industrial system. Technological and organisational changes are reflected in the competitive position of different regions in contradictory ways (see the fifth section). With regard to tertiary activities, development trends in rural areas are partially conditioned by the future role of the public sector. Yet there are clearly other important factors remoulding the service sector in rural areas. These include, among other things, demographic developments, increased tourism and a growing interest in amenity-oriented styles of living which contribute to the demand for services not only in urban fringes but even in some locations in classical rural areas. Here, too, the prospects for rural areas depend to a great extent on their connections with urbanised regions.

Network infrastructure and rural development: basic issues

Needless to say, developments in network infrastructure as well as in modes of transport and communication have played a major role in the socio-economic and spatial restructuring of rural areas. Among others, they have facilitated rural industrialisation and the growth of the service sector. To take another example, the dramatic increase in the level of private car ownership has affected settlement patterns. It has boosted mobility and contributed to the diffusion of urbanised forms of living to rural areas. A major, continuously growing, segment of the rural population nowadays commutes to local centres for work and services, although the repercussions of this transport 'revolution' have not been felt evenly among different groups of rural residents.

   In the following, the discussion of the role of network infrastructure in rural development prospects begins with the basic concepts and policy issues.

Physical and social infrastructure

The concept of physical infrastructure refers to the system of settlements and the transport and communication channels connecting them (a spatial network consisting of the nodes and links). In a wider meaning, infrastructure also includes the social-institutional structure, human capital and technological capacity of a society. In general, an up-to-date physical and social infrastructure is a necessary but not a sufficient prerequisite for socio-economic and spatial development.[4]

   From a short-run perspective, infrastructure is usually regarded as a cause of inertia. Because it embodies an enormous amount of physical capital, it cannot be changed rapidly. This implies that new economic and social activities have to adapt themselves to the existing infrastructure.

   Seen from a long-term perspective, economic and social activities have created the physical and social infrastructure facilities they require — for example, the transport routes, communication links and qualifications needed in their utilisation. This guarantees that transport and communication costs are not directly dependent on distances, but are conditioned by the roles which the regions concerned have historically had in the spatial division of labour.

In the light of the above considerations, a fundamental problem facing classical rural areas derives from the fact that their infrastructure — not only in its narrow 'physical' meaning but also in its wider 'social' meaning — has mostly been conditioned by an economy dominated by the primary sector and activities related to it. This raises the question of how much and by what means it could be flexibly modified or its utilisation improved according to the requirements of emerging economic and social activities.

Strategic development or derived demand?

In general, processes of change in the socio-economic sphere are relatively fast and flexible in comparison with the slower and more rigid ones in network infrastructure. These two have to adapt or to be adapted to each other. The two basic approaches available in the development of infrastructure could be characterised as strategic development and derived demand respectively. This setting is outlined in Figure 13.3.

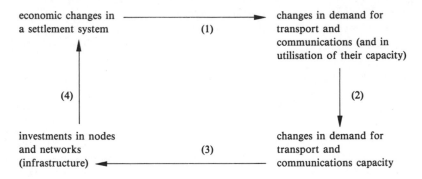

Figure 13.3   Investments in network infrastructure: the basic setting

Source: Adapted from Johansson, 1989, p. 6.

Strategic infrastructure policy aims at creating preconditions for socio-economic development in the long run; that is, supply comes first and endeavours to induce demand. This emphasis (link (4) in Figure 13.3) has been prominent, for instance when road and telephone networks have been built by public organisations in rural areas to advance the internal integration of national economies. Obviously, the most central issue of this strategy concerns the potential of infrastructure as a prerequisite for development; under which conditions are network infrastructure investments critical and efficient measures for purposes of socio-economic and spatial development?

From a short-term perspective, investments in network infrastructure are usually treated as derived demand, according to the chain (1)–(4) in Figure 13.3. This results from the fact that services based on infrastructure are utilised as intermediate inputs in various economic and social activities such as production and consumption. As a result, the relevant investment requirements can be estimated on the basis of the actual or predicted utilisation rates of the existing capacity.

It is apparent that there is no clear-cut dividing-line between the two approaches outlined in Figure 13.3, nor are they mutually exclusive. Interdependencies between supply-driven (or demand-inducing) and demand-driven investment criteria are complex in practice and the relevant time horizon is conditioned, among other things, by the technology in use. An additional factor complicating the analysis of network infrastructure investments is the fact that each form of infrastructure (roads, telecommunications, etc.) is produced by a specialised agency (or agencies) and there may be other organisations responsible for the provision of services based upon it.

Notwithstanding all these reservations, the distinction outlined in Figure 13.3 between the supply-driven and demand-driven approaches is relevant from the point of view of rural areas. This results from the fact that these two approaches imply very different issues concerning not only priorities in the allocation of infrastructure investments, but also the rationale for various regulatory practices in the utilisation of existing infrastructure capacity (see the subsection below on regulatory practices and policy challenges).

Infrastructure: A rediscovered factor

In the industrialised countries, the doctrine of regional development has been in a state of flux in recent years. Immobile, region and locality-specific resources have been emphasised instead of mobile ones, and, consequently, infrastructure-oriented thinking has gained ground in the analysis of spatial divisions of labour and settlement patterns. A lot of interest has been devoted to the 'bottlenecks' of infrastructure capacity, to the network requirements of the ongoing international integration and especially to the repercussions of new transport and communications technologies. In brief, infrastructure has been rediscovered both in regional development theories and in regional development strategies. From the point of view of rural areas, this poses a complex set of threats and possibilities.

As far as bottlenecks in network infrastructure are concerned, two related issues have been at stake. Firstly, it has been observed that the GNP share of physical infrastructure investments has been declining in many countries.[5] Secondly, because congestion is almost by definition a problem of urbanised regions, the construction of networks in order to relieve it tends to change the spatial distribution of infrastructure investments to their advantage. If there is no net increase in the total amount of infrastructure investments, rural areas, in consequence, lose their share. Obviously, the repercussions depend on whether this tends to delay the modernisation of their communication and transport networks.

Western European integration, the second important stimulus to the current policy interest in network infrastructure, is reflected in the 'grand dynamics' of spatial systems, and, consequently, in the derived demand for infrastructure investments. Leaving aside the genuinely uncertain long-term repercussions of the deepened integration, its more direct impact on the development of transport and communications in classical rural areas is realised mainly through special policies and programmes. In the EC policy they have assessed both conventional and advanced networks and preconditions for their utilisation.[6]

In addition, investments in international transport links induced by integration can in some cases have considerable local and regional impacts. They may cause a total upheaval in the logistical position of certain rural regions, changing them into important international transport corridors and having a major effect on their structural development (see Button, 1990; Johansson, 1989) This is, of course, not necessarily only a positive prospect, because it may result in negative externalities, as illustrated by the experiences of Switzerland and Austria.

As already noted, the potential of new technologies has received most attention in the discussion on the 'infrastructure approach' to regional development. It is briefly surveyed in the following section.

New networks: technology potential *vis-à-vis* policy challenges

The concept 'new infrastructure' can be used in two meanings. It refers either to technologically new infrastructure (e.g. broadband communications, TGV railways) or to the infrastructure which utilises conventional technology in new locations (e.g. new motorways). These two meanings are closely intertwined for the simple reason that the technology of new infrastructure networks is usually the most advanced available.

Emerging technologies, especially in communications, have aroused a lot of interest in analyses and speculations concerning the prospects for rural areas. The assessments presented vary considerably both in terms of time horizons and connections with the actual trends of change.

Can the rural problem be eliminated?

Paradigmatic commitments to the interdependencies between techno-logical and socio-economic changes are reflected in the assessments concerning the role of network infrastructure. Grand visions such as that of Andersson (1986) are inclined to highlight technological advancement as the driving-force behind socio-economic and spatial restructuring. Socio-economic factors and responses as well as providers and users of networks are not included in the discussion (see Janssen and van Hoogstraten, 1989).

According to Andersson (op. cit.), a fourth logistical revolution is currently emerging and it will undermine the structures created by the third one, the so-called industrial revolution. This break with the past is linked with the enormous growth of information processing and com-munication capacity. As a result of these improvements in telematics as well as in air traffic, the world economy will be increasingly characterised by the features of a discrete network. The continuity of places and regions is bound to decrease in importance in the sphere of economic and other activities, reflected in the changing relationship between the global and the local.[7]

The spatial context of Andersson's vision is the urban system. Its role will be strengthened and its core will consist of versatile and innovative 'C-cities' — centres of communication, creativity, culture and competence. With regard to rural areas, the implication is normative; they should be urbanised in functional terms. Following this line of argumentation, Batten and Wiberg (1988, p. 23), for instance, state in more concrete terms that the settlement system of rural areas should be changed from the traditional one formed by primary production towards

creating local environments in various parts of the nation (including sparsely populated municipalities) as nodes or junctions within a complex grid of networks to facilitate rapidly expanding service activities such as air transport, data-communications and creative educational skills.

This policy suggestion focuses on economic development and it refers primarily to the rural peripheries of the Nordic countries, where a large segment of the rural population already lives in local centres of various sizes and where the dependence of the centres on their hinterland has decreased in importance. Obviously, the vitality of these regions very much depends on whether these traditional central places are able to develop themselves according to the requirements of the modern economy towards nodal centres in the context of new functional multi-core or non-adjacent economic regions.[8] The isolating of the centres being a major hindrance to this pursuit, advanced communication and transport infrastructure will apparently have a potentially strategic role.

Yet, the realisation of the above-mentioned ambitious goal could not eliminate the rural problem completely. Some non-urbanised niches are bound to remain, and consequently, there will be, among others, persistent social problems concerning ageing population in remote villages. Also, new kinds of rural problems will grow in importance in northern Europe, as well as in other fringes of Europe; for example, the decay of the man-made cultural environment in the countryside will receive more attention. Furthermore, it should be emphasised here that the more traditional rural syndrome will not wither away in the Europe of the foreseeable future. Even if it could be gradually ameliorated in Western Europe, the former socialist countries, where it has so far remained latent, face it on a massive scale.

In short, the fact that the distinction between 'rural' and 'urban' becomes increasingly irrelevant in many spheres of socio-economic activities in many advanced countries does not imply the end of the rural problem. Instead, the need to recognise its variety is more pressing than ever.

Enabling technology?

In the discussion on the implications of new technologies for spatial development in general and for rural areas in particular, a good deal of interest has been devoted to the non-nodality properties of information technology (see, *inter alia*, Törnqvist, 1990). There is access to them almost everywhere, not only from specific terminal and destination points. This is in clear contrast to many existing infrastructure network technologies (including air travel).

Following this line of argumentation, several speculations on the repercussions of information technology and telematics on rural areas have dealt with a hypothetical situation in which their services would be fully available. Thus, they have concentrated on their potential impact in the case where the most advanced technologies would be utilised to the fullest extent possible in the framework of supply-driven network infrastructure policies (cf. Figure 13.3).

In that case, the non-nodality property of networks would considerably reduce the significance of physical infrastructure as a locational factor. In contrast, the importance of some other factors, such as psychological and organisational, might increase in affecting the dynamics of spatial economic changes. Thus, information technology would be a spatially enabling or at least ambivalent technology, contributing to the evolution of the spatial division of labour, decentralising it, undermining age-old hierarchical structures.

For more specific assessments concerning this technological potential, particular types of applications should be investigated in different rural areas. Interest in this kind of research has rapidly increased in recent years. With regard to tentative conclusions, the following two studies commissioned by the EC are probably representative.

A study by Analysys Ltd (Hansen et al. 1990) focuses on the economic costs and benefits of stimulating applications of telecommunications and information technologies in rural areas across Europe. According to the findings of the econometric analyses, the likely aggregate gains from investments in these are substantial. Yet there is a threshold effect in the sense that the benefit is reduced for extreme rural areas.

A study by Price Waterhouse (1990) evaluates four types of advanced applications of information technologies in rural areas. The potential of remote conferencing, teleworking, remote transactions and access to information are found to vary considerably. During the next ten years, remote conferencing as a public network service will be constrained by the scarcity of broadband links, and its benefits are likely to accrue mainly in urban fringe areas. So far, very expensive experiments have been failures; remote conferencing simply seems to lack something in comparison with genuine face-to-face contacts. The case of teleworking is different for this reason alone, that many of its applications are already feasible, and consequently, its constraints concern primarily organisational issues. The implications of remote transaction services for rural areas are conflicting. For instance, rural customers can receive better banking and retailing services over telecommunications links. Yet, as a consequence, rural shopkeepers will face increasing competition from urban suppliers, which obviously threatens local services. With regard to improved access to remote sources of information, the main conclusion of the Price Waterhouse study is that public administration, health and education services probably benefit most.

To sum up, there are indisputably potential benefits to be gained from telecommunications and information technology applications in rural areas. Yet there are major constraints to their realisation, especially in classical rural areas. The most critical factors are the regulatory practices concerning the provision of network infrastructure and the services based on it, as well as the determinants of demand for these services in production, consumption and distribution. With regard to research, the obvious implication is that the repercussions of new communication and transport technologies should be analysed contextually. Regulatory practices are discussed in the following section and demand is considered in the fifth section.

Regulatory practices and policy challenges

In general, the role of private and semi-private organisations is increasing in the provision of network infrastructure and services in western European countries. First and foremost the ongoing deregulation concerns the field which is changing most rapidly in terms of technology, that is, telecommunications, but it also has an influence on the maintenance and modernisation of the other systems of infrastructure as well as the services they generate.

Clearly, changes in the institutional organisation and regulatory practices of infrastructure investments and services are reflected in the prospects for rural areas in a fairly straightforward way. Firstly, deregulation tends to give demand considerations a more prominent role as an investment criterion. This effect is accentuated by the very high costs of some new infrastructure technologies.[9] This is bound to limit the coverage of some advanced transport and communication networks, and consequently, the case for special programmes for the purposes of upgrading rural infrastructure is indisputable. Secondly, low density, scattered demand for transport and communication services in rural areas contributes to less competition between parallel infrastructure systems, and consequently, service charges tend to be higher there. Yet it should be noted that this is a double-edged issue; from the point of view of an agency providing services, higher prices strengthen the rationale for further investments. Thirdly, deregulation undermines cross-subsidisation, that is, balancing the deficits of certain type of services with the surpluses of others, which has lowered prices for several transport and communication services in rural areas.

Needless to say, there are a number of factors modifying the impact of the above-outlined general tendencies in different rural contexts. Unfortunately, the possibilities of making more concrete conclusions on the spatial repercussions of deregulation and other institutional changes are rather limited, since so far there have only been a few systematic case-specific analyses of the ongoing changes in transport and communications policies from the rural point of view.[10]

As far as guidelines for policies towards rural areas are concerned, the foremost issue at stake is not the choice between public and private agencies in the provision of transport and communication networks and services based on them. Instead, the most fundamental decision centres on the criteria for the quality of these services as well as the resources for their provision.[11]

As far as institutions are concerned, a practice probably becoming more common is the one in which private or semi-public agencies are responsible for the provision of transport and communications services (telecommunications, bus, rail) in rural areas and local and regional governments set quality levels and provide subsidies. In general, the outcome is very much conditioned by the position of rural transport and communication issues, that is, the maintenance, modernisation and utilisation of networks in political agendas. In the long run, transport and communications services in rural areas also depend on the development of technologies suitable for their specific circumstances. This is also a task which is easily neglected without special development programmes.

Context for applications: service production and economic restructuring

The discussion above was confined to the prospects for the supply of transport and communications networks and services in classical rural areas. In the following, some factors affecting demand are considered. First, there is an introduction to the provision of services and then a discussion of the prospects for, and constraints on, economic restructuring in rural surroundings. Finally, some examples and concluding remarks on future development strategies are presented.

Services

In general, the (physical) accessibility of public and private services is worse in rural areas than in urban areas. In terms of economic analysis, this can be explained by economies of scale in the provision of services and by the discrete nature of some service facilities.

The problem of accessibility has become more difficult in many countries for the following two reasons. Firstly, the thresholds in the provision of services have been raised in order to increase efficiency, which has resulted in larger catchment areas. Secondly, the depopulation of the classical rural areas has eroded demand, leading to low utilisation rates of service buildings and facilities (see Batten and Wiberg, 1988).

This has supported further concentration and readjustment of the services provided — the whole chain of events is a standard example of the principle of cumulative causation. Yet it is worth emphasising that disparities in the provision of services in Western European countries are not geographically determined in the sense that problems would always be most difficult in the most sparsely populated and remote regions. As already noted (in the second section), the country-specific difference is important here. The second relevant point is that the greatest problems primarily concern certain groups of people, and only secondarily certain localities or regions. Accessibility as well as mobility is clearly linked to life-cycle issues: old and disabled people belong to the most disadvantaged groups. When public transport services have declined, possibilities for mobility have decreased for certain groups of people at the same time as the bulk of rural inhabitants have become very mobile. Thus, with regard to personal accessibility, the growth of mobility includes both features of transport-related welfare and those of transport-induced deprivation (see, for example, Nutley, 1984, pp. 357–58).

Given the problems outlined above, a number of new measures have been experimented with in Western European countries for the purposes of maintaining or improving services for rural residents. In many cases, such as in caring for the elderly, the introduction and utilisation of new arrangements in the provision of services depend mainly on available resources and organisational innovativeness, and not so much on further breakthroughs in technologies. In the transport sector, for instance, commercial services can be supplemented by services provided by statutory, voluntary and informal sectors. Practical solutions to the problem of low density demand in rural areas include, among others, various share-a-ride and dial-a-ride systems as well as community and social car schemes (Banister and Norton, 1988).

Yet it is also evident that the potential of new technologies in providing services in rural areas is far from being fully utilised. To take only a few examples, applications of new telecommunications and information technologies can be used to improve the quality and availability of health services (such as remote consultation with an expert through teleconferencing at a local non-specialised health centre), to create possibilities for distant work and teleshopping as well as to increase the accessibility of mobile services. As already noted, the realisation of some of these new options is conditioned by the modernisation of existing telecommunications networks.

Given the variety of problems and the varying level of infrastructure networks in rural Europe, generalising about the role of transport and communications systems in the provision of services for rural residents is obviously rather difficult. Yet it should be emphasised here that there are numerous promising experiments of new technological and organisational models currently being piloted. The large-scale utilisation of their results depend also on the qualifications of potential users, the upgrading of which provides a major challenge to various social experiments in this field.

Trends in restructuring

The ongoing structural changes in advanced economies are also reflected in the preconditions for economic development in rural areas, and consequently, in their roles in the spatial division of labour. Although this process of restructuring is usually conceptualised in terms of dichotomies, actual changes are characterised by several partly contradictory processes with country, locality and institution-specific features. The most basic problem concerns the issue of whether any new hegemonic model of industrialisation, urbanisation and regional development is emerging or whether the one argued to be such is only one aspect of a complex process.[12]

In any case, the main theses in the debate on restructuring can also be applied as a point of reference in the assessment of the prospects of rural areas. According to these the significance of marketing and international operations as well as R&D and product competition in particular grow in a modern economy. Uncertainty is characteristic to all these activities and firms try to reduce it through different forms of co-operation. From the firm's point of view, the resulting network relationship forms an important asset for competition, which it utilises for preserving and creating strategic resources as well as for improving its flexibility (see, for example, Christensen et al., 1990).

With regard to rural development, the basic problem concerns the extent to which the possibilities for creating strategic resources are dependent on distance, proximity and locally-specific factors. The obvious impediment to sparsely populated rural areas is clearly that firms in those surroundings, more often than in urban areas, have no dynamic local network for mutual co-operation — and they are more constrained in gaining access to non-local ones. This gives modern telecommunications a very important role. Although they cannot completely replace face-to-face contacts with customers or access to strategic information, they can be utilised for purposes of fostering decentralisation of decision-making autonomy and increasing interconnectivity between rural economies and the wider international economy (see, for example, Gillespie et al., 1991). However, the increased interconnectivity might also have negative implications for rural economies, because it tends to erode the protection of distance which has benefited local suppliers.

In addition to locational constraints, the present role of classical rural areas and less-favoured regions in the spatial division of labour sets structural obstacles in the path of their technological and organisational renewal. Resource-based processing industries, branch plant activities and traditional small firms operate mainly in mature sectors and are not usually on the leading edge of the restructuring of the industrial system.[13] Furthermore, it is improbable that the decisive stimuli for new technological and organisational models would come from the primary or services sectors, although these models are not sector-bound, but form, in principle, a possible strategy for increasing competitiveness in any sector.

In contrast, there are also certain potentially positive things from the perspective of rural areas. According to empirical evidence, new industries are not tied to metropolitan locations in any straightforward way. While emerging economic activities create their own production complexes, their locational window is open. Also, some new information services are locationally footloose. Yet the possibilities for successful restructuring on the basis of new industries obviously vary considerably in different types of rural area.

The success stories of new dynamic industrial districts are often explained by referring to high-amenity milieux and entrepreneurial culture. As regards the former, certain rural locations seem to have competitive advantages among relevant groups of people. In contrast, a dynamic entrepreneurial culture is by no means a typical characteristic in classical rural areas, many of which have for decades suffered from selective outmigration. It can be regarded as a result of, rather than as a reason for, successful restructuring.

By definition, restructuring is a multi-faceted process which cannot be compared in different regions on the basis of single indicators. For instance, observations on the relatively rapid diffusion of information technology into firms in some classical rural areas have an easily understandable rationale; branch plants have qualifications for utilising this technology with the help of their parent companies and they need it for purposes of upgrading their price competitiveness. In general, although there are numerous examples of technologically and/or organisationally modern firms on the rural fringe of Western Europe, on average these areas lag behind the core areas in restructuring.[14] The basic dilemma of classical rural areas continuously concerns the methods they need to employ to keep pace with the changes taking place in more central regions. It is exactly in the modernisation of rural economies that the strategic inputs of transport and communications are needed and their potential will be tested.

Although differences between rural and urban areas have become more fluid in terms of economic activities, there are and will remain regions where the potential for restructuring along the lines of the urbanised society remains very limited indeed. In these most marginal regions of Western Europe, very different strategies of economic development are needed. For instance, in infertile upland areas and in remote northern peripheries, where agriculture cannot be efficient and where it has been based on traditional small-scale farming, the preservation of landscape presupposes that the role of farmers develops towards that of park-keepers. The maintenance and improvement of transport and communication links and services in these regions would facilitate rural tourism and other sources of living for pluriactive rural households.

Top–down programmes and bottom–up initiatives

Problems in providing services have been identified and modernising the production structure has been tackled in numerous efforts on behalf of regional and rural development. Increased interest in local initiatives and resource mobilisation and in physical infrastructure such as telecommunications are examples of this.

Measures related to transport and communications systems can play a role both in top–down and bottom–up development pursuits. In the former case, the emphasis is usually on technology and physical networks. In the latter case the focus is on upgrading the qualifications of the potential users of available technologies as well as in testing new practical applications.

In the EC regional policy, infrastructure investments have played a relatively important role.[15] With regard to renewed policy emphasis and co-ordination, the Special Telecommunications Action for Regional Development (STAR) in the years 1987–91 has been, so far, the most important programme in support of rural areas. Its aim was to introduce advanced telecommunications services in the areas lagging behind. Under this programme, around ECUs 1,500 million were allocated from ERDF and national sources. About four-fifths of the funding were used for infrastructural advances and the rest for feasibility studies, promotion activities and demonstration projects. Among potential beneficiaries, small and medium-sized enterprises were the most important target group, and the idea was to place infrastructural measures into a more comprehensive development package.

Recently, an extension of the application side of the STAR, TELEMATIQUE, has been launched. It will operate until 1993 and is intended to support both urban and rural areas of the target regions. Another programme on telematics systems for rural areas, ORA (**opportunities for rural areas**), is a research and development scheme, the priorities of which include drawing up a typology of rural areas in order to indicate those most suitable for particular information technology services. ORA will investigate the social and technological preconditions for such services, measure potential demand and provide support for pilot applications.

In comparison, a representative rural example of the bottom–up approach to the introduction of modern technologies and the creation of a demand for services based on them is the Nordic telecottage movement.[16] A telecottage is a small-scale advisory centre for the introduction of information technology. In addition to data processing and telecommunications equipment, it may contain local TV production facilities, teleconference studio, telework equipment, databases and consultancy capacity. Telecottages have been mainly established on local initiatives but they have been supported financially from public sources. The aim of a telecottage is to inform local people about the basis of information technology, support its applications in agriculture and other economic activities, provide a place for distance working and in some cases serve as a local meeting forum.

Several hundred telecottages have been founded in rural areas in the Nordic countries since the mid-1980s. Their roles have, of course, changed in the course of time; some have become small-scale firms, and others have been linked to the educational system. More recently, some experiments have been launched along the same lines in some other countries, such as Ireland. In any case, the varied experiences of telecottages give a concrete basis for evaluating the potential of small-scale applications of information technologies in the context of peripheral and rural areas.

As already noted, priorities in investments in new network infrastructure vary a lot in the classical rural areas of Western Europe. In some regions there are still serious deficiencies in the infrastructure needed to provide basic services, whereas there are other regions where the emphasis has shifted to the construction and utilisation of new infrastructure technologies. In the future, this difference in the level of development could even become a potential source of conflict between various fringe areas in an integrating Western Europe.

In general, the experiences gained from the diverse development efforts of rural areas in Western Europe suggest that new forms of production, distribution and governance are not transferable from one country or region without modifications (see, for example, Oinas, 1990). Their evolution is conditioned by the prevailing production base, political and social institutions and spatial structure. This simple fact has important implications for strategies seeking to support revitalisation and restructuring. In these strategies, the relative role of infrastructure and the choice of emphasis between physical and social infrastructure is a case-specific issue.

Conclusions and policy implications

On the whole, the socio-economic and spatial development of rural regions in Western Europe is to a diminishing extent based on areal economic activities; land as a factor of production has decreased in importance. Contrastingly, the role of the countryside as a compensation area for urbanised society has become more prominent. It provides milieux for housing, leisure and tourism and is utilised as a reserve of both natural and cultural landscape. Consequently, the role of space as the basic resource of rural areas is accentuated. Competition over it intensifies in most accessible regions whereas there is a surplus of it in most remote areas.

From the perspective of rural areas, trends in production structure, organisations and technology have both positive and negative implications. New organisational models might contribute to decentralisation of decision-making from centres of markets and administration, while growth industries are locationally rather footloose and are not tied to urban agglomerations. In contrast, face-to-face contacts and utilisation of special services, which are more easily accessible in urban surroundings, play an increasingly important role in modern economic activities. Overall, these developments emphasise the strategic role of telecommunications in the adaptation of rural economies into a wider national and international economy.

At a closer glance, even genuinely rural areas in Western Europe are internally differentiated to the extent that it is a highly questionable practice to analyse them in terms of averages. This variation concerns both current structural characteristics and ongoing processes — and naturally, the problems of development and the strategies needed in alleviating them as well. With regard to the potential role of network infrastructure, for instance, this differentiation is evident in the comparison of the southernmost and northernmost rural regions in Western Europe. The former are still characterised by the rural exodus syndrome and by deficiencies in the provision of basic services. In contrast, the very thinly populated regions in the north are fairly well equipped with up-to-date infrastructure networks, but they face the intricate problem of how their small and scattered centres could develop into dynamic nodes in a modern international economy. As a consequence, the need to adjust strategies according to local circumstances is obvious, both in the provision of services and in the restructuring of economic activities.

This creates a potential conflict with the ongoing developments in infrastructure policies. These are, to an increasing degree, based on the priorities of the urbanised society as seen from an international perspective, and carried out in a more homogeneous institutional setting. The resulting emphasis on demand and competition is difficult to bring into accord with the requirements of rural regions. Although advances in network infrastructure technologies offer some new options, in the final analysis solutions are primarily conditioned by choices in transport and communications policies.

To sum up there are some priorities in policies which are worth emphasising:

1. Public procurement and R&D support for rural communications and transport applications are needed, because there is an urban bias in technical development in network infrastructure and services.
2. The modernisation of rural networks, especially in telecommunications, is a necessary precondition for the utilisation of their potential in rural development. This calls for special-purpose programmes. Also, modernisation should be ensured as an important target in regulatory practices concerning network service operators in a more competitive setting.
3. Universal service obligations should not be abandoned as a point of reference in policies, although in practice relevant measures (e.g. subsidised tariffs, differentiated service charges, etc.) have to be modified according to resources, technologies and specific circumstances.
4. Upgrading demand is an essential element in development strategies concerning transport and communications infrastructure and services in rural areas. It emphasises improvements in social infrastructure, especially in education. Measures should be employed in the context of an integrative programme which for its part presupposes co-operation between organisations at different levels.

Acknowledgement

Comments and suggestions by Andrew Gillespie, Seamus Grimes, Sven Illeris, Sten Wandel and Perttu Vartiainen have proved most useful in the preparation of the final draft of this chapter.

Notes

1. The dichotomous theories of contrast thinking have a long tradition in rural studies. They are derived from the classic *Gemeinschaft* v. *Gesellschaft* contrast introduced by Tönnies (1974; original 1887). These concepts were erroneously linked to particular localities — to the village and town as opposed to the city. Pahl (1966, p. 322) questioned the relevance of the urban–rural continuum, which according to him 'arose in reaction against the polar-type dichotomies, but there are equal dangers in overreadily accepting the false continuity. . . . Any attempt to tie particular patterns of social relationships to specific geographical milieux is a singularly fruitless exercise.

2. Widely differing figures can be and have been presented in regard to the size of the total rural population. Hall and Hay (1980), for example, estimate that in 1975 about 32 million of the total Western European population of *c*. 300 million lived in regions which were non-metropolitan in their classification. Yet they had to apply their classification (core, ring, non-metropolitan) in very different ways in different countries (for the criteria used, see Hall and Hay, op. cit., 32–83).

3. For the conceptual analysis of these processes, see, for example, Vartiainen, 1989.

4. Analytically, physical infrastructure consists of a set of attributes, not of a set of material objects, (see Youngson, 1967). It has two distinctive qualities: it has to be built in large units and it produces external effects. For the analysis of the concept and properties of infrastructure see Lakshmanan, 1989. Concerning the role of infrastructure in socio-economic and spatial development in general, see for example, Fullerton and Gillespie, 1988.

5. For the analysis of trends in the share of infrastructure investments and related macro economic issues, see, for example, Aschauer, 1989; and Peterson, 1990.

6. See, for example, Fullerton and Gillespie, 1988; Revolve, 1988; Ungerer, 1990; and also the fifth section.

7. There are several approximately similar interpretations of the long-term spatial dynamics of the information economy. In some of them, the socio-economic response is not totally subordinated to the technological imperative; see, for example, Castells (1989), who analyses the process of transition from the 'space of places' to the 'space of flows'.

8. Snickars (1989, p. 29) puts this concisely: 'The first role comes to a city by inheritance. The second role must be acquired through conscious decisions made to select collaborating partners in cities in similar or aspired positions.'

9. In particular, the lack of demand concentrations sets limits on the diffusion of nodal, capital-intensive infrastructure. For instance, there is no rationale for the forthcoming network of high-speed trains reaching the extreme fringes of Europe. The problem of spatial coverage does not only concern transport and telecommunications services, but is a relevant issue for example in the supply of energy. Natural gas, which is a potential substitute for electricity in many cases, is only available to a limited extent in Western European rural areas.

10. See, however, Sundberg and Carlen, 1989; and Gillespie et al., 1991.

11. From the rural point of view, an interesting solution to these problems is Eriksson's (1989) suggestion, which states that the provider of an infrastructure system would have to pay a 'tax' based on the number of non-beneficiaries. The resulting infrastructure fund could be used for paying

compensation or for developing appropriate technological solutions for providing network services in sparsely populated regions.

12. The break with the past has been argued to lead, for example, from the previous technological paradigm or mode of regulation to a new one, from price competition to competition based on product development, and from Fordist mass production to flexible, customised production. The one-dimensionality of the ongoing restructuration is overemphasised in these frames of reference in a rather similar way as the urban/rural dichotomy in rural studies. For a presentation of the supposed new model for industrialisation and regional development, see Storper and Scott, 1989; and for a critical commentary, Amin and Robins, 1990.

13. Admittedly, there are interesting exceptions. For the case of western Jutland in Denmark, see Hansen, 1991; and Illeris, 1992.

14. Concerning the introduction of information technology in sparsely populated regions, see Wiberg, 1990.

15. See, for example, Fullerton and Gillespie, 1988.

16. The underlying ideas of the Nordic telehouse movement can be found in the influential nineteenth-century Danish Folk High School movement, which emphasised group discussions instead of formal education as a method of training. For discussions of the telehouse movement, see Qvortrup, 1989; and Rieper, 1990; for a summary evaluation of social experiences with teleservice centres, televiewing, databases and distance learning, see Cronberg et al., 1991.

References

Amin, A. and Robins, K. (1990) 'The re-emergence of regional economies? The mythical geography of flexible accumulation', *Environment & Planning D. Society & Space*, 8(1), pp. 7–34.

Andersson, Å. (1986) 'The four logistical revolutions'. *Papers of the Regional Science Association*, 59, pp. 1–12.

Aschauer, D.A. (1989) 'Is public expenditure productive?', *Journal of Monetary Economics*, 23, pp. 177–200.

Banister, D. and Norton, F. (1988) 'The role of voluntary sector in the provision of rural services — the case of transport', *Journal of Rural Studies*, 4(1), pp. 57–71.

Batten, D. and Wiberg, U. (1988) 'Disparities in the provision of services between urban and rural areas: current situation and trends'. Working Papers from CERUM 1988: 22. Umeå.

Button, K. (1990) 'Infrastructure plans for Europe', in Gidlund, J. and Törnqvist, G. (eds), *European Networks*, pp. 95–118. CERUM, University of Umeå and Institute for Futures Studies. European Networks 1990.2.

Castells, M. (1989) *The Informational City: Information Technology, Economic Restructuring, and the Urban–Regional Process*. Basil Blackwell, Oxford.

Christensen, P.R., Eskelinen, H., Forsström, B., Lindmark, L. and Vatne, E. (1990) 'Firms in Network. Concepts, spatial impacts and policy implications', *NordREFO* 1990:1, 11–58. Academic Press, Copenhagen.

Cronberg, R., Duelund, P., Jensen, O.M. and Qvortrup, L. (eds) (1991) 'Danish Experiments — Social Constructions of Technology'. New Social Science Monographs, Copenhagen Business School.

Eriksson, O. (1989) *Bortom storstadsideerna. En regional framtid för Sverige och Norden På 2010-talet*. Carlssons, Stockholm.

Eskelinen, H. (1991) 'The Nordic model at the crossroads — the consolidated periphery in a state of flux?' *NordREFO*, 1991: 4, pp. 55-64. Academic Press, Copenhagen.

Fullerton, B. and Gillespie, A. (1988) 'Transport and Communications', in Molle, W. and Cappellin, R. (eds) *Regional Impact of Community Policies in Europe*. Gower, Aldershot, pp. 88-110.

Gillespie, A., Coombes, M., Raybould, S. and Bradley, D. (1991) 'Telecommunications and the development of rural Scotland. A Study for Scottish Enterprise'. CURDS, University of Newcastle-upon-Tyne.

Hall, P. and Hay, D. (1980) *Growth Centres in the European Urban System*. Heinemann, London.

Hansen, N. (1991) 'Factories in Danish fields: how high-wage, flexible production has succeeded in peripheral Jutland', *International Regional Science Review*, 14(2), pp. 109-32.

Hansen, S., Cleevely, D., Wadsworth, S., Bailey, H. and Bakewell, O. (1990) 'Telecommunications in rural Europe. Economic implications', *Telecommunications Policy*, June, pp. 207-22.

Illeris, S. (1992) 'The Herning-lkast textile industry: an industrial district in West Jutland', *Entrepreneurship & Regional Development*, 4, pp. 73-84.

Janssen, B. and van Hoogstraten, P. (1989) 'The "new infrastructure" and regional development', in Albrechts, L. et al. (eds) *Regional Policy at the Crossroads*. Jessica Kingsley Publishers, London, 52-66.

Johansson, B. (1989), 'Economic development and networks for spatial interaction'. CERUM Working Papers 1989:28. University of Umeå.

Lakshmanan, T.R. (1989) 'Infrastructure and economic transformation', in Andersson, Å.E. et al. (eds) *Advances in Spatial Theory and Dynamics*. North Holland, pp. 241-61.

Moseley, M. (1979), *Accessibility: The Rural Challenge*. Methuen, London.

Nutley, S.D. (1984) 'Planning for rural accessibility provision: welfare, economy, and equity', *Environment and Planning A*, 16, pp. 357-76.

Oinas, P. (1990) 'The scope of post-Fordism and local industrial policy', *Nordisk Samhällsgeografisk Tidskrift*, 12, pp. 48-56.

Pahl, R.E. (1966), 'The urban-rural continuum', *Sociologica Ruralis*, 6, pp. 299-327.

Persson, L.O. and Westholm, E. (1990) 'Europas jordbrukare väljer nya vägar', *Nordisk Samhällsgeografisk Tidskrift*, 12, pp. 40-7.

Peterson, G.E. (1990) 'Declining Infrastructure Investments', *Urban Challenges*, pp. 97-114. SOU 1990: 33. Stockholm.

Phillips, D. and Williams, A. (1984), *Rural Britain. A Social Geography*. Basil Blackwell, Oxford.

Price Waterhouse (1990) 'The economic impact of information technology and telecommunications in rural areas'. Final Report to DGXIII.F, Commission of the European Communities: Price Waterhouse, London.

Qvortrup, L. (1989) 'The Nordic telecottages: community services centers for rural regions', *Telecommunications Policy*, pp. 59-68.

Regional Utveckling i Norden. Årsrapport 1990/91. Nord 1990: 113. Nordiska ministerrådet, regionalpolitiska basprojektet, Borgå.

Revolve (1988), 'Constraints and requirements on the introduction of integrated broadband communication into less favoured regions of the European Community'. Main Report, SUS Research Limited, Dublin.

Rieper, O. (1990) 'Social experiments with information technology in peripheral regions in Denmark', in Heide, H.T. (ed.) *Technological Change and Spatial Policy*. 191-201. Netherlands Geographical Studies 112. Royal Netherlands Geographical Society, Amsterdam/Utrecht/The Hague.

Snickars, F. (1989) 'On cores and peripheries in a network economy' *NordREFO*, 1989: 3, pp. 23-35, Helsinki.

Storper, M. and Scott, A. (1989) 'The geographical foundations and social regulation of flexible production complexes', in Wolch, I. and Dear, M. (eds) *The Power of Geography*. Unwin Hyman, Boston, pp. 21–39.

Strijker, D. and van de Veer, J. (1988) 'Agriculture', in Molle, W. and Cappellin, R. (eds) *Regional Impact of Community Policies in Europe*. Gower, Aldershot, pp. 23–44.

Sundberg, L. and Carlen, G. (1989) 'Allocation mechanisms in public provision of transport and communications infrastructure', *The Annals of Regional Science*, 23, pp. 311–27.

Tönnies, F. (1974, orig. 1887) *Community and Association*. Routledge & Kegan Paul, London.

Törnqvist, G. (1990) 'Det upplösta rummet — begrepp och teoretiska ansatser inom geografin', in Karlqvist, A. (ed.) *Nätverk. Begrepp och tillämpningar i samhällsventenskapen*. Gidlunds, Värnamo, pp. 23–59.

Ungerer, H. with the collaboration of N.P. Costello (1990) *Telecommunications in Europe*. Commission of the European Communities, The European Perspectives Series, Brussels.

Vartiainen, P. (1989) 'Counterurbanisation: a challenge for socio-theoretical geography', *Journal of Rural Studies*, 5(3), pp. 217–25.

Wiberg, U. (1990) 'Informationsteknologins spridning in periferins näringsliv', CERUM Working Papers 1990: 1, University of Umeå.

Youngson, A.J. (1967), *Overhead Capital. A Study in Development Economics*. Edinburgh University Press, Edinburgh.

Chapter 14

Transport and the development of tourism: some European long-term scenarios

A. Bieber and F. Potier

Introduction

The importance of tourism in the evolution of the modern economy is now fully recognised. But, as with many leisure-oriented activities, predicting its future development remains difficult. The following chapter presents an attempt to derive some scenarios of tourism that could help in understanding the future spatial organisation of Europe.

Recently, political troubles have highlighted the extreme behavioural flexibility of modern tourists. In spite of this, we believe that long-range evolution remains a worthwhile subject of study for transport experts and regional scientists, especially in the context of liberalisation of the European economies.

This contribution is made in four parts.

1. A sketch of socio-economic dynamics as they have influenced tourist behaviour in modern society.
2. A brief description of the evolving relationship between the tourism and transport economic sectors.
3. A consideration of the congestion caused by mass tourism and its importance for transport and regional policies in many European regions.
4. A presentation of plausible factors for the future evolution of tourism and, subsequently, of three simplified scenarios for the possible long-term evolution of tourism in Europe.

Socio-economic dynamics and tourism in Europe

The three periods of tourism

Since the 1950s, in most European countries, tourism has become a mass phenomenon and is no longer the preserve of the wealthy few. The result has been a well-known and persistent process whereby the wealthier tourists, reluctant to visit democratised, congested resorts, have constantly introduced new forms of tourism in increasingly secluded and often more remote locations.

Three periods can be distinguished in the development of tourism. Elitist before the 1930s, it became group-oriented and conformist from the 1930s to the 1970s, and then more demanding and individualistic in recent years. The changes show how the industry has been evolving in a direction which, though ultimately favourable to mass production, is increasingly differentiated by superficial marketing, with a very recent trend towards segmentation by a major theme (physical fitness, cultural tourism, sport-related tourism, etc.).

The 'fragmentation' of holidays

At first confined to the long summer holidays, tourism gained further impetus as winter sports became popular. A winter sunshine market has subsequently grown strongly, and more recently people have begun to take short break holidays at the weekend, extended by one or two days.

These developments are indicative of a tendency towards more 'fragmented' holidays. This reflects in the first place how much more easily people can interrupt their work but it also reflects, in many highly interactive occupations, especially in the tertiary sector, the difficulty of breaking off altogether from work for a long period. Another reason why some people are fragmenting their holidays more may be that they are combining business travel with travel for pleasure which, taken to the extreme, can become a complete lifestyle.

New categories entering the tourist market

New age groups are entering the tourism market. One is the 60–70-year-old generation with decent incomes and abundant leisure, who are still taking holidays as they used to when working. At the other end of the age range, single adults and childless couples are a target group already much studied and sought after by the tourism and carrier industries, which are constantly proposing special fares for young people and couples to fill spare capacity between the business and tourism peaks.

Further, new categories of international tourists are arriving on the European market from Japan and some other East Asian countries, while, more recently, the political events in Eastern Europe hold out the prospect of major new sources both of tourists and of destinations. Further immigrant populations in Western Europe have been altering their holiday patterns in recent years. Whereas in the past they would nearly always go home for their holiday, they are now starting to entertain their families and friends in Europe.

The development of inter-continental tourism

For the countries of Europe, the relatively new competition represented by the spectacular development of inter-continental tourism is not yet much of a threat, except perhaps for skiing holidays affected by winter sunshine tourism. But several development factors seem likely to make the remoter countries more economically competitive in the years ahead:

- Unless there is another energy crisis, long-haul scheduled air fares will remain competitive, and charters continue to grow. On some scheduled routes, the cost is likely to decline with greater competition.
- Real estate and labour costs may continue to diverge between developed and developing countries.
- The effects of saturation and hence the self-destruction of resorts may be skilfully averted by a policy of rotating destination countries together with a few basic environmental precautions.
- Incentive travel will play a very favourable role in the development of inter-continental tourism.

The development of long-haul tourism has both direct and indirect effects on transport. The direct effects are easy to observe, with air transport becoming a greater force in tourism. The indirect effects are reflected in the greater importance of transport-related economic factors in the development of tourism facilities.

The behavioural flexibility of tourists: the Gulf War experience of 1990–1

In the classical vein of long-term forecasting, the temporary effects of minor political troubles can usually be neglected. However, events in the recent past have been of such a nature as to influence structurally the future of tourism in Europe. In particular the Gulf War and the revolution in the eastern part of Europe have already had substantial effects. Directly, they have modified the flows of tourism, sometimes drastically. Indirectly, they have led to much more cautious investment policies in the sector.

Combined with economic recession, the immediate impacts of the Gulf War were devastating. Air traffic losses at the peak of the crisis reached more than 12 per cent in Europe. For traffic to or from the Middle East, the decrease was 40 per cent in the same period. Tourist activity levels (measured by hotels and tour operators' patronage) decreased by 80 per cent in the Middle East, by 60 per cent in Turkey, Egypt, Greece and the Maghreb countries, and by 20 to 30 per cent in the Mediterranean 'quiet' countries (Spain, Italy, etc.).

However, the good results of the following summer period in many European countries showed that a large proportion of tourists simply postponed their travel decisions, with destinations changed to the profit of those countries (Italy, Spain, northern countries) unaffected by the proximity of unrest. Similarly, the Yugoslav civil war has had strong localised effects (downward for Greece and Yugoslavia, of course; upward, as a natural compensation, for 'quiet' countries).

Beyond these direct effects, tourist travel will indirectly be influenced by changes in the European air travel system that were attributable to the Gulf War. The contraction of traffic speeded up a move towards concentration and productivity, with negative impacts at first but with positive effects upon the industry in the long run.

- Concentration by means of selling ailing companies was accelerated by the war.
- 'Hub-and spoking', or network concentration, was also accelerated.
- A 'shake-out' of many travel agents has occurred, with its usual bad (social) and good (economic) impacts upon the industry.

In a general sense, the volatility in tourist behaviour induced by the Gulf War has amplified feelings of insecurity in many countries with respect to the stability of their tourist markets. All national tourism institutions speak about the urgent necessity to revamp their mass tourism facilities. All want more refinement, more quality, and all want to leave others the bottom of the market. Intense refurbishing of tourist facilities and refined marketing is likely to take place during the 1990s as the industry seeks an escape from the volatility of unsophisticated mass tourism.

What John Urry (1990) called the 'post-tourist' is more and more conscious of, and unaffected by, the artificial character of the resorts in which he locates his search of pleasure. He is likely to avoid potentially risky countries. The war in the Gulf might mark the decline of *tiers-mondisme* in the tourist industry. This is a crucial question for the study of Europe's spatial reorganisation in the next twenty years.

Tourism and transport: an evolving relationship

Evolution of the tourism industry

The long association between tourism and natural sites of exception has gradually changed. Originally a small-business, site-related industry, tourism has become capital-intensive, serving its interests by introducing a great many fairly comparable products in various regions and countries for each type of tourism. There have been two fundamental reasons for this:

- to reduce the risks associated with climate, economics and politics inherent in too much concentration on one site; and
- to reduce the adverse effects of excessive congestion, thereby maintaining the quality of the product.

In many regions or countries endowed with some minimum attraction such as sunshine, the tourism industry has been introducing large numbers of standard products for each type of tourism by relying on an artificial conception of nature. In recent years, site tourism has given way to product tourism, an irreversible trend on the supply side.

Sport and physical fitness are playing a greater role in shaping the industry's wares and in determining how individuals relate to tourism. Socially prestigious sports are strongly influencing the tourism habits of all age groups. Sailing, tennis, golf, skiing and mountain sports are central to many resorts' strategic thinking, especially as regards advertising.

These sporting infrastructures both support and speed up the 'artificialisation' and the proliferation of resorts. Whereas Venice, the Mont Blanc glacier and the Alhambra are unique, there has for some time been a shift towards the 'medieval town', the 'palm-lined beach' and the 'mountain and its guides', all of which can be reproduced in their hundreds. A further shift has been towards the water park or marina, the golf course, the tennis club, and the ski run, and all these can be reproduced in their thousands.

Taken to this extreme, this leads to the 'holiday club', which is just as interchangeable in style and clientele (i.e. what matters to its customers) as the hypermarket or the air-conditioned office block.

This form of standardisation is also a remedy for traffic congestion. It provides scope for negotiation with the hotel suppliers. It accustoms the tourist to a standard product towards which he/she can be guided, having regard to residual transport system capacity.

Transport modes and types of holiday

The positions of the different transport modes in the tourism transport industry fluctuate with changing holiday styles. Drawing on the classification in the Plan Bleu (1988), eight main types of European tourist can be distinguished. It is possible to assess in qualitative though not yet in quantitative terms how the transport mode is chosen for each type, distinguishing between two broad categories of tourist travel, short/intermediate distance and long distance, the dividing line between the two being roughly 1,000 kilometres.

1. The **'ordinary' holiday-maker**: families, taking a long stay at an ordinary resort. Most of these travel by car for short and

intermediate distances and by charter flight for long distances.

2. The **long-distance second-home resident**: this phenomenon is currently receiving a boost in the form of co-ownership and time-share as fairly flexible means of accommodation in highly sought-after areas. The sunniest countries now have an expanding sub-category, the international second-home owner who prefers air travel for north–south journeys.

3. The **wanderer**: mainly young, the tourists in this category are attracted by Eurorail and equivalent systems.

4. The **theme tourist**, mainly cultural, much targeted by coach operators though also by train and air transport. As the population ages and living standards rise, this market can be expected to grow, though it is already being adversely affected by congestion at the most popular cultural sites, a drawback which can only get worse.

5. **Conference participants** and **incentive travellers**, where the trip is directly related with the traveller's occupation: some travel in this category is provided as an incentive, some for tax avoidance reasons (benefits in kind). Air transport practically has a monopoly and carriers are actively participating in the development of very long-distance conference and incentive travel.

6. **Spas, fitness clubs** (especially salt-water cures): numbers can be expected to grow as the population ages. Since the trips involved are scattered and involve fairly short distances, growth should benefit all surface modes (including automobile), but air transport to only a lesser extent.

7. **Recreational tourist**: a fairly young adult or couple with few or no children. This tourist wants an active holiday with at least one sporting and one cultural component. Recreational tourists are increasingly relying on public transport and leaving the car at home, especially for the many fragmented holidays they take. The railways are offering special fares, as are the medium and long-haul airlines.

8. **Short-stay or weekend tourists**: for fairly short journeys to a typical second home or to visit family or friends, these travel mainly by car, but for longer journeys they may take the train or fly.

The four latter categories are on the whole expected to grow significantly over the years ahead. It is difficult to forecast more precisely in this field, especially for longer-term trends. A broad picture nevertheless emerges in which the dynamics of tourism have had to give way to more complicated patterns based on matching fast public transport modes (bus, high-speed train, air) with car rental. The result is that the major transport operators are playing an ever more important part in tourism, and this trend will be irreversible.

Role of the carrier

Transport is one of the essential components of tourism, while tourism constitutes one of the most profitable sidelines for transport undertakings and may in future by the only one offering scope for growth. It is noteworthy that all carriers now take a growing interest in their tourism clientele.

For coach operators, tourism now represents the only expanding activity. Another point is that in view of the basic product's value, a good deal of 'transport' added value may be maintained even though competition is on the whole high.

For the European railways, tourism, which in the nineteenth century was the strongest and steadiest passenger market, has now become secondary. Demand is very seasonal, with railways facing considerable peak loads on the traditional holiday departure dates. Incentive fares have been introduced both to attract new customers and to regulate demand by means of pricing. Completion of the European high-speed network will help to make the railways more competitive with air and road.

For air travel, scheduled services must be distinguished from charters. For the scheduled services, tourism is regarded as a supplementary source of clientele, to be encouraged by fare structure to fill time slots less used for business travel. For the charter industry, tourism in all its forms constitutes the market.

European charter traffic, with about 60 million passengers in 1988, is almost the equivalent in business terms to the entire scheduled services, which totalled just under 65 million passengers in the same year. Expressed in terms of passenger-kilometres, charters flew 120 billion and scheduled services 60 billion, demonstrating the predominance of charter flights for long hauls, especially from the larger generating countries (UK, Germany, Scandinavia).

Tourism has benefited from the growth of non-scheduled services and increasing numbers of companies are interested in this market; the European charter system is made up of some sixty companies, and the twenty leaders include all the major national airlines, for whom charters account for a substantial proportion of their tourism traffic.

The relative importance of charters and scheduled services in the future

One key aspect of the European transport outlook associated with tourism lies in the relative significance of charter and scheduled services. In the past, three factors favoured charters:

- the concentration of substantial tourism flows from the main generating countries on particular North–South routes;
- air transport regulations, which charters helped to get around;

- the significance of business clientele who to some extent enabled the leading companies to underestimate tourism clientele and leave the field to the charters.

Some observers expect these factors to operate for at least one or two more decades. The fact that most European air traffic will from 1990 be essentially tourist in the broad sense should ensure the maintenance of charters. But a majority of observers consider that the situation will now change because tourist flows, distributed over a greater number of airports, may come to resemble other flows in their geographical characteristics. Deregulation can be strongly expected to remove some of the flexibility advantages currently enjoyed by the charters. The introduction of high-speed rail networks and advanced telecommunications could lead to a long-term decline in airlines' business traffic. In the future, tourists will feature more prominently as a strategic objective for all long-distance transporters.

Transport's action on the tourism industry

One essential question in tourism forecasting concerns the bases of economic power and national interests in the development of the tourist industry. Each European country has major tourism operators, but the northern countries (particularly the United Kingdom, Germany and Scandinavia), where very powerful groups control the generation and destination of tourist flows, are contrasted with southern countries (like Spain, Italy and Greece), which are still essentially tourist destinations. The southern countries are highly committed to the tourism economy but their industries are less structured and therefore have less influence in organising mass tourism. France is an intermediate country, with a few medium-sized operators, in which organised travel is much less developed compared with the northern countries.

Among the major generating countries, a distinction is generally made between Germany and Scandinavia, which are real economic forces in the tourism field, and the United Kingdom, where cyclical demand fluctuations and low profit margins have, according to most observers, made the major operators highly vulnerable.

Another talking-point, in the destination countries more than the generating countries, is the respective position of carriers and destination operators in sharing the power to organise tourism flows. The general conclusion is that the carriers will strongly predominate. This has three consequences:

- The first is that the destination operator is in a very weak position, since he can be bypassed if the carrier decides to redirect tourism flows with an eye to aircraft occupancy rather than resort occupancy.

- The second is to induce the carrier, who takes considerable risks when he organises his service (arranging charter flights, setting fares), to severely squeeze the hoteliers' profit margins and even go into the hotel business himself. The threat is to the very independence of considerable segments of the hotel sector.
- Another effect is to concentrate professionalism in the hands of the carriers. This process is already supported by the relative power of the existing organisational structures in transport on the one hand and the tourism operators on the other. It is considerably strengthened by the emergence of computerised reservation systems which will tend to subordinate tourist choice to that of the transport company. The transport companies may even be tempted to present the hotels as a by-product of the route and the route as a by-product of what capacity the carrier has available. In this way, the concentration effects of introducing these reservation systems are a major element in strengthening the dominant positions of the large generating countries.

Tourist behaviour and its consequences for transport congestion

Tourist behaviour in tourist areas: a theoretical approach

Dean MacCannel (1976) suggested a conceptual model of tourism behaviour of considerable structural value for an analysis of the problems of tourism-related local transport. Theoretically, MacCannel suggests, a tourist is actuated by three interrelated underlying motivations which can be ranked as follows:

1. Participation in a 'contrived' form of tourism. This involves concentrating on the precise geographical scene prepared by the tour operator, perhaps in the theatrical sense of a scene, expecting to witness the enactment of some ritual associated with one or more sites, which the tourist has imagined before leaving. This 'core area' of touristic activity is basically working as a verification of preconceived expectations.
2. The tourist, afterwards, is seeking a slight change of surroundings without getting caught up in the theatricals, sometimes organised by the tour operator (trips arranged from the base), sometimes independently where there are gaps in the arrangements (walks through characteristic areas of the hinterland). These places are in their own way 'secondary scenes', attracting fewer tourists and so giving the less sophisticated tourist some feeling of integrating with the locality.
3. For the most demanding tourists, a third level of expectation is the

remoter hinterland region, less affected by tourism flows, giving the individual a more enthusiastic approach to tourism as a whole by once again experiencing the joys of discovery, chance, and getting away from the crowds, a fundamental aim at this third level of expectation.

Consequences for transport in tourist areas

The above model, based upon the trilogy of verification, integration and discovery, has definite consequences for the organisation of transport in tourist areas.

At the geographical heart of the tourist area lies the preconceived scene to be verified (site, beach, mountain, etc.), reinforced, in very many cases, by some sporting or cultural scene to liven it up. This has to function intensively because it has received very heavy investment, economic and symbolic. It will usually be congested. Large-capacity hotels are linked to sites by intensively used pedestrian walkways and short coach routes. They have serious parking problems for cars and coaches and are subject to much land and property speculation.

Next to the most heavily organised tourist centres come areas receiving moderate numbers of tourists. Coach operators and car-hire companies are interested in these markets, which consist of local circuits based on linking up secondary tourist sites which may be more of less specialised (archaeology, gastronomy, atmosphere, minor festivals). The common feature of these activities is that many take place in hinterland villages which may be particularly sensitive from the point of view of their economic, sociological or ecological balances. This category also includes urban tourism activities based on a pattern of partly developed and partly spontaneous circuits. This form of tourism is expanding strongly and arousing much optimism on the part of local authorities.

Discovery tourism, perhaps more elitist, cannot be reduced to its wholly self-produced components as in the old days of the rucksack. Today's trekker is of considerable interest to the carriers and to all the back-up services which will be accompanying him. Other more artificial forms of discovery make use of expensive technical facilities (helicopters, cars with guides and chauffeurs, small personalised charter vessels for sailing from island to island, etc.). In this case a sophisticated programme will involve sophisticated services, and customised transport services often very worthwhile for the local economy but expensive and only accessible to the wealthy.

Tourism and congestion: some critical aspects

No form of tourism is exempt from a gradual process of site destruction as a result of seasonal invasion and associated ecological and social problems. In the European context, unlike the developing countries, the social impacts appear less critical. Cultural shocks are less intense since the cultures are more similar in the first place. Even so, certain economic concerns remain, when one country finds that its tourism facilities are under the economic control of generating countries.

For some time there has also been anxiety about tourism-related crime. However, this is no threat to the policy of encouraging tourism in the areas concerned, so vital is the growth of tourism to the local economy. The same does not apply to the ecological impacts, which can literally destroy the attractiveness of a tourism area. Water and air quality, landscape, noise level, and safe travel are also threatened by the concentration and poor level of public facilities in many tourism areas. Central to these problems, for transport, are:

- the bunching of travel;
- the heavy dependence of tourists on cars;
- the difficulty of designing road and parking facilities used in a very seasonally concentrated way.

Local policy options to remedy congestion include:

- reducing travel bunching by special pricing, policies to provide information about best departure times and alternative routes, agreements with the hotel industry to change rental patterns, etc.;
- the promotion of seasonal public transport services to reduce dependence on cars. This applies especially to city tourism;
- forms of toll-based investment to facilitate the financing of seasonal facilities.

The need for new infrastructure

The coastal areas most suitable for the development of mass tourism in Europe are now characterised by three forms of concentration:

- the concentration and creation of exclusive tourism sites in areas located in the immediate proximity of the coast. The concentration is seasonal, with a tendency to fill up the low season with new tourism products. But with practical effect, the transformation of the coastline by accelerated urbanisation, is difficult to reverse. In some cases the over-densification has already resulted in serious deterioration of sites, which has to be reduced by costly rehabilitation programmes.

- the rapid and economically important growth of retirement homes. The liveliest resorts and the particularly attractive small coastal towns are acting as poles for the more scattered, suburban development of pensioners' homes. Associated building programmes are keenly sought by the local authorities, who see not only the immediate advantage of having the accommodation built but also practically permanent sources of employment and incomes.
- the accumulation of higher tertiary undertakings associated with advanced research and industry. Companies anxious to attract high-level senior staff in a keenly competitive employment market are increasingly locating close to tourism resorts. This boom in tertiary activities (and specialist secondary activities), though very desirable from the standpoint of the general economy, has serious consequences for the functioning of these areas and for the congestion of their infrastructures.

Rapid transit facilities have already become a critical problem. In areas that are ecologically and politically very sensitive there is a pressing need for the construction of:

- new motorways to provide additional capacity, as nearly all existing coastal motorways are already congested in the high season;
- in certain cases, high-speed railways (such as the TGV route to Nice in France);
- local road networks to improve access to resort areas, many of them mountainous and difficult to reach.

In many regions it is therefore clear already that infrastructure will be the key to future development. Will it be possible to build such infrastructures? The ecological sensitivity of residents in the north Mediterranean sun corridor poses one of the most difficult questions in this forecasting exercise. More forceful ecological opinions are a logical consequence of heavy development in these areas. The most affected are Spain, Portugal and Greece, but comparable problems may also become serious in some of the Alpine valleys (in which case Switzerland, Austria and even southern Germany would also be affected).

Factors of development and future scenarios

The most modest approach to future-oriented studies is to see the future not as something to be foretold but to be prepared for. Our standpoint will be to briefly discuss plausible factors of development for tourism, then to sketch scenarios representing three leading values, namely economic development, equity and ecology.

Ten general factors regulating tourism in Western Europe

From the above discussion, the following general factors favourable and unfavourable to the development of tourism in Western Europe can be distinguished:

- five probable favourable factors;
- three plausible unfavourable factors; and
- two unfavourable but improbable factors.

Five probable favourable factors:

1. Reduction in time and in costs for medium and long-distance transport (especially time for rail and costs for air), and reduction in hotel costs following present over-investment.
2. Reduction of political risks in the core of Western Europe. On the contrary, long-lasting instability outside the industrialised and affluent OECD countries.
3. Consumer lifestyles becoming more demanding and self-centred, as required by the development of the economy in general. Growth of a new attitude for Europe which is favourable to the display of wealth.
4. Weaker family constraints (young couples and adults without children, young pensioners, etc.). Greater freedom of movement.
5. With more people employed in the services sector, there will be more opportunities for and fewer constraints on more 'fragmented' holidays than in the traditional, secondary-sector occupations which used to predominate.

Three plausible unfavourable factors:

6. Congestion and gradual self-destruction through excessive density and artificiality of Europe's main tourism resorts. For some, the 'holiday style' they assume may soon become obsolete and unfashionable.
7. Emergence of and strong competition from new tourism countries (especially in Asia), as the leading generating countries step up their investment in those regions.
8. Some up-market suppliers may overestimate the consumption capabilities of their clientele (over-investment followed by lack of profitability and confidence affecting the sector as a whole, e.g. for leisure parks).

Two unfavourable but relatively improbable factors:

9. Protectionist tendencies on the part of the leading generating coun-
    tries ('modern' protectionism based on regulating the balance of
    payments by controlling tourism flows).
10. Long-term competition from artificial forms of nomadic behaviour
    referred to by Jacques Attali (1990). Two levels are possible: nomad
    behaviour based on videos and electronic networks; or the artificial
    paradise worlds of possibly legalised new narcotics.

Three scenarios for discussion

As a basis for long-term scenario building, three contrasting value
systems are assumed; economic development values, equity and societal
values and ecological values (see Masser et al., 1992, for a fuller use of
these value systems within future scenarios). Before developing the
scenarios, however, we will briefly summarise our personal view of the
past and present evolution of touristic activities, the main elements of
which are shown in Figure 14.1.

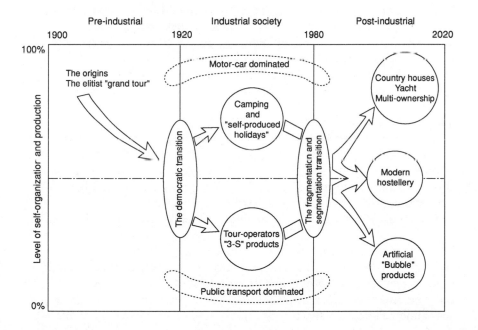

Figure 14.1   The evolution of tourism

From left to right, three periods are distinguished. Only affluent
societies have completed this threefold evolution, marked for them by
two transition periods, the first in the 1930s, the second in the 1980s.
The first transition is the massive democratisation of holidays that

took place in the 1930s, both in authoritarian and democratic countries, in association with what can be considered the apex of the industrial society. The second transition is the passage from the mass industrial-oriented societies to the more segmented and service-oriented post-industrial societies.

The vertical axis of the chart opposes forms of touristic development according to their level of self-production, with a range from completely service-oriented and 'organised' (0 per cent), to completely 'goods-based' and self-produced (100 per cent).

The pre-industrial phase, on the left, starts from a very elitist, largely self-produced and unorganised state of touristic supply. The democratisation process is characterised by the development, in the pre-war period, of the 'rucksack' camping style of holiday-making, and in the post-war period, of the tour operator mass industry.

In the transition of the 1980s, fragmentation of touristic activities, both across time and thematic dimensions, reflects the more refined and segmented aspirations of the tourist. A three fold basis of future activity is proposed, respectively dealing with:

1. the improvement of self-produced solutions through capital-intensive evolutions (secondary houses, mobile homes, boats, etc.);
2. a modernised hotel-based activity, aimed, through better location and better quality, at shorter vacations;
3. the 'resort' concept, highly artificial, with systematic attempts to overcome the absence of site-specific 'landscape' advantages.

The most extreme examples of this emerging philosophy are, for instance, the Centerparks facilities in Europe and the Disney installations in the United States and Euro-Disney. The idea of controlling the weather impediments through large bubble-like glass structures epitomises this direction of future evolution. This is the reason why, in Figure 14.1, we have coined for it the term 'bubble product'.

The foregoing suggests three deliberately contrasted scenarios:

THE ECONOMIC DEVELOPMENT SCENARIO
In this first scenario, the main process of market-oriented economic development is continued and even accelerated. The renewed growth in the economic core of Europe allows the perpetuation of the main past economic features of the tourist industry. These are the following:

1. The scene is dominated by large tour operators for organised and service-oriented tourism, the share of which increases with time.
2. Under the combined pressure of air transport interests and large hotel and resort groups, concentration and vertical integration are at work, with more and more multinational interests.
3. Touristic products slowly follow the upward movement created by

economic growth and its positive implications upon clients' willingness to pay. However, market segmentation is not accelerated since mass products are still classically based upon unsophisticated 'three-S' expectations (sea, sun and sex).

The main policy implications of this highly predictable scenario are relatively easy to sketch. From a transport viewpoint, economic and geographical concentration effects could be worsened by the restricted areas in which future investments would take place. Increased awareness of political risks in the Third World (and this unfortunately includes Eastern Europe) will probably focus future investments in 'quiet countries' in Western Europe.

The main problem associated with this scenario is the self-destruction caused by congestion and its drastic impact on the environment. Airport congestion, car-based air pollution, the difficulty of providing facilities for cars without subsequent destruction of landscapes, and water management problems are already growing exponentially in some highly concentrated areas of mass tourism.

Excessive economic concentration in air transport might also become a problem, associated with its expected deregulation. The constitution of quasi-monopolistic situations, without the classical regulatory countermeasures, accelerated by larger and larger global reservation systems, might become a domain of real concern.

THE EQUITY SCENARIO

Post-industrial societies will naturally consider service-oriented activities such as tourism to be a strong provider of future employment. Unfortunately, the development of such a society might involve higher costs in the long term, which, if not counteracted, would likely cause unequitable effects across both geographical areas and tourist types.

From a societal stand-point, highly labour-intensive activities can only develop for mass tourism if low-cost labour is available in the receiving countries. But the cost of labour in many Western European countries is tending to go up in the long run. In other words, one of the most exacting challenges in this field is to distribute sufficient surpluses to the labour force, without exceeding the willingness to pay of the unexceptional tourist.

Many observers of the touristic scene strongly believe that this challenge will not be met without the perpetuation and indeed enhancement of self-produced and local forms of tourism. The basic features of an equity scenario in this vein would be the following:

1. The scene would no longer be dominated by large tour operators from the sender countries. A homogenisation of activities would happen throughout Western Europe. Reception countries would gradually limit the volumes of in-bound tourists. They would begin to

have sender activities for their own populations, such as Italy and Spain in the early 1990s.

2. The idea of favouring 'proximity' (less than 1,000 km) tourism would be facilitated by the development of second-home ownership. A strongly car-oriented form of transport policy would be the most likely transport feature of this scenario, but high-speed and relatively inexpensive rail solutions might help.
3. The development of self-produced forms of tourism might be facilitated too by the active promotion of better 'thematic' facilities at the regional scale throughout Europe. Visiting not-too-distant tourist destinations with a sporting, cultural, gastronomic, etc. objective, would gradually be the main axis of a rather equitable touristic *art de vivre* in all regions of Europe.

The equity scenario is, to our mind, very favourable not only to car-oriented transport activities, but also to the coach and regional rail industries. It is not favourable to long-distance air transport. It also brings with it the decline of unsophisticated mass-tourism tour operators, to the profit of a new generation of tour operators. From an environment viewpoint, its strong house-building and car-orientation could create road congestion problems. This is why it cannot be considered also as an ecological scenario.

THE ECOLOGY SCENARIO

In common with the equity scenario, an ecological scenario would be based upon a strong regulatory activity, avoiding concentration at geographical, economic and societal levels. Factors in favour of an ecological scenario seem to exist already in the fragmentation of stays and in the segmentation of markets. Such changes are marked characteristics of the post-industrial age.

Fine-grain artificial resorts such as golf, swimming-pools (and even 'bubble products' such as Centerparks) could play a positive role in the development of an ecological form of tourism, provided they are built with care and are well spread in locational terms. The well-known Swiss policies of small and well-integrated resorts of traditional style would be much more in accordance with this scenario.

The basic features of the scenario are, to our mind:

1. The dissemination of resorts of traditional nature, serving fragmented markets and thematic touristic activities.
2. The avoidance of self-produced forms of tourism, through the maintenance of well-integrated, service-oriented facilities such as small but high-quality hotels. Their competitiveness, of course, is at stake and can be attained only, if as in the Swiss example, activity is not too seasonal.
3. The development of pollution-free forms of transport at the local

level, such as electric buses and rental cars. Strong promotion of hiking and bicycling, articulated with good public transport networks in the touristic areas would also help.

From a policy implications viewpoint, it is clear that an ecology scenario in tourism cannot be developed in a non-ecology-oriented society as a whole. This is why this scenario is credible only if vast changes happen in the conduct of affairs in industrial sectors, such as transport.

A second point is that any such ecological progress would have to be sustained by a reasonable level of economic affluence in the western part of Europe. Finally, one should stress the great difficulty to restore the ecological quality of highly industrialised mass-tourism locations, since they are often not located in affluent areas of Europe.

The ecological scenario appears as the most demanding scenario in the present context. Only a very profound change in the behaviour and motivation of modern tourists could in the long run encourage its realisation.

Conclusions and policy implications

1. Overall, tourism is generally expected to grow in the context of post-industrial societies. Democratisation of holidays is still in progress in many countries, particularly in the south of Europe. Transport progress allows more frequent departures by all modes. The leisure orientations of important groups (the young, pensioners, singles without children, etc.) are reinforcing this diagnosis of growth.

   But touristic flows are a volatile product. Political unrest, currency exchange levels, etc. can greatly modify local equilibria, both for tourism and transport. Moreover, the basic structure of tourism is characterised by more and more fragmentation, both socially and geographically. The corresponding markets or 'niches' are erratic.

   A first policy implication is relative to the great flexibility of transport systems in the future; demand will be highly volatile, supply will have to be very flexible. In this context, deregulation appears as a global feature well adapted to this future instability.

2. Congestion created by touristic concentration will be an increasingly important matter of concern. The littoral zones, in particular, are already areas where new transport investments are critical. The ability to build high-speed railways and new motorways will be more and more a source of intense local conflicts. In some areas, the drastic regulation of tourism might be imposed as the result of a lack of new transport facilities.

3. Proximity tourism, with its overwhelming motor-car orientation, appears as the most promising perspective in order to reconcile

growth and equity in this field of activity. Substantial ecological problems are, however, in view, which could be partially solved if electric propulsion of road vehicles progressively becomes a reality.

4. Long-distance tourism will of course remain in the realm of air transport. Costs of air transport evolution is a particularly difficult topic to forecast. Concentration, deregulation, streamlining of old-fashioned services are favourable to a decrease in costs. Long-term energy scarcity, relative decline of business traffic and congestion of airports are much less favourable factors. But, associated with long-lasting political unrest in Third World countries, a rather positive balance seems possible for Europe-bound long-distance tourism.

5. Three scenarios of the future evolution of tourism have been sketched in relation to the main orientations developed within the NECTAR Europe 2020 Working Group (Masser et al., 1992). They respectively put forward (A) economic development values; (B) equity values; and (C) ecological values. Let us recall their basic features:

A. The **economic development** scenario is based upon the perpetuation of the main past evolutions, characteristic of the industrial society. Large tour operators see their activity develop. Economic domination of the industrial core of Europe allows more and more southbound flows to the Mediterranean 'northern arch' in Spain, Italy and France. Political troubles in the Third World and in Eastern Europe may bring new flows of tourists to this sunny playground of Europe.

    Large congestion problems are expected with this scenario, especially in littoral areas. New motorways and high-speed railways would need to be built, against considerable local opposition and conflicts.

B. The **equity scenario** is, in our view, characterised by an important further democratisation of tourism. Due to obvious economic constraints, we see this type of development as non-service-oriented; on the contrary, the development of social tourism implies the growth of proximity tourism and massive self-production of tourism.

    The motor car with its pervasive character is the ideal transport tool for such a scenario. Substantial increases in tourist road traffic would, in this perspective, need much new road and motorway investment in touristic zones closer to the large cities. A new rural policy maintaining the quality of 'green regions' throughout Europe would be an important asset. Culturally, many cities could also develop as a basis for thematic tourism. Rail and coach transport would play an important role in this scenario.

C. The **ecology scenario** would also be based upon the dispersal of touristic activities throughout Europe, but it would be less self-produced and less car-oriented than the previous one. Modernised forms of hostellery maintaining quality at all levels of the price range, as in the Swiss example, would play a very important role in such a scenario.

The development of pollution-free local forms of transport, well articulated with good intercity rail and bus services, could, hopefully, reduce the pressure of conventional cars. This is the most promising and the most demanding scenario. At all levels (society, tourism activities, transport) it implies innovative policies which cannot develop without profound changes in the behaviour and motivations of tourists.

Selected bibliography

Ascher, F. (1984) *Tourisme. Sociétés transnationales et identités culturelles.* UNESCO, Paris.

Ascher, F. and Cazes, G. (1984) *Le Tourisme international et les transformations des espaces et des modes de vie.* Ardu, Institut d'Urbanisme de l'Université de Paris VIII.

Attali, J. (1990) *Lignes d'horizon.* Fayard, Paris.

Baudrillard, J. (1970) *La Société de consommation: ses mythes, ses structures.* Collection Idées, Gallimard, Paris.

Belet, D. and Colomb de Daunant, L. (1991) *Les Compagnies charters européennes — Stratégies pour les années 90.* ITA.

Boorstin, D. (1964) *The image: a guide to pseudo-events in America.* Harper.

Boyer, M. (1972 and 1982) *Le Tourisme, peuple et culture.* Seuil, Paris.

Cazes, G. (1989) *Le Tourisme international: Mirage ou stratégie d'avenir.* Hatier, Paris.

CEE (1987) *The European Community and Tourism.* CEE, Brussels.

Christine, M. (1987) 'Les Vacances', *Données sociales,* INSEE, Paris.

Dumazedier, J. (1974) *Sociologie empirique du loisir. Critique et contre critique de la civilisation du loisir.* Collection Sociologie, Seuil, Paris.

Futuribles International (1986) *L'Avenir du tourisme. Analyse et perspectives.* Dossier de synthèse prospective — Futuribles International, Paris.

INRETS (1989) *Concentrations touristiques et transports — Etat de l'art et prospective.* Actes de séminaire, December, Paris.

Jakle, J.A. (1985) *The Tourist — Travel in Twentieth-Century North America.* University of Nebraska Press, Lincoln and London.

Krippendorf, J. (1987) *Les Vacances et après? Pour une nouvelle compréhension des loisirs et des voyages.* Collection logiques sociales, L'Harmattan, Paris.

Lasch, C. (1980) *The Culture of Narcissism,* Sphere.

Le Plan Bleu (1988) *Avenirs du Bassin Méditerranéen.* Economica, Paris.

Lipovetsky, G. (1984) *L'Ère du vide. Essais sur l'individualisme contemporain.* Folio, Gallimard, Paris.

MacCannel, D. (1976) *The Tourist: A New Theory of Leisure Class.* Schocken Books, New York.

MacCannel, D. (1986) 'Tourisme et identité culturelle'. Communication no. 43, University of California.

Macé, H. (1989) *Prospective du tourisme littoral français,* in collaboration with HTL Council Direction du Tourisme, Paris.

Masser, I., Sviden, O. and Wegener, M. (1992) *The Geography of Europe's Futures*. Belhaven Press, London.

OECD (1989) *Politique du tourisme et tourisme international dans les pays membres de l'OCDE — Evolution du tourisme dans les pays membres de l'OCDE en 1987*. Paris.

O'Hagan, S.W., Scott, Y. and Waldron, P. (1987) *L'Industrie du tourisme et les politiques des douze états membres de la communauté*. CEE, Bruxelles.

OMT (1983) *Etude sur l'évolution du temps libre et le droit aux vacances*. Madrid.

OMT (1983) *Risques de saturation ou dépassement de la capacité de la charge touristique dans les destinations de séjour touristique*. Madrid.

OMT (1985) *Role des opérateurs touristiques transnationaux dans le développement du tourisme*. Madrid.

OMT (1988) *Rapport sur le développement du tourisme*. Madrid.

Pearce, D. (1988) *Tourism Today, A Geographical Analysis*. Longman Scientific and Technical, New York.

Pearce, D. (1989) *Tourist Development*. Longman Scientific and Technical, New York.

Preel, B. (1988) *La Quasi-industrie touristique française: quelques remarques pertinentes*. BIPE, Paris.

Preel, B. (1989) *La société des enfants gâtés*. La Découverte, Paris.

Riesman, D. (1964) *La Foule solitaire*. Arthaud, Paris.

Trigano, G. (1984) *Les Aspects économiques de l'industrie du tourisme*. Conseil economique et social, Paris.

Urry, John (1990) *The Tourist Gaze — Leisure and Travel in Contemporary Societies*. Sage.

Veblen, T. (1970) *Théorie de la classe de loisir*. Collection Tel, Gallimard, Paris.

Viard, J. (1984) *Penser les vacances*. Actes Sud, France.

Wackermann, G. (1989) 'Equipements techniques, services et attraction touristique internationales', *Annales de géographie*, no. 545, Paris.

Williams, A.M. and Shaw, G. (1988) *Tourism and Economic Development — Western European Experiences*. Belhaven Press, London.

Chapter 15

Communication, mobility and the struggle for power over space

E. Swyngedouw

A technological revolution of historical proportions is transforming the fundamental dimensions of human life: time and space. New scientific discoveries and industrial innovations are extending the productive capacity of working hours while superseding spatial distance in all realms of social activity. The unfolding promise of information technology opens up unlimited horizons of creativity and communication, inviting us to the exploration of new domains of experience, from our inner selves to the outer universe, challenging our societies to engage in a process of structural change. (Castells, 1989, p. 1)

In this chapter, an attempt is made to elucidate how the process of social and economic restructuring proceeds in and through a reconfiguration of the spatial organisation of society and its associated **transportation, communication and mobility** (TCM) patterns.

In the first part of this chapter, it is argued that economic and social power depends on the ability to command place; a command over place which is necessarily embedded in and organised through forms of territorial or geographical organisation. This command or power over place is predicated upon the capacity of capital, commodities and people to move over space. Changes in mobility and communication infrastructure and patterns, therefore, are not neutral processes in the light of given or changing technological–logistical conditions and capabilities, but necessary elements in the struggle for maintaining, changing or consolidating social power.

In the second part, then, the current restructuring of the temporal and spatial organisation of the practices of everyday life will be examined in the light of the argument developed in the first part. It is subsequently argued that the present mobility surge and accompanying technological change is part and parcel of a process of restructuring of power relationships; a process which is inscribed in and unfolds over space.

Finally, it is argued that the debate on mobility and communication as a technological discourse obfuscates the underlying power struggles, and is consequently unwittingly participating in a development which may in fact lead to the disempowerment and exclusion of particular social groups while propelling others to new commanding heights.

Annihilating space: exploring the dynamics of transportation, communication and mobility

The historical–geographical dynamics of communication and transportation

This chapter starts from two premises. First, social and economic change is inscribed in spatial or territorial organisation. It follows from this that (1) a particular spatial organisation corresponds with a particular political-economic fabric; and (2) that changes in space and society derive from the internal dynamics associated with the way in which socio-spatial relationships in a society unfold. These premises, in turn, suggest that changes in the pattern of spatial organisation (transportation and communication flows, mobility parameters) can only be understood, and hence changed, in the context of the socio-spatial dynamics associated with particular political-economic forms. In this sense, logistical, communication and mobility changes should be theorised as an integral part of a general and explicit historical–geographical theory.

Second, the very role of transportation, communication and mobility indicates a problematic condition. On the one hand, every social activity is *inscribed in space* and *takes place*. Meaning, representation and material life are produced through the 'spatiality' of the practices of everyday life (Bourdieu, 1977; De Certeau, 1984). We cannot escape place in the structuring of the practices of everyday life (Lefebvre, 1991). However, at the same time, spatial organisation, the historical–geographical expression of everyday life, posits itself as a problem, a barrier, a frontier which harnesses, imprisons, confines social actions within the given geographical configuration laid down by relatively immobile fixed infrastructures of social and regulatory practices. A railway, a motorway or communication line, for example, all liberate actions from place and reduce the friction associated with distance and other space-sensitive barriers. However, such transportation and communication organisation can only liberate activities from their embeddedness in space by producing new territorial configurations, by harnessing the social process in a new geography of places and connecting flows. For example, telecommunication channels massively accelerate the mobility of money capital, but can only do so through an elaborate network of communication infrastructures which harness mobility patterns again, enabling new flows while simultaneously excluding or inhibiting (the further development of) others. In short, liberation from spatial barriers can only take place through the creation of new communication networks, which, in turn, necessitates the construction of new (relatively) fixed and confining structures.

The historical–geographical dynamics of these premises will be explored in the subsequent sections.

Unraveling TCM dynamics

The dynamics of a capitalist market economy are associated with a particular temporal–spatial organisation of society in which TCM patterns are of paramount importance. Since this is not the place to give a full account of the dynamics of a capitalist market economy (for a detailed analysis, see Harvey, 1982), it will suffice in this context to summarise them briefly (see Harvey, 1985). We shall draw attention in particular to the role of changing transportation and communication systems, networks and technologies within the dynamics of a capitalist market economy.

1. A capitalist society is based on the circulation of capital, organised as an interlinked network of production, exchange and consumption processes with the socially accepted goal of profit-making as its driving-force. Accumulation of capital is the correlative of this circulation process. Put simply, in a market economy, economic agents invest with the intention to appropriate the surplus after the successful completion of a production and marketing process. The completion of the process augments the agent's initial outlay of (money) capital. Such successful completion of the circulation process is predicated upon the transportation (movement over space) of money, commodities and labour. Consequently, the circulation process is inscribed in and organised through the harnessing of geographical space. The perpetual flow of circulating capital is main-tained by means of TCM infrastructure and patterns. TCM-related technologies are therefore both a product of capital accumulation and a necessary support for the circulation of capital.

2. The above condition suggests that a capitalist market economy is necessarily expansionary. If the owner of capital does not accumulate, i.e. if an investment is not profitable, the entrepreneur will have to give up his/her social position. At an aggregate level, then, this necessity to accumulate implies the inevitability of continuous economic growth. An aggregate negative growth could not be sustained for other than a very short period of time without threatening the fundamental social relations on which a capitalist market economy is based. Zero growth is therefore incompatible with maintaining the social relationships associated with a capitalist market economy.

3. The expansion of the system is based on living labour. Without the application of productive labour, no production and consumption process along the lines outlined above can be maintained. No train will be constructed without the application of some form of living labour or move without a driver (or, in the case of unmanned systems, a systems controller); no telecommunication system will operate without a software programmer or logistical expert system.

4. As surplus is generated by living labour but appropriated by the owner of capital in the form of profit (or transferred to the state in the form of taxes, to landowners in the form of rent or to financial institutions in the form of interest), the above condition suggests that accumulation is based on an exploitative relationship. That is (if stripped from its emotive connotation), accumulation is necessarily the result of the application and appropriation of unpaid living labour.

5. Consequently, the circulation of capital through which accumulation takes place implies antagonistic social relationships, i.e. the entrepreneur-capitalist needs to safeguard his/her accumulation conditions, while the worker wants to assure his/her reproduction (short and medium-term survival). With a deepening and expanding division of labour in production, social fragmentation increases while power relations and tensions multiply (along class, gender, ethnic, territorial or other fractures).

6. This antagonism is expressed in the struggle for the control and appropriation of the surplus production through the circulation of capital. Given the territorial organisation of this circulation process, this struggle, too, is inscribed in and unfolds over space, and consequently alters the pre-existing geographical configuration. This struggle over space can be exemplified by conflicts over land use or over the distribution and allocation of resources and infrastructure.

7. In addition, individual entrepreneurs operate in an atomistic, and hence competitive, context in which they engage in a struggle with one another over the conditions of surplus production, appropriation and transfer. Consequently, a competitive struggle unfolds for the control over spaces of production and the flows of commodities, money and labour.

8. The latter two conditions (inter and intra-class struggle) make the capitalist market economy inherently and necessarily technologically and organisationally (and hence spatially) dynamic. The double competitive character of capitalism induces the need for continuous productivity increases and diminishing capital circulation times. These twin dynamics of innovation in and acceleration of the circulation of capital necessitate perpetually changing TCM systems and demand continuous changes in the geography of production, consumption and exchange.

9. A static capitalist society is therefore theoretically and practically incompatible with the above conditions. Absence of change under capitalism would lead to chaos, disorganisation and, eventually, to a radical change in the very cohesion of society. Stability in a market system is predicated upon perpetual change, upon continuous transformation. Stable historical–geographical patterns and relationships are incompatible with a coherent capitalist society. Further, static transportation and communication infrastructure and flows

would threaten the relative stability of our type of society and result in revolutionary change in the nature of social relationships that characterise a society based on capitalist market exchange. The sustainability of such a system is predicated upon perpetual upheaval in the way space is organised and controlled.

10. At any given time, the production and consumption system exhibits some form of coherence; a coherence which is relatively stable and cannot be changed radically overnight. This friction between the need for continuous change and the relative stability (fixity) of existing forms and relationships threatens the stability of the circulation process.

11. This instability of the circulation process erupts from time to time in problems of over-accumulation or over-production, that is, a situation in which capital (under its various forms) and labour lie idle side by side. For example, in the 1970s this condition took the form of a 'stagflation' crisis: that is, high inflation, high unemployment and low economic growth. Idle equipment, un- or underutilised infrastructure, over-production of commodities (cf. the expected over-capacity of automobile production in the EC over the next ten years) are examples of conditions of over-accumulation.

12. Such instability is contained by means of continuous restructuring and devaluation of over-accumulated capital and labour. Such devaluation can be exemplified by chronic or instantaneous devaluations of forms of capital: inflation, debt defaulting, unemployment, stock market crashes, bankruptcies, un- or underutilised productive equipment, abandoned private or public infrastructure, physical destruction of productive, consumptive or circulating capital, stockpiling of unsold commodities, deindustrialisation and so forth. Such devaluation of capital is always place-specific, but can easily ripple over space and erupt in a general crisis.

13. The need for continuous technological and organisational (and hence geographical) change in order to innovate and accelerate the circulation of capital on the one hand, and the creeping or rampant devalorisation processes on the other, perpetually reshuffles the geography of everyday life and produces new socio-economic geographical patterns. While older forms of infrastructure are devalued or become obsolete, others are created to reinvigorate the capital accumulation process. This restructuring process itself shatters existing power relations while creating new ones, without, however, transforming the basic antagonisms that define capitalism. The mushrooming of new spaces of production (such as Southern California, Baden-Württemburg, Rhône-Alpes) and the reconfiguration of others (London, Paris, Berlin) with their associated new commodities, transaction and communication technologies and patterns in the late twentieth century exemplify this process (Castells, 1989; Swyngedouw, 1991; Krätke, 1991).

Space, the final frontier: the limits of spatial organisation

The above propositions concerning the functioning of a capitalist market economy allow us to define and understand spatial organisation and its associated TCM patterns within the context of the circulation of capital. It goes without saying that the circulation of capital as outlined above is necessarily inscribed in space and organised through concrete forms of territorial organisation. Moreover, transportation and communication patterns are necessary carriers for the perpetual flow of circulating capital. The form of the technological, logistical and institutional structure of capital circulation as it is concretely organised at any given moment in time shapes the geography of TCM patterns. In other words, geography is actively and historically *produced* in a well-defined and relatively immobile physical infrastructural and social way. At any given moment in time, society will show a particular set of transportation, communication and mobility patterns which give coherence and form to the geography of everyday life. Whatever production or consumption process one imagines, it always presupposes the use and making of spatial organisation of a particular geographical landscape.

Vice versa, every change in the form of production and consumption unleashes infrastructural, socio-cultural and economic change in the pre-existing geographical patterning. However, this spatial organisation itself produces rigidities and friction. The technological, logistical and institutional organisation of the circulation of capital is, given its spatial anchoring, difficult to change in a relatively short period of time. For example, investments in the built environment, the physical-spatial organisation of the production and circulation process (through institution building, collective production and consumption equipment, transportation and communication channels and the like) create a fixed and relatively rigid geographical pattern. This holds true not only for the material characteristics but also for qualification structures of the labour force, level of salaries, union sensitivities, particular patterns of the division of labour, labour ethos, political commitments, institutional forms, cultural expressions and movements and so on. In other words, the production of what we referred to above as 'territorial organisation', a combination of economic, infrastructural and institutional-regulatory practices, is a historical product which simultaneously defines, shapes and transforms social relationships and daily practices.

Waves of time/space compression in capitalist societies

Those historically produced material and immaterial forms that define territorial organisation, and hence particular time-space paths of social and political-economic behaviour, are relatively permanent features, in particular *vis-à-vis* the rapidly changing conditions of the economic

Figure 15.1 AUDI advertisement, expressing the tensions between the necessary rootedness of capital in place and the desire to move it over space

Note: I am grateful to V.A.G. (United Kingdom) for their kind permission to reproduce the advertisement photograph.

process. The latter dynamism stems from the rivalry over the appropriation of surplus between and within social groups (see above). The basic contradiction between the relative immobility of the historical spatial structure on the one hand and the permanent need to revolutionise this very process of circulation on the other expresses itself as a fundamental problem.

This 'spatial problem' for capital is aptly illustrated by a recent advertisement for AUDI (see Figure 15.1). Published only a few days after the collapse of the world's largest real estate developers, the Canadian-based Olympia and York, the image captures well how the necessary rootedness of capital in place makes this capital vulnerable to devalorisation (illustrated by the non-performing Olympia and York sky-scraper in the London Docklands). It also highlights the utopian desire of capital to move the now idle real estate capital to more lucrative places and how the capacity to 'shift a lot of space quickly' is of critical importance for successful capital accumulation.

Harvey (1982; 1989) argues that the process to overcome the 'limits of space' and to accelerate the circulation of capital is achieved through the 'time–space compression' of spatio-temporal relationships. This process of 'time–space compression' is clearly expressed in the history of transportation and communication technologies which permitted the continuous progression of the 'annihilation of space by time' and the progressive elimination of the barrier of space for the circulation of capital (Hall and Preston, 1988). But this process necessarily brings with it the production of new spatial patterns whose barriers eventually have to be broken down again.

This inherent problem, i.e. the need for territorial organisation and coherence on the one hand and the necessity to continuously change the locational-organisational structure of capital circulation on the other, was brought home forcefully in a recent article by the Vice-Chairman of Philips, in which he addressed the effects of the continuously changing 'mosaic of uneven development', as expressed by the wildly fluctuating monetary exchange rates in the world's financial markets:

My final point about the external factors exerting an influence on Philips and others is the wildly *fluctuating monetary levels in the world markets*. The instability of exchange rates has completely distorted profit levels and made a shambles of long-term planning. *The influence on product locations is quite clear*.

There is a joke about buying a huge ship, equipping it with CAD/CAM automated production capability and dropping anchor on the shore of whatever country at the moment offers the best currency exchange opportunity. It isn't particularly funny, however, when you consider the costs involved in moving production facilities, which unfortunately cannot yet float. A Philips example: since 1985 Philips moved production of 14 inch TVs from the United States to Taiwan and now again to Juarez, Mexico.

Many companies could tell their own stories about second-guessing the world money market. But when hard-earned profit margin increases are wiped out by currency fluctuations, companies are forced to use resources that could be so much more valuably allocated elsewhere. (Jeelof, 1989; p. 86)

Both the AUDI advertisement and Philips's use of the metaphor of the ship exemplify the dynamics of capital to annihilate space by time and the desire to produce in a space-less world; that is, a world which is distance-free and operates within the hyperspace of a Star Trek dematerialisation beam. These examples simultaneously recognise the utopian character of space-independent production, the impossibility of space-less accumulation and the absolute need to engage place in the value production process. The desire for rapid movements of capital, commodities and people over space, taking advantage of unevenly produced geographical opportunities, equally suggests how the use of space and the production of territorial configuration is embroiled in the maintenance of the circulation process.

Moreover, the conditions for profitable production demand that the circulation time of capital is continuously shortened, or rather, that the time during which productive labour is performed on the circulating capital is maximised. Such acceleration or intensification of the use of capital is possible only by means of changes in the organisation of the production process, the market, the type of products produced, the flow of labour, money and commodities, and consequently, in the spatial structure of production and consumption. In this way, the acceleration and intensification of the circulation of capital can only be achieved through the breakdown of existing barriers imposed by the concrete historical spatial configuration. These transformations take place by introducing new technologies, new organisational forms of the production and circulation process, a renewed infrastructure and changed logistical and transaction systems (Läpple, 1976; Scott, 1988).

It is quite clear that this need to break down concrete forms of spatial configuration is accompanied by fundamental changes in the spatial fabric of everyday life and with often long and painful periods of deterritorialisation, destabilisation and restructuring. The current information revolution exemplifies this process of time–space compression (see Gillespie and Williams, 1990). This 'time–space compression' is also illustrated by the development and successful implementation of new process technologies. For example, computerised manufacturing systems coupled with new transactional and logistical organisation systems such as **just-in-time** (JIT) manufacturing accelerate the flow of capital (in a variety of forms, from money and labour to services and manufactured goods) and produce a new economic landscape (see Table 15.1).

Such transformation in the socio-spatial organisation of capitalist development begs the following question. Namely, if the devalorisation of spatial configuration is predicated upon the recomposition of territorial organisation, then space (or spatial organisation) is not only a barrier for sustained accumulation but also provides (a) possible

Table 15.1   Value impacts of spatial technological change and the formation of new territorial configurations associated with the introduction of JIT or circulation-accelerating methods

Organisational change	Empirical effect	Theoretical relevance
Logistical revolution	Generalised shortening of production and circulation time and gradual elimination of idle, dead or 'masked' production time.	Increased intensity of the labour process Reduction of fixed constant capital and improved productivity.
	Improved utilisation of machinery and organisational capital and of labour.	Shortened turnover time and accelerated circulation time. Reduction of delay, transfer, waiting and transaction time of capital.
Just-in-time	Savings of capital expenditure both of components and stocks. Reduction of the amount of capital in motion. Improved labour utilisation.	Ibidem + Reduction of fixed circulating capital
Quasi-integration/ externalisation[1] (new territorial configuration)	Ibidem	Ibidem + Reduction of circulation capital

Source: Expanded, based on Coriat (1990, p. 122).

Note: for a more detailed acount of the process of 'externalisation', see Swyngedouw (1991).

'solution(s)' to overcome the limitations imposed by the barriers of space. In the next section, we turn to this question.

Spatial Solution(s) and the Construction of New Spatial Frontiers

Both spatial and technological fixes are actively used as strategies to improve competitive positions, and consequently, both provide a series of possible solutions to delay or temporarily contain problems of over-accumulation. The dynamics of the production of space, i.e. the continuous valorisation/devalorisation of spatial configurations, and consequently, the continuous production of spatial unevenness, opens up two mechanisms of actively using and producing space. First, expansion in absolute space, and second, the restructuring of the space/technology nexus (the production of new relative spaces). The two processes are, as we shall discuss in a moment, mutually related.

ABSOLUTE SPACE, THE TRADE-OFF BETWEEN SPACE AND TECHNOLOGY
AND THE SPATIAL FIX: THE SPATIAL LIMITS OF SURPLUS VALUE
PRODUCTION

At any given moment in time, the geography of everyday life appears as an absolute (and uneven) space. This very unevenness of (absolute) space opens up the possibility of penetrating new spaces and integrating these spaces into a given space–technology nexus. For example, the 'spatial fix' (to use Harvey's terminology) is an attempt to spatially expand a specific configuration of the division of labour: the search for locations with a lower cost of production (of resources, components, labour force or regulatory systems), with a large reserve army of (potential) wage workers or with a promising expansion of new markets, exemplifies forms of spatial fixes in absolute space. Each of these strategies uses the historically constructed space as a means to temporarily resolve problems of profitability or of over-accumulation, and consequently, to stave off the always imminent dangers of real obsolescence and devaluation of capital. This expansion is predicated upon the extension (and improvement) of the flow of commodities, labour and money, and therefore of transportation and communication technology and infrastructure.

For example, the spatial solution in the form of penetrating and capturing new markets offered a temporary, but adequate, solution for the over-accumulation problems in the British textile industry in the nineteenth century. The proliferation of off-shore locations of branches of multilocational or multinational companies during the period 1955–85 is another example of the active use of space to (temporarily) contain the problems of over-accumulation (see Peet, 1987; Schoenberger, 1988; Swyngedouw, 1989). However, the concrete mechanisms of the spatial 'fixing' pursued change over time and coincided with the transformation of the spatio-temporal, infrastructural and institutional organisation of the mode of development. The extent and success of each of these strategies for the various competing forms of capital is, indeed, influenced by both the conditions that prevail in each of the pieces of the mosaic and by the way this mosaic of unevenness is linked with and integrated into the global system of capital accumulation through communication and transportation systems.

The choice between the spatial or technological-organisational fix is therefore relative and limited. For example, during a phase of intensive and sustained accumulation, spatial expansion dominates over the process of technological-organisational change, or at least, the two strategies are used side by side. The financial manager of a major Belgian Philips branch recently put it as follows:

If a product tips over the top of its life cycle, we move its entire production to low wage countries . . . although, in some cases, we may decide to fully automate its production here. This is what is happening at this moment with the Compact Disc. (Interview 23 April 1990)

This quote simultaneously illustrates the trade-off between space and technology as well as the limits thereof. As the innovation cycle shortens and new technological-organisational principles are introduced to deal with this need to permanently innovate and introduce new products, the old-style 'spatial division of labour' strategy along the product's life cycle becomes a less effective competitive ploy. Combined with other changes in political, industrial or financial market structures, the use of absolute space becomes more problematic and territorial reconfiguration (the restructuring of the space–technology nexus) becomes the preferred (and often necessary) strategy.[1]

However, as discussed above, technological-organisational change, taking place in the context of a historically produced territorial configuration is a difficult, slow and costly process which, moreover, distorts or reconfigures the productive capacity of the spatial configuration in which the activity is embedded. Spatial expansion, on the contrary, necessarily entails the occupation of new territories, which were either devalued in the past or were hitherto not yet fully integrated into the new space–technology nexus of the dominant mode of development. The 'spatial fix' through spatial expansion is limited in time. These limits refer to the — at any given point in time — absolute character of space. Those limits can be summarised as follows:

1.   the limits of absolute physical space;
2.   the limits of absolute space which are socially constructed.

This can be exemplified in the following ways (see Swyngedouw, 1989):

1.   Spatial market expansion is limited or at least conditioned by the (spatial and social) distribution of income and buying capacity, the pattern of uneven development, and the mechanisms by which the distribution of the produced value is organised.
2.   The possibility of penetrating and capturing new spatial frontiers (as markets, resource bases or labour reserves) is conditioned by the geo-political organisation of the world. For example, during the post-Yalta period, the spatial expansion of the post-war capitalist system was virtually limited to the Western sphere of influence despite a number of rather unsuccessful attempts to break down these barriers. Small wonder, therefore, that *Die Zeit* (15 November 1989) associated the crumbling of the Berlin Wall (and the accompanying opening up of Eastern space) as a possible basis for generating the upswing movement of a fifth Kondratieff long wave.

3. The integration of lower cost areas in the circulation of capital is equally limited in time. The dynamics of competition result in a gradual erosion of competitive advantages associated with spatial 'fixing'. In other words, for the individual avant-garde entrepreneur, a competitive edge can be secured by using particular spaces. However, this competitive advantage is eroded as others engage in the same strategy and the rate of profit starts to equalise. For example, exploiting spatial variations in labour conditions or wages loses its comparative advantage as the strategy spreads and the socially average conditions change. In short, the tendency for the rate of profit to equalise across sectors and over space gradually erodes the competitive advantage of the more profitable firm,[2] a situation which can be turned around only by means of producing new monopolisable spatial configurations.

4. The limits of time–space distanciation. The time–cost compression of the barrier of distance is determined by the technical limits of harnessing space in particular infrastructural forms of exchange and transaction (transportation/communication), production and consumption. Put simply, geographic expansion and penetrating (absolute) spatial frontiers demands a space–time organisation of the infrastructure, which, in turn, channels the circulation of capital in particular concrete ways. This technical-organisational fabric conditions the time–space structure of geographical patterns which cannot be easily revolutionised.

In sum, the technical-organisational, institutional-regulatory and political organisation of the world's geography — this is what I would refer to as the organisation of absolute space — at a particular moment in time conditions the characteristics of and limits the extent to which the spatial 'fix' can be used as an active strategy in the struggle for the production of value and over the distribution of surplus value. In the end, spatial extension as a strategy to contain the problems embedded in the circulation of capital simultaneously extends those very problems over space and contributes to undermining the very conditions and mechanisms that allowed for the temporal containment of these problems.

THE PERMANENT PRODUCTION OF RELATIVE SPACES: OVERCOMING THE LIMITS OF SPACE

The above-discussed limits of space, then, require from time to time a more or less fundamental reconfiguration of the territorial and spatial organisation of the production–consumption process. This process itself reconfigures the space–technology nexus and opens up new forms of spatial organisation (what Scott (1988) calls 'windows of locational opportunity'), and hence, spatial solutions. This relativisation of spatial relationships is to a large extent, but not exclusively, associated with a revolution in the technological-organisational mechanisms of reducing spatial barriers and an acceleration of the speed with which space can be overcome. With the emergence of each new phase of dramatic time–space compression through the acceleration of transportation and communication flows, the globe shrinks in relative terms as time-distances are shortened and relative positions of places *vis-à-vis* each other changed. Each logistical revolution relativises spatial relationships and produces a series of changes which produce a new geography and spatial pattern.

The dynamics of this process result in the continuous reshuffling of spatial relations, and consequently in the overturning of the old spatial order. Relations within territorial configurations (places) and between places are changed; relative positions alter as new flows appear and others are restructured. This continuously shifting see-saw between technology, space and territorial configuration shapes the historical geography of capitalism, produces an endless 'mosaic of uneven (historically and spatially) development' and creates an 'inconstant geography of development' (Storper and Walker, 1989). The production of new communication technologies and the subsequent acceleration of inter-place flows threaten existing relations of domination and subordination while new relations of power, control and exclusion come about.

Social power and changing TCM patterns

Powerful transformations.

Since the world-wide crisis and subsequent perpetual restructuring which has shaken the stability of international, national and local/regional relations since the early to mid-1970s, transportation, communication and mobility patterns have changed in rather dramatic ways. Andersson (1986) has argued that a new logistical revolution has transformed spatial relationships and flows in significantly new ways (Jansen and van Hoogstraten, 1989). These logistical changes reverberate through the production process and the transactional systems and alter consumption patterns. Evidently, such sweeping changes in TCM flows, patterns and infrastructure are not particularly new or unprecedented. As Figure 15.2 illustrates, transport modes have changed in dramatic ways in the past. Each new paradigmatic mode of transport reduces the friction of distance in important ways and coincides with long phases of growth and sustained accumulation in the capitalist world economy (Mandel, 1975; Grübler, 1990). It is equally clear that such changes have affected the socio-economic geography in quite important and often qualitative ways. Each logistical revolution changes our experience, perception and actual

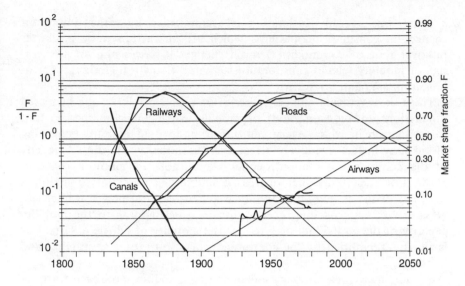

Figure 15.2 Transportation infrastructure substitution in the USA.

Source: Grübler, 1990, p. 189.

use of time and space, and consequently overhauls the established practices of everyday life.

First, the drive to accelerate and extend the accumulation process through changes in TCM technology has resulted in a massively intensified labour process and the introduction of a series of new commodities, from high-technology means of communication and transportation to information. In addition, we have seen the rise of new core sectors in the economy around advanced services, banking and finance and leisure. Each of these developments is predicated upon the introduction of new TCM infrastructure, while the latter, in turn, affects the composition and structure of the production process. In other words, the dynamics of change outlined above revolutionised the nature of the production process, and hence the flows of capital. This is associated with the globalisation of the economic process and the quest to accelerate the movement of people, money and commodities around the globe. For example, large sums of money can now be whizzed around the globe in 'the twinkling of an eye' (Smith, 1984).

Second, the interaction between changes in the production process on the one hand (through which new commodities and thus TCM-related technologies are generated) and the need to extend and accelerate the movement and flow of commodities from one moment in the circulation process to another has brought sweeping adjustments in transportation logistics and infrastructure (telecommunications, satellite systems, high-speed trains, modal shift to air traffic and so forth) and increased mobility (at least for some).

Third, this overall acceleration is accompanied by rather important changes in consumption patterns which are characterised by a shorter turnover time of commodities, rapid changes in tastes and an acceleration of mobility-related consumption activities (Benetton clothing, recreation, tourism, and so forth).

These developments embody a series of problems. First, the increased production (and consumption) of mobility-enhancing commodities lead to a situation in which every addition of individual mobility-enhancing means may in fact negatively affect average mobility. Hardin's 'Tragedy of the commons' is, indeed, equally applicable to mobility (Hardin, 1968). For each individual, increased mobility is essential to maintain positions of social, economic, political and/or cultural power, while, vice versa, we are approaching a condition in which adding to the mobility capacity of one individual may reduce the mobility of all the others. This is clearly exemplified by the enormous congestion problems in cities and in the air.

Second, many new mobility-enhancing commodities and/or infrastructures depreciate pre-existing ones as well as their related activities. The collectivity (i.e. the state) usually has to carry the burden associated with writing off or diminishing the negative consequences associated with obsolescent infrastructure which often hinders or blocks the introduction of more efficient technologies.

Third, the investment required to introduce wholesale shifts in TCM infrastructure often transcends the financial capabilities of individual companies. This then puts a heavy burden on the state to provide the conditions (expropriation of landowners, appropriation and clearance of sites, defusing discontent, etc.) and necessary investments for collective infrastructure whose benefit and other induced positive externalities are often privately appropriated (c.f. infrastructure for the high-speed train or the state subsidies for and investment in public transport in the London Docklands) in a socio-economically highly uneven and deeply unjust manner.

Fourth, new TCM commodities and/or infrastructure demand the restructuring of the organisation of everyday space and harnesses the experience of everyday life in new and relatively immobile flows and patterns. This restructuring, which revamps the existing spatial order, is riddled with conflict as different claims over the organisation and pattern of everyday life lays bare both the necessary spatial rootedness of social life and the unequal power relations through which the struggle over space unfolds.

Social conflict and mobility

Indeed, the social relationships through which the circulation of capital is organised are conflict-ridden. These conflicts originate from struggle both between and within classes and other social groups and can take many and highly variegated forms.

Inter-capitalist struggle is fought by means of, among others, the monopolisation of particular accumulation-enhancing technologies. This, in turn, depreciates the infrastructure of competitors which need to adjust or leapfrog technologically in order to survive. The competitive process, therefore, underlies changes in TCM-related or enhancing technologies or organisational practices which, in turn, change the spatial relations through which the circulation of capital is organised. In addition, TCM patterns as basic carriers of transactions between individual units of capital are deeply problematic in the sense that their effective use depends on the possibility of collective usage of the infrastructure while the individual units attempt to appropriate the effects privately. There is a perpetual conflict, therefore, between the need for collective infrastructure on the one hand and the necessity for private accumulation and private appropriation of the positive (external) effects generated through such infrastructure on the other (see Swyngedouw, 1991). This explains, for example, the role of the state in infrastructure provision and how the collective provision of such infrastructure is essential to maintain the competitive position of the infrastructure users.

This competitive process also takes the form of a struggle for the control over space. Changing transactional or communication patterns is conditioned by the control and power individuals (or companies) can exert over particular places and predicated upon the ability to change pre-existing spatial characteristics in a desired way. In addition, cashing in on the advantages (externalities) generated through new logistical or TCM infrastructures and flows depend on the capability of the individual firm to monopolise particular places. For example, the speculative fever in the built environment around planned high-speed train stations (in Brussels, London or Lille, for example) suggests that the competitive process does not only reshuffle spatial relations, but, in addition, is predicated upon monopoly control or command over particular locations. Consequently, changes in TCM patterns are associated with deep social struggle; a struggle which is both inscribed in space as well as unfolding as a struggle for the control and command over place.

The class struggle for the appropriation of surplus equally suggests the need, in combination with competition, to continuously adjust and change the flow of capital, commodities and people. Changes in TCM infrastructure and technologies are often associated with a reorganisation of capital–labour relationships at the level of the shopfloor as well as of the society as a whole. Moreover, the perpetual struggle for an accelerated circulation of capital through extending and restructuring capital's command over space is equally exemplified by the struggle over place as spaces of production and spaces of consumption. This tense relationship, which often leads to a variety of social conflicts and movements over and for the control of particular locations, suggests how changing TCM patterns are part and parcel of the continuous struggle for power.

Disempowerment and control over space: mobility as social power

The above argument shows how political-economic power is predicated upon the control over spatial flows; a control which can only be maintained and/or consolidated through the appropriation of specific places. This control is subject to intense social struggle. As every place that is used and organised in a particular social way is always social, new demands will challenge and undermine those patterns and install new conditions which pervert and mould the social relations in profoundly new ways. The changed mobility, and hence, power patterns associated with the installation of new mobility commodities and infrastructure, may negatively affect the control over place of some while extending the control and power of others.

For example, the planning and construction of the new high-speed train station in Brussels illustrates how new TCM infrastructure is associated with intense urban social struggle and political-economic change in the fabric of urban life. In particular, the further disempowerment of the poor in the control over their living-space is clearly exemplified by the development process which brings together local, regional and national government in an alliance with speculators and developers who will cash in on the anticipated higher rents and externalities generated by the new spatial configuration constructed through the high-speed train network; an alliance which leaves the former neighbourhood inhabitants dispossessed and driven out into other areas (De Corte, 1992). The dispossession is not restricted to the actual theft of the surplus value (in the form of future rents on which the speculators bank) embodied in their property as a result of the construction of the TGV station, but also by diminishing their individual mobility choice and control as a result of their removal from instant access to the existing train station (as they have to move out). The relative control the residents exercised over space is replaced with new control and power structures which command the geography of the new logistics system to their own advantage.

Therefore, the increased liberation and freedom from place as a result of new mobility modes for some may lead to the disempowerment and relative exclusion of others. This, in its turn, further accentuates social and economic inequalities. Given the importance and power of mobility, those trapped in place, stripped of their capacity to move across space, will suffer in an age in which mobility has become an even more profitable and extremely powerful commodity itself. The power of mobility does not only hold in economic terms, but cultural elites equally depend on their ability to command space (that is to easily move from one place to another) to consolidate the social power they command in their daily life. That is, cashing in on cultural capital (see Bourdieu, 1977) assets is related to the individual's capacity to construct a multiscaled and multiple identity; an identity which comes about in and through the command of place and the capacity to move across space. In other words, social power cannot any longer (if it ever could) be disconnected from the power or ability to move quickly over space. The necessary resources to minimise time–space distances and the unquestioned commodification of time–space compressing processes accentuates social, economic and cultural inequality. Being trapped in particular places and subject to processes of restructuring and depreciation undermines the control and command of the spatially imprisoned individuals and social groups, while this very restructuring and depreciation is organised by those Cyborg men and women whose ability to command place is predicated upon their power and ability to move over hyperspace (Swyngedouw, 1991; 1992).

This commodification of flows of capital, people and commodities is most dramatically exemplified by the flow of information through communication channels. Controlling and appropriating information has become an important vehicle for regenerating the accumulation process. This is aptly illustrated by the role of information technology in organising and setting the rules of the international financial markets as well as in the rise of global commercial information networks like CNN. The commodification and, hence, private appropriation of information as a key commodity in the capital circulation process has added new dimensions to social inequality. The exclusion of some social groups from access to commodified information, and hence to the power embodied in commanding information and information flows, has produced a new class of underprivileged. Road pricing or other linear methods of controlling or excluding particular social groups from getting over space equally limits the power of some while propelling others to the exclusive heights of controlling space and thereby everything contained in it.

Technological discourse and social justice

The debate on transportation, communication and mobility can therefore not escape asking serious questions about social justice and emancipation as mobility itself is part and parcel of the process of uneven development and of consolidating asymmetrical power relationships. Raising questions of social justice and exclusion may perhaps be considered to belong to an outmoded debate, but absence of these considerations cannot annihilate those who are caught in the doldrums of persistent deprivation and perpetual restructuring.

As we have attempted to demonstrate in this contribution, TCM patterns are far from neutral or value-free, let alone driven uniquely by a 'natural' process of technological change and scientific progress. Mobility itself is one of the arenas in which the struggle for control and power is fought. An important strategic weapon of the powerful in this struggle is the ideology of progress and the legitimising scientific discourse of scientists and engineers. Very worrying in this respect is the fact that the techno-discourse on control and engineering of TCM technologies and logistics obfuscates those underlying social processes and power relationships and is thereby accomplice to an order which serves the few while excluding the many. If questions of social justice in the debate and praxis of mobility are not again put high on the agenda, it may force itself on to the political platform very soon by means other than words.

Notes

1. The flexibilisation that took place during the 1970s and 1980s exemplifies the need for readjustment and territorial reconfiguration. The drive towards institutional, social, labour market, network or technological flexibility attempted to liberate the capital circulation from the configurational harness in which it was encapsulated. Reconfiguration — which is necessarily a difficult and risky activity — requires new material and immaterial relationships which are easily adaptable, adjustable and open to rapid and unforeseen changes. Flexibility, therefore, is an important vehicle for the construction of a new space–technology nexus and associated rebuilding of new spatial configurations. This spatial restructuring is exemplified by, for example, **just-in-time** manufacturing (see Swyngedouw, 1987) or the recent restructuring of the computer and telecommunication industry (see Cooke et al., 1992).
2. For a mathematical solution and numerical example of this process of equalisation of the profit rates, see Gouverneur, 1978.

Bibliography

Andersson, A. (1986) 'The four logistical revolutions', *Papers of the Regional Science Association*, vol. 59, pp. 1–12.

Bourdieu, P. (1977) *Outline of a Theory of Praxis*. University Press, Cambridge.

Castells, M. (1989) *The Informational City*. Blackwell, Oxford.

Certeau, M. de (1984) *The Practice of Every Day Life*. California University Press, Berkeley.

Cooke, P., Moulaert, F., Swyngedouw, E., Weinstein, O. and Wells, P. (1992) *Towards Global Localisation. The Restructuring of the Computer and Telecommunication Industry in France and the United Kingdom*. University College Press, London.

Coriat, B. (1990) *L'Atelier et le robot*. Ed. Bourgois, Paris.

De Corte S. (1992) 'Pokerspel rond een Station: De komst van de Hoge Snelheids Trein in Brussel', *Planologisch Nieuws*, vol. 12, No. 2, pp. 129–44.

Gillespie, A. and Williams, H. (1990) 'Telematics and the reorganisation of corporate space', in Soekkha, H., Bovy, P., Drewe, P. and Jansen, G. (eds) *Telematics — Transportation and Spatial Development*. VSP, Utrecht, 257–74.

Gouverneur, J. (1978) *Eléments d'économie politique marxiste*. Contradictions, Brussels.

Grübler, A. (1990) *The Rise and Fall of Infrastructure: Dynamics of Evolution and Technical Change in Transport*. Physica-Verlag, Heidelberg.

Hall, P. and Preston, P. (1988) *The Carrier Wave*. Unwin Hyman, Boston.

Hardin, T. (1968) 'The tragedy of the commons', *Science*, 162, pp. 1243–8.

Harvey, D. (1982) *Limits to Capital*. Blackwell, Oxford.

Harvey, D. (1985) 'The geo-politics of capitalism', in Gregory, D. and Urry, J. (eds) *Social Relations and Spatial Structures*. Macmillan, London, pp. 128–63.

Harvey, D. (1989) *The Condition of Post-Modernity*. Blackwell, Oxford.

Jansen, B. and Van Hoogstraten, P. (1989) 'The "new infrastructure" and regional development', in Albrechts, L., Moulaert, F., Roberts, P. and Swyngedouw, E. (eds), *Regional Policy at the Crossroads*. J. Kingsley, London, 52–66.

Jeelof, G. (1989) 'Global strategies of Philips', *European Management Journal*, vol. 7, No. 1, pp. 84–91.

Krätke, S. (1991) 'Cities in transformation: the case of West Germany', in Benko, G. and Dunford, M. (eds) *Industrial Change and Regional Development: The Transformation of New Industrial Spaces*. Belhaven Press, London, pp. 250–74.

Läpple, D. (1976) *Staat en Algemene Produktievoorwaarden*. Zone Special 1, Ecologische Uitgeverij, Amsterdam.

Lefebvre, H. (1991) *The Production of Space*. Blackwell, Oxford.

Mandel, E. (1975) *Late Capitalism*. New Left Books, London.

Moulaert, F. and Swyngedouw, E. (1991) 'Regional development and the geography of the flexible production system', in Hilpert, U. (ed.) *Regional Innovation and Decentralisation: High Tech Industry and Government Policy*. Routledge, London, pp. 239–65.

Peet, R. (1987) 'Industrial restructuring and the crisis of international capitalism', in Peet, R. (ed.) *International Capitalism and Industrial Restructuring*. Allen & Unwin, Boston, pp. 9–32.

Schoenberger, E. (1988) 'From Fordism to flexible accumulation: technology, competitive strategies, and international location', *Environment and Planning D: Society and Space*, vol. 6, No. 3, pp. 245–62.

Scott, A. (1988) *New Spaces of Production*. Pion, London.

Smith, N. (1984) *Uneven Development*. Blackwell, Oxford.

Storper, M. and Walker, R. (1989) *The Capitalist Imperative*. Blackwell, Oxford.

Swyngedouw, E. (1987) 'Social innovation, production organisation and spatial development', *Revue d'Economie Régionale et Urbaine*, No. 3, pp. 487–510.

Swyngedouw, E. (1989) 'The heart of the place. The resurrection of locality in an age of hyperspace', *Geographiska Annaler*, vol. 71(B), No. 1, pp. 31–42.

Swyngedouw, E. (1990) 'l'Espace, le Fordisme et le Limbourg', *Contradictions*, No. 58–9, pp. 115–51.

Swyngedouw, E. (1991) 'Spatial organisation as a force of production'. Mimeographed paper, School of Geography, Oxford University, 27 Mansfield Road, Oxford OX1 3BT, UK, 54 pp.

Swyngedouw, E. (1992) 'The mammon quest. "Glocalisation", inter-spatial competition and the monetary order: the construction of new scales', in Dunford, M. and Kafkalas, G. (eds) *Cities and Regions in the New Europe*. Belhaven Press, London.

Part IV

Chapter 16

Transport and communications innovation in Europe: policy implications and options

G. Giannopoulos and A. Gillespie

Introduction

This book has sought to see the whole issue of future transport in Europe from the social science perspective with which we have tried to address the substantive issues raised in the area of transport and communications innovation. Although technological innovation is, not surprisingly, a dominant theme of the book, the contributions have attempted to place technology within its broader economic, organisational, institutional, social and spatial contexts. Whereas an engineering or technologically led focus on policy issues would be interested in these broader contexts only in as far as they constrained the development or diffusion of the technologies concerned, the perspective adopted in this book has a rather different starting-point, and hence a rather different approach to the policy issues raised. In particular, we eschew the type of policy discussion which is premised on the implicit or explicit assumption that 'technological potential' has to be maximised. The mere fact that a technology or technological system is feasible is not sufficient to justify policy measures to bring about its realisation; such a justification would need to bring into play a complex, and inevitably political, array of other concerns beyond the narrowly 'technological', including the economic, social, cultural and environmental implications of postulated technological futures.

   In the above sense the material in this book has been 'innovative' in many views but especially in as much as:

1. It is based on a simultaneous analysis of both transport and communications systems. The analysis of technological innovation which we develop proceeds on the basis of a strong interrelationship existing between transport and telecommunications technologies, an interrelationship witnessed for example by a host of IT applications applied to the transport sector and which are presented.
2. It stems from a constant awareness that although technological changes in telecommunications and transport are the catalyst for spatial dynamics, they are only necessary but not sufficient conditions for these dynamics.

3. Despite most frequent analyses trying to capture a direct link between technological changes and spatial patterns, here we stress the interrelationship between technological changes, new organisational forms of production and spatial trajectories, new spatial distributions, etc.

4. We adopt a two-level approach, at micro and macro level, for studying changes in organisational and spatial structures. The micro level refers to the firm, i.e. changes in the intra and inter-corporate organisational structure and in the spatial organisation of production. These changes could manifest themselves through a new division of labour. The macro level is related to the industrial system as a whole and underlines changes in universal industrial behavioural rules, in regulatory regimes and in the spatial structure around which industrial systems are organised.

5. Finally, the analysis is probabilistic in nature in that no single, unique trajectory of change in the industrial and spatial structures can be identified for the future and the same applies to the development trajectories for transport and telecommunications technologies, since these in turn depend on the development trajectories of some other crucial elements, including technological innovation, the diffusion and application of technologies throughout the industrial system, and the institutional framework within which diffusion takes place (concerning, for example, the structure of markets and how they are regulated, standards, etc.).

In this final part, the attention turns to the policy implications and options associated with the theme of transport and communications innovation. Given the book's focus on European developments, and given the importance of transport and telecommunications in helping to forge a new, more integrated Europe, many of the policy issues which we discuss here would be best addressed at the European scale of decision-making, though they will also be relevant at national and subnational scales. Beyond our immediate concerns with Europe, nevertheless, many of these policy issues which will be synthesised in this final section, are also relevant to other transport and communications-intensive and high-mobility societies, whether in North America or East Asia.

It follows that the policy domains with which we are here concerned extend well beyond those concerned with innovation in transport and telecommunications. We are, for example, concerned additionally with the institutional and regulatory structures within which the development, deployment and utilisation of transport and communications take place; with economic and industrial policies which impinge upon the provision of transport and communications infrastructure or upon the demands placed upon these infrastructures; with spatial policies, whether at urban, regional or national scales, which influence the nature or patterns of movement and interaction; and with environmental policies and concerns which impinge upon transport, movement and mobility issues.

The policy formulation perspectives

Policy implications of changes in the economic, social and spatial organisation

The thesis of this book is that innovation in the fields of transport and communication needs to be understood within the context of broader changes taking place in economic, social and spatial organisation. Indeed, a number of the contributors see transport and communication innovation as essentially responding to new demands placed upon the transport and communication system by changes in this broader environment. It follows that in considering the policy issues and implications arising from the previous chapters, we need to encompass not only technological innovation in transport and communications, which we do in the following section, but also the transport and communication policy implications arising from these broader forms of innovation.

In Chapter 3, it was argued that transport and communications are, in both literal and symbolic terms, the carriers of new forms of economic organisation. Just as transport and communications systems have responded to the demands put upon them by previous shifts in economic organisation, so the current transition from what we characterised above as a 'Fordist' system of organisation to something different will impose new demands upon the transport and communications system. Although the nature of the 'something different' towards which we are evolving is a matter of debate, certain features, with important implications for transport and communication, appear to be clearly evident in the current period of transition.

In the realm of industrial organisation, for example, the evolution of the large, vertically integrated Fordist enterprise, with its extended spatial division of labour, appears to be evolving into a 'network firm' system of organisation, one more in tune with the need for constant product and process innovation and with the requirement to cope effectively with rapidly changing markets. The transport and communication implications of this shift are to accentuate the need for high speed, high-quality and long-distance 'highways' for the movement of goods, people and information. The development of advanced logistics, to take an example considered in Chapter 12, can thus be seen as the organisational response to demands emanating from the industrial system for higher quality, greater frequency, larger geographical coverage, shorter lead times and greater flexibility in the movement of goods.

One perspective in considering the policy implications for the transport and communications sector therefore concerns the innovations that are needed in order to facilitate the realisation of the emerging models of economic and social organisation; a policy to ensure, in other words, that transport and communications facilitate rather than constrain broader changes in economy and society. The types of policy that would be in line with this type of perspective include:

- policies to develop advanced transport and communication infrastructures at the pan-European scale, including high-speed rail, motorway networks, and broadband telecommunications;
- policies which encourage technological and organisational innovation in the supply of transport and communications services;
- policies which deregulate transport and communication markets, thereby permitting the more rapid adjustment of supply to changing demand.

Policies covering each of these areas of action are well represented in the European Community, in both transport and telecommunications domains. Examples include the Community's support for the high-speed rail network; the proposals agreed at the Maastricht summit to invest substantially in trans-European transport and communications infrastructures; technology development programmes such as DRIVE and RACE; and the implementation of policies to deregulate the supply of transport services (such as the easing of the restrictions on cabotage) and of telecommunications services (through the implementation of the measures put forward in the CEC's 'Green Paper' on telecommunications policy).

One policy perspective starts then from the premise that transport and communications play an important functional role within new forms of economic and social organisation, and that policy should facilitate the adjustment of the transport and communications systems to meet the new requirements put upon them. A rather different perspective on the objectives of policy questions whether the changes taking place in the domains of transport and communications are desirable in their own right, and, if not, whether something should be done to change the processes in the economy or in society that are bringing them about.

A good example of this type of perspective would be the environmental concerns surrounding contemporary developments in transport, in which the high consumption of energy, pollution and congestion caused by current trends in socio-spatial organisation are being increasingly questioned and challenged. Although technological innovation, such as in clean engine and fuel systems (Chapter 7), may help to ameliorate these concerns, some argue for more radical action to alter the conditions that are generating movement and hence causing the environmental problems in the first place. Examples would include measures to internalise the costs of transport which are currently externalised (such as pollution and congestion imposed on others), which would serve to substantially increase the cost of transport and, in the longer term, lead to forms of economic and spatial organisation which are less movement-intensive.

These contrasted policy perspectives should remind us that the objectives of policy need to be explicitly and clearly stated. Clearly very different policy prescriptions, with respect to transport and communications innovation, will emerge depending on whether the objective of policy is understood to be to facilitate or even encourage the physical movement of people and goods, or, conversely, to reduce the need for physical movement.

The changing context for policy

In considering the policy implications and options raised by the contributions to this book, we clearly need to make some assumptions about the broad parameters within the transport and communications issues to be considered. The difficulty in this respect is that the present and recent past appear to suggest that structural or epochal changes are in the process of taking place in political, cultural and economic spheres which create considerable uncertainties over the shape the future will take. These uncertainties inevitably impinge upon transport and communication policy issues, which is why a number of the contributions in this book, and the other book arising from the work of the NECTAR Europe 2020 group (Masser et al., 1992), utilise scenario approaches in order to explore alternative futures.

Even if there are uncertainties over outcomes, we can at least specify those aspects of the background within which to consider transport and communication policy issues which appear to be undergoing significant change. These are:

1. **The new socio-political environment**: the last decade or so has seen an increasing reliance upon market forces as a means of regulating the supply and demand of transport and communications. In a period of rapid technological change, the market mechanism clearly possesses many advantages as a means of deciding between competing options. In the longer term, the unfettered action of market forces may very well lead to the re-establishment of private monopolies in the transport and communications field, requiring reregulation. The legitimacy of competition within markets as one of the principal forms of decision-making within the transport and communications arena appears unlikely to be reversed, however.

2. **New value systems**: shifts in societal value systems seem to be occurring which put greater emphasis on the satisfaction of individual rather than collective desires. Such a shift, if continued through, obviously has direct implications for transport and communications, such as in modal choice, but also has significant indirect implications

in terms of the proliferation of 'lifestyle choices' and the growth of new forms of consumption and leisure. At the same time, however, and partly in contradiction with more individualised value systems, there is also evidence of a growth in environmental or 'green' value systems, the generalisation of which would have profound implications for the transport and communications domain.

3. **New methods of production organisation**: new forms of flexible and 'just-in-time' production have been developed to meet changing customer requirements and expectations, taking place alongside a clear trend towards globalisation (which in the European context is expressed most clearly in the formation of a single European-wide production system). These new forms of production organisation impose quantitatively and qualitatively different requirements upon the transport and communication systems, with general increases in the frequencies of movement, in the distance over which movement takes place, and in the required reliability of transport systems.

4. **New forms of spatial organisation**: developments in transport and communications have, of course, facilitated the emergence of complex forms of spatial organisation, in which much greater integration across space has taken place. Such integration can be seen at a variety of scales, including cities and rural areas, cores and peripheries within national territories, and between countries at the European scale.

5. **New technological possibilities**: last but by no means least, there has, as many of the contributions in Part II of this book have testified, been a revolution in the transport and communications field as a result of technological innovation. The 'informatisation' of both transport and telecommunications as a result of the application of microelectronics has transformed both, and also facilitated possibilities for their greater integration, as witnessed in the development of advanced logistical systems.

Taken together, these various elements of change in the environment within which to consider policy implications and options, point firmly to the conclusion that economic, social, organisational and spatial trends are bringing about a highly mobile society, in which the movement of people, goods and information have increased drastically and seem likely to continue increasing in the future.

Policies to facilitate innovation in the (broadly defined) arena of transport and communications, perhaps to resolve some of the contradictions and sustainability questions in the scenario of high mobility and increased movement, are thus of vital importance. It is to a consideration of such policy issues that we now turn.

**Understanding the interrelationship between transport,
telecommunications, and spatial-economic organisation**

Few changes are having a greater impact on the ability of firms and
countries to compete in global markets than the recent and ongoing
revolution in telecommunications and transport. The new capabilities of
information processing and transmission, as well as the enhanced
mobility of people and the movement of freight, are profoundly altering
features upon which the competitiveness of firms and the comparative
advantages of regions depend. The key forces generating a new industrial
and spatial structuring are embodied in the radical technological changes
currently under way in the telecommunications and transport industries.
Communications and transport networks can be regarded as the
'carriers', in both literal and symbolic senses, of new systems of
industrial and spatial organisation.

Technological innovation, associated with the ongoing technological
revolution, can be exploited by firms and production systems with the
intention of:

● creating new production processes;
● increasing the efficiency of office functions (back and front-office
  automation);
● improving the control over production processes from the managerial
  point of view (automated factory);
● creating new distribution networks (telebanking, teleshopping);
● improving the quality of existing products;
● improving decision-making processes;
● creating new relationships between the firm and its external environment (new relationships with suppliers, teleworking, databases as
  external information sources).

Each of these renewal processes obliges firms and institutions to
rebuild their organisational structures according to new principles for
achieving economic advantage through new managerial and technological
instruments.

The introduction of new technologies is an extremely complex process,
the result of profound cultural, psychological, managerial and organisational changes. New technologies both allow and impose internal
organisational changes for their adopters; they support the spatial relocation of production, as well as obliging new functional divisions of
labour. In other words, they have the potential to reshape the organisational structure of the firm at a micro-economic level, and the economy
at a macro-economic level, building new forms of social, economic,
managerial and corporate organisation. Technological innovation must
therefore be associated with major organisational changes, and the study
of the diffusion of new technologies among companies must be

associated with the study of these organisational dynamics.

The idea of communications and transport as the carriers of new industrial and spatial forms is of course not new. Many commentators have drawn attention to the historical association between advances in transport and/or communications technologies and changes in the nature of society, changes in the way the economy is organised, and changes in spatial structure and organisation.

In one sense, the very existence of the city can be understood as the spatial response to the severe limitations upon the movement of people, goods and information which prevailed before and during the early stages of the industrial era. As it was mentioned also in Chapter 3, 'to avoid transportation, mankind invented the city' (Schaeffer and Sclar, 1975, p. 8).

Adopting a historical perspective, Capello and Gillespie (Chapter 3) made it clear that technological advances in transport and communications have been instrumental in the establishment of a series of major economic, social and geographical developments (they purposely did not use the term 'caused').

This relationship between transport and telecommunications on the one hand, and economic, spatial and social development on the other, goes well beyond simple technological linkages and manifests itself in the joint capacities these technologies have to impact on the spatial structure of the economy. Just-in-time organisational forms of production, for example, require both advanced telecommunications infrastructures as well as a modern, efficient and reliable transport system. The lack of one of the two infrastructural systems would inevitably lead to inefficiency and to difficulties in sustaining this particular spatio-organisational form of production.

The organisational variable can be regarded as a fundamental and crucial 'bridge' to capture the linkages between technological changes and spatial dynamics. The relationships between these variables are neither linear nor uni-directional, being best regarded as a circular set of interconnections, making the definition of the original causes of changes not easy to define (see, for example, Giannopoulos and Curdes, 1992, p. 16). To present the argument in a linear narrative way, the circle must be 'broken into' at some point. Although we have chosen in this book to break into the circle at the point of technological change, reflecting the context within which we are writing, we contend that other starting-points would be equally valid, and possibly more useful in understanding the nature of contemporary transport and spatial–organisational–economic interactions and transformations.

The development trajectories for the industrial and spatial structures are related to the development of transport and telecommunications technologies, but these in turn depend on the development trajectories of some other crucial elements, including technological innovation, the diffusion and application of technologies throughout the industrial system, and the institutional framework within which diffusion takes place, concerning for example the structure of markets and how they are regulated, standards, etc. Thus no single, unique trajectory of change in the industrial and spatial structures can be identified for sure for the future (see also the analysis in Chapter 3 by Capello and Gillespie).

These elements can follow a number of different development paths, each of them leading to a different pattern of usage of transport and telecommunication technologies and consequently to the constitution of different industrial and spatial structure scenarios. For these reasons, we referred in Chapter 3 to three different possible scenarios in the development of the industrial and spatial structure and considered which of them is most likely to take place, given some key considerations. The transport policy implications of this most likely to happen scenario are presented in the fifth section below.

A final point that has to be remembered here is the well-known idea that transport and communications technologies in themselves are not sufficient forces for generating indigenous local economic development. On the contrary, they have to be thought of as strategic instruments to be exploited with reference to broader spatial-economic planning. Thus there is a clear need for integrated transport and communications systems to be developed in conjunction with broader spatial (urban and regional) planning. Only in this way will transport and communication networks be developed on the basis of the real needs and necessities of the newly emerging industrial and spatial system. In this way, supply-driven transport and communications projects with little or no connection with real demand requirements and needs can be avoided, and the future development of these leading technological infrastructures can be conceived rather in terms of their contribution to the creation of an integrated economic system for the Europe of 2020.

Policy issues concerning technological innovation in the field of transport and telecommunications

Private car transport

Private road transport for passengers is undergoing a profound technological transformation that started in the 1980s and is now in the peak of its evolution. By the turn of the century both the technology for automobile construction and the technology for traffic management and control will have produced a radically different environment for road transport. This 'environment', which is usually referred to as the **integrated road transport environment** (IRTE), comprises elements that can be classified in the following six broad categories (DRIVE, 1991):

1. the automobile's own technological development;
2. travel demand management;
3. travel and traffic information;
4. integrated urban and inter-urban traffic management;
5. driver assistance and co-operative driving.

The key factor for the development of the new systems is computer and telecommunication technology (**telematics**). However, considerable changes are also expected due to some recent breakthroughs in energy generation technology and the mechanical systems of the vehicles.

We are already faced with a situation where European, US and Japanese governmental organisations and industrial actors are competing with one another to be the first to supply the newest technological innovations in the market-place.

As regards **the automobile's own technological development**, several technical problems related to the automobile have been solved and new technological fields have emerged which promise further advances. Of these (described in more detail in Chapter 6) the most interesting as far as future policy formulation towards the use of motor cars is concerned, we note the expected advances towards more environment-friendly vehicles, aids to the drivers, safety and new energy sources. Automobile functions will become even more sophisticated and diversified, making cars more 'individual' to their owners.

The policy issues arising from these developments are many. On the one hand, the use of private cars is likely to become even greater than it is today and the corresponding demand for road space greater. On the other hand this use may not have the serious negative implications for the environment that current use of cars has, but the overall 'balance' is therefore a point that has to be carefully analysed in the future. The pressure for more space for the parking and circulation of these vehicles will nevertheless continue to increase. The critical factor will be the corresponding technological improvements in public transport vehicles, which will have to 'compete' with the new amenities offered by the private cars.

Related to the above is the issue of the **demand management** actions that will be probably due in the near future, in order to move travel demand to more suitable modes, and to obtain a better distribution of traffic both in time and in space. Such actions will be both necessary and indeed more acceptable in the future, provided of course that the public is properly informed. Another point to be made here is that the operation of any demand management action will have to be integrated with the other subsystems of the IRTE.

Current technological innovations allow a number of policy actions that will alleviate the problems associated with the use of private cars and allow greater utilisation and effective capacity in the existing infrastructure. 'Technological innovation' has been seen throughout this book as a term encompassing a wide range of products and applications not only for the mechanical parts of the vehicles but for the whole 'environment' in which they operate. The formulation of this so-called **integrated road transport environment** (IRTE) is based on advanced telematics applications which include the following:

- **Travel and traffic information** technologies allow for timely and accurate information to be given to drivers or prospective travellers on traffic conditions, routes, modes of travel, as well as other information that will assist drivers and travellers in the best utilisation of the available transport infrastructure.
- Urban and inter-urban traffic management technologies will permit **urban traffic control** (UTC), **automatic vehicle monitoring** (AVM), **parking management**, and other related actions for better and more efficient **traffic flow control, intersection control**, and **network control** in urban and inter-urban areas.
- **Driver assistance and co-operative driving**, whose functions allow for **intelligent cruise control** (ICC), **interactive route guidance** (IRG), **automatic debiting, co-operative detection and ranging**, i.e. range-finding, obstacle detection, etc.

A basic European approach to a suitable implementation path for all the above technologies is still to be found but their implementation in actual commercial practice will is expected to start before the end of this decade and will be gradually extended.

Freight transport

During the last few years a major research effort is under way in Europe directed to improving the performance of freight transport and road transport in particular. By using the capabilities of modern information and telecommunications technology, the whole operation and organisation of freight transport is being transformed towards a service capable of providing a high-quality service to the customers in terms of speed of travel, frequency, guaranteed times of delivery, etc. The aim is to integrate the freight transport operation into the **integrated road transport environment** (IRTE), i.e. the development and operation of an 'intelligent' road infrastructure and vehicles which will enable a smoother, safer and more efficient traffic flow and transportation process in general.

There are three general levels of **road freight operation** (RFO) that are the prime 'beneficiaries' of the new technologies. **Level 1** consists of the freight management and 'logistics' functions that have to do with the planning of the transport operation in the long term; the processing of the orders; the processing of the paperwork that accompanies each transport; cost control; keeping of statistical data; the monitoring of the cargo; and general finance and administration. **Level 2** is concerned with the monitoring of the fleet of vehicles which include functions such as route planning and vehicle scheduling; vehicle dispatching; vehicle (or more generally mobile unit) fleet monitoring and control. Finally, **level 3** contains the functions that deal with the vehicles themselves and the goods carried. It includes route guidance; trip planning; vehicle and cargo technical monitoring and control; consignment identification; and maintenance scheduling.

Information and telecommunication technology (IT) applications have been and are being studied for all these functions and levels so as to provide for increased efficiency and safety of operation. These applications include appropriate hardware and software, as well as the necessary organisational structures (orgware) that will make these applications most efficient at both the company level and the national or international level.

There seems to exist today a key division in telematics which influences the acceptance of systems by companies. When the system performs a task of 'data transmission' (e.g. sales order processing, dispatched goods invoicing, etc.), it is likely to have ready acceptance. By contrast, the 'decision-making' systems such as those for depot location, vehicle routeing and scheduling, or for strategic planning, are regarded more circumspectly by companies. The reservations of companies are many, but an important aspect is one of 'responsibility' and mistrust.

As a general rule, it is the larger-sized companies that are more willing to invest in new information technology and telematics applications. A fleet of ten vehicles would appear to represent a threshold for the acceptance of such applications. Below about ten vehicles, the operator requirement for telematics will be restricted to general management applications such as accounting. For larger fleets the applications will be more specifically related to freight transport and its associated activities.

There is an active field of research and practical applications for information technology and telecommunications in the field of freight transport in Europe. Indeed it seems that it is this particular field of transport which is the first to benefit from such technology. On the other hand both the IT industry and the European administrations (led by the EC) are now setting out the policies and standards for the particular applications.

Public transport

In this area lies perhaps the biggest challenge for policy options to alleviate the wider transportation problem in urban areas. Improvement of public transport will continue to be the prerequisite for a balanced and environmentally acceptable urban (and inter-urban to a lesser extent) transport system. Policy options to invest in improving public transportation services will be facilitated through current technological improvements in both telematics applications to public transport operation, and improvements in the performance of the mechanical systems of public transport vehicles.

There are usually seven main 'domains' or 'functions' that are identified in urban public transport operation and which more of less exist in every operating company (CASSIOPE, 1991):

1. Real-time control (operations management)
2. Scheduling
3. Passenger information
4. Fare collection
5. Maintenance
6. Strategic planning
7. Management information

In all the above functions, which can be further divided into subfunctions, there is today some significant telematics application that can be used to enhance operation and control of the system (identified in Chapter 8 by Papaioannou and Simoes). Efforts are now mainly directed towards creating an integrated structure for data handling and utilisation within one system of public transport operation, and using these data in all the above seven functions.

Technological advances have also been significant in mechanical systems for buses and other public transport vehicles. The suppliers of vehicles and other mass transit equipment offer a variety of technological 'extras' required in current operation conditions. At the same time safety regulations are now much more stringent, resulting in better quality systems from a safety point of view. Also, the need to reduce maintenance cost and time and to automate much of the work done manually have forced manufacturers to fit vehicles with a number of computerised systems.

The various areas in which mechanical improvements have been made lately include (see also Giannopoulos, 1989, pp. 149–207):

- safety (braking systems, seat design, vehicle interior design);
- security (alarm and other emergency systems, drivers' and vehicles' protection);
- passenger comfort (ergonomics, noise, air-conditioning, ventilation);
- vehicle aesthetics;
- warning systems for the vehicle's mechanical parts;
- energy efficiency;
- air pollution.

The technological innovations in all the above fields have been already partially incorporated in all major functions of public transport. The degree of penetration of all this new technology varies from country to country and operator to operator. It depends on a number of factors, some of which are the ownership status, the size of the operator, the competition, the operators' traditional attitude towards innovation, and the overall and local economy.

The adoption of suitable policies from the central and local governments to promote and encourage the use of new technologies in public transport, coupled with the appropriate financial motives, should remain or become a high-priority policy for all partners involved. The potential benefits from such a policy will include among others, better and more accessible public transport services, environmental improvement, promotion of the public transport role, reduction in accidents and overall better living conditions in our urban areas.

Therefore public transport enhanced by the use of new technology described previously and in the corresponding chapter can be and must be the key to a comprehensive approach towards solving transportation problems in urban areas, and should as a priority form part of the new integrated road transport environment for Europe.

Mechanical parts of vehicles — engines and fuels

If the long-term energy supply problems can be solved in the way discussed in the chapter by O. Svidén, then a number of new fuels have to be defined, produced and distributed on a large scale. It is not possible to define these new fuels yet. It has to be done in close collaboration with both the primary energy supply side and the vehicle engine research and development side. But with respect to their environmental properties, the following list of basic alternatives will probably have to be considered in a systems approach:

- Hydrogen
- Methane
- Methanol
- LPG, liquid petroleum gas
- Synthetic petrol
- Synthetic jet kerosene.

Furthermore, there is a range of non-fuel alternatives that have to be investigated in a systems approach. If one includes alternatives with electricity transmission to vehicles, we also have to look into the following possibilities:

- electricity by batteries;
- electricity by trolley on motorways;

- electricity by open-ended transformers in the road;
- electromagnetic levitation and propulsion.

Some three to four decades ahead, the world will have to abandon crude oil as a primary energy for transportation fuels. This event could be dramatic if a substitute supply is not planned well in advance. It also provides mankind with an opportunity to redesign the complete energy supply and conversion chain from mining and refining to combustion in the vehicle engines in such a way that it can meet the global ecological criteria.

The overall policy conclusion is that interesting new systems options do appear if the fuel supply system is related to the energy conversion method applied. If a very clean fuel, like hydrogen, is selected, a number of new direct conversions to electricity emerge. Furthermore, if petroleum fuel resources beyond the year 2020 will not be sufficient to supply the world demand of mobility, a new primary energy source has to be exploited in order to develop and distribute the new clean fuels required. By natural and historical analogy, these changes in primary energy substitutions take many decades to develop. Policy-makers should therefore now promote efforts already under way in the industry for research into and development of new sources of fuels that will eventually replace the fossil fuels when the latter become depleted.

Technological innovation in the field of telecommunications

The new technologies in the field are expected in the future to impose the widespread use of at least the following applications:

- digitalisation, which makes it possible to process much larger amounts and new forms of data (such as moving images);
- the use of optical fibres, which makes it possible to transmit information at considerably higher rates and at much lower cost;
- the integration of microelectronics components and software;
- the development of satellite links.

These advances, which are already in the process of becoming established, will bring about a decisive improvement in the way in which the human voice data and images are transmitted and processed, and will make possible the much more widespread use of communication networks which fully exploit their interactive potential.

From a user's perspective, the rapid increase in communications potentials embodied in the new communications technologies opens the way to the exploitation of competitive advantages on the basis of the achievement of more information and knowledge. Competitive advantages are now based on the capacities of new technologies to transmit, process, store and elaborate a greater volume of information.

Thus, the higher technological potentialities present major opportunities for firms to achieve competitive advantages. However, despite general beliefs, these opportunities are not provided by the simple adoption of these technologies, but by their *innovative use*, i.e. by the application of these technologies to produce new products, new processes, new transactional structures.

Since such innovative use of this technology undoubtedly requires also a high level of organisational changes, it is easily implied that the diffusion of new telecommunications technologies among users also requires organisational changes or at least a deep and thorough investigation of the possible interrelationship between this technology and organisation.

The primary message here is therefore that adoption of the new technologies of telematics and related technological change is not a condition for 'automatic' economic development and improved performance of firms. It is rather a chance given to these firms to achieve a better economic performance, but the capacity to exploit these possibilities depends on individual corporate strategies and on the capacity of each firm to link the technological changes to new business and organisational strategies.

Public policy should thus encourage computer networks development in areas with high potential demand density, such as central regions, where mechanisms such as network externalities could generate positive cumulative effects, and thus where critical mass could be achieved in a shorter time.

Positive network externalities, in fact, arise because the total number of subscribers to such new services has an important effect on the user value of each additional subscriber, and each additional connection has important effects on the user value of the network of existing subscribers.

The decision of the countries of the European Community to commit themselves to development of the ISDN network, i.e. a single network that will serve a wide variety of user needs by supplying a broad range of telecommunications services, must therefore be followed by policy actions to enhance the chances of their acceptance and wider acceptance by the users according to the above.

A top–down approach, i.e. an approach starting with national projects and then developing local ones, has been suggested in the corresponding chapter of this book as a more appropriate public policy to generate cumulative adoption processes. Nevertheless, to be efficient, these policies have to consider the geographical asymmetry in networks, which are created by following a top–down approach, only as a timing difference in investments among regions.

The implications

Inter-urban transport (passenger and freight)

All current indications point to the fact that long-distance movement of both passengers and freight (intermediate and final products) will increase in Europe over the next two decades. This will be accompanied, as far as freight is concerned, by an increase in short-distance final product movement, co-ordinated through new logistical systems. The consequence is a more intense movement of people from peri-urban or rural areas to regional or national urban centres as well as between urban areas for business and recreation or tourism. Similarly products from production sites will be moved more frequently and in greater quantities to storage centres and from there to the final market. Globalisation of markets will strengthen this phenomenon, augmenting the spatial distribution of products and thus their physical movements.

A rather strong pressure for long-distance business travel derives directly from the most likely scenario of 'network firms' presented in Chapter 3. This necessitates high volumes of movement between firms and (spatially diffused) customers, and between functions of multi-site firms (each of which is expected to be located in one place, avoiding duplication and thus inefficiency). The 'network firm' scenario additionally implies a high volume of business travel associated with co-operative agreements, which may well be international in scope, complemented by well-developed and advanced satellite-based video-conferencing systems.

Moreover, the 'make-together' form of organisation implies a high volume of information transmitted between firms, in the form of horizontal inter-corporate information flows. At the same time, high volumes of vertical inter-corporate information flows characterise this scenario, corresponding to the information requirements for asymmetrical but stable linkages with suppliers. Intensive intra-corporate information flows will also be necessary in order to develop the types of 'new management of territory' outlined above, involving the relocation of part-functions in one place, thus rationalising decision-making processes. It is clear that with such a relocation of activities in space, firms will need a constant flow of information, both horizontally (to develop decision-making processes) and vertically (because of the decentralised control system).

From the above discussion, the most compelling and immediate form of action for the policy-makers concerns the infrastructure requirements associated with this scenario. In an industrial and spatial system based on intense long-distance movement of people, goods and information, a wide range of transport and communications systems infrastructures will be necessary, including air freight systems, short-distance frequent-delivery road-based local systems, high-speed trains, air passenger travel, long-distance computer networks, and advanced personal communication services (i.e. video-conferencing, electronic mail).

The creation and operation of such an infrastructure must be today the main preoccupation of all European and inter-European governmental bodies. As the importance of national territorial transport infrastructure systems dissolves, the emphasis will be put more and more on infrastructure provision shifts towards advanced international transport and communications networks.

Spatial planning of transport infrastructure therefore needs to be developed in conjunction with the territorial planning of transport and communications infrastructure. An efficient and reliable logistical system to support the operation of this infrastructure in every way will require the contemporary existence of both advanced telecommunications and transportation networks.

Urban transport (passengers and freight)

As the funds and space for more 'private car-oriented infrastructure' become scarcer, urban transport in the Europe of the future will have to rely more and more on two areas of improvement: urban public transport systems, and the development of electronic aids to manage the demand for (urban) transport and to help improve the operation and exploitation of the existing infrastructure. The first is the subject of the next section of public transport.

The second involves the creation of a whole new 'environment' in which the system will operate, and which will ensure the most efficient and productive use of the available resources for the movement of people and goods. The formulation of this so-called **integrated road transport environment** (IRTE), is based on advanced telematics applications, most of which have been outlined in Chapter 6. It also requires a whole new organisational framework and governmental commitment so that the systems to be implemented are truly international and universally applicable.

For Europe, a number of policy and implementation actions are necessary in order to bring about this IRTE, the main ones being briefly the following.

On the **demand management** issue, actions are probably due in the near future not only on the principles but also on the standard technologies to be applied. There has to be early agreement on this if some concerted action is to take place. For example, the technologies for road pricing, and its principles, have been discussed for several years now but agreement on a common attitude is far from being reached. **Interactive route guidance** (IRG) and **automatic debiting** have until now developed separately. If unification becomes possible, it will open new possibilities for efficient integrated demand management measures, but this technical possibility should be considered now. Since some form of road pricing (toll) will probably be universally in operation in Europe by the turn of the century, the development of integrated electronic toll payment systems should be considered as a priority.

The second aspect of demand management is the fact that the operation of any demand management action will have to be integrated with the other subsystems of the IRTE. These two items are likely to be high on the agenda of many future European policy-making sessions, and will require tough political and policy decisions to be made before the turn of the century.

On the other issues facing the creation of a pan-European IRTE, the following are perhaps the more pertinent.

Development of **travel and traffic information** technologies, to help passengers and drivers make the best choices concerning their travel, will require development and application of technologies for 'data collection', 'forecasting models', and 'co-ordinated database network'. The last is considered to be the most important. The communications network, together with the equipment needed for user interaction, will develop in the near future along an independent path, derived from existing technology such as Minitel, Teletext, ISDN and similar. Apart from the quoted areas, where joint research and development effort is needed, there is no evident need for high-priority work in regulations and standardisation. End-user facilities for trip planning can be provided without difficulty by a series of different service providers.

What is also needed is, first, a preliminary indication of a possible choice of communication media and standards, and secondly, a reliable and well-established network of databases. On the other hand, it is to be noted that strong efforts in research and development are needed for a number of models, methods and systems.

In the field of **integrated urban** (and also **inter-urban**) **traffic management** there is a definite need for work to be carried out to rigorously test in practice the new systems developed through the technological innovations in the area, and for the setting of pan-European standards before any implementation takes place. The following points are most important:

- Agreement on standards for the USC (**unified short-range channel link**). This is perhaps the most difficult task. On the other hand, the possibility of using the same channel for **interactive route guidance (IRG)**, **user fee-financed infrastructure** (UFFI), as well as for other services and traffic management will open the door to a series of major improvements.
- Early commencement of an 'intelligent marketing' action, directed at local authorities. This action should concentrate on the possibilities offered by the urban IRTE, together with the need for a series of

integrated local prerequisites. Large towns and large-scale demonstrations should be included first in this action.

Relative to the same broad area of integrated urban traffic management are the following specific technologies that are currently under development or pilot application in Europe and elsewhere in the world.

Systems to broadcast information to drivers while they are travelling, known as RDS/TMC systems, are in the process of being installed in major urban (and inter-urban) areas. The success of the RDS/TMC will depend on the quality of the broadcasting features as well as on the accuracy, completeness and timeliness of the information broadcast. To achieve this, the collection of actual, up-to-date traffic data is of great importance. The introduction of the RDS/TMC infrastructure should be accompanied by the enhancement of existing (or installation of new) systems for monitoring traffic behaviour and detecting abnormal conditions. Due to the interregional nature of RDS/TMC, a strategy for coordination of different information centres is also needed.

In the field of **mobile telephony**, the selection of the **Groupe Spéciale Mobile** (GSM) system for pan-European application opens the way for other applications, and market forces are already strong enough to generate products with attractive cost benefit characteristics. However, additional effort is needed to make the best use of the options available in the GSM specification for road traffic applications. Therefore, based on the results of the investigations on dedicated GSM systems, harmonised requirements of particular GSM functions must be defined.

For **driver assistance and co-operative driving systems** and their major functions of **intelligent cruise control** (ICC), **co-operative detection and ranging** (CODAR), and **interactive route guidance** (IRG), the following can be observed.

The early implementation of ICC requires a choice of the method and technology for detection and range finding. The 'co-operative' nature of today's feasible solutions leads to the conclusion that an early agreement, on a European scale, between all the interested actors is necessary. Also possible commonalities in on-board equipment (if any) with the other elements of the IRTE together with the integration with roadside-based functions have to be carefully analysed.

Intelligent cruise control offers such great improvements in safety, efficiency, environment and comfort in driving that already many of the automobile companies or their suppliers are engaged in developing it for commercial use.

Interactive route guidance (IRG) on the other hand can be envisaged in the near future only for dense and congested urban road networks. This is due to the nature of the system itself, as well as to the time required by the local authorities to decide and to the effort and time needed for starting the system operation. On the other hand, IRG is a 'local' measure, in the sense that its effectiveness in a urban area will not depend on conditions 'outside' the town itself. Thus a European agreement on the general acceptance of the system is not necessary, although some action could profitably be directed at local authorities to show them the benefits and features of the system.

Finally, as regards CODAR, a basic European approach to a suitable implementation path is still to be found. Common efforts must be made to ensure that feasible options in this field are picked up and realised. Soon, efforts have to be made to get an official (CEPT) statement on a frequency band, for the possible implementation of CODAR systems (80 GHz are currently under discussion). This will concentrate R&D and provide a reliable basis for the technological investment required. The same is true for the development of a unified short-range communication system. As there are already systems available, a unification will only be possible for the next generation of systems.

The stage has been set and rigorous action is already under way both in the EC and other governmental and intergovernmental European bodies. European car manufacturers have also taken up the challenge, and their interest in common action is manifested by their readiness to contribute to common R&D programmes, for example by launching the Eureka programme PROMETHEUS.

Public transport

Improvements in the operation and provision of public transport systems will continue to be a major preoccupation for the future. Technological innovation promises better operating conditions as well as the easier operation of buses and other public transport vehicles. As the quest for better public transport services profits from technological innovation, policy options will improve and a better balance of modal split will be a feasible achievement. The increasing constraints for better environmental conditions, especially in urban areas, and the need to conserve energy resources, will give more and more weight to the implementation of new technologies in public transport which were presented in Chapter 8.

New developments in the area of **public transport** will also call for appropriate national and European policies. The basic policy elements, with respect to public transport operation, characterising the new era, are likely to be as follows:

1. Promotion of public transport will have to overcome both the 'traditional' competition of the private car, but also the increasing passenger needs which will be due to mobility and population increases. Public transport, however, can, and has to, play an important role in future urban area transport.
2. The application of a more competitive environment in public transport will normally result in lower operating costs and increased

productivity, but this may be to the detriment of applying new technologies if this will mean increased initial cost of investment and not very tangible economic results.

3. Outright 'on the street' competition may have little to offer in promoting the application of technological innovation in public transport. The optimum may be conditions of controlled competition between sufficiently sized (public or private) public transport companies in order to allow for the necessary investments.

4. The supplementary role of transport modes must be continuously promoted. 'Integration' may well be the key word for the transportation systems of urban areas of the future, and this calls for increased awareness and promotion of the application of new technologies. Both public and private transport, either urban or extra-urban will need to complement each other rather than compete with each other with public transport being given the role of the main transport mode in congested urban areas.

Mobility in rural areas

On the whole, the socio-economic and spatial development of rural regions in Western Europe is to a diminishing extent based on the economic activities of these areas; land as a factor of production has decreased in importance. On the contrary, the role of the countryside as a compensation area for urbanised society has become more prominent. It provides milieux for housing, leisure and tourism and is utilised as a reserve of both natural and cultural landscape. Consequently, the role of space as the basic resource of rural areas is accentuated. Competition will intensify in most accessible regions provided that the transportation system can play a successful role in providing mobility.

From the perspective of rural areas, trends in production structure, organisations and technology have both positive and negative implications. New organisational models might contribute to the decentralisation of decision-making from centres of markets and administration, while some growth industries are locationally rather footloose and they are not tied to urban agglomerations. In contrast, face-to-face contacts and utilisation of special service, which are more easily accessible in urban surroundings, play an increasingly important role in modern economic activities. Overall, these developments emphasise the strategic role of transport and telecommunications in the adaptation of rural economies into a wider national and international economy.

As regards, therefore, the implications of technological innovation in transport and communications for the rural areas, there are some priorities in policies which are worth emphasising (see also Chapter 13):

1. Public procurement and R&D support for rural communications and

transport applications are needed, because there is an urban bias in technical development in network infrastructure and services.
2. The modernisation of rural networks, especially in telecommunications, is a necessary precondition for the utilisation of their potential in development. This calls for special-purpose programmes. Also, modernisation should be ensured as an important target in regulatory practices concerning network service operators in a more competitive setting.
3. Universal service obligations should not be abandoned as a point of reference in policies, although in practice relevant measures (e.g. subsidised tariffs, differentiated service charges, etc.) have to be modified according to resources, technologies and specific circumstances.
4. Upgrading demand is an essential element in development strategies concerning transport and communications infrastructure and services in rural areas. It emphasises improvements in social infrastructure, especially in education. Measures should be employed in the context of an integrative programme, which for its part presupposes co-operation between organisations at different levels.

The prospects for recreational travel

Overall, tourism is generally expected to grow in the context of post-industrial European societies. 'Democratisation' of holidays is still in progress in many countries, particularly in the south of Europe. Improvements in transport technology will allow more frequent departures, greater reliability of travel by all modes, improved travel information services and a general improvement in all those factors affecting recreational travel. The leisure orientations of important groups (the young, pensioners, singles without children, etc.) are reinforcing this diagnosis of growth.

However, as the Bieber and Potier chapter demonstrated, touristic flows are a volatile product. Political unrest, currency exchange levels, etc., can greatly modify local equilibria, both for tourism and transport. Moreover, the basic structure of tourism is characterised by more and more fragmentation, both socially and geographically. The corresponding markets or 'niches' are erratic.

A first policy implication is therefore related to the great flexibility of transport systems in the future; demand will be highly volatile, supply will have to be very flexible. In this context, deregulation appears as a global feature well adapted to this future instability.

Congestion created by touristic concentration will be an increasingly important matter of concern. The littoral zones are, in particular, already areas where new transport investments are critical. In some areas, the drastic regulation of tourism might be imposed as the result of a lack of new transport facilities.

Long-distance tourism will of course remain in the realm of air transport. Costs of air transport evolution is a particularly difficult topic to forecast. Concentration, deregulation, and streamlining of old-fashioned services are favourable to a decrease in costs. Long-term energy scarcity, relative decline of business traffic, congestion of airports are much less favourable factors. But, associated with long-lasting political unrest in Third World countries, a rather positive balance seems possible for Europe-bound long-distance tourism.

In Chapter 14, three scenarios of the future evolution of tourism have been sketched in relation to the main orientations developed within the NECTAR Europe 2020 Working Group (see also Masser et al., 1992). They put forward respectively: (1) economic development values, (2) equity values, and (3) ecological values. Let us recall their basic features.

1. The 'economic development' scenario was based upon the perpetuation of the main past evolutions, characteristic of the industrial society. Large tour operators see their activity develop. Economic domination of the industrial core of Europe allows more and more southbound flows to the Mediterranean 'north arch' in Spain, Italy and France. Political troubles in the Third World and in Eastern Europe may bring new flows of tourists to this sunny playground of Europe.

    Large congestion problems are expected with this scenario, especially in littoral areas. New motorways and high-speed railways would need to be built despite considerable local opposition and conflicts.

2. The 'equity scenario' was characterised by an important further 'democratisation' of tourism. Due to obvious economic constraints, we see this type of development as non-service-oriented; on the contrary, the development of social tourism implies the growth of proximity tourism and massive self-production of tourism.

3. The 'ecology scenario' would also be based upon the dispersal of touristic activities throughout Europe, but it would be less self-produced and less car-oriented than the previous one. Modernised forms of hostellery maintaining quality at all levels of the price range, as in the Swiss example, would play a very important role in such a scenario.

    The development of pollution-free local forms of transport integrated with good intercity rail and bus services could, hopefully, reduce the pressure of conventional cars. This is the most promising and the most demanding scenario. At all levels (society, tourism activities, transport) it implies innovative policies which cannot develop without profound changes in the behaviour and motivations of tourists.

Some key horizontal issues

The need for integration

It is expected that advanced information systems will expand from networks within individual companies to open networks, and that the quality of the information processed in the network will improve. It is also expected that such systems will expand from within a particular industry to large community systems and to international information systems. Many companies have already created world-wide information networks that facilitate the flow of information necessary to control the logistics. Moreover, the introduction of road–vehicle communications systems will accelerate the sophistication of road transport (especially freight).

There is an obvious need, therefore, to create truly integrated services and networks that will allow for a multitude of tasks to be performed in the most efficient way.

The integration has to take place at both a geographical and technological level. At a geographical level, we are referring primarily to international networks, designed for long-distance transport and communications. Networks which are confined to national territories, whether for the movement of information or people, will be of limited use in sustaining the types of industrial organisation predicted, in Chapter 3, under the 'network firm' scenario. Technological integration is clearly vital for the development of international interconnected networks. Standards problems have to be overcome, both in the telecommunications and transport arenas, in order for genuinely border-less infrastructures to be developed.

Indeed the integration requirements go well beyond the geographical and technological integration of transport networks. Our recommendation is that a complete integration between transport *and* telecommunication networks will have to be developed. The increasing importance of standardisation and harmonisation, mentioned in the next section, refers not only to the two sectors separately but also to their combination.

It can easily be said that the strength and success of infrastructural development in the Europe of the future will be related to the implementation of technological and geographical integration of elements in *both* the transportation and telecommunication systems.

The need to standardise

Many of the developments in communications and information technology and in logistics will emerge in different ways, at different times and at different speeds. It is therefore difficult and not advisable to control these developments in a top–down manner. This will cause inflexibility and inefficiency. However, the proliferation of all kinds of systems may also be unattractive, and some kind of assistance in the required standardisation, or help in achieving horizontal and vertical co-operation is valuable. This is an important task for governmental organisations.

The need for monitoring and control

All over the world, deregulation and privatisation of public facilities are emerging. This will create possibilities for increased efficiency through increased competition amongst companies and countries. We do not for a moment doubt the necessity for continuation of these policies and trends. Indeed we have not even discussed it at any length in this book because it is only within a competitive and carefully deregulated environment that all the changes anticipated in this book can take place.

However, there is an important need to monitor the developments mentioned above. This need arises not only from the obvious reason to provide for stimulus and freedom, but also in order to avoid the danger that monopolistic tendencies will occur.

Thus governments should carefully observe what is happening in order to take appropriate action. This means that there is an important monitoring function to be performed. Many of the statistics that we are used to compiling today are not well fitted to achieving this task. Especially in the field of communications and the organisation of logistics, some efficient form of data collection has to be developed.

Institutional and legal issues

What the present situation demands from the modernisation of the physical infrastructure is not only repair, replacement and optimisation of existing systems, but also technological modernisation of entire systems, including their institutional and social components.

Also the debate on transportation, communication and mobility cannot escape asking serious questions about social justice and emancipation, for mobility itself is part and parcel of the process of uneven development and of consolidating asymmetrical power relationships. Raising questions of social justice and exclusion may perhaps be considered to belong to an outmoded debate, but absence of these considerations cannot remove the problems of those who are caught in the doldrums of persistent deprivation and perpetual restructuring.

As Swyngedouw (Chapter 15) has attempted to demonstrate in his contribution, TCM patterns are far from neutral or value-free, let alone driven uniquely by a 'natural' process of technological change and scientific progress. Mobility itself is one of the arenas in which the struggle for control and power is fought. An important strategic weapon of the powerful in this struggle is the ideology of progress and the legitimising scientific discourse of scientists and engineers. If questions of social justice in the debate and praxis of mobility are not again put high on the agenda, they may force themselves onto the political platform very soon by means other than words.

Consideration of the externalities

There are many obvious obstacles, such as social, technical, organisational, financial and legal barriers, to the establishment of truly integrated systems of transport and communications in the future. Some of the issues and concepts which would affect the future picture are summarised in what follows.

In order to achieve optimal usage of scarce resources, all of the costs that society has to pay for, in order to facilitate activities, have to be taken into account, and ideally be paid by the users of these facilities. In many cases this is not easy, and at present many costs, especially those related to environmental damage, are generated but not compensated for. Of course, the internalisation of external costs — also relevant in areas other than transportation and communications — could lead to significant changes in decision-making, and therefore are of the outmost importance.

The environmental concerns are likely to emerge in the developed countries in particular. The way in which these will affect development and operation of the transport infrastructure of the future is not very well understood yet and is an interesting area for future research. This involves the development of environmentally friendly (green) transportation systems, such as the recycling of waste products and the minimisation of external effects of transport operation (noise, pollution and accidents).

In areas where the spatial conditions are such that the infrastructure cannot be improved above ground, the development of underground facilities could help to overcome these problems. All of these developments will take place in various countries, and in various political and cultural climates. Such developments could be assisted by international co-ordination and co-operation, thus leading to improved economic growth and stability.

A plan for action

The priorities

We are in the midst of a profound change in the European socio-political and economic pattern of life. The characteristics of this change are developing from changes that are occurring gradually but surely in the political scene of Europe and the technological and organisational innovation that is making itself evident in almost every aspect of everyday life. Change is mostly felt in the ways we are communicating with each other (both data and information), manufacturing our goods and producing services, and transporting people and goods over space.

If the current aim of the EC countries is to become more closely associated, creating for the first time a specimen of the United States of Europe for the future, then these changes will be even more paramount, deeply affecting almost every aspect of life not only in the EC countries but also in the EFTA countries as well as those of Eastern Europe.

The message repeated by all forecasts of future demand in the field of transport is one of increasing quantity as well as quality of travel needs for both passengers and freight. The dilemma that has dominated policy-makers for the last decade will become even more pertinent, i.e. how to provide a level of mobility that matches the changing magnitude and pattern of demand, without at the same time jeopardising the quality of life in urban and rural areas.

The scale of the transportation problems that are likely to arise even in the near future must also be taken into account. Current estimates are that by the end of this century (only seven years away), assuming that the EC's Single European Market and the rest of the Maastricht Treaty provisions take effect within this time period, the twelve EC countries will be:

1. spending some ECU 750 billion (nearly one trillion US dollars) per year on road transport products and services alone. For all transport services (air, road, rail, sea, inland waterway) these figures are more than double;
2. devoting some 10 per cent (approximately the same as today) of every family's budget to transport;
3. experiencing annual increases in international traffic of as much as 7–10 per cent for freight vehicles and 4–5 per cent for private cars, while car ownership levels will continue to increase by the current 4 per cent per year at least until the year 2005;
4. suffering some 60,000 deaths and 2 million injuries (10 per cent of which causing permanent handicap) per year with a total cost to the economy of these accidents of anywhere between ECU 50 and 100 billion per year;

5. investing, however, something around 0.5 per cent of their GNP to new transport infrastructure if current trends continue, and more that 1.5 per cent of the GNP if one assumes a change in current policies and financial means to match demand (something rather unlikely to happen until 2000).

Faced with the situation European governments will have to be urgently seeking ways to ameliorate the situation with the least possible cost in both money and environmental terms.

The answer that the chapters of this book have striven to provide to the policy-makers, is that in view of two major current obstacles, i.e. scarcity of space for new physical infrastructure provision (especially in urban areas), and scarcity of funds — both of which are not likely to disappear soon — we must, as a priority, concentrate our efforts towards achieving positive results in the following areas:

1. fostering new, more efficient, patterns of spatial (land use) distribution and organisation;
2. consolidating new methods of production and distribution harmonised with these patterns;
3. achieving better management of traffic flows in urban and inter-urban areas;
4. improving the organisation and quality of transport services;
5. promoting universally available and efficient communication of data and information throughout Europe; and
6. supporting technological improvements to engines and fuels to reduce adverse effects on the environment.

Furthermore, a **European mobility policy** (EMP) is necessary for the near future, covering at least the period until the exhaustion of the fossil fuels (some forty years from now). The main aim of this policy should be to strike an optimum balance between mobility, economy and the environment. Such a policy cannot of course contain only an inventory of technological innovation opportunities, but it should try to define the limits and priorities for applying these innovations, as well as the action necessary in order to make these new technological and organisational possibilities a reality. In doing so, it will first have to identify why what is theoretically possible today is not yet operational, and which alternatives are to be explored further before taking up firm positions in a future action programme.

We believe that for each of the areas indicated above, one can mention a number of actions to be included when formulating the future EMP, and these have been already mentioned in the sixth and seventh sections above. In addition one can also mention the following.

More efficient patterns of spatial distribution and organisation

A different development pattern may now be seen to emerge as regards the European industrial and spatial system. This pattern is characterised by the globalisation of urban areas and markets to extend their influence throughout Europe. This trend will become strengthened and more evident after the European unification process that starts with the Single European Act in force since January 1993 in the countries of the European Community.

A 'make-together' form of organisation of production will accompany this spatial organisation pattern, and in return influence it further. Such development will imply high volumes of information transmitted between firms in the form of horizontal inter-corporate information flows, corresponding to the information requirements for asymmetrical but stable linkages with suppliers. Intensive intra-corporate information flows will also be necessary in order to develop the types of 'new management of territory' concepts, involving the relocation of part-functions in one place, thus rationalising decision-making processes. It is clear that with such a relocation of activities in space, firms will need a constant flow of information, both horizontally (to develop decision-making processes) and vertically (because of the decentralised control system).

Towards universally available and efficient European transport networks

As already stressed in the fifth section, all policies enhancing long-distance transport and communications infrastructures are to be greatly strengthened. They have as their prerequisite the development of efficient European-wide networks for information transfer and transportation. The development of international computer networks with **electronic data interchange** (EDI) applications will be required to deal with the mass of information associated with the new logistical platforms, as will the implementation of ISDN (the **integrated service digital network**).

In this respect a top–down policy approach to the development of the necessary advanced infrastructure (in a wider sense) networks, rather than the bottom–up local network approach, will be much more effective and efficient. Such a policy should be dealing with the implementation of international 'transport and information highways' rather than with local transport infrastructure and telematics networks improvements.

This approach to future European policy formulation, which has to start now, will have clear and far-reaching implications for the development of transport and communications infrastructures. Not only will this new industrial and spatial pattern be built on the assumption that long-distance, reliable European transport and communications networks are 'implemented', but also that these networks have to be 'integrated networks', both geographically and technologically speaking. The integration of these networks will permit the development of the industrial and spatial system outlined above, because a 'quasi-vertically integrated' form of organisation requires both an advanced communications infrastructure and a highly reliable complementary transport system.

Physical discontinuities in both transport and communication networks have to be avoided if the new industrial and spatial system in Europe is to be effectively supported.

With respect to this issue, it is very encouraging to see that within the European Commission preparatory work for the creation of the so-called 'Trans-European networks' has already started. These networks cover three basic areas: transport; telecommunications; and vocational training. For the first, the following five types of networks are being prepared: road; conventional rail, high-speed rail; combined transport; and inland waterways.

Working in parallel, a group of international experts have developed a project on Missing Networks in Europe for the Round Table of Industrialists, primarily concerned with identifying the discontinuities which exist today in European international networks, in both transport and communications sectors. The result has pointed out that both telecommunications and transport networks could perform much better if missing networks were addressed at five different levels (Nijkamp et al., 1990):

- hardware (physical infrastructure)
- software (logistics and information)
- orgware (institutional and organisational setting)
- finware (financial and funding arrangement)
- ecoware (environmental and safety effects)

The interest in avoiding 'missing networks' becomes more crucial once a spatial and industrial system is envisaged, as in this book, in which economic transactions are developed primarily at an international scale and where synergies among firms take place globally.

Better management of traffic flows

From the above, it follows that the interest in infrastructure over the past few years has by no means arisen only from the greater interest in the environment and the aim of sustainable development. Infrastructure systems are becoming more and more an issue also because of shifts in user requirements and technological innovation. In addition to improved means of transport (vehicles and vessels), upgraded regulation of traffic and transport flows, improved utilisation of network capacity and better alignment of the various transport modes and infrastructures are also needed.

So far, the choice has been an obvious form of modernisation of the physical infrastructure, aimed especially at combined renovation of different systems. Examples of the new way of thinking are the introduction of dynamic traffic control systems (e.g. congestion signalling, access ramp traffic control, tidal flow, rerouteing and information); various forms of logistic steering and on-line goods flow control, e.g. as expressed in the new transport concepts 'hub-and-spoke', logistic service centres, 100 per cent on time, and flexible distribution systems; and the integration of networks for picture, speech and data communication (ISDN, EDI).

References

CASSIOPE (1991) 'The computer-aided system for scheduling, information and operation of public transport in Europe', DRIVE I programme EEC/DGXIII, Deliverable 5.1.

DRIVE (1991) 'Dedicated road infrastructure for vehicle efficiency in Europe'. A programme of EEC/DGXIII, final report.

Giannopoulos, G.A. (1989) *Bus Planning and Operation in Urban Areas*. Avebury, UK.

Giannopoulos, G.A. and Curdes, G. (1991) 'Innovations in urban transport and the influence on urban form. A historical review', *Transport Reviews*, vol. 12, no. 1, p. 16.

Masser, Ian, Svidén, O. and Wegener, M. (1992) *The Geography of Europe's Futures*. Belhaven Press, London.

Nijkamp, P., Maggi, R. and Masser, I. (1990) 'Missing networks in Europe'. A study prepared for the European Round Table of Industrialists by the ESF/NECTAR Network.

Schaeffer, K.H. and Sclar, E. (1975) *Access for All: Transportation and Urban Growth*. Pelican, Harmondsworth, Middlesex.

Index